ORCHESTRAL MANOEUVRES IN THE DARK

PRETENDING TO SEE THE FUTURE

RICHARD HOUGHTON

www.thisdayinmusic.com

All rights reserved. No part of this publication may be reproduced, stored in a retrieval system, or transmitted in any form or by any means, electronic, electrostatic, recording, magnetic tape, mechanical, photocopying or otherwise, without prior permission in writing from the publisher.

The publisher makes no representation, express or implied, with regard to the accuracy of the information contained in this publication and cannot accept any responsibility in law for any errors or omissions.

The right of Richard Houghton to be identified as author of this work has been asserted by him in accordance with sections 77 and 78 of the Copyright, Designs and Patents Act 1988.

A catalogue record for this book is available from the British Library

This edition © This Day In Music Books 2018
Text ©This Day In Music Books 2018

ISBN: 978-1999592721

Front cover design by Chris Spurr @ Effection
Image research Liz Sanchez
Project management Neil Cossar
Book design by Robot Mascot
Printed in the UK by CPI

Eric's poster courtesy of the Pete Fulwell Archive at LJMU Special Collections & Archives.
Research Consultant: Professor Colin Fallows

Photo credits: Ian Plested, Francesco Melina, Innes Marlow, Neil Taylor, Lorenzo Suvee

Very special thanks to Mark Crouch for creating the omd-live.com website as it has been a very valuable resource in the compiling of this book.

Richard Houghton would like to thank Andy McCluskey, Paul Humphreys, Mirelle Davis, Neil Cossar, Malcolm Wyatt and Kate Sullivan

THIS DAY IN MUSIC BOOKS

This Day In Music Books
2B Vantage Park
Washingley Road
Huntingdon
PE29 6SR

www.thisdayinmusic.com
Email: editor@thisdayinmusic.com

Exclusive Distributors:
Music Sales Limited
14/15 Berners St
London
W1T 3JL

CONTENTS

EARLY YEARS	05
1980	95
1981	127
1982	146
1983	154
1984	180
1985	204
1986	226
1987-1988	256
1990-1991	273
1993-1995	300
1996	314
1998-2010	317
2011	363
2012	383
2013-2018	387

FOREWORD

WE LOVED THE ALBUM, FORMED A BAND AND LEARNT TO PLAY

My first OMD single was 'Enola Gay', on 7-inch vinyl with a turquoise cover and fiery sunset; you don't forget these things. My friend Chris went one better, managing to persuade his parents to buy the Orchestral Manoeuvres in the Dark album in the mistaken belief that 'Enola Gay' was on it. Our initial disappointment was soon dissipated; we loved the album, formed a band and learnt to play 'Electricity' and 'Messages'. We acquired a Siel Mono synthesiser which we put through an old tape echo to try to get the Humphreys lead sound. Almost. We wanted our own Gramophone Suite. I eventually persuaded my parents to buy *Organisation*, an album of gentle darkness beneath clouded skies, which I fell in love with aged 12 and still love today. When we were 17, Chris and I drove to Stanlow Oil Refinery one night on our way to the chippy in Oldham as a sort of homage. A two-hour detour to a 10-minute journey, *Organisation* recorded onto a TDK AD90 cassette in a beige Ford Fiesta. We were obsessive fans.

The first live show I saw was Dazzle Ships at Manchester Apollo in 1983. The set was magnificent - inspired by Peter Saville's superb cover design. Perhaps for this reason – a first gig always leaves an indelible imprint - *Dazzle Ships* is my favourite OMD album. It has an icy romanticism about it - the soundtrack of grey Eastern European capitals I'd never visited. Snow and spies and North Atlantic storms, and analogue songs about a digital future. I tried to tune into Radio Prague on a shortwave radio. The world was so much larger and more mysterious in those days.

'Stanlow' and 'Pretending to See the Future' and 'The Romance of the Telescope' and 'Silent Running' were my soundtrack; they shaped my character and inspired me to make music. They are as uplifting now as they were then.

PROFESSOR BRIAN COX

EARLY YEARS

Wirral, Merseyside, the late Seventies - Andy McCluskey, Paul Humphreys and friends appear in church halls and pubs under a variety of guises.

ANDY MCCLUSKEY

I had grown up in a very typical working class household. The eldest, and only boy, of three children in a semi-detached 1960 new build in Meols. The town had once been a tiny fishing village hiding behind the sand dunes on the exposed northern coast of the Wirral Peninsula. The 20th century saw the dunes replaced by a massive concrete sea wall and the sleepy hamlet became a non-descript suburb of Liverpool, the railway ferrying the commuters under the Mersey to their places of employment.

I remember that I could always sing. I would lie in bed at night reciting Rodgers and Hammerstein songs from my mother's albums of the film soundtracks. 'Oh What a Beautiful Morning' from Oklahoma! was my favourite. I'm not sure that my sisters enjoyed their eight-year old brother's mock baritone voice serenading them to sleep from across the landing, but I am confident that I was at least in tune.

My mother sang in the choir of three different Christian denomination churches. Disinterested in the sermons, but delighting in the hymns. My father could sing, but had to be pressed into doing so, and then only on rare occasions. Helen, the younger of my two sisters, received an acoustic guitar as a present aged 12. She abandoned learning to play it within months and I tentatively began teaching myself. That poor guitar was soon discarded again once I bought my first bass with the money I had asked for, for my sixteenth birthday.

Obviously, Paul and I were not in a musical vacuum. I had my personal heroes. Bowie, Kraftwerk, Roxy Music, Neu,

The Velvet Underground and Eno. And that is where I drew the line. Apart from a few rare exceptions the opinionated teen McCluskey thought everything else was 'crap'. I had long grown out of listening to show tunes, been through my Steve Harley phase (I did like his early albums because they were not 'conventional' pop music) and I only accepted music perceived to be challenging and innovative. It was my friend John Floyd who got me into Roxy and the Velvets. I am eternally grateful for his influence on me.

I recall that Paul was into Genesis and Queen. I think that I influenced him to move away from the prog rock, though I suspect that he still listened when I was not at his house as I would likely have been scathing and judgmental as only I could be when it came to music that I 'disapproved' of.

Of the two of us, Paul is the more intuitive musician. He possess an uncanny ability to conjure a perfect melody from the fewest notes. I am so fortunate that we met musically. Blessed that he tolerates my overthinking and determination, and honoured that he still trustingly offers up his most beautiful sonic creations for me to twist, torture and butcher to suit my own vision.

PAUL HUMPHREYS

As a kid, I was always messing with electronics, doing experiments and building things. When I was about three years old, we had the house rewired and I remember being with the electrician all the time, fascinated by all these wires. And from then on, I was just fascinated with cables and electrics, electronics and the possibilities of what they could do, and what I could make. From the age of 12, I used to get my Auntie's old radios that didn't work and start messing around with them. At 14 I started building things. I didn't have any money to buy things or to buy many parts. I used to bastardise old circuit boards to make new things.

When the band started, I was always looking for an alternative to the music that was around at the time and so was Andy. And then we found it. I heard 'Autobahn' on the radio and it really was the first day of the rest of my life. I thought, 'That is the future of music and I want to do that!'

I have a brother who's 11 years older than me, so growing up, all the music I ever heard was coming out of his bedroom and that was The Beatles, the Rolling Stones and Led Zeppelin, which probably had a subliminal effect on me – at least, The Beatles probably did, without me realising. But I never wanted to make that kind of music.

ANDY MCCLUSKEY

Paul and I knew of each other. He came to my school when he was seven. His father died when he was very young and now his sister had also passed. I think his mother, having lost her husband then her daughter, moved up to Wirral to be closer to her sister for moral support. Paul and I would see each other in the playground. He was the year below me, but a few of my friends got streamed down a year. Them being in his class at school glued us a little tighter. We knew of each other but weren't really friends.

Then I went to the local grammar school and he went to the comprehensive, so we weren't at the same school after leaving Meols Church of England County Primary.

Paul saw me in Meols Park just after my 16th birthday when I was about to start sixth form. He and his mates were still at school and about to do their exams. He saw me walking around the park carrying my bass over my shoulder, as one does to 'accidentally' advertise they have a new bass guitar! You don't see kids walking around with bass guitars over shoulders these days.

A deputation came knocking on my door. I recognised Paul but none of the others. He said, 'My mates are in a band and need a bass player. Would you be interested?' I nodded, 'Yes.' This was the beginning of what would eventually become The Id - Paul's friends from Hilbre Comprehensive School and I. We rehearsed in an art studio, which a friend's dad rented above the fish shop in nearby Hoylake. It *really* stank of fish!

I become the singer by accident. I joined as bass player, because they had a singer, Graham Johnson. Within a month the guys asked me,

↑ Paul outside 3 Frankby Road in Meols, the house he grew up in and where with Andy made their first recordings

EARLY YEARS | 7

OMD - EARLY YEARS

↑
Andy creating a conceptual landscape art piece

traffic control operator. He's had a great life without pretending to be a singer. That's how I became a lead singer. Completely by default. My entire musical career has been one rolling accident!

GRAHAM JOHNSON

The long hot summer of 1976. There was an end of year concert at which Equinox were to perform - Andy McCluskey, Neill Shenton, Gary Hodgson and a drummer. Paul was holding a piece of foil in place of the fuse in Andy's amp (friends for life!) during the audition in front of the music teacher and Andy had modified the words for the song to 'Myriads of Merry Minstrels' (normally 'Myriads of Masturbating Minstrels'). However, he slipped on the final chorus - the teacher's face was a picture!

Gary's father ran his own business and Gary used his van - a grey Austin A60. One bench seat, which could hold three at a push, with a few of us on the floor in the back. The floor under the seat was all but rusted through, leaving a metal flap that the seat was attached to and bounced up and down on.

I remember Paul was slowly building an electric piano and I asked him if I could solder some joints. I did one and was stopped for bad soldering - a

'Would you be the lead singer?' 'But I'm the bass player.' 'We've heard you singing backing vocals. You're much better than Graham.' I responded, 'Well, he's your mate. I'm not telling him. You tell him at school when I'm not there.' Graham Johnson got the heave-ho, for which he's eternally grateful. I've seen him subsequently and he's been a very successful pilot and air

dry joint (the solder turned dull instead of remaining shiny).

After Equinox, the rest of the band, without Andy, started another and needed a singer. They got one, but he was unfamiliar with Free's 'All Right Now' so I sang it for him to show how it went - and we had a new singer!

Gary came up with the name Electric Flux and the Teslas (well, he was studying electronics) although, strictly speaking, it ought to have been Flux Density and the Teslas, as the Tesla is the unit of magnetic flux density. Anyway, I was never a good singer (I'm still not) so we didn't last long, and Andy came back for the musicians and formed The Id with them.

Andy was always singing some ditty or other. I don't know whether he made them up or whether they were some obscure songs he knew. One was about the world's greatest, long-distance thrower-upper - able to cover 48 square yards. Another was about never wanting to be a rock'n'roll star - never wanting to get that far.

JULIA KNEALE
by Andy McCluskey

I was painfully shy as a child. Eczema and asthma didn't help. I would shred my wrists, ankles and the back of my knees to ribbons overnight and awake stuck to the sheets. To get up I'd have to rip the bedclothes off tearing the dried scabs away with them. Walking to school like a robot because it was too painful to bend my knees and being called 'lizard skin' in the playground didn't do much for

The Id at The United Reformed Church Hall 1978 - Julia Kneale and Andy

self-confidence. Neither did our home. Due to my father's gambling addiction we could never afford anything new. I mean nothing! The lounge carpet had a floral pattern that didn't repeat properly as it had been cut together in so many pieces from its previous homes. Under the staircase there were enough oily car parts to build a complete Ford Cortina, and when my alcoholic grandmother managed to walk to our house she usually wet herself whilst sitting on our sofa. Add three messy kids and racing greyhounds that regularly defecated all over the place - you could see why I was reluctant to invite my friends in.

My shyness was worse around girls. I could not believe my luck when Julia Kneale let it be known through a mutual friend that she fancied me. How could I resist?

Julia was attractive and creative. A poet and aspiring book writer. I was besotted. She was my first love. But sadly she was unable to see it. Nothing that I could say or do would make her feel loved. We met at completely the wrong time. Julia had experienced a traumatic childhood and her parents were recently separated. When I wandered innocently into her life I had no idea that she was at the threshold of a nervous breakdown. Neither did she. The last thing Julia needed was a relationship with a moody teenage boy who would tip her emotions over the edge.

The relationship was volatile. I would spend most nights in Julia's third floor bedroom at her mother's maisonette in West Kirby because her insecurity required me to remain. I was delighted to stay with the girl who I had lost my virginity to (she still says that I can't have it back). Each night would be a blur of beautiful lovemaking and excruciating argument. Exhausted by morning, I would depart for an early bus back to my house, grab breakfast, and head to Art College. Fortunately, my old Calday School mate Martin Wesson and I had secured our own room. Crawling under the table to sleep, I'd beg him to tell the lecturers that I had gone to the shops to buy pencils.

I can't remember if I asked Julia to join The Id or whether it just seemed a logical move, as we were inseparable. She could sing adequately but was a lyrical and poetic genius. Paul and I created a simple repetitive motif consisting of five bass notes and two organ chords, which sat perfectly on Malcolm's drum groove. Julia adopted the track insisting that she would sing on it. No one argued. It became 'Julia's Song'. She owned it! I am still convinced that the text is about me, though she swears that it is not.

Julia and I spent a lot of time in the company of our friend and fellow Id band member John Floyd. His parents had split up and he didn't seem to be able to live with either so rented a flat in Birkenhead. By the time the three of us had paid for the bus to his place, there was no money left for food, the electricity meter, nor the gas fire. John had lifted a floorboard and hotwired into the ceiling lamp of the flat below. As long as they kept the light on the three of us could huddle under coats on a dirty mattress in the middle of the floor and listen to Bowie's *Heroes* album on repeat. That second side felt even bleaker when you could see your own breath indoors!

We would walk up the hill in Claughton village to hang around in the derelict church. Very gothic and eerie! It was there that John 'married' Julia and I. Conducting the ceremony in a flamboyantly tortured romantic poet's style.

He really was Percy Bysshe Shelley, and sadly died almost as young.

Outwardly, Julia and I probably seemed the perfectly matched teen couple of artistic hippies. The reality was much more dramatic. Constant drama.

Her insecurities were deepening and she insisted that we become engaged. She was desperate for some emotional life raft to cling to. Essentially, I was being asked to prove that I loved her. The engagement idea did not sit well with my parents who were already worrying about their son that only came home for breakfast. The insecurities turned to anxieties and then depression. Diagnosed with Reactionary Depression Breakdown, Julia was admitted to a psychiatric ward. After we had both visited the hospital on the first day, her mother turned to me, 'Whilst she's safe in here and sedated you can end this relationship. For both your sakes this needs to stop.'

After we separated Julia continued to write to me. It was difficult to know what to say or whether I should even reply in case it just prolonged the agony for us both. This is the subject for my lyrics in our song 'Messages'.

Almost forty later, I find myself introducing Julia to a sold out York Barbican audience and she tells a beautiful story of her song before the band plays its only performance on that tour. Especially for her.

Julia qualified as a registered mental nurse. She is a specialist in five areas of counselling, is a BSc in health and social welfare with psychology and these days works mainly in the field of dementia.

She's lived in York for 31 years and rescues animals. The German Shorthaired Pointer and unruly parrot called Schubert are much easier to deal with than musicians!

*Julia Kneale tells more of her story and days in The Id in her book *Moods, Memories And Other Manoeuvres* (2014) for which Andy wrote the foreword. You can contact her on Facebook to order a copy.

PAUL HUMPHREYS

Andy and I were in several bands pre Orchestral Manoeuvres in the Dark. Equinox was the first, which I was basically the roadie for, and that migrated into an eight-piece band called The Id, very prog-rock and yet indie, with three singers and lead and rhythm guitar. It was all very rock. I came in as a keyboard player who couldn't play. I was learning as I went. I was in charge of noises to begin with, until I got myself an electric piano and an organ and started to add some noises into the equation. I felt I was to The Id what Brian Eno was to Roxy Music, just a sonic and noise making addition. I was 16.

Andy and I started to write all the songs. Several written during this period ended up on the first OMD album - like 'Electricity', 'Julia's Song' (with Julia Kneale) and 'Misunderstanding', which ended up on the second album.

After many rehearsals we had with The Id, Andy and I used to stay behind, messing around, and realised we had so much more in common musically than all the others.

NEILL SHENTON

John Floyd, my best friend at junior school, and I were fascinated by electronics and gadgets. We read *Practical Wireless* (hand-me-downs from a radio ham neighbour) and tried all kinds of daft experiments with valve radios, usually ending with blown fuses and one of us getting electrocuted. John's mum was very liberal in her attitude to us learning by dismantling 240v devices. Many people thought we were a little odd but, because we were gregarious, we didn't really get picked on in school until much later. We were inseparable until we went to different secondary schools.

Throughout my life I've been obsessed with music. My Mum told me that when I was three years old I'd stand in front of the telly, copying Jet Harris and Paul McCartney with my tin guitar. I was clearly destined to be a bass player. At secondary school, music was a major subject of study. Not music lessons. There was no such thing at our school, except for extra-curricular guitar sessions that seemed to my gang of hairy, rock and underground music fans to be aimed at girls playing folk, therefore the enemy of music.

A few of us had older family members with money to buy albums who introduced us to different kinds of music. John's older brother was the nearest thing I knew to a hippy, playing Canned Heat and Frank Zappa music. Paul's older brother was a prog fan and my brother loved American music, particularly Crosby Stills Nash & Young,

↑ Pegasus on stage at Deeply Vale, with Duncan Lewis on bass, Andy on vocals and John Bleasdale on guitar

Simon and Garfunkel and The Beach Boys. It was his friends who introduced me to the loves of my life - Led Zeppelin and the early incarnation of Yes.

Gary Hodgson and I were in the group, which started going to see bands in 1973. We saw Mott the Hoople supported by Queen, and that certainly shaped my thinking. I wanted to be in a band. We were lucky enough to see all kinds of wonderful bands: Pink Floyd, Lou Reed, Genesis, Thin Lizzy. We'd see bands every couple of weeks - thanks to the wonderful promoter Roger Eagle, who was also responsible for Eric's and who put on so many great nights at the stadium.

It was in woodwork lessons where we really started nurturing the seeds of a band. The teacher had pretty much given up on us but indulged our efforts at making electric guitars so we sat around and talked about music, read *Sounds* and *NME* and thought about being in a band. My brother bought me an acoustic guitar in 1975 and Gary got a lovely Les Paul copy. I put a pick-up on the acoustic and we learned a few chords. We persuaded the headmaster to allow us to practice in the school and Equinox was born. We performed at a school concert, playing an instrumental composition of our own, probably akin to punk. The music teacher and folk-strumming girls were highly disparaging.

This is where the Meols connection started. I rode my bike from Greasby to Gary's in West Kirby or Meols to meet Paul, going around to his house (listening to Genesis and Steve Hillage). More planning went on here and I got to know lots of the local musical characters, hanging about at the rehearsals of a band called Pegasus, the nearest thing to a prog-rock band I'd seen up close.

Another Yes fan that was part of the Meols scene joined Pegasus. He was different to the rest, more arty and a little contrary. This was Andy, who'd been at school with John Floyd. We reconnected at this time. Andy and I shared a love of Yes. He was the only person of my age group I can remember admitting to it.

GARY HODGSON

I went to Hillbre High School with Paul. I played guitar. We had a band in school called Equinox and Pegasus were our rivals. They were a prog-rock band and we were doing more electronic stuff. Equinox rehearsed above a very smelly fish shop in Hoylake in my Mum and Dad's house, and at a place in Greasby – long since knocked down - by which time we were getting a bit more serious.

Andy and Paul were with us. Paul used to 'play' the radio. He'd take a radio apart and get it to make weird noises before getting into playing keyboard.

Then Paul and I went to Riversdale College, although we spent a lot of time taking the train in the opposite direction, going to Freshfields, near Southport, walking across to the golf course, picking cigarette ends off the pavement and smoking them.

ANDY MCCLUSKEY

Paul was the roadie; he didn't play anything. He had technical knowledge and I remember the first time we ever played, at Hilbre school hall in some music festival. In the soundcheck my bass-head blew the fuse. Paul removed the fuse, wrapped it in foil from a cigarette box and put it back in. But the spring wouldn't hold properly. It was now too big. He hid behind the bass speaker, pressing this fuse, in serious danger of being electrocuted. That was the first time Paul was on stage with me musically.

Humphreys and I had actually been on stage together previously at Meols Primary School when, independently of each other, we'd done something naughty in class and were made to suffer lunchtime detention. We were sent into the hall to stand on stage whilst everybody else ate their food and laughed at us. Only when the entire school had finished were we allowed to come down off the platform and have lunch. Neither of us can remember what we were being punished for.

There was one other thing we subsequently discovered we had in common in primary school. Although in separate years, both of us were in recorder groups but couldn't actually play. We each adopted the same tactic, sitting on a table full of girls, miming in hope that they would cover up for us. And we both got found out!

As well as playing with Paul's school friends, I had mates at my school who were in a rock band. These included Duncan Lewis and Gary Kewley. Gary wanted to enter a Battle of the Bands competition. Even though we weren't a band, we still went down to talk to them about it. 'Look, we'll be a band if they'll have us.' Gary said, 'I play guitar. What are you going to be?' 'I'll be the drummer.' 'OK. Have you got a kit?' 'No.' I couldn't afford a drum kit. Then I started playing guitar and it hurt like hell. Duncan had a Fender Jazz bass copy. It was chocolate brown or dark burgundy and it was the sexiest, heaviest thing I'd seen in my life. It had these cutaway curves and the shape of it made me think, 'I want to be a bass player. It's only got four strings, they don't hurt as much to play as a guitar does and I can't afford a drum kit!' So it was a slow process of edging towards wanting to get a bass.

I'd started working with Paul's friends but, because we were both in Meols and the others lived elsewhere, Paul and I were closer. That summer I also started buying German import records. I had a paper round on a Sunday morning. It didn't pay much but I'd get enough money to buy an album the next Saturday. I'd go to Liverpool in the morning, buy a record and we'd listen to it at Paul's house whilst his mother was at work. I only had my mother's mono Dansette player from the '60s but Paul, with his electronics knowledge, had built a stereo. That's how we started listening to those imports together. We developed this symbiotic relationship. I would go to Probe Records in Liverpool on Saturday morning to buy Kraftwerk or Neu or whatever was in the German import bin, then I'd go to his house.

Objects for mechanical tapes
– why hard + square – round? spherical?

Recorded machines – played back and distorted through echo + fuzz + wah-wah + phase etc. also down stubaphone.

[Diagram: amp and mechanical sound connected to speaker with microphone, labelled 4'6", with note: either direct to tap or amplified + combined with other.]

	Speaker 1	Speaker 2	
phase 1	mech	mech	each phase lasts 20 secs and effect gradually builds in to end of 20 secs when it is max.
2	"	distort	
3	mech	total distort	
4	distort	distort	
5	total distort	mech	
6	~~total distort~~ distort	distort	
7	mech	total distort	

swapping

That's how it started. I got acquainted with him musically through his mates, but on Saturdays we'd hang out together if we weren't going to rehearse.

This was before Paul was in The Id. I had my bass and Paul started to make things that created noises and we began to experiment very early on in the second half of 1975. It was always at Paul's house on a Saturday. There was no space at my little through-lounge semi-detached with Dad home, Mum, two sisters and several greyhounds. My bedroom was 6' by 7'. Impossible to get more than me in. We began our journey at Paul's at 3 Frankby Road, Meols. Listening to records and Paul cannibalising any piece of audio gear he got his hands on. He built a thing we called the Noise Machine out of circuits he got from a diagram book. It just made a horrible noise - we'd shove it through fuzz-boxes and echo machines (all borrowed) and one speaker cab we made ourselves. We had no money. Everything was begged or borrowed but never stolen. Though it was seldom given back, usually because Paul had dismantled it for the circuits inside, so we couldn't return things. People got wise to us in the end and wouldn't lend anything!

So we just started making weird noises. We had an 'instrument' called the tuba-phone, a four-foot long cardboard tube that had carpet rolled up on it. We put a piece of plastic pipe inside then taped an old penny whistle thing to it. It became like a didgeridoo. Then we shoved a microphone in the end and put it into the echo machine. It was the most weird, ambient shit.

You can hear some of those songs on the free giveaway with the second album, the Dindisc compilation, all the really strange ambient stuff we made. We didn't have any keyboard. That was before we actually had something we could play a melody on.

DUNCAN LEWIS

Andy and I were in a band together when we were in the local youth club scene in Meols. Among the first gigs Andy and I played was when we went busking in Liverpool. We had a couple of out-of-tune acoustic guitars and only knew three chords. Where the lifts came up from James Street station we could keep warm and worked out that if we started to play when we heard the lift coming, we could get away with just playing those chords as people stepped out. Nobody was going to gather round to hear us play.

One song had a lyric that went something like, 'Spaceship, spaceship goes so fast, spaceship, spaceship shoot on past, planet Earth's no stopping place, since there came the human race.' It was pretty desperate. But it went

Andy's hand drawn notes for the 'tuba-phone'

OMD - EARLY YEARS

↑
Pegasus bass guitarist Duncan Lewis in the studio with Andy

→
German electronic band Kraftwerk released their album Autobahn in November 1974

over our three chords - E, A and D. I can't remember how much we made but to two young lads it seemed like a king's ransom.

Music was it for us. There were so many bands based along that little coastline. We would just swap gigs at the local church halls. We'd go up to Heswall and support the Heswall band of the day, or we'd go to Moreton and do the same there. Most of the gigs were church youth club-based and it was happy days creating our own nights and events.

My band was noisy, prog-rock outfit, Pegasus. Completely the wrong band for Andy. We truly were the un-coolest prog-rock band and Andy was already looking towards the angular, cool art-type bands. He did the right thing and jumped ship pretty quick. He'd finish a rehearsal with us and say, 'Right - I'm off to do some stuff with Paul.' We'd all pack up and he'd wander off. It was like, 'He's gone to see the other woman.'

Then one day he came back after he'd seen Kraftwerk in Liverpool and said he was leaving Pegasus because he'd absolutely seen the future and what he wanted to do with his music.

PAUL HUMPHREYS

I'd seen of Kraftwerk with their electronic drums. It was like knitting needles hitting pads with wires and I thought, 'I'm going to build one of those. And I did!

I went to the library in Liverpool, I spent a lot of time at the library in those pre-internet days and

DISCOVERING ELECTRONIC MUSIC

I was very fortunate that when I started being seriously interested in music, it was prog. I didn't have much money. I bought *Yessongs* second-hand and battered it to death. I was into Steve Harley and Cockney Rebel. But once I got to 15, that's when you start to establish your sense of self and utilise various elements to determine who you're going to be and how you're going to present your identity. In the tribal days, before the post-modern era where everything got detonated and you could have a bit of everything and mix and match, the clothes you wore, your haircut and the music you listened to were very much how you defined yourself.

I was also very interested in art, particularly alternative art. I liked Dada, not Impressionism but Dada specifically, because it was really weird and fucked up and asked you a question. I was to get more and more into conceptual art, so when it came to music I was fairly quickly getting tired of what I already saw in 1974 and '75 as the clichés of rock music - guitar solos and so on. We all hitchhiked to Cardiff Castle in 1975 to see Status Quo, who we didn't give a fuck about, and Curved Air and Hawkwind, who I wanted to see. I thought that was much more interesting than Quo, who came out with long hair, 'Duh, duh, du, duh, duh!' and flares. It was just, 'Yeah, yeah, yeah.' Whereas Bob Calvert came out like nutty Biggles in a leather-flying cap, a megaphone in one hand and a fucking machine gun in the other. I was like, '*That* is interesting!'

I was on a journey of looking for something alternative and in the summer of 1975, about the time of my 16th birthday, was in the bathroom at our house. There was a little transistor radio on the shelf and they played 'Autobahn' by Kraftwerk. I just went, 'Boom. What is that?' It ticked every box I didn't know I even had. It was weird. It was electronic. It was different. Yet it was melodic and mysterious, because it was foreign.

Off I went to Probe Records in Liverpool on the train with my Sunday paper-round money, looked in the German section, found *Autobahn* and got the album. I went to see them play later that year - on September 11th, 1975 at the Liverpool Empire. I sat in seat Q36. The trains weren't working. There was a bus service.

Wolfgang Flür says in his autobiography that I came and knocked on the door and told them, 'I'm throwing away my guitars.' No. It was a Sunday night. I'd just started in the sixth form at Calday Grammar School. I had to get the bus back to the train to get home because it was school the next morning. I'd never have knocked on the door of the Empire Theatre and introduced myself to them. I was just turned 16 years old and still had a 'fro and flares and a Dr Who scarf.

Paul and my journey into making electronic music was helped by a guy at Calday Grange called Graham Gates. He was a keyboard player and had a Selmer pianotron. I think we bought it from him for 25 quid. We finally had something we could play a tune on. It's a weird thing that plucks metal bars, kind of like a harpsichord, and has a long pickup. And then we bought a Vox Jaguar organ.

ANDY MCCLUSKEY

OMD - EARLY YEARS

I found circuit diagrams of a drum box.

I thought, 'What's a drum kit?' It's a kick drum, a snare drum, a hi-hat and a cymbal. So I took the circuit diagrams of those and built them on separate circuit boards.

I sold my Subbuteo kit to help pay for my first keyboard. I sold whatever was in the house! I had a massive Subbuteo collection. I labelled everything. I even painted the numbers on the backs of the players. I actually built a Subbuteo stadium. I put the baize pitch on a table then made stands all around out of cardboard. I hadn't thought that reaching over the stands would make it harder to play the game. The first stand I built was too high and you couldn't play, so I had to make it lower.

DAVE FROST

Paul Humphreys placed a local ad selling his extensive Subbuteo collection – boards and many teams - to raise cash for keyboards. My friend called at Paul's house in Meols and Paul's mum sold the lot to him for a few pounds. My friend still lives locally, is a regular like me at the Railway Inn, and still has the whole collection. Many of the boxes have Paul's handwriting on, with notes about teams, formations, etc.

SUBBUTEO

I moved to Meols as a nine-year-old in 1972. I lived in Park Road, not far from Andy and Paul, although I didn't know them. When I was about 13 or 14 I was a newspaper boy for NSS Newsagent's at Station Approach, Meols. One day I saw a notice on the board in the window advertising Subbuteo teams and accessories for sale. I was an avid collector so called the number to arrange to go around the house, just off Banks Road. I think it was Frankby Road. When I arrived, to my surprise a lady who worked at the newsagent's answered the door. She was really nice and I knew her well and we laughed, saying, 'So it's you I spoke to!' She explained that her son was selling all his Subbuteo because he was buying either a musical instrument or an amplifier. I can't remember which, but it was over 40 years ago. He had loads of stuff, but I could only afford the teams. I still have them in my loft. Move on nearly 40 years and I'm talking to a friend, Adrian Nicholls, and it emerges that he's related to Paul and mentions that Paul's mum worked at NSS for quite some time in the 70s. I described her and it became apparent it was her I bought the Subbuteo from all those years ago. I became a big OMD fan, but never realised until then I'd relieved Paul of his beloved Subbuteo.

PAUL HAMBLET

JULIA KNEALE

I think it's true to say that when Andy and I met at Liscard Art College, Wirral, in 1977, it was at the wrong time in our lives. Andy, 18, was studying a foundation course, producing large-scale canvases of dark, moody landscapes and such-like in thick-layered paint daubed with a palette knife. I still have one that he painted on hardboard. It's travelled with me all over the country, surviving several house moves. A few classrooms down the corridor, my own preferred medium for art was either smudgy pastels or ink drawings. I seemed to favour intricate details and shading, such as on birds' wings and flower petals. Two different artistic styles there, and given our personalities at the time, one would have expected it to have been the other way around.

 I was the more theatrical and demonstrative one, with my heart on my sleeve. He was more distant and preoccupied somehow. We were both high maintenance types in our own ways and, more often than not, clashing about something or other. I remember a set of Beswick ducks from my wall going west on one such explosive occasion. Yes, you've guessed it. It was me. If there had to be an 'our song', Bryan Ferry's 'On The Radio (Oh Yeah)' sums it all up for me. Perhaps Andy might say something by Kate Bush, but one thing's for sure, we both loved 'Heroes' by Bowie. Once in my attic bedroom, Andy, the late great John Floyd (of Radio Waves and The Id) and myself were singing and dancing dramatically to 'Heroes' and my mother yelled up the stairs, 'Stop showing off!' The woman obviously didn't recognise genius when she heard it.

 For all its exhausting craziness, our relationship was interspersed with some wonderful times. I tell more of this and my days in The Id in my book *Moods, Memories And Other Manoeuvres* (2014) for which Andy kindly wrote the foreword. It seems to be as rare as hens' teeth now.

 These days I'm a private, somewhat reclusive old dear, preferring nature, animals and writing, as opposed to anything flamboyant and dramatic, so the thought of appearing on stage with a globally renowned band, was terrifying me to say the least. Would I be able to hobble on arthritic legs up the stage steps? Would I trip over some errant wires and end up crowd surfing in my hometown of York? Would my microphone work? But, do you know, once I was up there and chatting to the band behind the scenes, it was just like old times, which only goes to show Nobody puts Julia in the corner. All is well.

NEILL SHENTON

I remember the first band I saw play in front of an audience was Hitlerz Underpantz. The singer

I USED TO DRINK VODKA UNTIL I DISCOVERED Hitlerz Underpäntz

The ultimate sound in migraine rock

If you want to jump on the bandwagon and be cool, get into HITLERZ UNDERPANTZ today.

↑
Hitlerz Underpantz
gig flyer

and main songwriter, Adrian Pratt, was much more musically talented than most and could really perform. If they reminded me of anyone it was the Bonzo Dog Doo-Dah Band. I recall Andy playing some gigs with them. I can't remember if he sang and played bass.

We were inspired to play all this in front of this audience at the United Reformed Church Hall in Hoylake. Some of us made an effort to change our look; I wore all white. John Floyd had a suit with cravat and stood with a glass in one hand and cigarette in the other. My clearest memory of the performance was 'Yugoslavia'. I looked across and had a side-view of John, Andy and Julia Kneale in full flow. They looked amazing, so happy and at home. Then I remember everyone saying how brilliant it was.

The second outing was what can only be described as short. This was an exciting development, at a club called Digby's in Birkenhead. We took to the stage and during the first or second song Andy tried to remove the mic. from the stand. The cable was taped on and offered more resistance than the connections in the mic itself so the wires came out. Someone leapt on stage and tried to throw a punch at Andy. *Neill Shenton*

ANDY MCCLUSKEY

The gig was a disaster. Made worse by seeing the other band playing that night at Mr Digby's… Big In Japan. It made me feel that our music was not very contemporary.

NEILL SHENTON

John (Floyd) and Andy were studying art and I think their teachers must have had some difficulty unpicking who had done some of their submissions. John, with his independence, became a magnet for many characters, holding parties that went on for days. John introduced me to Eno's music; an absolute revelation. We all loved Roxy, but this was something quite different. We wore out *Taking Tiger Mountain* and *Here Come the Warm Jets*. Then there were Bowie's German albums. All this, more than the punk revolution, drew lots of us together, something different from the past, signposting that everything can go into a musical mix. Andy was greatly influenced by this sound and ethos, before he fell in love with the Germanic influence of Kraftwerk and other electronica.

A new band was born and needed a name. My girlfriend and I were studying psychology A-level at Birkenhead Tech and had learned about Freud's dimension of personality, The Id; the uncoordinated drives and desires, perfect.

We left the room above the fish shop and looked for somewhere else. We found Greasby Library had a room in an adjacent building to rent and moved there, every Saturday afternoon. It was here we got to know Julia, Andy's very cool girlfriend, a little better. She appeared too cool to really talk to us oiks, but I imagine our well-established crowd was a little daunting. We no longer carried equipment on buses. Gary learned to drive and his Dad allowed use of his van. Not surprisingly, the van was stopped by the police more than once, but no charges pressed or anything illicit found. Hair was still long, clearly grounds for suspicion.

In that library, the band and songs took better shape. Gary and I played guitars; Steve, bass; Paul, piano, and Andy, John and Julia sang. It was a fearsome noise. A song called 'Rock and Roll' was a statement against rock traditions and anti-guitar. Andy wanted a deliberately horrible, out of tune, racket of a guitar solo and I was quite capable of delivering that. I think it was an early expression of anti-guitar sentiment.

Another song was called 'Yugoslavia'. I didn't ever quite hear the lyrics. Andy, Julia and John sang, and it was reminiscent of a march. I remember playing a part with an echo, using a Copycat machine, trying for a spacy balalaika effect. Another magnum opus was inspired by 'And You and I' by Yes.

The most enduring songs were 'Electricity' and 'Julia's Song'. I remember Julia working on the words right there. We played round and around that theme, so she could fit it all together. The version with all of us contributing and her singing was far more visceral and exciting than any that made it to tape. 'Electricity' was brighter, obviously, with that piano tune, but still a steam train of a sound.

PHIL CUNDLE

I went to the same school as Andy, Calday Grange. He was a year ahead of me, me living in Hoylake and him in Meols. I saw him every day as he caught the same bus. I never knew him personally but used to be in awe, as he didn't adhere to the school rules as such. Being a grammar school in West Kirby, regulations were fairly tough regarding uniform, hair and school bags. Andy hardly wore a jacket, had long fuzzy hair and a duffle bag with Hawkwind painted on the front. Back then there were a lot of gangs, notably Hawk (Hoylake and West Kirby). They'd go around looking for fights. Andy was associated with the 'hairies', boys who had long hair, loved heavy music and smelt of petunia oil. Being peace loving, they seemed to be left alone. However, this didn't happen to my mate and I who, after a few pints at the White Lion (Paul's local) at West Kirby, got chased by members of Hawk. My friend got beaten up and I escaped running down the railway line.

I saw Andy and his then-band - I can't remember the name - play Meols Church Hall. They went down very well. My Dad managed the Blue Anchor pub in Hoylake and advertised for staff in the paper. Andy applied and got interviewed by Dad, but unfortunately said he couldn't work most weekends as he was in a band, which at that time was the beginning of OMD.

I got to see Orchestral Manoeuvres in the Dark many times at Eric's in the next few years and although I emigrated to Australia soon after, we managed to see them back in May 2013 at Liverpool Empire on a trip back home.

THE ID, ST ANDREW'S CHURCH
11 August 1977, Hoylake, UK

ANDREW DOWDEN

I was in Paul's class at school. Most of his close friends were heavily into music, some of them were also involved with The Id. Collectively they were known as the 'hairies'. I seem to remember ex-Procol Harum guitarist, Robin Trower being one of their heroes. Perhaps the love of electronic music came later, saying Paul always had keyboards rather than guitars.

Andy and Julia Kneale always hung out together. One night I bumped into Andy in West Kirby. He said he was no longer in a relationship with Julia and was giving it six months to make it with OMD. We all know now how that drive and determination paid off.

I saw lots of early gigs, including pre-OMD related incarnations like Pegasus, Radio Blank and The Id.

The Id played St Andrew's Church, Hoylake with Mainline Junction on 11 August 1977, then twice in October played Hoylake Reformed Church with State Sympathy then Jasper and Hard up Heroes. Also that month they played Mr Digby's, Birkenhead with Tripicata and Rising Sun. The gig at Mr Digby's, a proper club in Birkenhead, was probably a step up. I saw The Jam there on their In The City Tour on 7 July – 7/7/77, a significant palindromic date in the year the two Sevens Clashed.

I seem to remember Andy thought my dancing … err, should I say pogoing, wasn't quite what the group wanted to be associated with. Things were of course moving on and The Id, later OMD, wanted to be at the vanguard. These gigs were well attended, even the ones in church halls. The group was developing quite a following.

DAVE BALFE
Teardrop Explodes, Big in Japan, Zoo & Food records, Blur manager

I first met Andy in 1978. I was 19 and Andy about the same. I've just looked it up, he's three months older. Wirral's finest and probably only punk band, Radio Blank, had recently come to an end and I, together with guitarist Alan Gill, had then formed the determinedly post-punk (long before that was even a genre) outfit, Dalek I Love You. One evening we found ourselves visiting a church hall gig in Hoylake and among the still prevalent bunch of long-haired, wannabe prog and heavy-rockers was a band with something a bit more modern about it - The Id.

But only a bit.

The band's musicians had the defining shoulder-length hair and swollen flares that we short-haired, tight-trousered punks sneered at as being from a now long-dead, grossly unfashionable era, just over a year earlier. True, the singer's hair was a little longer than we could comfortably accept, but it was unusually curly and somehow not quite irredeemably hippy.

Andy was definitely doing something interesting, something with more talent than most, something approaching contemporary. This was such a rarity, as to be almost impossible in those days. I remember admiring two songs in particular

OMD - EARLY YEARS

The means to an end. by FAT JULIA

①
The means to an end
A sinful distress
Writing down meaningless words
Vaguely off hand
So the rest of the band ~~can lea~~
Can learn from the bees and the birds.

②
Concentrate businessmen
Haven't got long
Planets are ruling your heart
Stilettos and thighs
May be burning your eyes
But it keeps you from falling ~~apart~~.

③
Heavy, but generalised
~~this~~ Sordid and wet
Someone advised me to die
Blowing your mind
Coz you know what you'll find
When you're looking for pigs in the sky.

④ Under the influence
Rotting our nerves
Cutting us off at the mains your grandmothers
Nearing the end with ~~a dog~~ friend
Is something ... do when it rains.

- 'Electricity' and 'Julia's Song'. I went up and spoke to him after the show, got to know him. So began a period where we'd meet occasionally to talk music and go to each other's gigs.

I was frequenting the musically cutting-edge Eric's Club, Liverpool, playing there occasionally. If Andy hadn't already been, I wouldn't be surprised if it was me who first dragged him along to sample its grimy, new wave delights. It was the possibility of playing at this deliriously cool venue, rather than the dreary pubs and church halls of the Wirral, that inspired in us all the urge to make music that was different and was for tomorrow rather than just emulating yesterday.

I remember bending Andy's ear many times that he ought to ditch his unforgivably hippy band and join us in Dalek, which he eventually agreed to do. I think three or four gigs across Merseyside over the next month or two, we played together, our set including 'Electricity' and 'Julia's Song'.

Dalek I Love You was, I still think, one of the most excitingly innovative bands I ever worked with. We were the first band I'd ever seen, much less played with, that used a synth, backing tapes and a drum machine. This combined with our then passion for anything 'surrealist' to create an anything-goes approach that was a joy to be part of, and enormously imaginative.

The trouble with this particular incarnation was that there were too many chiefs and not enough Indians. Andy, Alan and I all wrote songs and insisted on singing them. We were also all strong-willed individuals with views as to where we should be heading stylistically, in that excitingly crucial moment in British pop culture where punk had played out its hand but the next wave of musicians felt there was now a whole new virgin musical territory to expand into.

Because of this, I think, after those few gigs, Andy wisely decided to go his own way, which we thought was fair enough. It was all very amicable. When he and Paul reappeared a few months later as Orchestral Manoeuvres in the Dark we weren't enormously surprised to find the backing tapes/synth combination we'd used was being employed to annoyingly more modern effect as a more stripped-down electronic duo. Though we were definitely flabbergasted by the band's name.

The final chapter of the tale came a year or so later. Again, I'm guessing as to the timescale. By then I'd fallen in with a bunch of Liverpool musicians from Eric's and formed an indie record label with Bill Drummond - Zoo Records. At that point I think we'd put out singles by The Teardrop Explodes, followed by Echo and The Bunnymen, and were managing both. Out of the blue, Andy (or was it Paul, his then manager?) got in touch and asked if we wanted to put out a track they'd just recorded on their custom-built equipment in Paul's garage. It was 'Electricity', a song

←

Julia Kneale's original lyrics to 'The Means to an End' later known as 'Julia's Song'

EARLY YEARS | 27

I knew very well and held in high regard.

I've often looked back on the mistake I was just about to make and tried to work out why I did it - telling them to go and record it again because, I insisted, it sounded a bit too rough. I strongly suspect I was just trying to act superior, play the big label head to my old mates. It was ridiculously stupid of me - but I was only 20.

Instead they sent it off to Tony Wilson, who wisely stuck it straight out on his Factory label. It became the electronica classic that's now known and loved by us all.

Andy and I have remained friends over the centuries since these ancient events, but now we meet in big houses rather than bus shelters. Every time I think back to this era I feel enormous envy for our teenage selves. Despite all the insecurities and fears we undoubtedly had, we were nevertheless in a time when everything stretched out ahead of us, rather than disappearing far off in our rear-view mirror as it is today.

ANDY MCCLUSKEY

First time I ever heard the name Dave Balfe was when Malcolm (Holmes) had his snare drum stolen from the room above the fish shop in Hoylake. He saw the drum when he was walking past a tiny music store in Liverpool, underneath where our studio would be a couple of years later. He went in and said, 'That's my snare drum! Where'd you get it?' The guy responded, 'Oh, somebody just came in the other day to sell it. I've got his number.' It was a young man called Dave Balfe, who just happened to go on to discover Blur and live in a big house, a very big house in the country! We obviously forgave him about nicking Malcolm's snare drum, because a few years later I was in a band with him. In the summer of '78 I did some gigs with Dalek I Love You. They'd originally been a punk band, Radio Blank, but Dave steered them into being more electric, more weird

I always thought that Dave would ultimately be on the management or record company side of the business. He was the only one of us teenage hopefuls who had who had any kind of holistic overview. However, his entrepreneurial determination extended beyond just liberating Equinox's equipment. There was a music shop in Wallasey where Dalek I Love You acquired their Kawai synth free of charge, and Radio Blank had a trick whereby somebody would stand under the metal grille of a shop in Birkenhead with a mic stand that had a solid metal base. The accomplice across the other side of the street would go, 'Ready? One, two, three ...' and run across the road, jump to the top of the grille as the mic stand smashed the glass ... just grab whatever they could and leg it! That's how they got several items of musical equipment.

BRENDAN COYLE

Andy frequently came to my friend's house in Stanley Road, and I still have a recording from when he rehearsed there with The Id. He'll remember my bands The Games and Some Detergents. We had a deal with Frank Hessy's music store in Liverpool to get any Roland synthesisers or Yamaha straight off the showroom floor. Andy was like a scout, showing up at many of our gigs just to see what our set-up was.

GARY HODGSON

We were quite serious as The Id and doing quite a few gigs. Then, The Id became Orchestral Manoeuvres in the Dark and the rest of us were sacked off, a mass-sacking. I think Paul Collister had something to do with it.

Andy and Paul didn't like the guitar thing at all. Living so close together they spent a lot of time knocking ideas about. Andy had more enthusiasm from the start and definitely wanted to be a pop star.

The Id – Steve Hollas, Andy and Gary Hodgson

OMD - EARLY YEARS

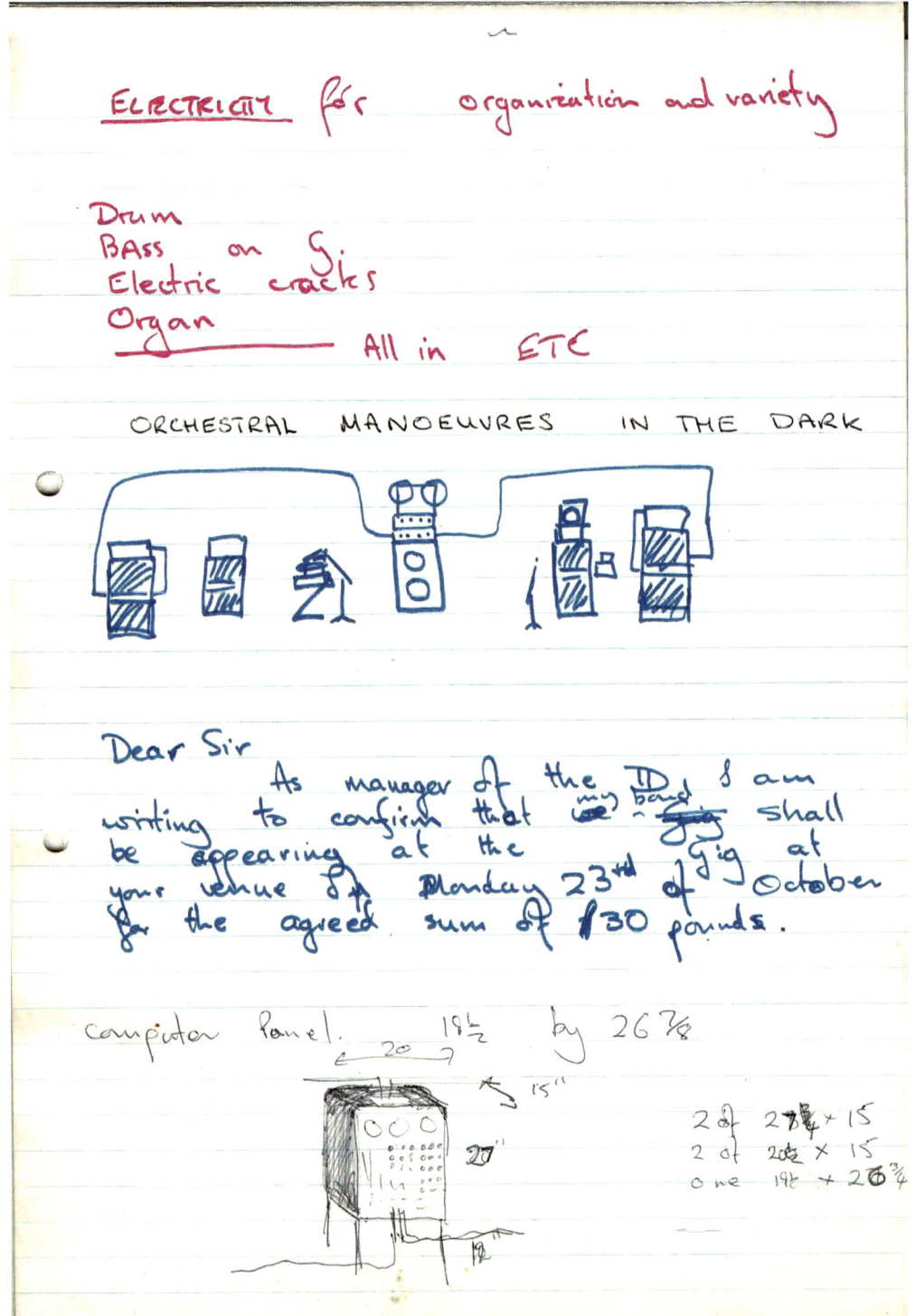

Paul left college to do Orchestral Manoeuvres in the Dark and I was left there on my own for a short while. I got a job doing electronics for the RAF and never looked back. Then several years later, after OMD had made it, I got involved as a roadie.

I couldn't tell you exactly when The Id ended. It wasn't long before that first Orchestral Manoeuvres in the Dark gig. Some of the songs on that first album are Id songs. We'd play 'Electricity' and 'Julia's Song', although perhaps not quite as well as Orchestral Manoeuvres in the Dark did.

ANDY MCCLUSKEY

The Id ended after we played at Eric's in August 1978. Gary, Steve Hollas and Paul Humphreys were leaving Riversdale Tech College. The former two were going to get jobs. It seemed a natural time to end The Id and play something more akin to the style that Paul and I now envisaged that we could actually do live.

DAVE HUGHES

I think the first time I came across Andy was when I went with a few mates to see The Id somewhere on the Wirral in early '78. Apart from 'Julia's Song', I don't think we were greatly impressed with the material but noticed they had some good equipment and thought Andy had an interesting look.

We were both going to Eric's Club as punters, so there was a bit of a crowd there, and we were coming from across the water, so were like a sub-group of foreigners in Eric's.

Andy came to an early Dalek I Love You gig and again we were socialising. We did a demo tape in a school hall and nicked Malcolm (Holmes) to play the drums on the demo. That was the first link, the first person we used from OMD, and the first time we worked together. Then Dalek I Love You started playing gigs with Alan Gill and Dave Balfe. We felt we were going down pretty well. We were doing Eric's and a few other trendy places, but Alan was quite shy as a singer and Dave Balfe was very pushy so suggested Andy, Malcolm (Holmes) and Martin (Cooper) get involved in a big variation of Dalek I Love You.

Andy's notes on 'Electricity', the stage set-up, a letter to Eric's and a drawing of the light box

EARLY YEARS | 31

ERIC'S

Eric's was home to the alternatives and outsiders. The thinkers, the questioners, and outcasts.

They built it and we came. Jane Casey was the Queen. Shaved head and black lips. Everyone was in awe. I certainly was. Smart, sexy and terrifying! There was Bernie, Boxhead and Yorkie. Holly Johnson, Pete Burns. Wylie, Cope, McCulloch and Paul Rutherford. DJ Norman, Doreen on the door. Balfe, Broudie, Budgie, and Bill Drummond. The same family of faces every time that you attended.

The 'house band' were Big in Japan. A supergroup in reverse. They all became famous afterwards. Lead singer Jayne (Pink Military), lead guitar Ian Broudie (Lightning Seeds), drums Budgie (The Slits, Souixsie and the Banshees), bass Holly (Frankie Goes to Hollywood) Balfe (Zoo, Food Records), rhythm guitar Bill Drummond (Zoo, The KLF). They are remembered for having just one bloody awful song that consisted of repeated shouts of 'Big in Japan'. It was chaos on stage but they managed to get a tolerable version on record.

My favourite Eric's groups were Echo and the Bunnymen and The Teardrop Explodes. The early Bunnymen had the drum machine, which made them less rock. Will was always stage right with his swirling guitar effects, Les stage left looking like a schoolboy but rolling these fantastic bass patterns and Mac in the middle all big eyes, hair and lips pouring out his acid lyrics. The Teardrop's songs were fixed on the best bass lines by Julian Cope, and Paul Simpson's organ playing was as cool as he looked. Their song 'Camera Camera' gave me the opening lines to our song 'Almost.' Echo and the Bunnymen, The Teardrop Explodes and Orchestral Manoeuvres in the Dark all played their debut gigs on Thursday nights at Eric's within a few weeks of each other. All three bands played Eric's together on one night at the end of 1978. We were on the small stage at the back of the venue and the others were on the main stage. Rather an appropriate staging metaphor of the fact that we were outsiders, even amongst the outsiders, for the three reasons of looking like unreconstructed hippies, being from the other side of the river, and playing electronic music.

ANDY MCCLUSKEY

PAUL HUMPHREYS

I think the catalyst for The Id ending and OMD coming into being was that Andy and I had lost interest in The Id. We were more interested in our electronic thing rather than the rock thing. We ended up firing members of The Id until there were only two of us left, then thought, 'Do we still want to be called The Id? Let's think of something more interesting.'

We called ourselves VCL 11 for a while. The 'Radioactivity' sleeve is like a radio and on the back is a picture of a circuit board. The old radios used to print the circuit boards and valves needed to go in them, and one of the valves is a VCL 11.

When the band started, I was always looking for an alternative to the music that was around at the time. So was Andy. Then we found it. I heard 'Autobahn' on the radio and it really was the first day of the rest of my life. I thought, 'That is the future of music and I want to do that!'

ERIC'S

Summer 1978,
Liverpool, UK

ANDY MCCLUSKEY

I got asked to play with Dalek I Love You and did several gigs with them. Martin (Cooper) guested with them as well that summer. But singing other people's songs? I wanted to do my own.

That summer there were things happening at Eric's which were changing the way we thought about it all. Eric's was the place where everybody went to hear the interesting touring bands. Not the Genesises or Yeses, but Devo, The Clash, The Cure, XTC, Pere Ubu. We went to Eric's every week. If you look at an old flyer, there were at least four or five things every month you wanted to go and see. It was just interesting and felt like everybody in the crowd in Eric's ended up being in a successful band.

That summer, The Human League released 'Being Boiled' and we were like, 'Fucking hell, where's this come from?' And we were standing in Eric's when the DJ played 'Warm Leatherette' by The Normal. I went to ask about it and came back to the bar, saying, 'That's English! Somebody in England has been listening to what we're into and they've made a record.' People were now making records of electronic music. I think The Human League played Eric's that summer. Dalek I Love You played Eric's with a tape machine and drum machine and a mannequin dummy on stage. They newspapered the back of the wall to customise it and create a happening or event. For us it was, 'This is much more interesting than a rock band.'

↑
Paul's soundchecking at Eric's, Liverpool

EARLY YEARS | 33

OMD - EARLY YEARS

Paul and Andy at unknown gig (top) and Paul and Andy at Eric's with homemade electronic drum box to Paul's right

Andy on stage at Eric's, Liverpool 1978

EARLY YEARS | 35

They had this talent night on a Thursday. The Id played a Thursday night just before we split up. Paul and I went and knocked on the door of the office of Eric's when we were there watching a gig, saying, 'Erm, Andy and Paul from The Id. Do you remember we played here a couple of weeks ago? Could we come on Thursday night and play, just the two of us? We'd like to play our electronic music that we've really always been writing but we've always changed it to play with a rock band.' 'Yeah, sure. What are you called?' 'We'll get back to you on that.'

Paul had a friend who also did electronics. He was a year older than Paul, had left Hilbre school and was now a Visionhire engineer. He had a Visionhire van, a tape recorder, which he called Winston and a recording studio in his parents' garage at their house. So we said to Paul Collister, for it was he, 'Could we record some backing tracks on your tape recorder? And go and do a gig, just the two of us?' He said, 'Yeah, okay, I'll help you.'

DAVE HUGHES

We did a few rehearsals and a couple of gigs; I remember one at Eric's and one at the MVCU (Merseyside Visual Communications Unit) in Liverpool.

But it didn't move on from there, because Alan Gill wasn't very keen in the first place. He wanted to sing his own songs and it was all songs Alan and I had worked on. Andy also had ambitions to be a writer.

Then Dave Balfe went off and joined Big in Japan, which just left Alan and I. Everybody who played Eric's seemed to be getting demo sessions off major labels. We were given some money by Phonogram to go and do some demos. My Dad had to sign the contract, as I was still 17. Explaining that to him was quite weird.

Within that set-up, we were working with tape machines and synths. Andy enjoyed that side of things. There was something that happened on the Wirral that I think was an inciting incident, because our side of the river was quite synth-based, whereas Liverpool was traditional guitar groups. There was a break-in at a music store on the Wirral, resulting in a few synthesisers and organs floating around the black market. I think we both picked up stuff from that, which put us on that sound ladder

The whole thing was quite light-hearted, but suddenly we had an album. Then Alan and I fell apart after recording the album. We went to Rockfield to record it and it just petered out. We didn't fancy gigging. Alan didn't want to perform at all and we weren't sure we were going to get another record.

ERIC'S
12 October 1978,
Liverpool, UK

JOHN DOWIE
comedian, musician
& writer

The thing about talent is, you can spot it a mile off. I've spotted it three times. Once, in the early 70s, when I performed on the same bill as an aspiring singer, writer, comedienne. Her name was Victoria Wood. A short time later, I spotted it again. Three men with dyed blond hair performing their debut gig. I watched them do their soundcheck and knew they were going to be massive. That was The Police. The third time it happened was in 1978, in Eric's, a club in Liverpool's Mathew Street, where I'd been booked to do my act. Two young men opened the show. I watched their set. One of them performed with the help of a reel-to-reel tape recorder and a collection of synthesisers that looked as though they'd been rescued from a skip at the back of Argos. The other plucked a bass guitar, sang, and hopped about in baggy trousers. They were, clearly, young and inexperienced. Just as clearly, they were young, ambitious, and packed with talent.

Thanks to the late (and much missed) Tony Wilson, I did a few more gigs with Orchestral Manoeuvres in the Dark. Only now they weren't opening the show – I was. Not long after, we went our different ways. I went into the world of Fringe Theatre. They went on to *Top of the Pops*.

↑
Eric's flyer showing Orchestral Manoeuvres in the Dark's first concert on October 12 1978 supporting John Dowie

EARLY YEARS | 37

OMD - EARLY YEARS

WE NEED A NAME

We were still called VCL 11, but thought, 'That's not the right name.' Roger Eagle from Eric's phoned and said, 'We need to advertise the gig. You need to give us a name.' We only had about four hours to decide on the name. We ran around to Andy's house. He kept all our song titles written on his wall. We thought, 'Let's just pick one that says we're really not like any other band.' One of them was 'Margaret Thatcher's Afterbirth', so we could have been called that. MTA!

Fortunately, we chose 'Orchestral Manoeuvres in the Dark'. We had a lot of song titles that were linked to possible musical experiments. The idea for 'Orchestral Manoeuvres in the Dark' was that we were going to use some classical samples and recordings of orchestras. It's a running theme throughout OMD. Andy and I have always been fascinated with war. So the manoeuvres were that we were going to put war noises like machine guns and things across classical music, and 'in the dark' because we didn't really know what the hell we were doing. So that was going to be 'Orchestral Manoeuvres in the Dark', which never actually saw the light of day as a song.

PAUL HUMPHREYS

→

Andy's strangely matter of fact notes about the band's second ever gig at the Factory in Manchester, commenting on the PA system and a new disco song he's working on.

STEPHEN MORRIS
Joy Division & New Order

The passage of time plays many tricks. Some on the soul, some on the body, but mostly the mind. It's the memory that suffers most. The past seems to grow more and more porous with each passing month. Until absolute certainty becomes uncertain speculation. It'll never happen to you of course … until the day it does. The trouble with this recollection is that while we can all agree it actually happened, the when and where are a little ambiguous.

What exactly can I tell you of memories of Orchestral Manoeuvres in the Dark? Not an easy name to remember, I know I thought that. That they are from Merseyside. That's fairly solid ground. Maybe I should start there.

Mathew Street, Liverpool. I had my first gig with a band called Warsaw. A Saturday afternoon matinee at Eric's, sometime in August 1977. Manager Roger Eagle gave many bands their first gig here. Roger was good like that. A lovely man, he loved music and had a good ear. Without him many things would not have happened the way they did.

The band Warsaw became Joy Division and in October 1978 we had recorded two songs for the Factory Sample, Factory's first excursion into vinyl. Sometime later that month I crossed paths with two young men who called themselves Orchestral Manoeuvres in the Dark. That's where things get a bit murky and confusing. Old age is most likely to blame.

Andy and Paul are sure they

October 27th Friday

We played the 'Factory' in Manchester - a club which is run by Tony Wilson. Paul Collister the Sound Man/Manager/Electrician/Van driver - you name it mixed us through a 2,000 watt PSL hire P.A. using a stramp 16.2 desk.

We seem to be getting enough gigs to keep us happy so we are concentrating on building new equipment. Paul has the electronic percussion nearly finished and I am building some large back-drops which are proving more difficult than I had imagined.

I have been trying to write a disco song for about 3-4 weeks but it is just not coming - actually we have not written anything for over a month. By the next concert I hope to have the backdrops and the drums fully operational. Paul (H) will play the drums on stage - purely to show people what is making the noise.

OMD - EARLY YEARS

played their first gig with Joy Division at Eric's on 12 October 1978. I on the other hand think we may have played Kelly's in Manchester on that date. But we definitely did meet in October '78 in some North West club or other.

I remember our first meeting well. It was a shared interest in musical equipment and a shared love of the music of Kraftwerk and electronic music that first got us talking. I was assembling my drum kit on a sticky carpet in front of a well-trodden stage. Andy and Paul were nearby, setting up their small collection of keyboard and boxes. I could be wrong, but I don't think there were any actual synthesisers. Their largest bit of gear was a reel-to-reel tape machine. Andy, spotting my black flying saucer shaped Synare 3 drum synthesiser, came over for a nosy. Syndrums were cutting edge items in 1978. They were used mostly for the 'pew pew' drum sound, a 70s disco trademark. In the wrong hands though, they could do much more than that. Andy, never having seen a drum synth before, was interested. He asked what I used it for. 'Weird noises mostly,' was probably my unhelpful reply before moving on to ask what they used the reel-to-reel for. The tape machine turned out to be the third member of the band. I confess I was dubious. Using tapes live sounded a bit risky to me.

But OMD carried it off surprisingly well. There was a lot of space in their sound. Andy, Paul and the reel-to-reel looked cool together. They had that self-confidence all Liverpool bands seemed to have. They had great songs too, electronic and fresh sounding.

I'm biased - I've always liked playing with bands without drummers. They made my life easy. Took up less room. Probably Rob Gretton, our manager, passed on Tony Wilson and Alan Erasmus' address at Factory to them. One thing I do remember for certain, the pigeonhole 'synth pop duo' hadn't been invented then.

We played several Factory nights with OMD. Being drummer-less they were easy to accommodate on tiny stages with two other bands on the bill. We'd wind them up, getting them to go on straight after the Amazing Aynsley the fire-eater. How he got on the bill I really can't say. It must have seemed like a good idea at the time. The trouble was after he finished his death-defying act; the stage was engulfed in a cloud of noxious fumes. The fallout from the lighter fluid gas that was Aynsley's main tool of the trade - after fire of course. The stench was horrendous and made breathing very uncomfortable and unpleasant. Health and safety would've had a field day! We would toss a coin to decide who'd go on next. If we lost it'd be best of three.

I'd hate to think this was anything to do with their short time with Factory. Though sticking with Peter Saville for the artwork was a very good idea. Tony would rave enthusiastically about the sleeve design for 'Electricity.' 'You should see Saville's sleeve idea - brilliant! Black on black.' That sleeve along with the cut-out design he did for the first album are probably two of Peter's finest.

ANDY MCCLUSKEY

We put our tapes together, got Paul Collister to drive us over, and got our gear. We didn't have a synthesiser so borrowed one from the art college. We created ourselves for one gig and we went down there.

We can't remember when we played Eric's. I always remembered the date as being September but could never find anything that proved it. Then we found a flyer that says October 12th: 'Making their first appearance since the demise of their parent band The Id, Orchestral Manoeuvres in the Dark, supporting John Dowie.' John Dowie was going to be on Factory Records and was being championed by Tony Wilson.

I've spoken to Stephen Morris about how we supported Joy Division that first night we played. He said, 'Yeah, I remember that gig. Eric's, Thursday night, yeah. We came over from Manchester.' I said, 'Do you remember you were setting up?' He said, 'Yeah, I set my drum kit up on the floor and you and Paul were talking to me about my Syndrum.' I said, 'Was it October 12th? I've looked at your website and it says you played a Rock Against Racism gig at Kelly's.' And he said, 'Yeah, we did play there.' I said, 'How do you know?' He said, 'Because I've got the receipt. We got paid 30 quid. Are you sure it wasn't August?'

So the date of our first performance seemed in dispute, but the fact we supported Joy Division is not in dispute. Or is it?

The owners, Pete and Roger actually semed to like what we did, even though there were less than 30 people in the crowd, mostly our friends and family, who probably left after we came off stage. So perhaps only 10 people watched the main act. They said, 'the artist you've just played with is from Manchester and we've got this reciprocal relationship with some guys in Manchester who are running a club night called the Factory. Do you want us to see if we can get you on down there?' And we said, 'Yeah, okay.' We were going to do one gig but decided to do two because we'd been offered another gig. 'Okay, we'll do two gigs.'

GARETH BRENTNALL

I recall the first gig at Eric's in Mathew Street. We were there pretty much every week in 1978 and '79, seeing all the punk greats – The Clash, The Stranglers, etc. Orchestral Manoeuvres in the Dark were like nothing anyone had heard before. We liked it so much that the boys had to rewind the Revox for an encore.

OMD - EARLY YEARS

Andy and Paul in Meols, '78

→ Andy's list of gigs from 1977-1978

ANDY MCCLUSKEY

It was bloody terrifying playing Eric's as a two-piece. There is safety in numbers! In the early days Paul always played side-on looking across the stage. I was facing the audience. All 30 of them. A few family members, friends and the odd Eric's regular who could actually be bothered to leave the bar and look at us. I recall a smattering of almost sympathetic applause from the more generous of our mates but stony silence from all others. However, I do also recall being really delighted with ourselves for daring to do it. Those early gigs seemed quite attritional. There was often a sense of antagonism from an audience that was usually pretending to be rather blasé, or who were punks and couldn't get off on an electronic duo with a tape machine.

As well as Winston on stage we had a box that we had made ourselves from an old panel bought at a radio spares convention. Dozens of coloured lights that we arranged to keep flashing. Tony Wilson asked us what it did. He was most disparaging when he found out it was only for show. 'Stop pretending lads. You need to fuck that thing off and just be honest. One day you will be surrounded by real computers up there'. Another Wilson prophecy that came true.

SYNTH PROBLEMS

Paul had the Vox Jaguar organ and Selmer Pianotron but no synth. We were borrowing synths. We had a friend, Adrian Pratt, who had been in Hitlerz Underpantz and had a synthesiser. We borrowed that and, if we couldn't we'd borrow a Kawai (from Dalek I Love You) or the Roland sh-1000 from the art college. There was one in Whetstone Lane in Birkenhead and I knew the guy there because we did a musical piece for them, a performance one night in Birkenhead, where we put loads of chains and things into the piano and couldn't play it. We just free-formed in a very alternative way, which is exactly what we did to the piano at Ridge Farm when we recorded 'VCL XI'. You can hear this piano with all this metal in it, going 'clang clang clang'. We were practicing for that.

One gig we did at Eric's, we borrowed a synth that Paul didn't know how to utilise. He said, 'I don't think I know how to make a sound that we can use in the song 'Dancing', so what are we going to do?' I said, 'We just won't play it.' 'Yeah, but it's on the tape.' 'Get the tape recorder in here.' 'We haven't got a spare spool.' We spooled it onto the floor and left it, so there was a quarter-inch tape of 'Dancing' backing track left at Eric's because we couldn't play it that night.

ANDY MCCLUSKEY

BUYING THE FIRST SYNTH

PAUL HUMPHREYS

For the first four or five OMD gigs we didn't actually own a synthesiser. An electronic band without a synth! We knew two people on the Wirral who had synths and borrowed theirs. It made it very difficult, because I had to invent sounds as I went - it wasn't the days of pre-sets. I had to wing it every night, and we hated having to do that.

Andy's mum had the Kay's mail order catalogue, and in there was

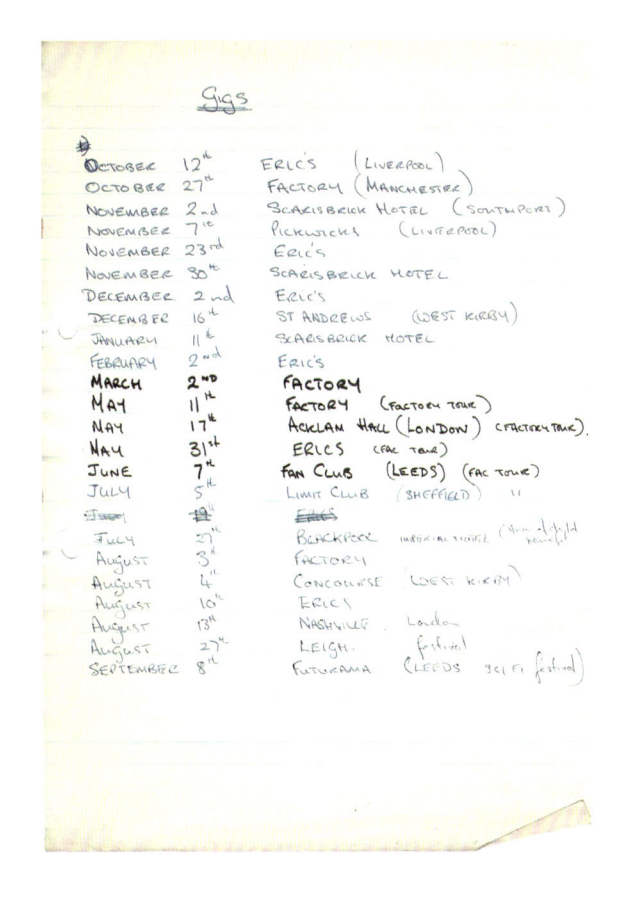

EARLY YEARS | 43

OMD - EARLY YEARS

Paul and Andy in the back room at 3 Frankby Road

a Korg synth, £7 something a month over 36 weeks. Andy and I used to get the money together to pay that off every month.

So we finally got ourselves a synth, which was pretty shit really. It was just variations of the sound, 'EEEEEEEEEEE'! We'd process it through all kinds of effects we made, just to make it sound interesting. But that was our first synth and the only synth on the first album.

ANDY MCCLUSKEY

We thought, 'We can't keep borrowing bloody synths. Paul doesn't know what to play on them.' You borrow it on the day of the gig without a frigging clue what to do. 'What do these buttons do?

The one we bought was £7.76 for 36 weeks, paid for out of our dole money. I think the dole was £14 a week then. Half of that went to my mum for my keep, and half of what was left went on that synth, with the other £3.50 for a couple of pints of beer and the train to Eric's.

We both made decisions in the summer of '78. I had a place at Leeds Polytechnic to do a BA in Fine Arts, which I'd chosen because they did sculpture and because they had a recording studio, the two things I was interested in. I was delighted that I got in, because there were only 40 places and 800 applicants. But I decided to take a gap year. My family were okay about it: 'You've got your place, that's fine. You're going to university, so if you want a year to chill that's okay.'

For years and years when I was in the band, I always assumed I would go back to university and do my fine art degree. I thought, 'Any minute now the band will stop.' I'd done a foundation year, and my work was obviously good enough, because it got two people into university.

John Floyd, a year younger than me, who was also in The Id, went to art college and did nothing but still wanted to go to university. He said, 'I haven't got anything to show them. Can I borrow your portfolio?' I agreed that he could.

My portfolio included photographs of my art - me wearing masks, me standing in this lighting installation. There

↑
Paul and Andy and equipment at the back of 3 Frankby Road

was no sign of him in the photos. When he was interviewed, they asked, 'Why are all these photographs of somebody else?' 'John Replied' 'Oh that was my mate. I was taking the pictures and he was modelling the masks and sculptures. He's in the photographs just to give it scale.' He blagged it and got in. So my portfolio got me into Leeds and him into Nottingham (I've still got photographs missing from my portfolio that he never gave me back).

Paul was offered a job with Post Office Telecommunications - BT as we know them now - to go to London to be trained as a telephone engineer. He was so interested in doing music that he never told his mum he turned it down. She would have been livid if she'd found out. He just went on the dole like I did.

Neither of us looked for jobs. We just went to Paul's house every day and wrote songs. That was when we wrote the rest of the first album, and some of what became the second album. His mother was working. She still worked at the newsagent's six days a week. Fortunately there was nobody else in the house. Apart from one occasion when she was ill. She was upstairs with a really bad cold, we were writing 'Bunker Soldiers.' We laid the drum sound and bass down on the tape and it just went on for five minutes. The tape would run out and we'd wind it back, then add the vocals and wind it back, over and over again. This must have gone on for three hours. Finally, the door opened and his Mum appeared, saying, 'It's a very nice song, but do you know any others?'

The difficulty came the next year for me, when I decided to not go to university. I'd also got a job because we needed more money for more gear. We were up to our eyeballs on our £14 a week, so I joined the Civil Service. Because I had 'A' levels, I could be an executive officer. I got £64 a week, a considerable improvement on my dole money. So for three months starting in the summer of '79 and just before my birthday I went to work in the Cunard Building right down on the Pierhead in Liverpool, processing cargo entries for Her Majesty's Customs. God, it was boring.

I got that job just as 'Electricity' was coming out on Factory in May 1979. By that stage, we were doing quite a lot of gigs: Factory package gigs with A Certain Ratio, John Dowie and Joy Division. We'd play Blackpool Imperial Ballroom, F Club in Leeds, the Nashville Rooms in London, the Limit Club in Sheffield. Phil Oakey says he saw us there.

ERIC'S
23 November 1978, Liverpool, UK

DEE WILIAMS

My memories of OMD stretch back 40-plus years. I regret to say initially they were based on lust for Paul Humphreys, but this is a story of the band's music's influence on all stages of my life. Born on the Wirral and brought up in Ellesmere Port, the 'wrong side' of the peninsular, the Wirral's a strange place, the M53 motorway neatly dividing us into two halves. The Western side is affluent, green and rural and overlooks the River Dee, including leafy Heswall, West Kirby, Hoylake and Meols. On the Eastern side, where I come from, it's far grittier: the industrial part, with all the factories (many now closed, contributing to a run-down feel), the Vauxhall car factory and refinery where my dad worked. OMD found inspiration in the industrial landscape of Stanlow, but what Andy and Paul's beautifully-crafted song omits is that the refinery stinks, and my Mum - long before awareness of pollution was recognised - worried about the effect all this had on the lungs of her young family.

I had a very happy childhood, although money was tight, with four older brothers, the 'baby' of the family and only girl, quite spoilt. My brothers were heavily into the Wirral music scene and three became massive OMD fans.

Eventually Dad got a car for work, and there were often fights among my brothers as to who was allowed to borrow it. There was a sure-fire way to secure 'custody': saying it was needed 'to take our Dee on a trip to the seaside', either Hoylake or West Kirby. My brothers all liked going over to the 'posh' side, believing the girls were of a superior quality. They also believed the music scene - the real object, not the beach - far superior: everybody seemed to be

↑ Eric's flyer showing Orchestral Manoeuvres in the Dark on the same bill as Teardrop Explodes

OMD - EARLY YEARS

in a band then, and I was ordered to disappear sharp-ish, do my own thing, so took a friend Penny.

Abandoned one day with Penny for company, we were in some sort of church hall or similar with a band playing, and I noticed the most beautiful man I'd ever seen. Paul Humphreys. Not that I knew his name. He was leaning against a wall and drinking. I saw him again about three weeks later on another expedition to the posh side and later yet again. Asking around, I was able to discover his first name. I was totally in love.

Weeks later, I saw what I believe was my first sighting of Andy, again at some gig at a hall. This Leo Sayer lookalike was part of the band.

I eventually made it to Eric's in Liverpool. People rather romanticise about it now, with benefit of hindsight, but I remember it as a complete dive. Leaning against the wall with Penny, I remember getting quite filthy. The whole experience was actually rather uncomfortable; we were under-age and plastering ourselves with make-up, not sophisticated. I saw Paul and Andy play there, late 1978 I think. I can't remember much about the event, other than they were the support.

JOY DIVISION

We must have played about eight concerts with Joy Division in 1979. I remember thinking how Ian Curtis's dancing style was not unlike my own. I loved Hooky's bass riffs and Stephen's metronomic but unusual drum patterns. These two elements were the foundation for Barney's (he prefers being called Bernard now) guitar parts and Ian's dark vocal intoning. Before Martin Hannett produced them they were more rock/punk. He imposed his vision on them and they adapted their arrangements to be more like that sound thereafter.

The first time that we played a gig with them we saw Stephen setting up his kit on the floor in front of the stage. We had never seen a syndrum before. It was amazing how that one drum completely altered his drumming sound and style, and the listener's perception of the whole rhythm track.

ANDY MCCLUSKEY

→

Andy's notes from playing gigs at Eric's and in Southport

ERIC'S 23rd November

Supported by the Inadequates and the Teardrop Explodes.

A minor disaster — Foldback amp burnt out so we played without foldback.

New songs that we could not play. Borrowed PA — the Bass bins of which were rubbish. A reporter from the Echo was there + says he will come and see us again.

Southport 30th Nov

Using H.H mixer we were loud and perfect. We had retreat to more easy musical ground but still included a song we had written that week using electronic percussion on the tape — for the first time. A good performance with favourable audience response.

DECEMBER 2nd ERIC'S

A last minute booking to replace the Cabaret Voltaire. We played supporting Danny Miller (Normal) / Robert Rental and Fray Bee. Had long conversations with Danny about Rough Trade and 'Alternative' bands.

The Matinee was a very good performance — we played the same set that we played at Southport. Unfortunately the 16 year olds did not really like us. The evening was very different — we played well, but the mixing was most erratic, and we became so fed up that Paul + I finished the set Early. Many people congratulated us — and we got a reasonable response from a fairly full Eric's.

We had our back-drop screens up for the 1st time and they looked very

OMD - EARLY YEARS

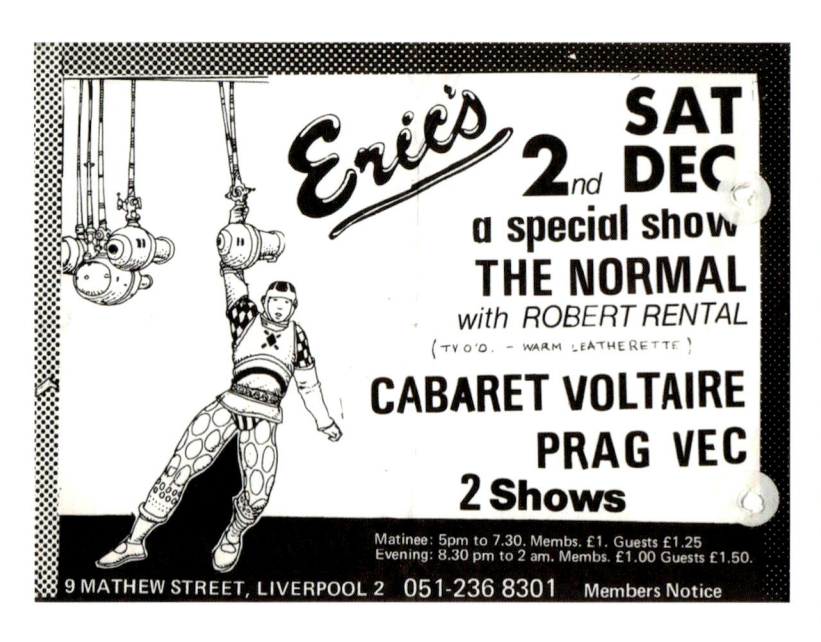

Eric's flyer for Saturday 2 December 1978 when OMD replaced Cabaret Voltaire

ERIC'S
2 December 1978, Liverpool, UK

ANDREW DOWDEN

Orchestral Manoeuvres in the Dark played Eric's on 2 December 1978 with Robert Rental and Daniel Miller of The Normal and Mute Records. I think The Human League were supposed to play but weren't able to get there from Sheffield due to snow on the Pennines. Come closing time the snow had reached Liverpool, but we managed to make it home. The entry fee was £1. Two weeks later, they were back at St Andrew's Church, Hoylake, supported by the Tings, entry 40p.

I owned a Selmer Pianotron, the keyboard used for the lead on the Factory Records version of 'Electricity'. Andy wanted to buy it as theirs was on its last legs. They used a different synth for the Dindisc version. I've still got the Piantron.

One time I got a lift back from Liverpool with Andy and Paul. The talk was of Granada TV using one of their songs as background music. Granada taped the record and spliced the tape, so the melody repeated but didn't include the vocals. Tape loops? That was cutting edge technology back in the day, and OMD used them with Winston, the TEAC four-track tape machine.

DANIEL MILLER
Mute Records

I was obsessed by music from a very young age, from before I can even remember. I learned to play a couple of musical instruments in my early teens and had ideas in my mind of what I wanted to do and sounds in my head I wanted to create but couldn't do it with my limited technical ability. That was always very frustrating.

I was in bands at school, playing blues-based music, but when I went to art school to do film and TV in late '69, I heard a bit of electronic music and it started to really fascinate me. Ron Geesin gave a complementary studies lecture at our college and brought along an early AKS Synthi. He'd just bought it so he didn't know how to use it, but brought it for us to play with. The raw sound of the oscillator just turned me on.

Then I started playing with tape loops and white noise, experimenting with the soundtracks of films we were making at college. I didn't have any access to electronic musical instruments but did have access to tape recorders at the college so could use other instruments and screw them up.

Then I started to get into early Krautrock bands using electronics in interesting ways, like Amon Düül, Can (who weren't strictly speaking an electronic band but were using electronics within the context), Tangerine Dream, Klaus Schulze and Kraftwerk, around the time of 'Ralf and Florian.' 'Autobahn' was a massive change for me. I was quite into drony electronic music but this was more rhythmic and poppy, melodic, humorous and ironic. I got into that very heavily and then felt I had to start creating electronic music myself somehow.

A combination of punk, cheap synthesisers and cheap recording equipment opened the door. I was travelling and also working as a DJ and assistant film editor. When punk happened, all the barriers were blown away and it seemed possible to do anything you wanted in music. Synthesisers were coming down in price with the early Japanese synths available on the second-hand market. All these things came together, and I thought, 'If I don't do it now, I'm never going to do it.'

I was working so could afford a second-hand Korg 700S for £200 and a four-track TEAC tape recorder for a few hundred pounds. I was off and running, recording in my bedroom. I got to the point where I thought, 'I quite like what I'm doing and I'm going to make a DIY single.' So I put out my first single, 'Warm Leatherette/ T.V.O.D.' as The Normal. I started to meet other like-minded musicians, artists like Throbbing Gristle and Cabaret Voltaire, and met Robert Rental at a Throbbing Gristle gig. I'd heard his single and really liked what he'd been doing. The people at Rough Trade, distributing the single, were really supportive and encouraging.

A promotion company called Final Solution, who did a lot of left-field gigs in London at the time with Joy Division and people like that, were putting on a night of 'new' electronic music and asked me and Robert individually if we wanted to play. Neither of us felt we could do that solo, so we got together and did it as a duo. We did that one gig, with the Cabs and Throbbing Gristle, then got offered three dates with pragVEC, including dates in Manchester and Liverpool. They were an eventful three dates. We went to Manchester and played the Russell Club, the original Factory. It was there that I met Tony Wilson for the first time. He was just about to start

Factory Records and showed me the artwork for his Cabaret Voltaire single.

The next night we played Eric's in Liverpool, and the opening band was Orchestral Manoeuvres in the Dark. They played 'Electricity' and remember thinking, 'My God, that's an amazing pop song.' We talked a little bit and they were asking me how to put out a single and stuff like that. I said they should get in touch with Rough Trade.

OMD are definitely still regarded as one of the key artists of that era. They still sell out huge venues. They're still working and they're still making music. There aren't many bands from that period whose early records have stood the test of time, but theirs really do. Like a number of bands of that era that are now very active again, people are really beginning to respect OMD and appreciate them. They were having commercial success in that they had hit singles and albums but, like many of their contemporaries, like Depeche Mode, they were making music you wouldn't think of as obviously commercial.

They're a band that people really respect, and their records still sound great today. They continue to be very active and most importantly they have a good sense of humour, which is probably why they're still going strong!

ST ANDREW'S HALL

16 December 1978, West Kirby, UK

ANDY MCCLUSKEY

My sister Helen became tired of hearing our father complain that I was wasting my time on music. 'Have you actually listened? she asked him. 'He's playing tonight in West Kirby, why don't you go?' He did, after he'd been to the greyhound races. Just managing to sneak in at the end, he caught 'Electricity.' Later that evening when I finally arrived home I was greeted with a rather contrite, 'I came to your jig' (as he was wont to say). 'That 'Electric' song is actually good.' Praise indeed!

His attitude was much more supportive after that.

RICHARD TRACEY
Andy's cousin

It's dark - blessed relief. I've escaped from an awful party on Darmonds Green, just around the corner from the gig. The hall is half-full. The reel-to-reel tape machine (Winston, as I now know) springs into life. 'Ladies and Gentlemen, welcome to tonight's performance of Orchestral Manoeuvres in the Dark'. This is no 'local band', this is meant to be something else.

TONY WILSON

We went down the Factory, supporting Cabaret Voltaire (possibly 27 October 1978), and met Tony Wilson off the telly. Then we 'blagged' him. We sent him a cassette.

He said we sent a reel-to-reel that over-recorded Val Doonican or something, which is bollocks. We sent him a cassette, saying, 'We met you at Factory. Can we get on Granada Reports?' That was the independent regional television news programme for the North West after the main news at six o'clock. Tony was a newsreader but because he was into music he persuaded Granada to get bands in and put them on. It was amazing. That's what we were trying to do. We were trying to blag our way on. We'd seen The Human League on there and thought, 'Well. we've met him. We can get on.' He said, 'No, I can't get you on. But I'm starting a record label.'

What we didn't know was that he was hugely underwhelmed by us. The cassette we sent him was rotting in a bag. It was only his wife Lindsay bending his ear, going, 'That's the sort of thing you should be signing'. Tony was a genius at rewriting history. So one week it was, 'Bunch of long-haired hippies from Liverpool doing electronic music' to 'You guys are the future of pop!' We swore at him, using a word beginning with F, saying, 'We're not pop, we're experimental. But if you want to offer us a record, we'll say yes to that.' So after we'd played literally two gigs, we got offered a record contract with Factory Records.

ANDY MCCLUSKEY

↑
Paul, Andy and Martin onstage at St Andrews Church Hall West Kirby December 16 1978

EARLY YEARS | 53

CHRIS DOCHERTY

I am a Hoylake boy and went to your gigs at St John's Church Meols and West Kirby the Concourse youth club, so I can say I am a long-standing fan. Around that time of my early fandom I was listening to the Radio 1 Annie Nightingale show late in the evening in my bedroom when she announced 'here is an interesting new record by a band from Liverpool called Orchestral Manoeuvres in the Dark'. We (Wirral) have been 'robbed', I exclaimed to myself and have always been miffed when Liverpool takes the credit for our proportionally large talent pool in Wirral. So, you can perhaps thank Annie for helping you along in those obscure days.

SCARISBRICK HOTEL
11 January 1979, Southport, UK

MARTIN COOPER

In the early days I played saxophone on 'Mystereality,' a song conceived with Andy in my bedroom using Winston, the tape recorder, with sax heavily featured. I was at Art College in Sheffield and during the early shows my part was played on Winston. In the holidays though, Andy and Paul asked me to join them on stage to play live, along with a version of Lou Reed's 'Waiting for the Man.' I jammed along with them. It was, and is, unusual for them to jam.

Later that year I joined Andy and Paul for a few shows, including gigs at St Andrew's Church Hall, West Kirby, Southport's Scarisbrick Hotel, and at Eric's, Liverpool (as Orchestral Manoeuvres in the Dark).

The Scarisbrick gig was my first in a proper venue. Unbeknown to me, my family turned up to give us support. I also doubled as crew as the proud owner of a little, much-loved blue Morris Minor van. I transported some of the equipment there and back and was very popular as I had wheels.

Winston appeared at all these shows. It was owned by Paul Collister, an old schoolfriend and the manager at the time. He named it after Winston Smith, the main character in George Orwell's *1984*, a novel avidly read by Paul and I, brought to our attention by a song of the same name on David Bowie's *Diamond Dogs* album.

DAVE FAIRBAIRN

When Orchestral Manoeuvres in the Dark landed their first gig at Eric's club in Liverpool it seemed to me they'd hit the big time. Although it was only a Thursday night, it was nevertheless at the coolest venue on Merseyside. Playing on the same stage where we had seen the likes of Devo, Iggy Pop and The Jam was a big deal. And they got paid - a crate of Heineken.

Although the Eric's scene has gained legendary status over the decades I remember the audiences at those gigs as slightly lacking in enthusiasm. I realised later that apart from their friends and family who had gone along, 75% of the audience consisted of members of all the other Liverpool bands, there merely to check out the competition. No way were *they* going to clap.

The first gigs I recall OMD played outside Liverpool were in the basement of the Scarisbrick Hotel, Southport, where, for a change, the audience were visibly enjoying themselves. I think I even spotted three people dancing.

I seem to remember my job title on that occasion was 'roadie', consisting mainly of getting things out of the back of Andy's mum's

↑
Martin Cooper with Winston

maroon Ford Cortina, putting them on stage. I also had the job of assembling the stand on which Winston was placed (centre-stage). It consisted of lengths of angle iron, like giant Meccano, held together with gutter bolts. We thought it was 'high-tech'.

A year or so later I was present at a meeting with the band and their then-tour agent, Chris Hutchens from the Bron Agency at their offices in London. Bron had a roster of some of the big rock bands of the time and OMD was one such big name. He'd compiled a list of all the gigs OMD had done to that date, including their early local gigs, the Gary Numan tour, and their own UK and European tours. In total, they'd played just over 100 shows. At the same time, they had two albums in the charts, a couple of hit singles and were about to start a major UK concert tour. This was no conventional rock'n'roll story.

LINDSAY READE

There are many myths around the creation of Factory Records which have gone into the annals of history via words and screen. One such story is about the Sex Pistols gig in Manchester being the catalyst for the beginnings of Factory. I don't remember Tony (Wilson) ever talking about it. What was more important was his music show, *So It Goes*, on which the Sex Pistols eventually appeared. Tony later dissed the programme and said it was mainly 70s rubbish, but that doesn't tally with my memory. When the two-series show was axed by Granada, Tony had the bit between his teeth and simply had to get involved in some other way with the music world. We both wanted to in fact.

Tony was an intelligent impresario, but his musical taste was suspect. He was more excited by the youth culture that inspired punk rather than the music itself - in other words the movement more than the content. I wasn't so much, knowing it to be a passing phase, although I did enjoy a few punk bands/artists. I was always open to a good tune, from whichever quarter.

Because of Tony's involvement with *So It Goes* and continuing role as a presenter of *Granada Reports* (with a spot for playing new musical talent), he was sent literally bucket-loads of cassette tapes.

One day, driving somewhere together, I noticed a bag-full of these cassettes. He was uninterested (overkill, I expect) but I wanted to see what sort of stuff was on there. Factory was in the early stages of birth, in fact had a recent delivery with the pressing of an EP ('The Factory Sample'). I thought we'd been scraping the barrel by giving John Dowie the same space on the first EP release as, say, Joy Division (much as I liked John as a person). Also, despite Tony's huge enthusiasm for A Certain Ratio (who he was managing), I was singularly unimpressed. Hence, it seemed relevant and important to pay attention to the offerings made by other bands.

I put quite a few cassettes on, which were rapidly tossed straight into the rubbish department. The OMD tape appeared after a while and Tony was all for putting that in the bin too. I told him to hang on, 'Let's give it another listen'. He was still somewhat unsure, but I felt strongly there was something there. I remember telling him I could hear this music in the charts. He must have been feeling indulgently fond of me that day, because he patted me on the knee and told me, in that case, 'We will put it out on Factory just for you.' His very words.

I was quite pleased. At this stage of the development of Factory I felt equally as involved as Tony. Whatever people say about Tony's financial inheritance, it was our marital savings that paid for the early Factory recordings. It was only later that I became disassociated.

One of the reasons I felt pushed out was a day I clearly remember after Factory had released 'Electricity' (FAC 6) with the inspired Peter Saville cover - a kind of musical black on black braille. Tony came home from work and announced he'd done a deal with Carol Wilson at Dindisc for OMD. He'd sold the rights for £5,000 (I think). All without my involvement or any discussion whatsoever. I don't think he'd been all that impressed by the group as he saw them as commercial rather than controversial. But that wasn't the point to me.

It was this kind of no-debate behaviour that helped eventually to end our marriage (though I was guilty on other counts). Like the day he came home and told me he'd bought a house he'd seen with Alan Erasmus. I refused to ever live in it. Silly girl, that and Factory were worth a fortune and I left the marriage with nothing.

PETER SAVILLE

We were in the same place at the same time. The incentive was Andy and Paul sending in a demo tape to the fledgling Factory Records, sometime in '78, just after our first release.

Factory as a venue started in '78. May and June saw the first dates at the temporary Factory club. The Factory was no more than what we now call a 'night'. It was just four 'nights', every other Friday for two months. That was the beginning.

The legend, according to the film *24 Hour Party People*, is that it was Alan Erasmus's suggestion to call it the Factory. He and Tony were driving around Manchester, seeing signs saying 'Factory closing', as with the de-industrialisation of the city. Alan quipped, 'It would be great to see a sign that says, 'Factory opening'!' It seemed a fairly obvious choice in Manchester.

I got involved with Tony and Alan in the nascent stages of Factory, just to be part of this incredibly exciting and seemingly important thing – the post-punk

OMD - EARLY YEARS

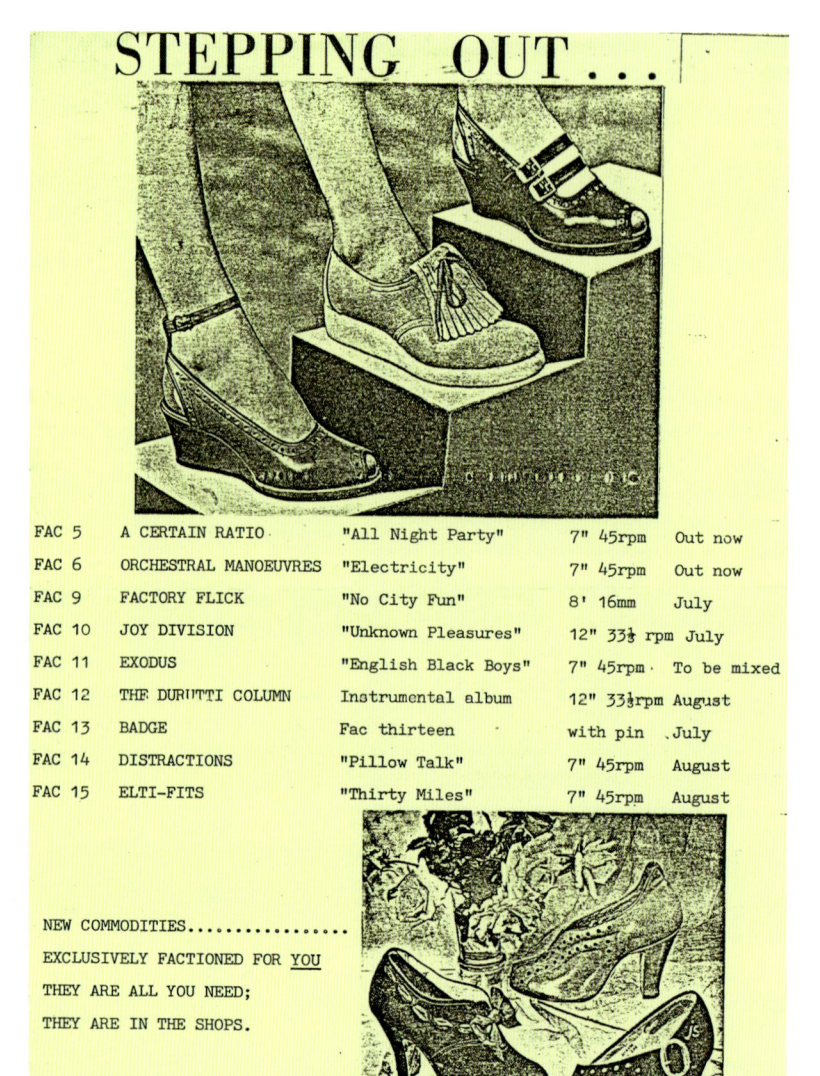

STEPPING OUT...

FAC 5	A CERTAIN RATIO	"All Night Party"	7" 45rpm	Out now
FAC 6	ORCHESTRAL MANOEUVRES	"Electricity"	7" 45rpm	Out now
FAC 9	FACTORY FLICK	"No City Fun"	8' 16mm	July
FAC 10	JOY DIVISION	"Unknown Pleasures"	12" 33⅓ rpm	July
FAC 11	EXODUS	"English Black Boys"	7" 45rpm	To be mixed
FAC 12	THE DURUTTI COLUMN	Instrumental album	12" 33⅓rpm	August
FAC 13	BADGE	Fac thirteen	with pin	July
FAC 14	DISTRACTIONS	"Pillow Talk"	7" 45rpm	August
FAC 15	ELTI-FITS	"Thirty Miles"	7" 45rpm	August

NEW COMMODITIES..................
EXCLUSIVELY FACTIONED FOR YOU
THEY ARE ALL YOU NEED;
THEY ARE IN THE SHOPS.

↑
A Factory Records flyer listing the latest releases

→
An early review of 'Electricity' stating that this duo are the future of pop music

→
Eric's flyer showing OMD on the same night as Teardrop Explodes

The best of the current crop is 'Electricity' by Orchestral Manoeuvres in the Dark on Factory. A danceable song which squeaks and sucks in a most intense manner, backed with a masterpiece more than its equal 'Almost'. Buy this record or be forever tastefully inferior. This duo are the future of pop music. Fact.

Eric's Dates

Members Notice
051-236 8301
9, Mathew Street,
Liverpool 2.

JANUARY/FEBRUARY

			members	guests
Sat Jan 20	**THE DAMNED** + Malchix	Matinee 5pm	£1	£1-25
		Evening	£1	£1-50
Thu Jan 25	Rock against Racism benefit with **China St** and **The Glass Torpedoes**		75p	75p
Fri Jan 26	**BETTE BRIGHT & the Illuminations** plus The Late Show with **The Moderates**		£1-25	£1-75
Sat Jan 27	**ADAM & THE ANTS** + The Straits	Matinee 5pm	75p	£1
		Evening	£1	£1-50
Thu Feb 1	Reggae with **IGANDA** + The Names (RAR)		75p	75p
Fri Feb 2	The 1979 Show with **Ded Byrds/Malchix/Teardrop Explodes/Orchestral Manoeuvres in the Dark**		75p	£1
Sat Feb 3	**THE HUMAN LEAGUE** + guests	Matinee 5pm	75p	£1
		Evening	£1	£1-50
Thu Feb 8	**THE LEYTON BUZZARDS** + Misprints		75p	75p
Fri Feb 9	From the USA **MOON MARTIN** (Big City R&B: he wrote 'Cadillac Walk' for Mink deVille)		£1	£1-25
Sat Feb 10	**GANG OF FOUR** + guests	Matinee 5pm	75p	£1
		Evening	£1	£1-50
Thu Feb 15	to be announced			
Fri Feb 16	to be announced			
Sat Feb 17	**STIFF LITTLE FINGERS** + guests	Matinee 5pm	£1	£1-25
		Evening	£1	£1-50
Thu Feb 22	to be announced			
Fri Feb 23	**NATIONAL HEALTH** plus the Late Show with **Inside Out**		£1	£1-50
Sat Feb 24	**WIRE** + guests	Matinee 5pm	£1	£1-25
		Evening	£1	£1-50

PLEASE NOTE: All evening shows start at 8.30 pm. On Fridays the main band will be on stage at approx 9.30 pm. When they have finished i.e. 11 pm admission will be 50p to see our new 'Late Show' Cabaret for the Eighties. You may of course see both shows for the price of admission to the first.
On Saturday the main group will be on stage at 10 pm and the support will play after they have finished

We are open every lunchtime (12 - 2pm) except Sundays for membership enquiries, badges and T-shirts. Call us on 051-236 8301 for our 24 hour answering service.

new wave – that was happening. I was still at college. My closest friend there, Malcolm Garrett, was already working with Buzzcocks, and getting together with Tony on the Factory project was a way of being involved too, which I felt was important. I went to meet Tony at Granada Television one day and just said, 'Can I do something?' He said, 'Yes okay, do a poster.' So I did and through the year there were a couple more.

We had a few nights through 1978, loosely under the title of 'The Factory'. Then at Christmas, on Tony Wilson's initiative, we temporarily joined the ranks of the independents and released a single, purely with the intention of it being a springboard for some of the groups who had played the Factory but didn't yet have a record deal.

There wasn't an agenda to have a record label. That would have seemed an overly-ambitious and adventurous notion. I'd just graduated from college and knew that sooner or later I was going to be en route to London to find work. Alan was footloose as ever in Manchester, and Tony had a very demanding full-time job with Granada. It's not as if we were sitting round looking for something to do. Also, we had no experience in the music business. We were not musicians, nor producers, nor managers. We weren't actually involved in the music industry, although Tony did have a late-night music show on Granada. We were just trying to facilitate something that seemed important. And that was Tony's sense of vocation – to realise possibilities.

We released a 7-inch double EP, intended to help the artists get a record deal by virtue of having something on vinyl – hopefully to fast-track them to the next stage. I put Alan's address on the back of the EP - Factory Records, 86 Palatine Road, Manchester 20. An unexpected consequence of that was that Alan Erasmus's flat was inundated with demo tapes. We reccived demos from all around the country from people who had a new label to write to, even though it wasn't a label! The postmen were bringing them in sacks, and in among those bags of demos was a tape from two young men on the Wirral calling themselves Orchestral Manoeuvres in the Dark. And that tape was a demo of 'Electricity.'

I wasn't opening the bags, but Tony gave me the tape and said, in a slightly disparaging way, 'Listen to this. You might like it. I don't. It's not my cup of tea. But Lindsay loves it.' Lindsay was his wife. He said, 'Lindsay thinks it's good. Tell me what you think.' I said, 'Who is it?' He read the label and said, 'They call themselves Orchestral Manoeuvres in the Dark, and it's called 'Electricity.' I decided I liked it there and then, without even hearing it. The name Orchestral Manoeuvres in the Dark and the fact that it was called 'Electricity' was all I needed. Thank God it was good.

My feeling was based on four or five years of loving Kraftwerk, probably the most significant influence on my cultural development. There were other groups I liked – particularly Roxy Music – but that was a stylistic affinity. I got something profound from Kraftwerk at the age of 18. It was a step-change moment in my cultural education. And the name of this group alone made me think of Kraftwerk.

A graphic designer whose work was enlightening was the Swiss typographer, Jan Tschichold. Later pieces of his work were classical concert programmes in Germany and Switzerland. His being formerly a Modernist and then ultimately a Classicist informed by Modernism was an influence on me. There was a subtle 'technological' dimension to Tschichold's work and he is probably the greatest typographer of the 20th century. There's a precision in the work, which has a technical sensibility about it and I was very taken by this and how it was coming through in his presentation of these classical music programmes. I wanted to try to be able to do something like that … and suddenly a group called Orchestral Manoeuvres in the Dark come along.

At some point in '78 I discovered a fascinating book of avant-garde music scores, including Stockhausen and Cage and how they scored their music in an unconventional, non-conformist way. Because the music itself was radical they had to find radical ways to score it. The normal notation was not really apposite to the sound of two cars reversing, for example. I picked this book up

←

Andy and Paul outside Eric's

OMD - EARLY YEARS

as abstract reference.

Suddenly the opportunity arose to work with Orchestral Manoeuvres in the Dark. I went to listen to that tape with great expectation and hope and wasn't disappointed. It was a raw energised proto-Kraftwerk kind of thing, and I loved it.

I said, 'Tony, please could we do this? Can we do this single for them?' And the combination of my passion for it and Lindsay's lobbying led to him saying, 'Oh fucking hell, yes, okay we'll do it.'

It was agreed that Factory Records would release a single for OMD following exactly the principle that we would do a limited release, and all being well that might help take them to the next stage and they might get a record deal with somebody. Which is exactly what happened.

Whenever I'm asked to describe the founding Factory 'principle' I say, 'Well, actually Orchestral Manoeuvres in the Dark fits exactly what we thought we were doing.' Joy Division don't. Joy Division chose to stay and said, 'Why don't we release our album on Factory?' That was never imagined. What was imagined was that we could have the vision to believe in somebody at proto-stage and be a springboard for them into the industry proper. So OMD followed the path of what we thought we were doing.

As a consequence of the agreement to do a single, it was arranged that I would then go and meet Andy and Paul at Cargo Studios in Rochdale. Ultimately, we met in the pub.

What was interesting, when we met, was that I had more affinity with them than some others in the Factory entourage. Tony and I had a certain affinity, but he was several years older than me, and that can make a difference. You might have some background in common, but they can feel a generation away. Tony and I got closer as we got older, but I didn't have as much in common with the people I was meeting from the other groups as I did with Andy and Paul. Particularly Andy. He and I got on from the beginning.

Andy said to me occasionally that if the group hadn't worked he'd have been a geography teacher. I can believe that. He and I might have had different points of view, but found common ground really quickly. At that first meeting I talked to them about my avant-garde music scores book and they liked that. We talked a lot about Kraftwerk.

Andy was from a middle-class background in the Wirral in the same way I was from a bourgeois middle-class background in Hale. He easily could have been a friend from school or college. I like Paul too, but he was always a little quieter. Andy's much more outgoing.

When I left the pub in Rochdale that day I felt I had a new friend. Often, we meet people and they're an acquaintance, but occasionally we meet somebody and think that person might become a friend. And he did.

I knew what I wanted to do for the sleeve for 'Electricity'. I wanted a score, so they roughed out a score for me. I talked to them about a

→
Review of the Factory Records night from Acklam Hall, 17 May 1979

radical score and how I wanted to use it and they gave me a sketch and I turned into an artwork. We made a very special sleeve for the Factory version of 'Electricity.' It was good. It's still one of the best things I've ever done. I think they liked it too. And it inspired a lot of black on black for the next 40 years in every field of graphic design.

DAVE FAIRBAIRN

The bright lights of Manchester: the Factory Club in the heart of the Hulme Estate. I had the task of operating the unique lighting system Paul Collister and the band built themselves: coloured fluorescent tubes that stood vertically in custom-made base units, the sort of lights normally seen in chip-shop windows in those days. The effect on stage was surprisingly impressive.

There was another dramatic event that night. The gig was going well - the first three or four songs at least kept the audience's attention. Then something changed. In preceding weeks John Peel had been playing the Factory Records release of 'Electricity' on BBC Radio One, and when the first bars of Paul's electric piano clinked out across the Factory Club that night the audience went mental. Everybody started dancing and jumping up and down! I knew then this was the start of something big.

ANDY MCCLUSKEY

I was initially disappointed about the sleeve for 'Electricity', as I wanted to design it myself. I'm quite determined about my own art, but I do, thank God, recognise other people can be better than I am. We said, 'We've got an idea' and Tony said, 'Yeah, okay, but we've got this guy to do sleeves. He's great. He's finished his degree.' And when Peter said, 'I want to do this with it', I thought, 'Yeah, this guy's probably going to do something much more interesting than my rough design. Let's see what he does.' Because when I met Saville I just thought, 'He's on another planet to me, this guy.'

Peter Saville has always been like my big brother. He's always been just a few years ahead of me. He's always more intelligent, more erudite, cooler. If I didn't love him I'd want to hate him, but I love him dearly.

That was the beginning of a journey. By total chance, we signed to Dindisc Records and left Factory, walked into the Dindisc office and there's Peter Saville. We said, 'What are you doing here?' 'Oh, I've just become their in-house artist. What are you doing here?' 'We've just signed to them. So you'll be doing our sleeves. Ta-dah!'

FACTORY NIGHT
Acklam Hall, London

FOUR diverse samples of current Mancunian Factory products: dopey comedian John Dowie; a cute pop duo called Orchestral Manoeuvres In The Dark; A Certain Ratio of young men desperately portraying themselves as artists; and finally Joy Division, whose unequivocal energetic approach was doubly welcome after the engaging but ultimately tedious naivety of the preceding players.

Making a rare appearance in the capital, Joy Division certainly deserved the affection of the few who heard their insistent, well-defined pop. Fronted by a jerky, disciplined singer in Ian Curtis, they were as exciting to look at as they were to listen to.

The singer's twitching robotic outbursts between vocal contributions provided the visual equivalent of relief through movement from the confined claustrophobic rhythms of drummer Stephen Morris and bassist Peter Hook, constantly clawed at from the inside by Bernard Dickins' nagging guitar playing.

Also interesting to a lesser extent, were A Certain Ratio ("Looking for a certain ratio" — from Eno's "A True Wheel"), who were last Thursday very conscious of their roles as artists, what with their uniformly severe haircuts and baggy trousers.

In contrast Orchestral Manoeuvres In The Dark, a keyboardsman and bassist vocalist, played airy electronic pop, like Kraftwerk during their lighter moments. Cute at the moment. Hope they don't get coy with it.

Out of the four samples Factory had on display, Dowie's daft humour was the least attractive. Still, his presence proves the eclectic, adventurous nature of the label — which in Joy Division, definitely has the basis for a solid future. — CHRIS BOHN.

OMD - EARLY YEARS

↑
Hand made poster for Orchestral Manoeuvres in the Dark appearance at Eric's on 27 April 1979

→
Advert for the gig at Acklam Hall on 17 May

→
Andy's hand drawn ideas for the 'Electricity' single

64 | EARLY YEARS

DINDISC

In the summer of '79, after 'Electricity' had been released, Tony Wilson said, 'You are the future of pop music' and we were like, 'yeah right.' He said, 'You should be having hits and be on *Top of the Pops*. We're too small, but I'll send it out to all the labels in London. It'll be like a demo and we'll see if we get interest.' One person was interested - Carol Wilson, who'd just started Dindisc. That was her present from Richard Branson after signing Sting to Virgin Publishing and making millions. She got in touch and said, 'Have you got any more gigs?' We said, 'We haven't got one for about two or three weeks.' She said, 'I'm really interested in you guys.' So we said, 'Well, if you want to come up, we'll play a gig.' She came to Meols and Paul's Mum's back room, sat on the sofa with Dave Fudger, her A&R man, and we played our entire set, which was probably seven songs. And that was it. She went, 'Oh great.' We played to an audience of two and off she went. We assumed that this would be the last time that we would ever hear from Carol. Fortunately we were very wrong!

ANDY MCCLUSKEY

OMD - EARLY YEARS

| ELECTRICITY | 21 MAY 1979 |
| WAS RELEASED | |

Music mechanics tuning up in the garage

by Fiona Shacklady

IT ALL seems very makeshift... music-making in a garage.

But for a local duo of talent, their lock-up garage could just be the first stepping stone to fame.

This month, Andy McLuskey and Paul Humphries — known collectively as local group "Orchestral Manoeuvres in the Dark" see their first record go on the market.

The two are helping to make an impact on the record buying public without taking the, by now, old-hat punk rock line.

Their single, "Electricity", is an attractive interpretation of the sounds from their electronic "music making" machines.

Forget the days of two guitars, a drummer and a singer, calling themselves a group. This duo produces a mature and sophisticated sound. Their single has touches of the smash "Oxygene", released by the French artist, Jean Michael Jarre, a year ago.

They probably wouldn't like you saying that... nobody likes to be linked, albeit tenuously, with somebody else's ideas. But face it, that single gave Jarre a very nice monetary reward.

Andy, a voluble, dark haired musician from School Lane in Meols, and Paul, the quiet, fair partner in the duo, have been together for a couple of years.

Both 19, they went to different schools — Andy to Calday, Paul to Hilbre — but over the past months, have been keeping musical company.

Local clubgoers may have heard their music at "Eric's" in Liverpool—a club where some of the up and coming bands in the area play their first public notes.

But says Andy: "Most people we know seem to think our music is a bit weird."

Andy is bass guitarist and singer-writer. With Paul on keyboards, electronic percussion and lending a helping hand writing, it adds up, in my opinion to something a little bit more special than some of the sounds around at the moment.

WORTH

But such is their lack of finance — their permanent state of poverty—that between them they've improvised on a number of their musical instruments.

Paul, who tried his hand at engineering, has designed — and it works—an electronic percussion "music box". With their other equipment, their worth as a group—at least materially—runs into a lot more than just a couple of hundred pounds.

The strange sounds their "music machines" make are an integral part of their whole performance. Andy adds: "We couldn't make the same sort of sounds without our percussion for example."

The two of them rely heavily on the electronic equipment and it's understandable. No way could they turn out the range of music playing standard guitars and drums.

The boys are definite: "We are not part of the new wave musical movement. That's just a passing phase."

Some people might call it cheating perhaps that the reason for the brief return to basic rock from the punk bands over the last year. But Orchestral Manoeuvres don't think so. "This is the way music is going," they say.

In a bid to make the big time, the two practise regularly. "We tried to work at Paul's house, but it just wasn't practical," so now it's back to the garage.

Surrounded by mattresses hanging from the garage ceiling, in a bid to block out the sounds from the streets, they pour their heart and soul into their sounds. Now they're hoping other people's cash will pour into their pockets.

In harmony... Orchestral Manoeuvres in the Dark. M30679

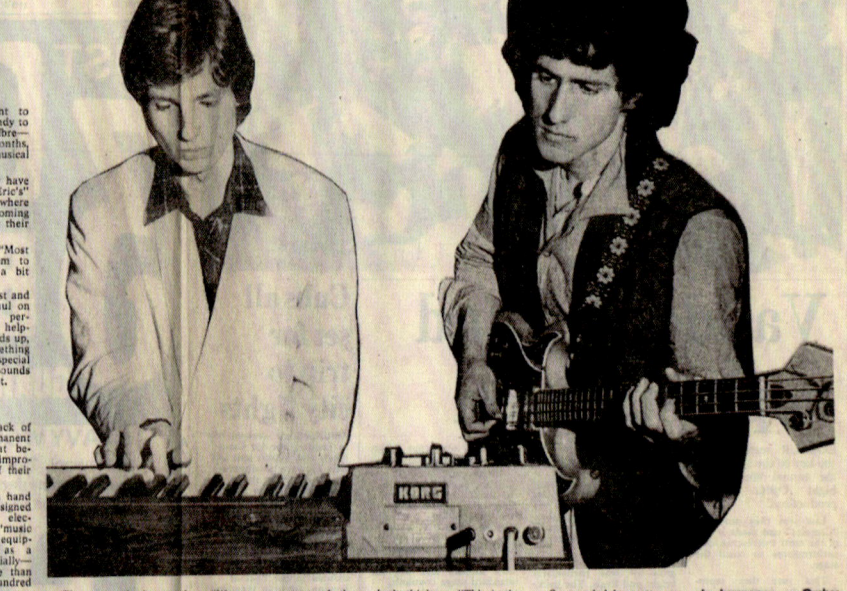

↑
Possibly the first major press feature on Orchestral Manoeuvres in the Dark in local paper *The News*

IMPERIAL BALLROOM

25 May 1979,
Blackpool, UK

ANDY MCCLUSKEY

When we played Blackpool's Imperial Ballroom, Carol Wilson was on her way to a holiday in Scotland, on the Friday just before a bank holiday. She'd driven up from London with Mike Howlett, her boyfriend, and the traffic was horrendous. I remember watching Joy Division, and standing in the audience talking to these two girls, saying, 'Oh yeah, they're really cool, aren't they? Did you see us on stage earlier, by the way?' And they said, 'Yeah, we're their girlfriends.' I went, 'Oh, sorry.'

So we were loading out, and Carol and Mike got to Blackpool just as we were putting our stuff in the van. She said, 'I've missed you. Read that on the way home.' And she hands us an envelope. We begin heading home in the Visionhire van, Paul Collister is driving, Paul H is in the back with the gear and I'm in the front seat. I pull down the visor with the little light on and open the envelope. 'She's offering us a seven-album contract.' 'No way!' 'Yes, yes, yes!' 'Read it, read it.' 'Okay, I'll read it. I'll read it again!' It was £30,000 for recording and £35,000 advance for publishing. 'It's seven albums and it adds up to £250,000! Aaaargh!'

It was amazing, driving home from Blackpool with a contract offer in our hands. How we didn't crash I don't know, because I'm sure we were all just screaming. The band had done seventeen gigs and we were eight months old.

CAROL WILSON

My favourite recollection of OMD is of two specific gigs: one, the first time I saw them, and the other just after their first hit. I used to visit Eric's in Liverpool most Saturdays to see if any new local bands were worth signing to my label, Dindisc. When OMD came on stage, I knew I had struck gold. They had fantastic tunes, were pushing out the boundaries of electronic sound, and had a charismatic frontman with a great voice, in Andy McCluskey. I was always particularly interested in innovation and originality, which they had in spades musically, but also I liked Andy's unique way of dancing on stage, which I thought gave the whole package an edge. When my colleagues at Dindisc saw them, some said 'but you've got to stop Andy dancing like that!' Typical of the record business - they want all the new artistes to look and sound like the old artistes. I didn't ask Andy to 'stop dancing like that' and, some time later, stood at a gig watching 2,000 teenage boys all doing the 'Andy dance' after OMD's first hit. How legends are born.

At that time, record companies traditionally gave their groups a bit of money to live on, plus a recording budget which would buy them about four weeks in a studio to make an album. OMD asked for all the money up front so that they could build their own studio in what I recall to have been some sort of abandoned warehouse in Liverpool. It seems strange, looking back, that I didn't have any hesitation in handing over enough money to buy a flat in Central London, with no evidence that they even knew how to build a studio. But we all knew in our hearts that they would be massive one day.

THE F CLUB
7 June 1979, Leeds, UK

JOHN F. KEENAN

I never worked at Eric's but ran the equivalent club in Leeds, The Fan Club (formerly The F Club). I promoted OMD a few times and was partly instrumental in obtaining their deal with Dindisc. 'Electricity' was a popular number at the club, as was 'Enola Gay' later. I put them on the bill for my first Futurama Festival, on a Factory tour with Joy Division, John Dowie and A Certain Ratio.

Later, when they were famous, I promoted a date on their major tour at Tiffany's in Leeds. Unfortunately, their stage-set wouldn't fit into Tiffany's and I had to move it to the Queen's Hall, a week or so later. I sold about 3,000 tickets, but due to massive snowfall, half the people couldn't get there. My phone was going for weeks after, people asking for refunds. I offered free admission to any of my other shows with an OMD ticket. It seemed to work, but I reckon it cost me money in the long run.

It was me who put Carol Wilson, who was starting up a new label, Dindisc, a Virgin offshoot, on to them. I was at Virgin HQ when 'Souvenir' had just been completed. I'm not sure if it was Carol, but someone at Virgin played me a preview. It sounded fantastic, especially the piano on the intro. I still think it's their best track.

LIMIT CLUB
26 June 1979, Sheffield, UK

> **ORCHESTRAL MANOEUVRES IN THE DARK:** 'Electricity' (Factory). If Mike Oldfield was ten years younger and a Tubeway Army fan this is what he'd sound like. Prissy keyboards tink about in a *Sooty Show* outtake. As Beverley remarked, who wants to listen to a bunch of scousers whining about electricity anyway? Certainly not me.

> **ORCHESTRAL MANOEUVRES IN THE DARK:** 'Electricity'/'Almost', (Factory). There are a million uncomfortable art records this week, the majority of them as shoddily despatched as they are ill-conceived and bogged down in undergrauate juvenilia; only OMITD have taken the time to refine their sound until it commands your attention. (The rest proceed as if effort were a bourgeois concept. Bah!) Still, these are two men with synthesisers and drum machines who manage an optimistic trot on the A side (redolent of Hot Butter meeting Kraftwerk) and a lush and slow flow on the backside that would be a hit if there were such places as discos for slugs. If you're allowed to say such things these days, the whole thing's packaged with as much taste as it is played. that's buggered *their* credibility.

PHIL OAKEY
The Human League

The first time I encountered Orchestral Manoeuvres in the Dark was in the summer of 1979. A tour featuring Factory Records artists had a date in town and we went to the Limit Club to catch a performance by Joy Division, who had a track on a compilation put out by our former label, Fast. Although their album was causing a buzz, underground so far, Joy Division had yet to put out a single, whereas 'Electricity' had been in the shops a couple of weeks. To the best of my recollection I was sat with Tony Wilson and Alan Erasmus while Andy and Paul played their set.

We'd released our first album a couple of months earlier to mass indifference and I certainly felt threatened by newer, younger bands that actually seemed to know what they were doing. But 'Electricity' was a great record. And to follow it with 'Red Frame/White Light', a personal favourite of mine, put the seal on it. It still took me years to admit OMD were making better records than we were.

Now with the struggle to make good behind us (one way or another), I only care how good the music is. Withstanding and overcoming the crazy technological arms race of 80s pop; OMD produced a series of lovely singles and a set of treasured albums. They're still doing it and they're still on my mix-tape.

STEVE LAMACQ
BBC 6 Music DJ & journalist

I'd have been 14 or 15 when I started listening regularly to John Peel's programme. It was a classic case of a lot of that generation of kids who were in their mid-teens upwards, getting into him. Although we read the reviews in the music press, John Peel gave you the opportunity to hear new music. You knew some of the bands in each programme, but it would also be full of stuff, which was brand new, and very much the cutting edge.

Peel's reputation was built on

↑ David Hepworth (top) review for 'Electricity' and Gary Bushell also reviews in summer '79

↑ Factory records 45 single of 'Electricity'

EARLY YEARS | 69

Original artwork ideas by Andy for gig poster and single

him discovering bands that no one knew they were going to like. He was the best A&R man in the country. He'd find bands that were making new and interesting music, music, which was constantly evolving, and bring it to the masses. Six months later these bands would be signed to a major label and a year after they'd be in the charts and on *Top of the Pops*.

The thing about Peel is that you trusted him. If he'd filtered out these records, however bonkers they sounded, there was a reason he was playing them. He could hear things in records that you couldn't and the fact that he was playing them was an endorsement like no other. That's why we all looked up to Peel and why he was so respected throughout his career. It's something a lot of deejays, myself included, have tried to replicate.

I'd listen on a transistor radio with a single cream-coloured earpiece. It was very hard taping records off the radio, because I had a very clunky radio cassette player, and taping something would alert my Mum and Dad to the fact that I hadn't gone to sleep. But with the aid of a torch and a bit of paper I started writing three-line reviews of some of the records Peel played. I marked them out of three. If a record got three stars, that was top of the range. Two stars was worth taping, one was okay, and none meant it was rubbish.

One of the first records I ever gave a three to was this record, the like of which I'd never really heard before, called 'Electricity'. I understood guitar music by this point - punk and new wave and some of the things, which had started to flow out of those things. But I had never come across much in the way of electronic music apart from 'Autobahn' by Kraftwerk and some of the disco music that had an element of electronica about it.

I'd never heard a record like 'Electricity.' I thought it was so fascinating and new and wonderful but at the same time so understated. It was a terrific pop song but not based on any of the machinery pop songs employed, so I became absolutely fascinated.

Peel played it twice in a week. In those days there was no way of going away and listening to a record for yourself. You were completely at the mercy of the DJ as to what you were going to hear and whether you'd get to hear this record again. The second time, I was so excited he'd played it again that I thought, 'Wouldn't it be the best job in the world to be able to just find curious records and play them to people?' Of course, it felt completely unachievable to a kid living in a tiny village in Essex whose population at the last census was 1,003.

I went to Parrot Records in Ipswich on the Saturday afternoon and bought a copy of 'Electricity.' I was strangely fascinated by the black on black sleeve. I'm not sure I even knew what Braille was at the time and the whole thing was so enigmatic. 'Electricity' is a record, which is like the dark corner of the room, a song that came out of the shadows, and the sleeve gave nothing away. I was used to sleeves that had pictures of bands on, most of them standing in front of brick walls. There was nothing to give away who these people were. It just said, 'Winston the drum machine.' You'd look at the sleeve and go, 'Wow, drum machines! What are these things?'

The Peel programme opened up a magical world of records and OMD's 'Electricity' was one of those records. It opened a doorway to the mysterious and marvellous world of music

Orchestral Manoeuvres sharing the bill with Certain Ratio and Joy Division at The Nashville Room, London

that lay beyond. I've still got the copy I bought from Parrot Records. It's still one of my favourite records from that era.

ANDY MCCLUSKEY

When 'Electricity' came out, John Peel played it and it sold all 5,000 in a week. Holding 'Electricity' in my hand for the first time, at the age of just 19, that black thermograph sleeve, was an incredible moment: 'We made this. This tune we wrote when we were kids is now a record. We have made a bloody record. Wow!' That was quite something. To actually have an artefact in your hand, something that was of your creation was incredibly powerful. What a feeling.

Myself, Paul Humphreys and Paul Collister drove in the Visionhire van down to 86 Palatine Road in Manchester, the offices of Factory Records. It was Alan Erasmus' flat. There we opened these boxes of 'Electricity' from the factory, took each one out of the white sleeve and put it in the black one. Every single one of those original 5,000 was bagged by myself, Paul or Paul Collister.

Paul Collister was very bloody useful. He was also very good at mixing sound, considering he was mixing us on an old PA head with just microphones in. Because we only had six channels on stage: bass, treble, volume. No faders and no proper mixing desk, just a head. The guy with the tape recorder, van, and studio in the garage had become so essential that he was effectively doing everything else that Paul H and I could not!

VINCE CLARKE
Depeche Mode, Erasure & Yazoo

I'd always been a fan of folk music (guitar and voice); because it was something I could create myself. After seeing the movie, *The Graduate* for instance, I bought the songbook, learned the chords and sang the songs. When I first heard 'Electricity' in 1979 I could immediately relate to it because it was similarly accessible. Here was music I could work out and play. No grandiose production or 70mph guitar solos, just synthesiser, bass and drum machine. 'Electricity' is a classic pop song, simply but perfectly arranged, and the B side, 'Almost', made me realise electronic music need not be robotic and cold but emotional and indeed, soulful … a true revelation.

AL HINE

I first heard 'Electricity' on the John Peel show one summer evening when he played the *Sounds* inky music paper 'Alternative Chart' top-three from the 26 July 1979 edition. The plinky-plonky melody stuck in my head all night and most of the next day. I rushed out and bought that edition of *Sounds* so I could get the record details and order it from my record shop. Sadly, they could not get it so I called my sister, who lived in Falkirk, and asked her to get it from legendary Scottish record shop, Brucie's Records. Again, all copies had sold out.

John Peel came to my rescue about a month later, when he played the Dindisc remix - my local record shop had no difficulty getting Din2 and I was hooked. It took me 25 years to finally get a Factory Records pressing. I have, for what it's worth, obtained all the 7-inch singles in that *Sounds* chart. I had most of them anyway, bought in 1979, but eBay has made record collecting so easy, if expensive!

LEIGH MUSIC FESTIVAL
27 August 1979, Lancashire, UK

ALTERNATIVE CHART

SINGLES
1. XEROX, Adam And The Ants, Do-It
2. ELECTRICITY, Orchestral Manoeuvres, Factory
3. EXPERT, PragVEC, Spec
4. NAG NAG NAG, Cabaret Voltaires, Rough Trade
5. HEART SURGERY, Glass Torpedoes, Teen Beat
6. YOU, Idols, Ork
7. GANGSTERS, Specials, 2-Tone
8. SOMETHING'S GOING WRONG AGAIN, Buzzcocks, UA
9. MARTIAL TIME, Warriors, Object
10. I CAN'T COPE, Protex, Polydor
11. GET READY, Walter Steding, Red Star
12. DNA, Murder The Disturbed, Small Wonder
13. BOYS DON'T CRY, The Cure, Fiction
14. PLAYGROUND TWIST, Siouxsie And The Banshees, Polydor
15. DISCO DUMMY, Jah Wobble, Virgin
16. REALITY ASYLUM, Crass, Crass Records
17. ELECTRIC HEAT, Visitors, Deep Cuts
18. EINE SYMPHONIE DES GRAUENS, Monochrome Set, Rough Trade
19. GET OFF THE PHONE, Heartbreakers, Beggars Banquet
20. NO FUN, Doctor Mix, Anon

RICHARD TRACEY

I hitch-hiked with my friend Russ to a place I didn't know existed, never mind knew where it was, or how to get there, to see the Factory/Zoo Records coming together of Liverpool and Manchester. I had long hair, so the police emptied my bag on the street and searched me. I got to the gate and found I had no money. Outraged at police brutality, the organisers let me in for free.

Tony Wilson was striding around the field in a billowing white shirt and tan leather cowboy boots. I pitched the tent among just

↑
Adam and the Ants hold 'Electricity' off No.1 in the *Sounds* Alternative Chart

OMD - EARLY YEARS

JOY DIVISION / ECHO & THE BUNNYMEN / ORCHESTRAL MANOEUVRES IN THE DARK / TEARDROP EXPLODES / THE DISTRACTIONS / A CERTAIN RATIO / CHAOS

Leigh Valley Festival

Due to the (avoidable) attentions of the drug squad, your reviewer missed most of Orchestral Manoeuvres In The Dark. What he did see — a song called "Mr Reality" with taped saxophone, the future hit "Electricity" and a passable electronic version of "Waiting For My Man" (which, at least, came out into the open about the frank Velvets influence of most bands playing) — didn't alter his impression that he'd rather listen to the nice record, thank you. A good live sound — the two members playing keyboards and occasional bass, the rest of the instruments on reel to reel — a reasonable if gawky presence, and awful clothes (that's important!).

↑
Orchestral Manoeuvres are joined by Zoo and Factory records acts for a bank holiday festival

→
Dindisc press release from Sept '79

a few others, and watched the Teardrop Explodes and Echo and the Bunnymen. OMD did their thing, but there was no dancing in the crowd. It suddenly seemed very late. I decided that staying overnight with no money or transport wasn't the best idea. I found my way backstage and asked for a lift home to Meols. Tent down, we piled into a silver Ford Cortina estate. Paul Collister was driving, Paul Humphreys was in the front, a girl sat on his knee. I don't know how many of us were on the back seat. Hours later we made it home. But, I regret forever not seeing Joy Division.

FUTURAMA FESTIVAL QUEEN'S HALL

8 September 1979, Leeds, UK

DAVE SIMPSON
Guardian music critic & author

Orchestral Manoeuvres in the Dark, as they were then called, were actually the first band I saw play live. I'd got the day off from my Saturday job in Asda to go to the 'World's First Science Fiction Music Festival' – Futurama at the Queen's Hall, Leeds. I'd gone mostly to see Johnny Rotten, whose new band Public Image Ltd were headlining, but for a teeny punk, Futurama proved a gateway to a whole new musical world. I became aware of this even before we got through the doors, seeing hordes of people queueing – all older than us - in weird and wonderful clothing, with a lot of black. Punk was fading, the synth-pop revolution was beginning, and my iron-on Sid Vicious T-shirt was as uncool as they came.

We were halfway through the entrance when I heard what I thought sounded like the *Magic Roundabout* theme from outer space, which turned out to be 'Electricity' by OMD. They were dressed like bank clerks, not rock'n'rollers. Andy McCluskey sang and played bass but most of the music seemed to emanate from a Revox reel-to-reel onstage. I'd only ever seen bands on *Top of the Pops*, and had heard Kraftwerk's 'Autobahn' on the radio, but none of them looked or sounded like this.

Over the next few hours, I encountered more of this strange, futuristic-sounding new music, from the likes of Cabaret Voltaire and Joy Division – who both played synthesisers, the music took me to places in my head I never knew existed, and I wanted to explore more. The Sid Vicious T-shirt went in the bin

ORCHESTRAL MANOEUVRES IN THE DARK

They were only 17 & 18 years of age and met in an off beat rock band called the Id in 1977. The band broke up in mid '78 due to 'personal and musical conflicts' (the usual excuse), whereas the truth of the story is that both Andy McCluskey's and Paul Humphreys' feet smelt something terrible.

Andy & Paul lived quite near each other in place called Meols in Wirral and decided to join forces and form their own band. The name of the band had to be decided and the first and most simple name that came into their heads was 'Orchestral Manoeuvres in the Dark' and so the band was born.

Suffering with what seemed an interminable 'foot problem' the boys decided to perform as a duo, with the exception of taking on their manager, confidante, father-figure and electronics whiz kid Paul Collister.

A band like Orchestral Manoeuvres in the Dark need a man like Paul Collister. Andy & Paul make their 'Orchestral' sound themselves by laying down backing tracks on tape first and performing the main melody live with Andy on vocals and bass and Paul on keyboard and back up vocals. Live performances require split second timing by their manager Collister who doubles as sound engineer with special responsibility for 'Betsy' their tape recorder.

By February 1979 the boys had their first song on tape. It was called 'Almost' ("B" side of 'Electricity')and was sent to the newly formed Factory Records' boss Tony Wilson. It was Wilson's wife who got to hear it before he was about to rush to the betting office one cold morning in February. 'Eureka' said Tony, and before you could recite Tolstoy's War and Peace the single was released on the Factory label.

Orchestral Manoeuvres in the Dark embarked on the few local gigs in and around Liverpool including eight successful gigs at Erics, about three at Manchester's Factory and the odd gigs at Sheffield, Leeds and London.

Meanwhile back in London the new record company DinDisc is on the lookout for talent and Carol 'Big Ears' Wilson gets to hear O.M.D. (we'll call them that from now on - look at the ink we save!). 'Eureka' said Carol, and realising she and Tony Wilson speak the same language, a deal was set up whereby DinDisc distributed this piece of futuristic pop art.

Press release - DinDisc.
Sept 79.
by Eugene Manz.

and 'Electricity' into my record collection as I glimpsed a world of possibility beyond Sham 69 and the UK Subs. With hindsight, that concert probably started the journey, which led to me writing about music. Thank you, OMD.

PETER SAVILLE

The strange thing between me and them is that our pathways stayed relatively parallel. Factory was not a business and wasn't in a position to employ me. It was vocational; we were doing it for the love of doing it, not for money. I had to get a job, and that would have to be in London. I wasn't going to be able to work as a graphic designer or art director in music without being in London. So I was on a fast-track to London in '79, and they were on the Factory springboard to being signed. With fateful serendipity, they signed to the same woman who later that year employed me, a woman called Carol Wilson, who was founding Dindisc Records for Virgin as a kind of pseudo-independent.

Carol had run Virgin Publishing successfully, and Richard Branson gave her the backing to found her own label. The idea was that Dindisc would look a little bit like an independent, because that was the cool thing at the time. As Carol was founding Dindisc, the Factory single brought both OMD and me to her attention and by the end of '79, OMD were signed to Dindisc and I was employed as the art director.

So we kept working together. For the next few years we were colleagues. It was an important time for them and an important time for me. And the parallel autonomy that worked from the outset carried on working. The things I wanted to do – my own visual pathway, my progress – seemed to have to continue to have touch points with what they were doing.

It was never difficult for me to do an OMD cover. Their first album featured a particularly British interpretation of hi-tech; it was something I wanted to do. And it worked perfectly for them. It came out of their need for some stage equipment and through working with Ben Kelly (who designed that equipment for them) I found the graphic equivalent.

The cover of the second album, *Organisation*, went rather awry due to my inexperience. The idea was good, and I'm still very pleased with it, but I was not pleased with the way it printed. But I liked the idea. A landscape was a nice idea.

The title for *Architecture & Morality* came from my girlfriend at the time, Martha Ladley, who was reading *Morality and Architecture* by the architectural historian, David Watkin. We shared the title with Andy, because Andy was a friend and we would see him, see them, quite often. Whenever they were in London for a record company event or *Top of the Pops*, there would be a conversation between Paul and Andy and about wardrobe. Clothes were not something they were very interested in, but I was. So I always helped them in those early years. It was social as much as it was work.

Andy re-phrased the title *Architecture and Morality*, and the next one, *Dazzle Ships* came from a work by artist Edward Wadsworth that I drew his attention to. This working coherence, this interwoven practice, was similar to the nature of my work with Joy Division, and New Order.

With Andy he'd say something, then I'd say something, or I'd say something and he'd say something. It was actually more connected, more interwoven. Nascent ideas would organically develop between us. I'd have something I was into and that would be a catalyst for something he was into, and vice versa.

There was some commercial expectation with OMD, not from the group but because the work was within the industry (rather than Factory) we had to accept there would be some compromise with respect to commerciality.

We had a certain amount of fun that went astray when making a video together. Which, when I see it now, is actually quite good but in 1981 was probably about 10 minutes ahead of its time. It was too passive and ambient but actually looks quite cool now. It was for 'Souvenir.' It was a new experience and I've fond memories of that.

The thing I distinctly remember from those early days, once I'd met them and when I saw them perform, is how ad hoc and hard work it was for them to set-up. They had a manager who was a friend and a little bit of a liability. He was the manager because he had a van, as is often the case with groups at the beginning. They were setting everything up themselves. I think they had a few fluorescent tubes and their equipment. I remember feeling sympathetic towards them because it was all lo-tech by necessity, yet the ideas they were pursuing were hi-tech.

That led to me turning to Ben Kelly, a friend I made in London, an interior architect and designer. I introduced them and we had this idea to ask if he could create some sort of space-frame support – desks, effectively – for their synthesisers and sequencers. Something that would be very portable and they could put together almost like Meccano. Ben designed a utilitarian space-frame set. It wasn't a stage-set from a point of view of a backdrop, but what they needed, such as the stands for their equipment, and Ben turned them into semi-sculptural objects.

It was this notion of a space-frame for their equipment, which led me to ask Ben, 'How might I do a space-frame album cover?' That was the beginning of the first album cover, me thinking 'How can I use the least amount of cardboard to hold a record?' As an idea, it was a conceptual proposition. From that the lozenge die-cut pattern came – a type of perforated steel Ben often worked with interiors that are actually used as a machine guard. Ben was transposing it into other situations. He did a doorway in

Covent Garden for a client using this perforated sheet metal and said, 'Take a look on the way home.' I went and there was the perforated pattern that was going to become the album cover, a convergence of 2D and 3D. The spirit of hi-tech, manifesting itself across disciplines.

Their music was hi-tech and technology was informing the shape of the things around us and how we were living. My interest in music was always as a soundtrack to life. I'm no more interested in music than the average person, perhaps even less so these days.

I am interested in music as a fundamental part of the art of our time. I'm interested in how the ideas channelled through music connect to other aspects of living. It's the holistic thing I'm interested in, and that was very relevant with OMD.

The first experience with their first album, with Ben Kelly and their set, that was very holistic.

AUTUMN 1979

ANDY MCCLUSKEY

The autumn of '79 was busy. We signed a contract and were supporting Gary Numan. We were so absolutely gobsmacked that the music we'd been writing for several years but not thought of as publicly 'acceptable' had started to be seen as quite interesting and not just a pile of nonsense. We thought, 'Who's going to buy this? This is too weird.' Despite what Tony Wilson said. Despite this crazy woman giving us a contract. It's not pop music. It's not going to sell. Instead of taking our 30 grand and going into a recording studio for a couple of months, and only having a couple of reels of tape to show for it, we thought, 'Why don't we build our own studio?' We found space in Liverpool at the back of Curly Music Store, at the back of Hessy's, looking out on to the White Star pub next to Probe Records on Button Street.

In between doing the Numan tour and Christmas, quickly as we could, we built a studio, recorded the album and gave it to them. It sounds like a garage recording because it was a garage recording. We produced it ourselves. It's incredible. A subsidiary of a major record company lets you build your own studio, doesn't come up to listen to it, doesn't A&R it, then you give them the album and they go, 'Okay, great. We'll release it.' That shouldn't happen, but it did.

We were budgeting for failure. We thought, 'When they drop us, at least we'll have a recording studio, then we can carry on making some records and go indie or whatever.' So we created the Gramophone Suite on the first floor of a five-storey warehouse in the centre of

Liverpool, in the Old Pool, off Whitechapel Street, around the corner from Matthew Street and Eric's. All the floors above us were abandoned. We bought a plate reverb, which we put upstairs on the floor above. The problem was, if you soloed in a quiet song, you could sometimes hear the pigeons coming through the windows cooing on it and flying in and out. Then somebody nicked the lead off the roof, five storeys up, and before we finished the record it rained, and it was coming through our ceiling.

The last song we were doing was 'Pretending to See the Future' and if you solo my lead vocal you can actually hear the water dripping into five or six buckets that were around the room. But we didn't have time to stop. We promised the label this record before Christmas so it could be released in February and I just had to fricking sing in the rain. It was nuts! But we delivered it.

They'd released 'Electricity' in the autumn and unfortunately, because Gary Numan had a couple of hits, Radio 1 said, 'Oh, this is just copying Gary Numan', which really pissed us off, because we were there before him. This is the thing with Numan. He was very kind to us, but we were a bit grumpy about the fact he'd come along when we were doing electronic music before he was. We'd been doing it 18 months, for several years really, but off the radar. But we'd been OMD for at least a year before he'd had a hit and we were a bit miffed. Just as miffed as The Human League were when they found out about us and we found out about them and Phil Oakey thought we'd nicked their idea.

It was like, 'We heard your record and saw you play, and all it did was convince us that we need to come out of hiding.' I was talking to Phil in June 2018 when we finally met for the first time and I said, 'Apparently we're supposed to hate each other', and he said, 'Yeah, apparently so.' I said, 'Weird thing is, we'd been going as long as you and we wrote 'Electricity' when we were 16 in 1976,' and he said, 'Oh, well we didn't start until 1977.' But at that time it was, 'We were a day before you. You copied us!' It was really competitive.

We thought we were the only people in England remotely interested in trying to be electronic. It was just strange when Numan and The Human League came along, and we discovered Cabaret Voltaire and Warm Leatherette. 'Hang on, other people are doing it.'

If you read about Kraftwerk in the mid-70s, it was usually taking the piss out of them and criticising them. Most of the weekly music paper 'inkies' didn't get it. It was the antithesis of what they thought real rock music was. We just thought, 'Yeah, these guys don't get it.'

Then of course punk came along and we said, 'That's not the future either. That's going up

OMD - EARLY YEARS

Paul, Andy and Winston during the Gary Numan tour

a cul-de-sac. The future is clever and intellectual, not anarchic and disruptive and negative.'

It was an amazing period. What had happened was all these little groups were working in vacuums in cities around the country, all independent of each other. Because, although we were reading the same music papers and were listening to the same radio stations, what we were really influenced by was so underground we thought, 'Well, nobody else is listening to this.'

We got a few plays for 'Electricity', which was released four times in the end, once by Factory and three times by Dindisc. I don't think it ever got higher than No.92. People think it's a hit. It's become part of the landscape now. It's a huge part of our history and we close our sets with it like it's a hit.

After we toured with Gary Numan, we did that tour exactly a year later and headlined it, selling it out after 'Messages' and 'Enola Gay' had been hits.

GARY NUMAN
Musician

Memory is the most unreliable thing, and the passing of time just adds to the problem, but my memories of being involved with OMD are all good. For me 1979 was an extraordinary year and, towards the end of it, I was due to start my first ever tour. Finding the right support band, one that would enhance each concert evening, was extremely important. I didn't want to find some talentless nonsense that, by simply being awful, would make me look good. I was confident enough (or arrogant enough perhaps) that I would be able to hold my own against anyone I toured with. But, I did want to find a band that were firmly Electronic, and had a sound uniquely their own, and one that actually wrote good, catchy songs. OMD were perfect. Not only were they a perfect fit musically, they were literally a perfect fit when it came to size. Just two performers, and a tape recorder (called Winston if I remember correctly) stood between them. They could do their set and be cleared off the stage in minutes. Quite handy for making sure I would always be on stage on time. I had no idea just how good they were though. Most nights I would sneak out to the side of the stage while they were on and, from my little hiding spot, would listen to some of the best pop songs ever written. To this day, whenever I hear an OMD song it takes me back to the incredible excitement of those early days. I found out not long into the '79 tour that they had a few problems financially so I invited them to travel with us and took care of transporting their gear (I think). As I say, memory is unreliable. I do remember it being a fantastic experience though. I watched them rise rapidly from support band to arena superstars quickly after that tour was over. I felt a tiny twinge of pride and connection whenever I saw or heard them, for years afterwards. Still do at times. Which brings me to my second big OMD encounter. I believe it was late '93, or around there somewhere, and I had just finished yet another UK tour when I received a most interesting and unexpected offer. OMD were about to go out on another arena tour and wondered if I wanted to go along. It was perfect timing, on many levels. First of all I hate it when tours end. Life feels slow and boring until you eventually adapt back into normal life, so the idea of going back out again straight away was very appealing. My own career was struggling at that time, one of it's many up and downs, and so the idea of playing arenas, and being seen by large numbers of people that were mostly unaware of how my music had evolved since '79, was also very appealing. Mostly though, it would be good to be touring again with OMD. The

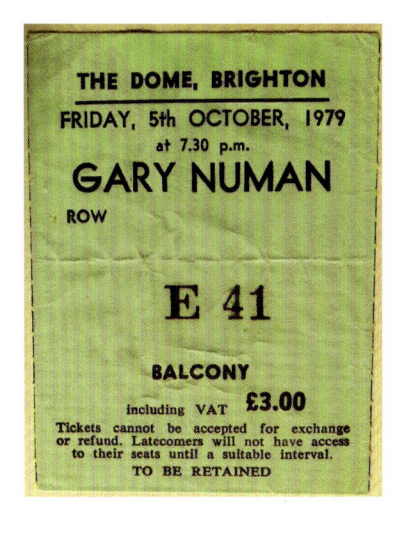

↑
Ticket for Gary Numan at The Dome, Brighton October 1979

EARLY YEARS | 81

roles were reversed this time though. I would be opening for them. It was a unique experience for me not to be headlining my own shows and I found that change to be a glorious shedding of anxieties and pressure. It was probably the most easy, stress free tour I've ever been involved in. Attendance? Not my problem. Production nightmares? Not my problem. Every little hiccup or worry (that usually drops firmly on my shoulders)? Not my problem, not on that tour anyway. I soaked up that happy environment 24 hours a day. It was just a fantastic experience. Both times.

ANDY MCCLUSKEY

Gary Numan worked in Beggar's Banquet record shop on a Saturday to get some extra money, just before Tubeway Army exploded and had two No.1 singles. He was still working there in May 1979 bought 'Electricity' and got his manager to phone the number, because Paul Collister's number was on the back of the sleeve. The manager phoned up and said, 'We're looking for a support band for Gary Numan.'

After three months in my nine-to-five job, processing cargo entries, I left and remember being quite anxious as to what my parents would say, because I'd been unemployed for a year, just got this job and was going to leave again. Fortunately, they were great.

Mum said, 'You'll spend the rest of your life wondering 'what if?' if you don't at least try it, so do it. Otherwise, you might be 40, 50 years old, thinking 'I wonder what would have happened if….' And Dad said, 'Listen son, if it doesn't work out the Civil Service is still going to be there.' They were great. I subsequently found out that they spoke to my uncle and they were pulling their hair out in anxiety: 'I can't believe he's just got a really good job and he's wanting to do this bloody music. But we can't say no, can we?' So they were outwardly supportive but they had their doubts.

We hadn't received our advance from Virgin, but Gary Numan said, 'Come on my coach. Put your gear in my truck. One of my guys will do the lighting and one of the guys from the sound crew will do your monitors.'

We did that tour with Paul Collister doing front of house sound, trying to find a couple of quid a day for monitors and lights. Gary's security guy, Big Mick, took a shine to us and went out and introduced us every night on stage.

Paul Collister gave us 60 quid. He said, 'Go and get a shirt and a pair of pants for the tour.' Paul had come back and had two shirts and a tie, but had spent less than me. Collister kicked off at him because he'd got two shirts, and Paul said, 'But there was two-for-one and a tie, and I've spent less than Andy.' 'That's not the point!' We wore the same shirts and trousers every night on that tour without them being washed or ironed. At Wolverhampton Civic

Hall, we were standing on the staircase ready to go on and Beryl, Gary's mum, came up and said, 'Lads, have you got five minutes? Can I iron those shirts for you?' We said, 'yeah, but don't smell them!' It was like a family, on the road together.

Gary was a few months ahead of us. He'd been nothing until six months earlier and suddenly he was huge. I met him recently and he's just such a lovely person. He was unbelievably generous to us. Of course, it suited him because there were only two of us. He had such a massive stage-set with the curtains that he could only get two guys with a tape recorder in front. So it worked both ways.

CITY HALL
21 September 1979,
Newcastle, UK

SEAN CHURCHILL

My first experience was being ejected from the bar of Newcastle City Hall at the tender age of 13, at the Gary Numan concert to a life-changing OMD singing 'Messages', my favourite song then and now. It's the one and only time I heard 'Red Frame/White Light' live. I've now seen OMD 62 times, the last being the Sage in Gateshead 2017.

EMPIRE
25 September 1979,
Liverpool, UK

IAN URMSON & STEVE GUARD

The 17-year old me and my best mate jumped on a train at Runcorn to see Gary Numan, who was No.1 in the charts with 'Cars.' As we settled down to the journey, we got talking about the support band. 'Tell me again who's the support, Ste'. 'Orchestral Manoeuvres in the Dark,' he replied. 'Have you heard owt by 'em?' 'Nope, but they're a local band and their single has had some good reviews in the music press.' A young lady sat opposite us who took a sudden interest in our conversation. 'They're really very good,' she said. 'How do you know?' Ste and I asked, looking down our noses at this eavesdropping woman. 'Oh well, I co-wrote a song on their album.' 'Yeah, right,' was the cynical reply. 'Honest. It's called 'Julia's Song'. I'm Julia,' she explained. 'You heard much of them anyway?' she probed. Ste said, 'They're support to Numan tonight. That's where we're going to now.' Her eyes widened. She shrieked, 'Really? I didn't know that.'

We carried on chatting about

music in general as we pulled into Lime Street station to say our goodbyes and the usual, 'Hope you enjoy the gig' as she marched around to the stage door to bang on it and force her way in. I'm not too sure how that conversation went with Andy and Paul, but she didn't seem too happy. We went to the gig and sure enough it was a great evening. The stand-out from OMD was 'Electricity.' When we got the album a little later, there it was: 'Julia's Song.' Julia Kneale did indeed accompany us on the first part of a long journey loving the work of Andy and Paul.

APOLLO
26 September 1979, Manchester, UK

DEE WILLIAMS

I remember going to the Liverpool Empire in 1979 with my friend Penny when they were supporting Gary Numan. My dad came to pick us up after and we were both furious - we wanted to stay behind, wait at the stage door. I feel ashamed thinking about this now - the luxury of being taken safely home to Ellesmere Port instead of having to make three bus changes, my kind old man worried about our safety.

The next night, one of my brothers drove me and Penny to Manchester to see them at the Apollo. He was reluctant, but wanted the car to get to the gig, and the deal was 'No Dee, no car'. Manchester seemed very exotic.

A couple of days later, another brother drove us to Birmingham to see them again, him looking to impress a particular girlfriend. It was a Sunday and Mum was furious as we only got home in the early hours, with school the next day. She was also mystified as to why I wanted to see the same band three times in a week.

I also developed a serious OMD record-buying habit from an early age. I had to have as many singles and albums as I could possibly afford. Even with a Saturday job to supplement my pocket money it was still hard to afford what I wanted. When *OMITD* was released, I wanted the different LP covers. A kind man in the record shop in Ellesmere Port very kindly allowed me unofficial credit so I could collect each coloured sleeve.

DAVID RICHARDSON

Andy often refers to seat Q36 when talking about the night he first saw Kraftwerk. I wish this story had some sort of synergy and I could remember my seat number. Sadly not, but it was somewhere in the middle of the balcony. As for Andy, it was the night that changed my life. I'd gone to watch Gary Numan, hoping to be blown away by this strange alien of a man and his music. Instead I was transfixed by the support act with a weird name, made up of a seemingly hyperactive frontman who sang, danced and played bass like his life depended on it, a still and very focused keyboard player pumping out some strange noises and even better melodies, and a four-track tape recorder they named Winston. They seemingly occupied just one tenth of the stage, yet the noise they made filled the room and grabbed my attention like nothing had ever done before. It was a eureka moment. After years of dieting on disco and punk rock, this was it – the sound I'd been waiting for. Gary wasn't half bad either.

HAMMERSMITH APOLLO

27 September 1979, London, UK

DEBBIE BULL

I was 11 when I first saw OMD with my sister Anji, supporting Gary Numan. It's probably my favourite gig. It was the start of an addiction, which has seen me attend over 160 shows. In 1983, I

↑ Press advert for 'Electricity' featuring Winston by the River Mersey

EARLY YEARS | 85

did every single night of the UK tour. It took me two years to clear my credit card, but was worth every penny. My other favourite shows were Dazzle Ships first time around, the Museum of Liverpool, the Royal Albert Hall and the six Punishment of Luxury shows I saw, Andy singing to me on my 50th birthday in Offenbach. And when Anji and I saw OMD support The Thompson Twins in Fort Lauderdale in 1986, we nearly got arrested for drinking wine. Who knew the legal age for consuming alcohol was different?

ANJI BULL

I adored Gary Numan. However, I wasn't quite prepared for the impact OMD would have on me. The following year I saw them on *Top of the Pops* with 'Messages'. That's where my real love started. Come 1981 I was starting to follow them at gigs and that November at my spiritual home - Hammersmith Odeon - I got my nickname, 'Oi you, Uxbridge'. In the early days I didn't know who was who, a little like Ant and Dec today. I called out to Andy, not remembering his name, calling, 'Oi you!' The name stuck. The worst thing about that gig was coming out to the back, seeing Mum and Dad rocking away. They loved it. How uncool.

I ended up meeting like-minded fans from all over the country, and we'd travel from gig to gig, known by the band as the 'Barmy Army'. In those days, money was short but as long as we had a ticket and the money to get to some random place in the UK, we were all set. Sometimes this meant jacking work early, jumping in my friend Mirelle's Mini and hacking it up the motorway in time for the gig. Often this meant no money for digs or food. We were not against buying a single sandwich and sharing that between as many as eight of us. Or going into Pizza Hut ordering one pizza and eating it between us. It wasn't uncommon for one person to get a room and x amount of people to bundle in. I've slept in the tour bus when the band was in a nice hotel. I've spent a night in the bath, on a floor, and shared a bed with five other people. In freezing winter, when it's been sub-zero and there's been snow on the ground, I've spent the night at Ipswich train station as we didn't have any money for digs, one sleeping bag rotated by at least four people every so often during the night.

DAVE HUGHES

Andy came to me when 'Electricity' had got quite hot and Dindisc decided they needed a bit more scale on stage. They called me in to do the keys on those first big tours, which I was happy to do.

But as it was all going on, the

Dalek I Love You *Compass Kumpas* album came out and got some great reviews. So although I was playing with OMD there was always this background of, 'and this might happen as well.'

The gigs were still light-hearted. They weren't too slick early on. Andy and Paul had done the Gary Numan tour so had an idea of which songs worked, but it didn't feel that different to the amateur Eric's nights.

Then it started to get quite serious as the buzz was building. Andy was learning how to control the audience and build it up, which songs were doing it and which songs were killing it, so it started to come together.

I enjoyed it when we were getting tighter. We were suddenly playing through great PA's and the synth sounds were amazing. We were really, really loud and it was quite rock'n'roll in a way, a big contrast to the lower key stuff that we had started off doing at Eric's.

We had some disasters on the way. There were a couple of gigs, like the Huddersfield one, where all the equipment broke down. One gig I quite enjoyed because Mally's pads were triggering everything. Every time he hit a pad, all the pads went off, so the sound was like a bulldozer because every single hit contained every sound.

We had to do some numbers without rhythm. It was quite weird following the tape when you didn't know where the rhythm was, so there was some chaos. And some things the manager, Paul, built just weren't roadworthy.

Some of the gigs on that tour were tiny places. The stage set-up they had, with those racks they'd made for the synths and stuff, didn't fit on the stage. The set-up looked quite cool on a big stage but they just looked like pieces of mad scaffolding in a club like JB's in Dudley, which has a capacity of a hundred-odd.

We got back into Liverpool, I think it was the university, and we were getting cheered onto the stage. I thought, 'Ooh, what the hell's happening here? We haven't played a note.' I knew we were getting articles in the press. They

↑ Live review in October '79 edition of *Sounds* at The Hammersmith Odeon

EARLY YEARS | 87

OMD - EARLY YEARS

were bubbling under by then.

I never really enjoyed performing that much. I was much more interested in studio work and dabbling myself. I had a creeping feeling that playing the same songs every night already seemed a bit uninspiring. And we were on rubbish money, so it was a struggle. We were usually travelling with five of us in the manager's car. It's a fantastic thing to do when you're that age but I'd already realised I couldn't wait to get time off and get back into the studio. When we were rehearsing mid-tour, or after the first couple of gigs, this song emerged that Andy had written, 'Enola Gay.'

Honestly, the chords were like a Chuck Berry song or something. Everybody was very excited by it and the record company loved the tape of the rehearsals we made. I thought, 'If that's the way it's going, that's way too poppy for my liking.' I loved their more obtuse stuff. But that's why I'm not rich. I couldn't pick a hit single to save my life!

To me they hit on a really interesting alternative that didn't sound like anyone else. If they'd gone up that avenue, with things like 'Romancing the Telescope' and some of their great B-sides, that would have been great. My favourite album is *Navigation: The OMD B-Sides*. That's where they were experimenting. I think the originality on that is tremendous. But that doesn't pay the bills and doesn't make you a star.

So 'Messages' appeared. We'd done a couple of gigs overseas, the first time I'd ever been abroad. All that was very exciting and we got called back from Brussels to do *Top of the Pops* on a really shitty little plane. Travelling back was quite terrifying. But it was amazing being on *Top of the Pops*.

We also did the *Old Grey Whistle Test*, and I only had two ambitions in life. One was to be on the *Old Grey Whistle Test* and one was to be in the *NME*, so I hit that pretty well.

We went over to America. We did Hurrah's and that was quite cool. The audience were quite hip and we went down pretty well. But Philadelphia was like a country and western club. I enjoyed it, because of the contrariness in playing to all these cowboys. I liked the look on their faces. They didn't know what on earth we were doing, because it was quite a new sound, they hadn't heard anything like that and we looked 'out there' as well, even though we didn't think anything about the way we looked.

I had a talk with Martin Cooper and told him I'd be leaving at some point because it wanted to build a studio and do stuff in there. I think I suggested Martin to them and he took my place. They were friends anyway, so that was an easy process.

There are a couple of sides that I just think are genius. They show a great sensibility. But if I'd stayed with them, I'd have got them to do more of that, and ruined their careers.

→
Andy's studio notes for their debut album recored at the Gramophone Suite, Liverpool

88 | EARLY YEARS

SONG	PAUL	ANDY	TAPE
✓ MISUNDERSTANDING	PIANO ORGAN	VOCALS	RHYTHM BASS GUITAR
JULIA'S SONG	ORGAN PIANO	VOCALS	CLAPS BASS RHYTHM DRUMS
ELECTRICITY	PIANO ORGAN	VOCALS BASS	DRUMS CRACKS
✓ VCL XI	SYNTHI Piano	PIANO VOCALS	ORGAN I ORGAN II BASS I BASS II
UNDERGROUND	ORGAN PIANO	BASS VOCALS	GUITAR GLISANDO GUITAR I+II
✓ DANCING	SYNTHI ORGAN VOCAL	BASS VOCAL	RHYTHM RADIO PIANO SYNTHI

Telephone

✓ MR Reality   Julias - Teen 2

Organ End.

Rhythm

Misunderstanding   FOXTROT 1. 15½   MR REALITY
                     WALTZ 17¼   TELEPHONE SONG
                                        UNDER COVER
ELECTRICITY   TEEN B1 10⅜   UNDERGROUND
(not used)   10⅜   END on organ Fade.
                     BALANCE 3/10

Telephone   Teen /2 + B NOVA TEEN 12¾ Balance
                     FOXTROT 11¼ 6½ B NOVA 11 Balance
                     Foxtrot 1   6½

OMD - EARLY YEARS

Malita Hayes reminisces with Gary Numan and Andy about their 1979 tour

CIVIC HALL

1 October 1979,
Guildford, UK

MALITA HALES

They came on stage and introduced themselves as Andy and Paul, then introduced the TEAC reel-to-reel machine as Winston. They hadn't played a single note and I was already hooked. I still am. My thinking woman's crumpet is Winston and I share the band's love and enthusiasm for certain oil refineries and inanimate machinery. I've also influenced the music tastes of my children, with my eldest daughter Rachel an avid fan.

GAUMONT THEATRE

3 October 1979, Ipswich, UK

LINDON LAIT

It was my very first gig. I was 13 and my parents let me go on my own by bus into town. I was blown away, by these two guys on stage with a reel-to-reel in between them. Andy's bass guitar had a chrome plate that kept catching the spotlight and shining across the audience. Although I went to see Gary Numan, the first ever band I saw was OMD.

CAMDEN BALLROOM

8 December 1979, London, UK

STRAIGHT MUSIC PRESENTS

TALKING HEADS

WITH GUESTS

ORCHESTRAL MANOEUVRES IN THE DARK

ELECTRIC BALLROOM
184 CAMDEN HIGH ST. NW1 (NEAREST TUBE CAMDEN TOWN)

FRI/SAT — 7/8th DECEMBER at 7·30

TICKETS £3·00 (inc.VAT) IN ADVANCE ELECTRIC BALLROOM BOX OFFICE. TEL: 485 9006
LONDON THEATRE BOOKINGS, SHAFTESBURY AVE., TEL: 439 3371; PREMIER BOX OFFICE, TEL: 240 2245, OR ROCK ON RECORDS, 3 KENTISH TOWN RD, NW1, TEL: 485 5088, OR £3·00 ON NIGHT

ADAM CLAYTON
U2

In 1979 U2 were an Irish band with half a step on the ladder to becoming regulars on the gig circuit in the UK. We still hadn't released any recordings on Island Records and were largely playing songs that would not make it onto our debut album.

Paul McGuinness, our manager, had pulled some strings to get us bottom of the bill at a Talking Heads concert - they were one of our favourite bands, hailing from NY and Art school, had bucket loads of Bohemian cool and played a jerkey funk that sounded otherworldly. They also had a girl bass player and bass players were always the most approachable members of a band and were

↑
Little known Irish group U2 also shared the bill at the Electric Ballroom but remained unlisted

frequently the way to build relationships between bands.

OMD a synthesizer duo from Liverpool were also on the bill, playing before the Heads and in a prestigious position, they would be our first challenge to make contact. Usually the headline act in such situations would use all the time in the afternoon of a big London show to run through sound checks but the Heads were mindful that we would all need some time on the stage.

This meant that we had the thrill of seeing and hearing them sound check - it was always revealing to see how musicians sounded individually and how they interacted with each other. It was also when we got to meet Andy and Paul from OMD.

As a duo using synth sounds they were not competitors to us, and it was understood that we all brought something different to that night's bill and like us, down to earth and open rather than playing it cool like London bands.

Andy also a bass man, hybrid mixed with front man / singer was affable and friendly and we struck up a conversation about the merits of various amps and bass guitars which always breaks the ice!

Andy was waiting for their sound check and as we were talking, the Heads finished and left the stage. We took a little more time to talk and then to our surprise and pleasure, Tina Weymouth, the girl bass player, walks by and starts to talk to us in her NY accent. I tried to keep my composure and Andy and I part charmed, part awkwardly flirted and expressed our open admiration for her and the band's success. Much to our surprise she was very blasé and said how tired she was as they had been on tour for six months and really needed a break.

This was not what we were expecting, though nowadays I would know what she meant! Andy and I looked at each other knowing full well that that was all we ever hoped for: a good run of six months of work to hone our bands' skills would be a validation that we had a career. Fortunately this was waiting just around the turn of the year and both of us achieved that goal and many more…

ERIC'S
28 December 1979, Liverpool, UK

CHRIS WILSON

My favourite gig was a joint one with Dalek I Love You at Eric's, billed as The Farewell to Winston Tribute Concert. They must have just recruited Malcolm Holmes as percussionist. I was a huge Dalek fan and think they hadn't played live before.

We travelled down from Leyland in a knackered Hillman Imp and parked on the car park that was

→ Eric's poster showing the 28 December A Tribute To Winston gig

MEMBERS NOTICE

Eric's Dates

051-236 8301
9 Mathew Street
Liverpool 2

			members	guests
Thur 29 Nov	TOURS		75p	£1
Fri 30 Nov	SIMPLE MINDS + The Portraits		£1-10	£1-60
Sat 1 Dec	THE POP GROUP + The Delta Five	Evg Only	£1-35	£1-75
Thur 6 Dec	JUNK ART + guests		free	50p
Fri 7 Dec	THE MODETTES + Wah Heat		£1-10	£1-60
Sat 8 Dec	JOY DIVISION + Section 25	Mat 5 pm	£1-10	£1-35
		Evg 8.30	£1-35	£1-75
Thur 13 Dec	STEEL PULSE		£1-50	£2-00
Fri 14 Dec	Jak Jones presents The PIRATES + The Nice Men		£1-25	£1-75
Sat 15 Dec	EDDIE & THE HOT RODS + guests	Evg Only	£1-35	£1-75
Mon 17 Dec	THE DAMNED + The Victims		£1-50	£2-00
Wed 19 Dec	THE BEAT + God's Toys		£1-25	£1-75
Thur 20 Dec	Open Eye Christmas Party with THOSE NAUGHTY LUMPS / THE MODERATES / ROY WHITE & STEVE TORCH		75p adv	£1 door
Fri 21 Dec	Lesley Palmer presents a Christmas Reggae Party with THE MIGHTY VHYBES + I SOCIETY + THE PEOPLE'S SOUND SYSTEM		£1	£1-50
Sat 22 Dec	ERIC'S CHRISTMAS PARTY with THE TEARDROP EXPLODES + ECHO & THE BUNNYMEN	Mat 5 pm	£1-10	£1-35
		Evg 8.30	£1-50	£2-00
Thur 27 Dec	Skeleton Records present THE ZORKIE TWINS / JUNK ART / ATTEMPTED MUSTACHE / THE POSERS / TIM BYERS		75p	£1
Fri 28 Dec	A TRIBUTE TO WINSTON featuring members of ORCHESTRAL MANOEUVRES IN THE DARK and DALEK I		£1-10	£1-60
Sat 29 Dec	A Rhythm & Blues Special with LEW LEWIS and BAD MANNERS	Evg Only	£1-35	£1-75

Hours of Opening: 8.30-2am (Matinee Saturdays 5-7.30pm) We are open between mid-day and 2 pm daily except Sunday for badges, posters, T-shirts and membership enquiries.
SHOW TIMES: On all shows except Saturday the support will be on stage at 9.30 and the main band at approx 10.45. On Saturdays the main band will be onstage at 10 pm and the support group will play at approx 11.30 pm. The door admission price will be reduced when the main band have finished their set.
MEMBERSHIP OF ERIC'S is £1-10 yearly. A member is entitled to sign in two guests, and to benefit from reduced admission prices. Membership application forms are available from the Club. Call us on our 24-hour answering service 051-236 8301 for further information.

The Cavern. We went straight into the club to get warm and enjoy the smell of damp that was always worst near the toilets. They played each other's songs, but my abiding memory of the night is that after playing 'The World', Andy said, 'That was Dalek I miming to their last single'. It was pretty obvious that they had mimed as the song had just faded out. So maybe all the Dalek parts were mimed? Anyway, it was tremendous fun, OMD doing songs from the forthcoming LP.

I can't remember whether Eric's was busy - but my recollection is that it wasn't, possibly because between Christmas and New Year all the students went home and OMD, being from the Wirral, weren't that popular with the hip crowd.

ANDY MCCLUSKEY

We recorded 'Red Frame/White Light' in a London studio in downtime overnight right at the end of 1979. Dindisc were looking for a single to release ahead of the album. Carol Wilson was doing it on the cheap. We stayed on Richard Branson's barge in Little Venice and I woke up the next morning with a bloody drill bit coming through the wall about three inches above my head. We had it cheap because it was being renovated.

'Red Frame/White Light' was released as a single just before the album came out and got to No.64. The 'future of pop' wasn't looking terribly certain. Carol realised that our recordings were a bit amateur and we didn't really know what we were doing in the studio. She persuaded us to go into Admission studio with her boyfriend, Mike Howlett as producer, and he re-recorded 'Messages' from scratch. Initially, I absolutely hated it. It was missing all the key ingredients I liked. We couldn't get the same synth sounds we had previously. I remember Peter Saville saying, 'That sounds really good', but I was not convinced.

I get 'demo-itis'. I can't get used to re-recordings. It would take me months, sometimes years, to accept what we'd actually done was okay. I wasn't arrogant but I was difficult to live with because I was bleeding for this 'art' and it hurt because I could never remain objective after long studio sessions. People would say, 'Your life must be great', but I was living on my nerves. I wish I could go back now and say, 'Andrew, chill. It's such a great time. You're going to do *Top of the Pops*. You're going to travel the world. Enjoy it.' Sadly, I didn't really enjoy it at all. I was just so tense all of the time. I was a bag of nerves.

ORCHESTRAL MANOEUVRES IN THE DARK 1980

1980 saw the release of two albums; *Orchestral Manoeuvres in the Dark* and *Organisation* and three singles, 'Red Frame/White Light', 'Messages' and 'Enola Gay'.

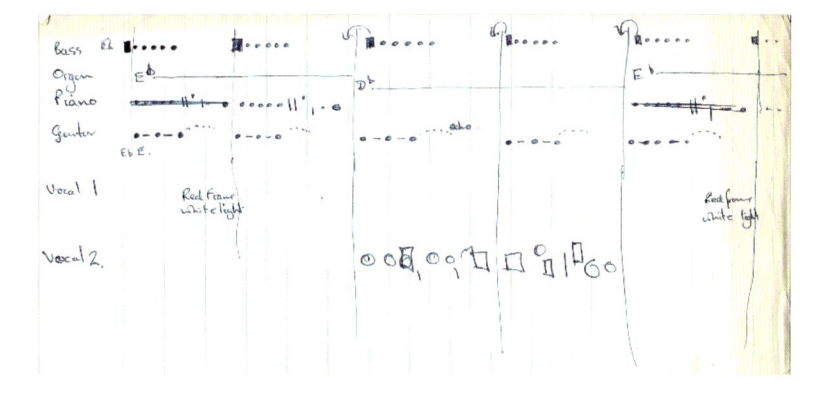

EFFENAAR

6 January 1980, Eindhoven, The Netherlands

ANDY MCCLUSKEY

Invited to play this club in Eindhoven, we drove down to Harwich to get the ferry to Hook of Holland. It was myself, Paul H, Paul Collister, and Malcolm as our 'roadie.' That we were offered a concert before the album was even released is indicative of the forward thinking in Belgium and Holland at that time.

The first time you go abroad under your own steam is very exciting! I remember having Dutch money and thinking how incredibly colourful it was. It looked like toy money. When I was younger I lived on my nerves, so whilst these early experiences were exciting, they were also terrifying. Every time we went somewhere I was really, really anxious. I was constantly in a state of turmoil.

↑ Early notes for 'Telephone Kiosk Song' later known as 'Red Frame/White Light'

OMD - ORCHESTRAL MANOEUVRES IN THE DARK 1980

RED FRAME/WHITE LIGHT WAS RELEASED

1 Feb 1980

RED FRAME/WHITE LIGHT

The phone box was our office. Neither Andy or I had a house phone, neither of our families could afford one. We used to have people call us at a certain time at the phone box, and we would keep other people out of the box because we were waiting for a call. Amusingly people would actually answer it if it was ringing as they went past and it would be, 'Is Andy or Paul there?' Then in 2017, it was taken away without anyone knowing. But thankfully after an extreme amount of fuss caused by ourselves, and many our fans, it's been reinstated. It's got a lock on it, but it's the actual phone box and the number still is 632 3003. It's probably going to be like a mini museum, and you'll have to phone up to obtain the code to get in if you want to explore it. It sits right next to the Railway Inn pub in Meols and people have made pilgrimages to that phone box since we began.

PAUL HUMPHREYS

↑
'Red Frame/White Light' single on Dindisc

PAUL HAMBLET

I played football with friends in Meols Park. When OMD started to become famous, around 1979, the phone in the box would ring all the time and we'd race to answer it. We were always greeted with the same question: 'Are Paul and Andy there?' Calls came from all over the world. I even spoke to someone in South Africa. Recently I was in The Railway Inn and saw the council taking the box away. I tried to explain they were removing a piece of music history, but they weren't amused and still took it. It's good to see it's back now.

ERIC'S
15 February 1980, Liverpool, UK

MALCOLM HOLMES
OMD drummer 1980 - 2013

I always consider my first gig with OMD to be this one. I'd known Andy and Paul a while, playing in early bands on the Wirral with them and helping out Winston the tape recorder, playing along with him. I did a bit of roadie-ing in Holland for them and spent time rehearsing at their studio, the Gramophone Suite. We'd huddle around a gas fire in the winter of 1979 and play songs from the first album.

I was using a brand-new state of the art electronic drum, built by the band's manager. It never worked. It was made from a few drum practise pads wired to a couple of circuit boards, with a bass drum pedal attached to a switch. It looked great for 1979 but was never going to go into mass production. It would certainly never be available at Curly Music, the shop below the studio.

Every time I used the bass drum pedal it would move a couple of inches forward, left or right. I nailed the pedal to the floor and it still moved. I'd hit a pad with a stick and destroy the crystal mic. buried under the drum skin that triggered the circuit board. Even as a naive little drummer I knew the kit wasn't going to last.

We needed a production rehearsal to try the gear out and make sure the crew knew what they were doing. The Gramophone Suite wouldn't be any good because of space, noise and humping the gear up three flights of stairs. So where else could we use for our production rehearsal for our small, intimate gig at Eric's club that held a few hundred people? Of course, the Liverpool Empire. One of the biggest UK venues, including one of the biggest stages you're ever going to play on.

I'd been to the Empire as a punter to watch bands. I'd never been on the stage or in the venue when it was empty. We arrived and trucked onto the stage with our few square feet of gear, including my electronic drum kit, 12 or so lights and the out-front mixing desk, firmly plonked in Row D because the cable only stretched that far. We huddled together in the middle of the stage, as we did when

↑
Andy on stage at Manchester Polytechnic February 1980 and Dave Hughes and Mal Holmes (using half-acoustic and half-electronic kit)

OMD - ORCHESTRAL MANOEUVRES IN THE DARK 1980

↑
Promo shot for the first album showing the custom stands for the tour that used the album lozenge design (Dave Hughes on the left)

we rehearsed at the Gramophone, only with no gas fire. Andy, Paul, Dave and I were completely swamped by that huge stage and an auditorium with 3,000 empty seats. It was daunting. Even with no one in the Empire it was intimidating. It scared the life out of me.

I remember looking out from my kit as we were setting up, wondering if we'd ever play here for real. 'Nah, no way,' I thought. Little did I know we'd take the place apart on many occasions, and it would become a very special gig for me, always to be treated with respect.

We started the rehearsal and someone turned the house lights off. What has always stayed with me is the view from the kit when the lights go down in a venue like the Empire. Exit signs. Yep those green exit signs. From the stage it gives the gig a sense of size, depth and scale. There's never been a gig at the Empire where I've not had a big smile on my face, watching those green lights looking back at me.

Next day was the Eric's show. I'd been out that afternoon to Top Man, buying the best electronic pop band threads I could find for 15 quid. A white shirt that buttoned up diagonally. A must-have shirt for any self-respecting electro-pop drummer showcasing his state-of-the-art drum kit that never worked. I also bought a pair of baggy kecks, like the ones Biggles wore in his Spitfire. Sorted.

I walked on stage for the Eric's show. The ceiling above us was very low and I immediately banged my head on one of the lights, to the joy of the crowd. Not cool. The gig got better for me, even though the drums wandered around the stage with every hit.

The tour started with a great gig in our hometown, people queuing down the street to get in. It was the start of things to come. I just needed to stop banging my head on the lights. And replace the Biggles kecks.

ORCHESTRAL MANOEUVRES IN THE DARK

WAS RELEASED

22 Feb 1980

ADVISION

Because the first album didn't sound very professional Carol Wilson persuaded us to go into Advision with her boyfriend, Mike Howlett, as producer, and he re-recorded 'Messages' from scratch. I absolutely hated it. It was missing all the key ingredients I liked. We couldn't get the same synth sounds. I remember playing it to Peter Saville. He said, 'Yeah, that sounds really good' and I went, 'Are you sure?'

We'd worked on it for two days. It was the worst case of demo-itis. I was terrible in recording studios. I'd write a song and have a vision of it, but my ears never heard in the final version what I'd originally imagined. It would take me months, sometimes years, to accept what we'd actually done was okay.

ANDY MCCLUSKEY

ANDY MCCLUSKEY

On the release of the first album, we were invited to perform on our first national TV show, *The Old Grey Whistle Test*. The broadcast sound is terribly embarrassing but in the studio we made new fans. The 20-year-old McCluskey was dismissive of ZZ Top as beardy old rockers, but they loved us. Years later we discovered they used to play our first album at their concert before they went on, were inspired to try using synths and drum machines and credit stealing their moves used in the *Eliminator* single videos from the way I rocked my bass on *OGWT*.

EDGE HILL COLLEGE

22 February 1980, Ormskirk, UK

BILLY GRAVES

I bought the first album from Probe Records in Liverpool, from none other than Pete Burns. A year or so later I met Jacci Newman, my first girlfriend and first love in a school disco at St Thomas the Apostle High, Skelmersdale. When we were together, she bought me *Organisation* as a gift and we listened to it over and over. Soon she became a fan too. Jacci and I were together for about four months until her family moved to Wrexham, North Wales. We tried the long-distance thing but sadly it just didn't work out. We were both devastated, with a few tearful phone calls. Jacci saved up her pocket money and bought some OMD records, which she played all the time, thinking about me. We lost touch.

In 2005 I moved to Adelaide, South Australia, with my young family. One night in June 2016, I had a vivid dream about Jacci's Dad, in which he said, 'Look after Jacci for me.' After a few days I searched social media, managing to find her younger brother, Ashley, discovering that the night I had the dream Jacci's father passed away. I wrote a short letter to Ashley passing on my condolences.

A few days after the funeral, Jacci contacted me thanking me and after exchanging a few messages we discovered we were both single. We started chatting every night, laughing and reminiscing.

In October 2016 Jacci came to Adelaide for a holiday. I showed her the *Organisation* album she bought me. All the memories came flooding back and we wondered if the fingerprints on the vinyl were ours. Jacci returned to the UK in December and it was obvious our love had grown, and we couldn't be apart, starting to plan a new life together.

Visiting the UK in June 2017, we saw our old stomping grounds and spent a few nights in Liverpool, where I showed Jacci the old Gramophone Suite, where Probe was, and where Eric's used to be. We're returning to the UK in May 2019 to get married, framing my copy of *Organisation*. OMD will always be a very important part of our story. To this day, the beginning of 'Enola Gay' - the ringtone I have for when she calls - still gives Jacci tingles.

UNIVERSITY OF EAST ANGLIA

2 March 1980, Norwich, UK

PAUL CURTIS

I can't control myself, jumping madly every time I see them, totally losing myself in the music. At Cambridge during the Architecture & Morality comeback tour, Andy and I tried to outdo each other during 'Electricity.' Another time at UEA I was bruised for over a week from dancing injuries, while at Ipswich Regent one time I felt cold air coming through to my knee. I'd cut through my jeans on an ashtray on the back of the seat in front. I didn't stop dancing, but when I got back home I had to jump into the bath to soak my jeans off.

STEVE MADDOCK

In March 1980 I was in the back of a car going to watch Judas Priest at Manchester Apollo when 'Electricity' came on the radio. There started a 38 year and counting love affair of the best band in the world ever. I bought that self-titled first album and it did exactly as it said on the tin when listened to at night. 1). Turn lights off; 2). Put record on. Lights from the stereo give you magical Orchestral Manoeuvres (that look and sound stunning) in the Dark.

What's on at Eric's, Liverpool February / March 1980

MUSIC HALL
4 March 1980, Shrewsbury, UK

MARK BOOTH

I was at Coppenhall Comprehensive School in Crewe, Cheshire and my good friend, Chris Doyle, lent me his black die-cut copy of *OMITD*. When I got home, I turned on my Dad's stereo and put it on. Straight away I liked the poppy songs, 'Messages', 'Electricity', 'Bunker Soldiers' and 'Red Frame/White Light', but the ones that really got my attention were the darker ones, such as the slow-burning 'The Messerschmitt Twins' and moody 'Pretending to See the Future.'

I reluctantly gave it back to Chris, telling him I thought it was brilliant and I had to get a copy. I saved up for two months - blue die-cut, orange inner sleeve - and almost wore it out.

Chris told me about an upcoming OMD concert and asked if I'd like to go. I jumped at the chance. I remember the lights and how loud it was. I sang along with the band. The die was cast.

When Andy started again with a new line up, I was overjoyed and delighted with the *Sugar Tax* album. I'd just moved to the US when *Universal* came out and sat alone in my Minneapolis apartment it was a little slice of home and familiarity, especially 'Walking on the Milky Way.'

DAVID GRAY

We arrived early at the Shrewsbury concert, met the band and were given lots of freebies. That same summer, OMD were playing a televised concert at Nottingham Playhouse. Me and my friend, Nick, quickly bought three tickets and set off. Being 18 we had no inhibitions and promptly walked straight into the Playhouse and watched our heroes for the whole day. Unfortunately, I missed the last train back to Stoke, sleeping on Derby station.

CIRCLE
16 April 1980, Ghent, Belgium

ANDY MCCLUSKEY

We played in Ghent and it was bass, mid, high frequencies with a very small PA. But we were only playing to a maximum of 200, 300 people.

We blew up our sub-speakers so the PA boys, unbeknownst to us, unscrewed them, took out the sub-speakers from the disco speakers and put ours in theirs. Two days later, we'd just done our soundcheck in Brussels and the police turned up. They wanted their speakers back. So the first time we ever played in Brussels, there was no bass. We just had mid and high frequencies. And there was no backline on stage. It must have been the tinniest gig we ever played.

The truck went missing in Amsterdam. They parked it on a bridge, which apparently was illegal. They got towed. But at least the gear hadn't been stolen. We got that back.

There were four of us by then. For the tour in February 1980, we asked Malcolm if he wanted to play with us. Although Martin had played with us when we were a two-piece, he couldn't play with us all the time. He had to finish his degree in Sheffield. So we asked Dave Hughes, another keyboard player, who was in Dalek I Love You, if he wanted to play with us. Dave toured with us and he's in the 'Messages' video and was on our first *Top of the Pops* appearance.

PARADISO

21 April 1980,
Amsterdam,
The Netherlands

ANDY MCCLUSKEY

We were kids from the suburbs. The Wirral ain't Toxteth. It's way over in the leafy suburbs of Liverpool. It's not even Birkenhead. And Amsterdam? Prostitutes in windows? Drugs were legal? You could walk in and out of sex shops? Everybody just wandered off, wide-eyed and brainless, like lambs to the slaughter. We didn't have a clue.

↑
Paul and Andy dressed as 'bank clerks'

After the soundcheck we were back at the hotel and the promoter came rushing in, crying. There were squatter riots all over Amsterdam and right outside the venue they'd built a barricade. 'The gig is cancelled' he wailed! 'Okay, don't cry, we can come back another day.' We tried to comfort him. 'I'm not upset about the bloody gig,' he snaps. 'The fucking police have bulldozed the barricade into the canal, and my car went in too!'

That night, instead of playing the concert we went driving around the city in our tour van. It was a war zone. Ranks of police with riot shields, Molotov cocktails being thrown, buildings on fire, debris littering the streets! We had never experienced anything like this in our lives.

LES BAIN DOUCHE

28 April 1980, Paris, France

ANDY MCCLUSKEY

This seemed the height of Gallic decadence. The venue was an old public baths, lit by candles. There were bloody ducks swimming in the smaller pools. The audience was so cool and sophisticated and Humphreys almost broke his ankle stepping down from the stage after the gig.

I was approached by this incredibly elegant older woman who complimented us on the concert, asking if I would like to accompany her and her friends for dinner. Amazingly I agreed. As the hours slid past the friends disappeared. Turned out that Antonia was fascinated by Marie Antoinette and apparently also by me! She claimed to be Marie reincarnated. I was hoping I wasn't Louis XVI and about to lose my head. We walked and talked through the streets of Paris. She delivered me back to the band hotel bathed in chill morning light. I know this happened, but it's as a dream. Unfortunately, the spell was broken when I climbed into a car full of inquisitive band members, trying to sleep on the drive to Lyon, being mercilessly ribbed and bombarded with a million questions. They refused to believe that all I'd done was walk around Paris until dawn with Marie Antoinette.

→
Andy's handwritten notes for 'Messages'

MESSAGES
WAS RELEASED

2 May 1980

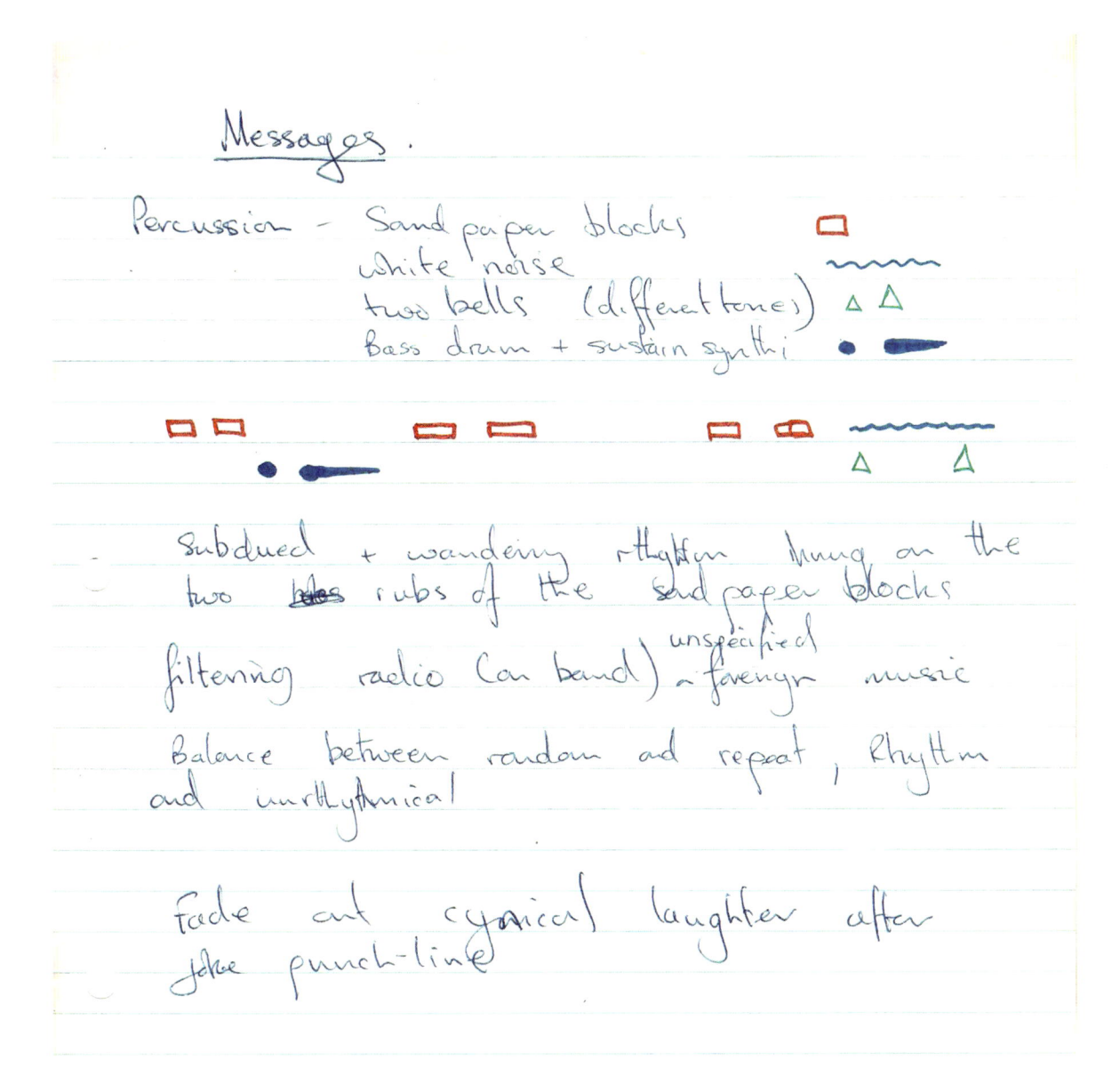

Messages.

Percussion — Sandpaper blocks
white noise
two bells (different tones)
Bass drum + sustain synth

Subdued + wandering rhythm hung on the two rubs of the sandpaper blocks

filtering radio (on band) unspecified foreign music

Balance between random and repeat, rhythm and unrhythmical

Fade out cynical laughter after joke punch-line

Paul and Andy in the Gramophone Suite, Liverpool

MARK RICHARDSON

One day in 1980, my mate from school came round my house and asked if I'd go with him to a local record shop. He persuaded me to fork out £1.09 for my first OMD single, 'Messages'. Thank you, Phil Redmond.

18 MAY 1980

ANDY MCCLUSKEY

A terrible clash of emotions! Just as our band is breathing the intoxicating oxygen of success, the air is sucked out of our lungs at the news of Ian Curtis' death. Hearing that Ian had committed suicide was such a shock. Someone that we actually knew. Had admired. Played concerts with just so very recently had decided that he could not go forward in life. And yet here we were doing Top of the Pops, having our first hit single and flying to America. Our brains were conflicted. Our hearts torn apart.

SIMON HOPKINS

One Thursday evening in 1980, doing dreaded Mr Crow's maths homework, I had half an ear and half an eye on *Top of the Pops*. New wave was all the rage and crashing guitars the order of the day. Then there was something way different, a melody, a hook, a synth. I'd been looking out for a different sound for months, getting intrigued by the upcoming use of synths, and there that Thursday night was the sound I was looking for. I'd found 'Messages.'

DAVE FAIRBAIRN
Working at The Gramophone Suite

Separated from the recording studio by sheets of plasterboard nailed to a timber frame was the OMD office. I worked there with Paul Collister in 1980/81. The rather flimsy construction of the walls meant the soundproofing of the studio wasn't exactly 100%. So management and admin work was carried out amidst a backdrop of either the band rehearsing or the latest OMD composition being constructed.

I was aware then that Andy and Paul had a very different approach to songwriting compared with anyone else I knew. Instead of starting by strumming a few chords on an acoustic guitar and throwing words and melody over the top, OMD built their music piece by piece, like musical Lego.

I'd be doing the VAT return and next door a drum machine would click and pop constantly - the same pattern all day. The next day it would have gained a hi-hat and that too would repeat over and over throughout the day, punctuated only by the whir of tape recorders being re-wound. About the third or fourth day it would have grown a bass drum. On one memorable occasion Andy spent days and nights perfecting the foundations of a particular composition and when Paul started adding organ and synth melodies Andy went to the library and brought back books about B-29 bombers. And so it became a song.

In the spring of 1980 when the band was finishing a tour of Europe I received a call from Carol Wilson of Dindisc. Exciting news: she'd got them what was to be their first *Top of the Pops* appearance, to be recorded the following day. The band would have to cancel their scheduled return by ferry and fly back

↑
Paul at the desk in the Gramophone Suite
Photo by Francesco Mellina

OMD - ORCHESTRAL MANOEUVRES IN THE DARK 1980

immediately to get to BBC TV Centre in time. There was one slight problem; they wouldn't be able to bring their instruments back with them. Dindisc had been told by the BBC they would have to make a new recording especially for *Top of the Pops* and wanted me to hire a whole set of replica instruments.

I was pretty certain the acts on *Top of the Pops* just mimed to their records, but having been assured by the record company they would pay for everything I set about hiring like-for-like instruments. I had to find a number of different sources to get everything I wanted and be sure it was all delivered to the *Top of the Pops* studio in time. Sure enough it was all there awaiting the band when they arrived, only for them to quickly establish none of it was necessary, as they would after all be miming to the record!

Turned out that the story about re-recording the song was a subterfuge to placate the Musicians' Union - in reality you just turned up with a tape of your record and pretended it had come hot from the studio. That's why when you watch that first performance of 'Messages' on *Top of the Pops* they're not playing their normal instruments. And did anyone notice that the tape recorder in the background is not Winston, but an imposter?

It was an interesting job! I was paid £50 a week, not bad considering Paul, Andy and Paul Collister's wages were all £20 less (although the band did get £10 a day when they were on tour).

TOP OF THE POPS, 1980

I was 12. Too young for gigs or even the musty-sounding, late-night armchair experience of *The Old Grey Whistle Test*. But OMD's version of The Future, carried into our Midlands living-room via the minimalist Morse code of 'Messages', felt like a siren's call – already different from the bombastic school play version of Orwell and Ballard presented by Gary Numan's Tubeway Army. For a start, OMD looked a bit like older 'me's – a touch spoddy, unruly hair, untrained dancing. I recognised them. And in 'Messages' was encoded a melancholy I would appreciate in many future OMD songs – one that mourned idealistic visions, or unfulfilled promises of what The Future would deliver. In the 'Messages' lyric the communication technology by which McCluskey's ex-love torments him is unstated (although he's thought of burning these messages), but the beautiful electronic suspension of the music makes you feel these dispatches are actually in the ether, and somehow they always will be (remind you of anything?). Many years later, Andy McCluskey would tell me he regarded Kraftwerk and the subsequent wave of electronic pop musicians of which OMD were part as 'the last Modernists'. Their faith in technology brought new sounds and textures to music, but their songs knew that utopia would remain a hollow hope, a beautiful dream.

DANNY ECCLESTON
SENIOR EDITOR, MOJO MAGAZINE

ANDY MCCLUSKEY

We'd just finished the European leg of the tour and were leaving the hotel in Belgium to get the ferry when a guy came running out: 'Stop, stop, stop!' Oh shit, somebody's not paid. He said, 'Telephone!' We went to the phone and it was, 'Guys, you've charted.' I think we were No.53. They obviously couldn't get people that week to come in live, so they'd gone down that far, offering *Top of the Pops* to us. We didn't get the ferry. For the first time in my life, I went on an aeroplane, because we had to fly from Brussels to London.

We had to go into the studio and record 'Messages', because the Musicians' Union insisted you had to demonstrate you had played the record. You'd do it the day before. You'd do the best you could in three hours and it would sound utterly shit. However, before you got there the tape op had put the master on tracks 23 and 24. The Musicians' Union guy would come down, sit there and you'd say we're just going to set up the mix now. Do you want to go to the pub and have a drink and come back?' And he'd leave. The engineer would mute the new playing, push up 23 and 24, mix it and - there you go - it sounds just like the record. Because it was the master tape, so it was the record! Most of the Musicians' Union guys knew what was going on, but they heard you playing it and they'd go, 'Yeah, that is him singing it, they played it.' Just occasionally, you got somebody who was a stickler and you had to use your

↑
Peter Saville-designed 'Messages' sleeve complete with pen

ORCHESTRAL MANOEUVRES IN THE DARK 1980 | 109

OMD - ORCHESTRAL MANOEUVRES IN THE DARK 1980

↑
Smash Hits feature with Andy and Paul with Winston and 'Messages' lyrics

three-hour piece of crap and could hear it on *Top of the Pops* and you'd go, 'Ooh, that sounds rough. Jesus!'

I still didn't have a telephone at my house. I still lived with my parents. Paul lived with his Mum. I'd gone to the Red Frame/White Light telephone box on the corner of Greenwood Road, kind of equidistant between our houses, and phoned Paul Collister, who had the call from the record company to say 'Messages' had reached No.13. I was on my way to Paul's, he was on his way to meet me and we collided at the top of his road on the corner of Birkenhead Road. We were jumping up and down, grabbing each other. I remember standing opposite the Railway Inn, on the corner, like schoolboys. 'Number 13! We're in the top 20! We have a real hit!'

Next time we did that was about five years ago at the Tate Modern, when Kraftwerk played 'Antenna' there. We never thought we'd hear it live. We were holding each other by the lapels, jumping up and down like schoolboys, going 'its 'Antenna'!' So we still have the energy in there somewhere. We can still be fan-boys.

PAUL HUMPHREYS

That was an amazing feeling, doing *Top of the Pops*, a show we'd watched as kids. We were just amazed to be in the BBC, going through the process and seeing how tiny everything was in the actual production studio. It looks so huge on the screen and it was this tiny little studio with five stages and hardly anywhere for people to be. They were nearly getting mowed over by cameras moving and had people ushering them around so not to crush them.

To actually stand on that stage, we were absolutely terrified. But we did it and that was such a milestone. I think that was the first of 29 *Top of the Pops* appearances.

We finally had credibility after that with people on the Wirral. We'd made it. We weren't making any money, but we'd made it.

HURRAH'S
MAY 1980, NEW YORK, USA

We were supposed to go the day before, but had to go back to London to do *Top of the Pops* and 'Messages' for the second time. So we ended up flying to New York on the day of our first show. We were on stage about 1am, the equivalent of 6am in the UK. But we were young. We could do it. We were at Heathrow the day before, on a payphone going, 'Where are we in the charts? Oh great. *Top of the Pops* again? So don't get on the plane? Okay, we'll come back. Cancel the flight!'

Why we were going to New York I haven't got a clue, because nothing was released and nobody was playing us apart from a couple of college radio stations and some real deep underground stations. The first album had just come out, but it wasn't released in America. You could only get it on import. However, we got invited to play two nights at Hurrah's Club in New York, which was pretty cool, so people had obviously heard about us.

When we landed none of us thought we'd need dollars, so we never thought about changing any money. At JFK airport this skycap came up, asking, 'Wanna hand with your luggage buddy?' We agreed, 'Yeah, great.' We were totally gormless. We didn't realise we'd have to give him a tip. He put all the luggage outside and said, 'There you go' and put out his hand. We were like, 'Oh shit. Er, has anyone got dollars?' 'No.' Our manager got out a five pound note, at the time worth $12.50, and gave it to him. We're thinking, 'That's loads of money.' He snarled, 'What am I supposed to do with that? Wipe my fuckin' ass?' Welcome to New York!

We were kids from a suburb of Liverpool and here was the Empire State Building. Police cars that go 'whoooo-whooooo.' Fire hydrants. Policemen with guns. It was like nothing on earth, like we'd been parachuted into the future. We didn't sleep for four days. I think the first time we slept was on the plane back home - we were wide-eyed and living on adrenaline.

We didn't have any money. We didn't have anywhere to stay. We went to New York and made an arrangement with Hurrah's that the barmaids and their friends would each have a band member to stay with them. Which is where Paul met his wife. Maureen had gone, 'Oh he's cute. I'll have him'. And she did! She was at the American ballet theatre in New York. She'd moved there from LA to study dance in New York. She was a good ballet dancer.

We were driving ourselves. We played in Boston and there was a support band. Problem was, we never had backline. Everything had to be plugged into DI boxes, and after the changeover all our stuff was plugged into the wrong boxes. We started to play and it was like World War Three. After about three songs, I threw a wobbler and walked off stage. That was the end of the gig. I'm surprised we ever got invited back to Boston. We then went to Philadelphia and then came home. We'd done four gigs on the east coast of America with no money, driving ourselves in a crappy hire car. It was nuts. Why the hell we went I don't know. But Paul met his wife!

ANDY MCCLUSKEY

ENOLA GAY WAS RELEASED

26 Sep 1980

PAM HILTON

It was 3am in the morning. After dancing the night away at a club called Patches in Oxford Street, Sydney, Australia, we went to a very late night/early morning cafe called Oddy's. A song was playing on the jukebox. It was 'Enola Gay.' I played it another three times and the very next day I went to the record store and ordered the album from the UK.

PAUL CHAPMAN

In early 1980 I took a detour on the way home from school to buy the latest *Smash Hits*. The lollipop lady asked what I had, and when I showed her said, 'Oh, my son was in that a few weeks ago.' I assumed her son was a music fan like me and had a submitted letter published. My Mum struck up a friendship with the lollipop lady and a few weeks later went round her house. When she came home she said, 'You'll never guess what - the lollipop lady's son was on *Top Of The Pops* tonight.' I asked what band he was in and she said it was a strange name, 'Orchestra something.' I dug out my earlier copies of *Smash Hits* and eventually found a copy with the lyrics to 'Red Frame/White Light' and a photo of Andy and Paul. The lollipop lady was Andy's mum! When 'Enola Gay' was released, I was very kindly invited round to the McCluskey's house, where I met Andy and he signed my copy of 'Enola Gay.' Living in a small town like Meols, it was amazing to think we had pop stars as neighbours!

BOB ALLEN

'Enola Gay' helped me come out in '81, in a humorous way. A friend played this song for me. I had a crush on him, but he was straight. We were hanging out, getting stoned, and when 'Enola Gay' was sung I heard 'You Know You're Gay.' I was relieved to hear OMD confirm I was gay but was confused when they sang, 'You should have stayed home yesterday.' I brushed it off. Maybe I shouldn't come out yet. On further listening, seeing the

↑ On holiday in LA a friend of Paul's arranged for a behind the scenes tour at Universal Pictures lot where Paul and Andy posed next to Enola Gay

song title, I realised I got the lyrics wrong, but not before sharing with my friend that I was gay. He laughed and said, 'You dummy!'

ANGELIA DARNBROUGH

'Enola Gay' changed my life. I'd never heard synthesised pop music before and the single launched my love for new wave. It was refreshing to dance to a new beat and listen to lyrics that really meant something, instead of songs about love lost.

NEIL TOMPKINS

I was an 11-year old struggling with the onset of early puberty, trying to get to grips with starting secondary school. I heard 'Enola Gay' on my Dad's car radio and again on my radio and knew this was mine. This piece of music – the synthesiser hook, the bass-line, the lyrics – this was my music. I did all sorts of pocket money earning chores to raise the £1 needed to buy the single on the Saturday after it was released.

I wanted more. I'll always remember that first time, and every time I hear 'Enola Gay' I'm transported back to September 1980.

ANDY MCCLUSKEY

To keep receiving his dole, Paul took a job as a bricklayer's assistant. It's hard to imagine Paul carrying a hod, helping refurbish Hoylake municipal baths. Whilst Paul was out justifying his dole

↑ Andy's research notes for 'Enola Gay'

money, I was round at his mother's house and wrote 'Enola Gay' on my own in the back room. I didn't have a drum machine as we didn't yet own the CR-78, but I had the chords, the bass-line and the melody. To this day, I still can't play that melody at full speed. I wrote it slow and showed it to Paul, and he played it. I think it's the first song either of us had written on our own.

There was a film called *Urgh! A Music War* containing music from all the UK bands from '79 and '80, filmed by Americans realising there was something going on. They filmed several of our tracks at Portsmouth Guildhall on 19th September, 1980, the biggest venue that we had headlined up to that point. They used a version of 'Enola Gay' before the drum machine was added, the version we had been debuting all year.

For Paul, it was an adopted song. It wasn't really his baby. And Paul Collister thought it was absolute cheesy shite. The two Pauls were saying, 'We don't want that. That's not cool. That's pop rubbish. Forget it being a single. We don't even want it on the album.' But we played a demo to Carol Wilson and her eyes lit up. She said, 'That's the hit that's going to break you, guys.' Paul Collister goes, 'We don't want it releasing. It's cheesy crap and it's not going to do them any good at all.' That was the first time I think there'd been a real split in the camp. It's hard to imagine a band manager saying he didn't want to be associated with something that would go on to sell five million copies!

After Mike Howlett's success producing 'Messages', we were persuaded to go to Ridge Farm Studios in the summer of 1980 with him and record the next album, that was to be *Organisation*. We took a couple of the multi-tracks from our studio, which had a 16-track machine and we could drop in and make another eight tracks around them, but most of it was re-recorded from scratch. Which again caused problems for me, because I was used to the demo we'd done. But you throw it all away and start again. It was difficult.

It was mixed at Advision, where we recorded and mixed 'Messages.' The record company were convinced they had a hit. I remember Mike Howlett arriving. He was playing 'Enola Gay' on a cassette in his car and I thought, 'It just doesn't sound right.' I said, 'I want it remixing and want to re-sing the vocals.' The record company weren't happy, 'You what? But it's gone. It's been cut. It's at the pressing plant.' I said, 'I don't care. It's not right.'

I put my foot down and said, 'No. I want to re-do the vocals and want a remix.' I got my way. I recently heard the version they wanted to go with and I was right. I sang it better the next time and it was a better mix. Or maybe I'm just used to it.

'Enola Gay' was released despite the initial resistance of the two Pauls and was rather successful. Everybody thinks it was a No.1, but it got to No.8 in the UK.

Early the following year we flew to Italy for a TV show and were asked to do press interviews.

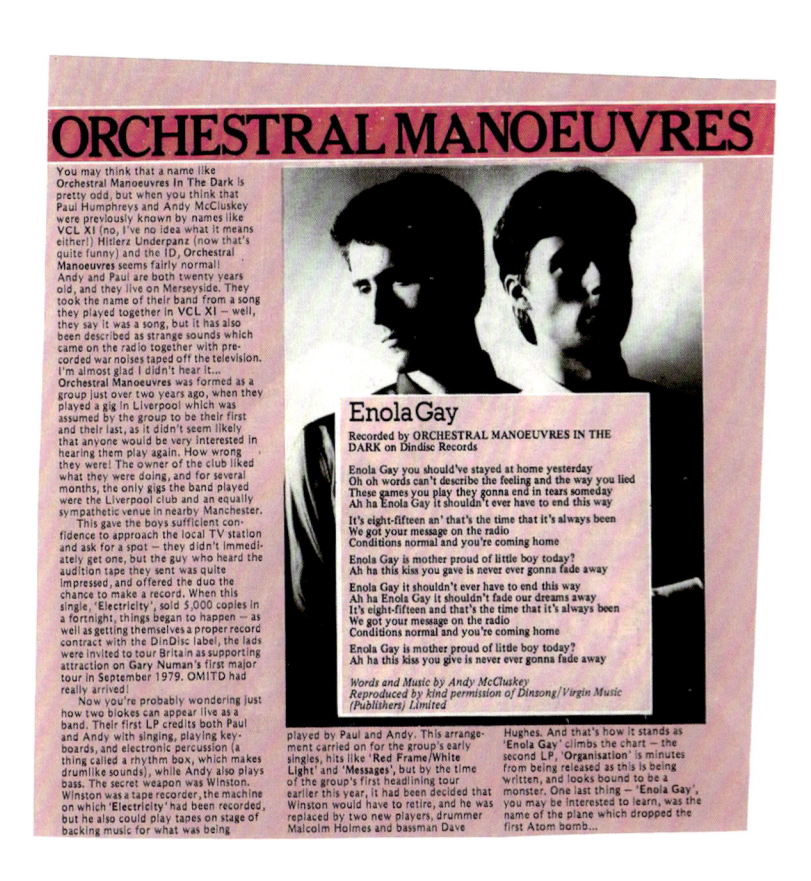

ORCHESTRAL MANOEUVRES

You may think that a name like Orchestral Manoeuvres In The Dark is pretty odd, but when you think that Paul Humphreys and Andy McCluskey were previously known by names like VCL XI (no, I've no idea what it means either!) Hitlerz Underpanz (now that's quite funny) and the ID, Orchestral Manoeuvres seems fairly normal! Andy and Paul are both twenty years old, and they live on Merseyside. They took the name of their band from a song they played together in VCL XI — well, they say it was a song, but it has also been described as strange sounds which came on the radio together with pre-recorded war noises taped off the television. I'm almost glad I didn't hear it...

Orchestral Manoeuvres was formed as a group just over two years ago, when they played a gig in Liverpool which was assumed by the group to be their first and their last, as it didn't seem likely that anyone would be very interested in hearing them play again. How wrong they were! The owner of the club liked what they were doing, and for several months, the only gigs the band played were the Liverpool club and an equally sympathetic venue in nearby Manchester.

This gave the boys sufficient confidence to approach the local TV station and ask for a spot — they didn't immediately get one, but the guy who heard the audition tape they sent was quite impressed, and offered the duo the chance to make a record. When this single, 'Electricity', sold 5,000 copies in a fortnight, things began to happen — as well as getting themselves a proper record contract with the DinDisc label, the lads were invited to tour Britain as supporting attraction on Gary Numan's first major tour in September 1979. OMITD had really arrived!

Now you're probably wondering just how two blokes can appear live as a band. Their first LP credits both Paul and Andy with singing, playing keyboards, and electronic percussion (a thing called a rhythm box, which makes drumlike sounds), while Andy also plays bass. The secret weapon was Winston. Winston was a tape recorder, the machine on which 'Electricity' had been recorded, but he also could play tapes on stage of backing music for what was being played by Paul and Andy. This arrangement carried on for the group's early singles, hits like 'Red Frame/White Light' and 'Messages', but by the time of the group's first headlining tour earlier this year, it had been decided that Winston would have to retire, and he was replaced by two new players, drummer Malcolm Holmes and bassman Dave Hughes. And that's how it stands as 'Enola Gay' climbs the chart — the second LP, 'Organisation' is minutes from being released as this is being written, and looks bound to be a monster. One last thing — 'Enola Gay', you may be interested to learn, was the name of the plane which dropped the first Atom bomb...

Enola Gay
Recorded by ORCHESTRAL MANOEUVRES IN THE DARK on Dindisc Records

Enola Gay you should've stayed at home yesterday
Oh oh words can't describe the feeling and the way you lied
These games you play they gonna end in tears someday
Ah ha Enola Gay it shouldn't ever have to end this way

It's eight-fifteen an' that's the time that it's always been
We got your message on the radio
Conditions normal and you're coming home

Enola Gay is mother proud of little boy today?
Ah ha this kiss you gave is never ever gonna fade away

Enola Gay it shouldn't ever have to end this way
Ah ha Enola Gay it shouldn't fade our dreams away
It's eight-fifteen and that's the time that it's always been
We got your message on the radio
Conditions normal and you're coming home

Enola Gay is mother proud of little boy today?
Ah ha this kiss you give is never ever gonna fade away

Words and Music by Andy McCluskey
Reproduced by kind permission of Dinsong/Virgin Music (Publishers) Limited

---

However, we were surprised to be led into the hotel conference room. 'What's going on?' There were about 30 journalists there. We didn't think people in Italy were that interested. We were introduced, 'Andy and Paul, welcome to Italy. First question please.' 'Hi. how does it feel to be No.1 in Italy?' We said, 'Is this *Candid Camera*? Is this a joke?' 'No, it's our surprise. We didn't want to tell you. You're No.1!'

Paul and I had no intention of being a pop group. It could not have been our intention, because we weren't writing pop songs in our heads. And then 'Enola Gay' became No.1 in Italy and France for three months.

The record company's attitude to making videos was, 'If it goes in the top-40 we'll make a video.' Well, it went straight in the top 40, so they said, 'We need a video now!' We said, 'Er, we haven't got time. We're going on tour.' We were rushed into the ITN TV news studio and recorded about two hours of us playing against green screens. They dropped in some clouds and that's the video to this day of 'Enola Gay.' The cheapest video you've ever seen in your life for a song that sold five million.

↑
Smash Hits informs its readers that 'Enola Gay' was the name of the plane which dropped the first atom bomb

ORGANISATION WAS RELEASED

24 Oct 1980

NEIL HOLLIDAY

I bought *Organisation* purely on the basis of 'Enola Gay' and for a long time it was the only track I really listened to. But this dark track at the end of side one just blew me away. I played it to my friends, who were equally impressed, and it became a sort of anthem with which we judged other songs. At art college, I was beset by students who wittered on about The Doors or Led Zeppelin, but OMD captured my heart and when things were tough I could lie in the dark and mutter, 'I can't imagine, how this ever came to be', the song playing in the background. 'Statues' was the song that really woke me up to what they could do.

JO CHAPLIN

I told a boy I fancied, Steve Chaplin, how good *Organisation* was. Being a music geek, he bought it too. It was a far cry from his AC/DC and Deep Purple albums. We later married and had our wonderful children. He still buys me their albums and we still go to their gigs.

ANDY WATSON

I first heard *Organisation*, a timeless symphony of complex soundscapes, in the mid-Eighties when OMD broke the US. I've been captivated by it to this day. 'VCL XI' sounds as melodic and fresh as the first time I heard it, and I kissed my future wife

---

ORCHESTRAL MANOEUVRES IN THE DARK: Organisation (DinDisc). If only this twosome would cease clinging to the idea of being a serious "experimental" band and go all out for the shameless synth-pop single, then at least we'd be spared these endless retreads of a rather limiting format. Apart from the nice 'n' sleazy "Motion And Heart", they haven't the substance to sound convincing when attempting to be anything but clever and superficial. Another "Electricity" would seem to be in order. (5 out of 10).
— *Mark Ellen*

for the first time to 'Stanlow'! The music worked, and now my whole family loves OMD.

LANCE HARDY
author & television producer

I remember playing both sides of *Organisation* back to back throughout the autumn of 1980, doing the same with *Architecture & Morality* a year later. Those albums changed my life. Nearly 40 years on, I still feature OMD tracks in my television production work.

FRIARS CLUB
1 November 1980, Aylesbury, UK

MARTIN COOPER

The Friars Club held a special place in my heart as a unique, exciting venue, a small club with an intriguingly evocative name. I enthusiastically read band reviews in the *NME* from there about many of my musical idols as a teenager. David Bowie performed there at the start of the Ziggy Stardust tour, which I was lucky enough to see the following month in Liverpool.

In the summer of 1980, when I joined OMD, *Organisation* had been released and we were embarking on a major UK tour. The dates were announced and to my delight the Friars Club was to be the first show. Truly momentous!

I was joining the band as a keyboard player/saxophonist and after only a couple of weeks of intense practising and a crash course in synthesisers we headed down south. There we had a long and boring day of production rehearsals at the famous Shepperton Studios, holed up in a cold, cavernous hangar with no creature comforts and very little time to actually rehearse. The day was all about production, lights and sound. It felt very new to me and I remember feeling desperately overwhelmed, tired and anxious.

Today we have wonderful instruments to play and at the press of a button pre-programmed sounds appear. But in those early days the synths I used were very basic – two Roland SH01/02 mono synths and a Vox organ. The Rolands had no presets or memory, so each synth needed to be quietly and quickly programmed manually between each song. I had to carefully jot down in a little notepad each configuration, then I'd quickly refer to my notes in the dark. This was very stressful. I'd have been lost without my little black book!

What a great and memorable gig though, that first visit to The Friars. I remember sharing a room with Andy (probably the only time I ever did), reflecting on the show together before finally going to sleep.

←
Original vinyl album of the group's second LP *Organisation*

←
Mark Ellen from *Smash Hits* gives *Organisation* 5/10

OMD - ORCHESTRAL MANOEUVRES IN THE DARK 1980

ANDY MCCLUSKEY

This was a step up for the band and I found myself with many more songs to sing without a bass guitar in my hands. Frankly, I was my usual terrified and stressed out self. I recall asking our tour manager Chris McMurray what I should do when I didn't have my bass on. He suggested, 'Find a happy face in the audience and smile back. Once they've smiled, you can move to the next face, and the next, then the next. One by one you will engage the audience. It's now your job. You are the lead singer.' I spent the concert endeavouring to carry out his instructions. I felt a sham, like I was pretending to be a lead singer and was going to get found out. However, it seemed to work. I've spent 38 years pretending to be a lead singer and I'm still hoping not to be found out!

COLSTON HALL

3 November 1980, Bristol, UK

JON SHEARD

'Stanlow' was a soundscape unlike anything I had heard before, conjuring up a vision of the place that is quite remarkable. Several years later, I moved to Liverpool and whenever I drive past, that music fills my mind.

I was overwhelmed by this concert. The music was so clean and modern sounding, yet some of the tracks were very danceable. I felt this was an intelligent band that had a lot to say.

CIVIC HALL
6 November 1980,
Guildford, UK

DAVID NORTON

It felt as though no time at all had passed between my being a 14-year old at Guildford Civic on a cold November night in 1980, watching the band take to the stage one by one to the pulsing industrial sounds of 'Stanlow', and another bracing November night at Reading's Hexagon Theatre in 2017. Stood in almost the exact spot in different venues, I continued to experience the amazement and awe I had 37 years previously. My hair had lost its colour and my joints were less supple, but my youthful passion still glowed in abundance.

Choosing one gig is difficult, but a stand-out memory is Cardiff's St David's Hall in June 2007. Prior to the gig, my then-wife and I were fortunate to spend several hours with Martin Cooper around Cardiff Bay, drinking coffee and taking in the sights. I always had a soft spot for Martin and Malcolm, so the chance to meet up again after all those years was a dream come true. My daughter Daisy was born a couple of days later, prematurely. I'd even packed the maternity bag that day, in case she was born that night, to the sights and sounds of *Architecture & Morality*.

APOLLO
10 November 1980,
Glasgow, UK

KEN LOGAN

I'd been a fan since hearing a session on John Peel, and the release of 'Electricity' cemented my love of electronic music. I'd been listening to Kraftwerk for a couple of years, along with Klaus Shulze and various other knob-twiddlers, like John Foxx. I joined the OMD fan club and received a photocopy of a

← OMD grace the cover of music weekly *Melody Maker* on 8 November 1980

hand-written letter with my name at the top together with a selection of badges, a fan club number, a fanzine-type newsletter and a floppy disc containing 'Stanlow' and 'Once When I Was Six'. I bought everything I could get my hands on, including the orange/blue version of the first LP and 'Electricity' 12-inch, still in my loft.

Fatal Charm supported them. Hearing OMD live was fantastic. They sounded just like the record. The baggy trousers and jumpers, smart shoes and Andy's trademark sway, with the bass high up his body, made the show come alive.

OMD were the epitome of UK synth-pop to me. Their brand of electro-pop had more depth and soul, explored darker themes and focused on the technical abilities of the equipment in far more depth than their contemporaries.

GEORGE BROWN

It was my first gig. My friend Alistair got the tickets. He read the *NME* and knew which bands were worth seeing. Glasgow Apollo was a venue with a fearsome reputation, with a 15-foot high stage and a balcony that swayed when the audience got excited. OMD came onstage in darkness to the intro of 'I Betray my Friends', Andy stood with his back to the audience. The crowd erupted and were on their feet, including all of us upstairs on that unsteady balcony. As Andy turned around, his jaw fell and a look of absolute terror crossed his face, confronted by 3,000 baying Scots. After a full set and an encore, the band returned. They didn't have any songs left to play, so rewound Winston and unleashed a second euphoric rendition of 'Enola Gay.' As the audience left I noticed how different they looked. The Clyde in the Seventies was a depressing place to grow up, but this crowd was different – excited, confident, optimistic. They looked like the future, and I was going to be part of it.

ODEON THEATRE

11 November 1980, Edinburgh, UK

LES WESTON

We had a couple of drinks before. OMD opened a great gig with 'Stanlow'. Discussing it on the way out, my work colleague said, 'I wondered whether my claustrophobia would kick in. I seem to be cured, as I was obviously fine.' I was in shock, thinking, 'What if he threw a wobbly during the show? We could have been thrown out!' Needless to say, he wasn't invited to any more gigs.

APOLLO

12 November 1980,
Manchester, UK

STEPHEN RICKETTS

The neon lights of the theatre reflected in the wet pavement. The sound of cars passing by was heightened by the noise the tyres made as they struggled to grip the rain-soaked asphalt. Night had fallen while we stood in the queue, impatiently waiting to be allowed in. It would have taken more than the usual foul autumn weather of North West England to dampen the spirits of our excited little group. We were 15 and this was our first rock concert.

I tightly gripped my battleship grey OMD T-shirt and Organisation tour programme while finding my seat in row D of the front circle, which cost me £3.25. I jealously eyed those lucky fans in the first two rows. I knew they would be allowed to stand up at the front of the stage once the concert started.

The lights went down and there was movement behind the net curtain covering the stage. I could see keyboards on top of industrial looking stands and a drum kit in the middle at the back. The curtain parted as shadowy figures strolled out, greeted by a cheer from the crowd. From beneath the instrument stands, bright white lights began to pulse in time to a slow melodic chug of industrial sounds.

'Stanlow', I blurted out involuntarily, my announcement lost in another cheer. The first synthesised notes rose up from the stage and crashed down on me in a wave of sound that sent a shiver though me. The notes sounded like an out-of-tune violin being played by an

↑
Press advert for the
Dindisc release of
Organisation

orchestral ghost. The following 90 minutes were spent basking in a type of new sound. 'Doot de doot music', friends called it. Not real music, my parents had complained, enduring continuous replaying of the LP on the turntable. But to me it was a revelation.

JENNY BEVERIDGE

I fell in love with Orchestral Manoeuvres in the Dark after seeing them on *Top of the Pops* in 1980. I vowed to meet them and as a first-year at Newcastle Polytechnic I travelled to Manchester to stay with a friend studying at UMIST.

At the Apollo I stood in awe, watching Andy, in heaven from beginning to end. I'm not sure how but a roadie offered me a backstage pass. I eagerly accepted, but once there I wasn't entirely sure what to do. Paul had Maureen beside him (or on top of him!). I thought, of course, they're pop stars, and deserve glamorous American girlfriends.

Andy gave me a burgundy wool scarf as a memento and wrote to me - a letter from the Wirral and postcards from around Europe. I posted the scarf back soon after, as it appeared in one of the concert programmes and I thought he should have it back.

I've seen OMD perform many times and thought 2017's performance at the Sage in Gateshead was the best ever. The atmosphere was electric and it was good to see fans of all ages.

From having my bedroom plastered with OMD posters and memorabilia, playing the early vinyl repeatedly on my navy blue portable record player to having 'Enola Gay' as my ringtone nearly 40 years later, I find it incredible that a naive girl out of her depth at 20 would have a chance to still see OMD perform three times in just over a year at Gateshead, Liverpool and even sailing on one of the seas with them.

CHRIS HAY

Growing up in a place now called Tameside, seven miles from Manchester city centre but with an identity crisis – not considered Cheshire or Manchester - I imagine the top of the Wirral has a similar 'problem' with Liverpool.

In 1979, aged 13 and starting to listen to music, Dad took us to Belle Vue Speedway, where they played snippets of tunes between race announcements, where I remember hearing a catchy tune that turned out to be 'Electricity.'

I bought the album. I was the only one in my school with the LP. A couple of years later we had a record player in the fifth-year common room, so I'd take that plus *Organisation* and *Architecture & Morality* into school. I remember 'Enola Gay' over the speakers in school one morning, a geography teacher deciding to do an assembly about the history behind the song.

The first time I got to see them was on the Organisation tour. It was my first ever gig (I won't count The Dooleys at the Tameside Theatre the year before).

At Hyde Sixth Form, I told the deputy head I'd lost my ID card. I gave my date of birth as 1965 instead of 1966, making me 18. She knew what I was doing but ran with it. I needed it to take out membership at The Hacienda and have fond memories of an OMD gig there, trying out new material. People talked in subsequent years about a mysterious track called 'Heaven Is', me thinking, 'I was there for that'. That gig is a legendary OMD event, a bit like the Sex Pistols at the Free Trade Hall. I went on to train as an army photographer and still use photography as a Cheshire Constabulary crime scene investigator.

I saw OMD at Manchester Academy in 2017 on the Punishment of Luxury tour with my eldest, doing his Master's at Chester. His Mum said I was, 'Getting him into old man's music'. I didn't force him to listen to OMD or make him go. He robbed all my CDs, made his own mind up.

ANDREW DOWDEN

Backstage at the Apollo, the band's manager was the only person not having fun. He yelled at Mally Holmes, who jumped off his drum-riser at the end, 'Don't do that again! If you break your leg that's the end of the tour!'

GAUMONT THEATRE

15 November 1980, Ipswich, UK

JUDITH BROWN

After an Ipswich Town FC home match, my friend Lynn invited me along with her to the Gaumont. I gladly accepted, and it was a brilliant concert. In the early days, they finished with the atmospheric 'Stanlow.' I've been along to see them every time they've returned.

↑
Judith Brown's ticket for the gig in Ipswich in November 1980

OMD - ORCHESTRAL MANOEUVRES IN THE DARK 1980

Mal, Andy and Martin smash the video games at a motorway service station after a gig

CITY HALL
17 November 1980, Sheffield, UK

GREG STURROCK

Aged 14, I was at my cousin's, who was playing a single with a grey braille sleeve called 'Electricity.' I was instantly hooked, for life. 'Red Frame/White Light' was bought along with a copy of 'Electricity' with a standard sleeve and the first album. I was then itching for the next release and news of tour dates.

The dates came out and I was gutted to find the closest was 40 miles away and on a school night. Begging and pleading began with Mum and Dad, eventually wearing them down with the promise that I'd be on the last train back to Leeds so Dad could pick me up. I got there early to check the walk back to the station, a cracking evening had until OMD played probably one too many songs. A mad dash was required, which Sebastian Coe would have struggled to make, with the inevitable result - the train pulling away from the platform without me. A phonecall home and hell to pay, Dad drove all the way, threw me in the back seat and didn't speak to me for a week … possibly a month.

On a more positive note, pre-concert I popped into the loo and who should walk in but Mally, so at school the next day I mentioned nothing of the missed train but let all my pals know I had a wee stood next to the OMD drummer.

ODEON
18 November 1980, Birmingham, UK

PAUL NETHERWAY

As good as they were, what stood out was what happened after. Generally, at the Odeon, if the bands were willing a few fans would be allowed backstage afterwards to meet them. After this show I was one of hundreds waiting, hoping to be lucky enough to be chosen. The group were clearly willing to meet as many fans as they could, and in a move I hadn't witnessed before, or indeed since, the doors were opened and everyone waiting was allowed back into the stalls. The band spent ages having photographs taken, signing programmes and tickets and just chatting to everyone. That they went to this extra trouble convinced me they were something very special. They still are.

ANDY MCCLUSKEY

If people have waited you do want to stop and talk to them. But there's a tipping point. If it gets to more than 15 or 20, you know you're going to be there for quite some time.

It's a moral dilemma. You don't want to walk past people and ignore them if they've waited. You're honoured that they care that much and you'd like to give them something back. But you just can't do it. Doing the theatres in the early Eighties, there would be so many people waiting for autographs out the back that, whilst the crew were breaking down the stage we would invite the audience in, and we'd have rows and rows of people in the seats and they'd all walk past us and we'd sign something. Sometimes the signing sessions after the show would go on longer than the show. We did that because we were so excited that people wanted to meet us and loved our music so much.

KING GEORGE'S HALL

19 November 1980, Blackburn, UK

JULIE DAVIES

OMD were so much part of my formative years from my first

↑ OMD on tour in 1980 waiting to soundcheck

concert at King George's Hall, and for the next five or six years at various places across the north of England before real life got in the way. I probably saw them 15 times in those years and met them most times - those were the days when you could just smile and work your way backstage.

MARK WARRINER

I started collecting OMD records, tapes and CDs from all around the world back in 1980 when I bought 'Enola Gay'. I have all the tour programmes and fan club letters and the tickets from having seen them over 30 times.

HAMMERSMITH ODEON
17 December 1980, London, UK

MARTIN RICE

I was up on a college trip to the Stock Exchange so dragged most of the class along. The superb 'I Betray My Friends' was played as the intro in pitch darkness before the curtains opened to dry ice and 'Stanlow.' Andy lost his shirt during the encore as the stage was mobbed.

ARCHITECTURE & MORALITY 1981

Architecture & Morality was released 8 November 1981 preceded by the singles 'Souvenir' in August and 'Joan of Arc' in October

RICHARD MANWARING
house engineer, The Manor Studios

'Joan of Arc had a lark, in the park …' We'd worked hard on 'Maid of Orleans' and Andy was jokingly giving the lyrics a different spin. The whispered vocal double-track had been added and apart from the mix, I felt the song was complete. I was smiling all the way through the playback and really didn't want to fade down the unstoppable end to three minutes 46 seconds. OMD and I were recording at The Manor, a residential studio north of Oxford owned by Richard Branson's Virgin Records and developed by Phil Newell, Mick Glossop and Barbara Jefferies. It was magical place to create.

My own first musical influences were from the Sixties – I loved the strong melodies with a voice that connected emotionally. So hearing the catch in Andy's voice really made a mark. I was sure if I was affected, everyone else would be! The very memorable melodies, with an emotive vocal against cold electronics is a great combination.

For me the Eighties was a time when we weren't thinking about particular chart success, it was about making the song sound as good and as different as possible. OMD were flexible enough to take on ideas I suggested, technically as well as musically. The *Architecture & Morality* album has a great mix of immediately accessible songs with others that develop with listening.

There were meetings with OMD regarding recording in early 1981 - the basis of the songs that came to make up *Architecture & Morality* had already started at the band's 16-track set-up in Liverpool. Engineering and co-producing with the band allowed me a more fluid role in the studio. I would sometimes find myself listening at the back of the control

OMD – ARCHITECTURE & MORALITY 1981

Paul and Andy on the cover of Smash Hits, March - April 1981

Andy's personal notes for songs on Architecture & Morality

room while they balanced the instruments on the console. The band knew what they wanted to hear. Although the sounds were generated electronically, the parts were all played manually – not programmed. Only the rhythms on the Roland CR-78 drum machine were programmed. I was open-mouthed at Paul and Andy's ability and accuracy in playing the 1/8 note bass parts.

Although Andy and Paul were the creative force, drummer Mal contributed greatly, none more so than on 'Maid of Orleans.' Recording at The Manor was from 19 July to 16 August 1981. The band were then busy promoting the Mike Howlett-produced single 'Souvenir', which meant mixing at Mayfair Studios in Primrose Hill didn't start until Sptember 8th through to the 18th. The running order on any album is crucial and in hindsight I think it was very brave to lead not with any of the three singles, but 'The New Stone Age'. However this jarring, seemingly bleak song, 'Oh my God, what have I done this time?' really set the marker for what the listener could expect from the album as a whole.

Architecture & Morality has a big warm sound that definitely comes from the analogue synthesisers coupled with The Manor's Helios desk and the Ampex MM1200 tape machine. I liked to record 'hot', enjoying the tape compression that added to the sound.

I don't recall any artistic or musical differences; my overriding memory is the smiles and laughter of recording together. At the time of working on a project you have no inkling of its impact. You just do your best. It is great to realise that the affection for the album and the band continues.

NEW STONE AGE
   Muddy — Too much plate.   Bass Synth
  Guitars up. Clip down intro   up + grand?
    Use chock as highlight run up to 2nd vocal.
GEORGIA — Bass end — watch Rumble
     B/D + Riff should cut through more
Sealand.
   Melodica?   Rise section — Blend
   B/D — tom?   Hammerium up into strings!
                    More tape echo + Harmoniz
  Bouncing echoes on B/D at end of
vox over the prophet — not both but
just the last beat to give single echoes
Trim chords after vocal te one set.
JOAN OF ARC   faster?

Glock — harmonizer. Backing vox's louder + harmonizer
Strings — louder on intro — <u>dynamic</u>
Take out pink noise as snare comes in
Bass Guitar? running Peasoup hat.

JOAN OF ARC

B change — lift any + Mello a touch to emphasise change
NOISE PIECE radio interference around the beginning
drop. Organ rattles after 1st drop | grey chant not too loud in intro
Second ½   something in the middle of
the end | Bring up backwards Harmonica
in Middle
SHE'S LEAVING
  Vocal up — snare a bit drier
  Melody down at End. Back plate off a few things
Try organ in just before vox enters

HAMBI HARALAMBOUS
musician & film director

My own band was also signed to Virgin but the first time we actually spoke was at one of Richard Branson's parties at the manor. OMD are recording in the studio but had to stop for the party. He was sat on the floor against the wall with Andy and Paul as Lesley (my girlfriend) and I walked past. Richard then grabbed Lesley to the floor for a bit of a drunken hug. Andy immediately suggested that I chin him. Being a peace loving guy I gave that a miss but appreciated Andy's direct way of dealing with things.

DAVE HUGHES

I was working on a track with a similar sort of choral feel to 'Souvenir' with those soft fade-in washes, and they liked it. I made them a copy of the tapes and let them have a play.

About 1983, Martin and I were working on a soundtrack. It was the first soundtrack I ever did, for a film called *Hearts in Armour*, an Italian Warner Brothers film (*I Paladini* in Italy). We saw the boss of Warner's Publishing and he said, 'I'm not sure about giving you the chance because this film needs a really strong melody. Something as great as Vangelis did for *Chariots of Fire*. Or,' he said, 'something like this.' And he put 'Souvenir' on. Martin went, 'I wrote that.' The guy was completely gobsmacked. He called an assistant in. He didn't believe it. The assistant went out and you could see him through the glass, nodding his head, saying, 'Yeah, he did write it.' That clinched the deal for us to work on the film, So it came back to me in a karmic sort of way, helping them out with 'Souvenir

MIKE JOHNSON

My connection to OMD started at high school, aged 13. Our forms or house groups would have their own theme for assembly, each head of house determining the nature. Fortunately for me, our housemaster liked to play music during the introduction and arrival and this would continue for a few minutes to allow us time to settle down. I remember being fascinated by the strange haunting sounds and melodies of a particular set of pieces. As I left assembly one day I asked my best friend what it was we were listening to. 'Oh, that's Orchestral Manoeuvres in the Dark,' he said. 'All those tracks are from their current album, *Architecture & Morality*.' I ran home that day and pestered my mum to buy me the album as a very early birthday present.

KARL HUDDLESTON

In 1981, I was 17 when I started attending new wave dance club, Phases, in the San Fernando Valley, Southern California, having emigrated from Northern Ireland seven years earlier.

One night, standing on the edge of the dancefloor waiting for a good song, the DJ came over the mic. and said, 'This is my favourite song right now, so I want everyone to dance.' She let the turntable loose and 'Electricity' came out of the speakers loud and proud. I hopped on the floor and lost my mind. I couldn't believe what I was hearing. Next day I went and bought the album.

WHISKY A GO GO

14 & 15 April 1981, Los Angeles, California

MARTIN COOPER
OMD keyboards/ saxophone

My first visit to Los Angeles was also the band's first concert there, in a small 250-capacity theatre. I remember waking ridiculously early, due to the time difference, sneaking out of the room, leaving Mal in the other bed. I wandered around the quiet, empty streets of LA for hours. What a culture shock it was for a young lad from Wirral. We were staying at the

↑
Martin Cooper on stage during the Architecture & Morality tour

small Tropicana Motel on Santa Monica Boulevard. The motel surrounded a pool with palm trees and it all seemed so exotic and sophisticated. It was also the first time I heard the phrase, 'Have a nice day!'

I went for breakfast in a cafe adjoining the motel, a bustling, vibrant place called Dukes, which served huge portions of eggs, hash browns, French toast etc. I'd never seen anything like it before and didn't realise there were so many different ways to fry an egg.

Later, it was off to the pool for a lazy couple of hours in the sun before the soundcheck. Having never experienced such heat before I was completely unprepared for it, ending up bright red, burnt from top to toe. Mal was hugely amused. I went onstage that night with full-blown sunstroke! I felt a complete fool, in quite a lot of discomfort. I imagined everybody was looking at me on stage, glowing in the dark.

COMMODORE BALLROOM
20 April 1981, Vancouver, Canada

ANDY MCCLUSKEY

The excitement of my first ever day in Canada was dampened by having to sit in the motel room and do 23 consecutive telephone interviews to promote the gigs for the days ahead. I managed to escape for five minutes, running 100 yards to the water's edge of the Straights of Georgia, wrestling off my shoes and socks and dipping my toes in the Pacific. I had this thing about collecting Oceans and Seas by paddling in them. Well, if you're going to travel the world you may as well collect something!

BREAKING AMERICA

America was very frustrating for us. In 1980 we did our first few gigs there, playing Hurrah in New York and Boston and Philadelphia. The first time in New York was just incredible. I felt like I was in a scene from *Kojak*.

We were playing bigger and bigger places around Europe, but every time we went back to America we'd be playing tiny clubs and couldn't get on commercial radio. It was only college radio playing us. You really need the infrastructure to break America and college radio can only get you so far.

Branson did a stupid deal. There was us, XTC and a few other bands and he did a package deal with CBS. He basically threw us away on this longer deal. It was a constant source of frustration. After a couple of years we realised A&M Records wanted to sign us but it took us ages to prise ourselves out of that deal. It wasn't until *Junk Culture* that we actually got on to A&M, and 'Locomotion' was a minor hit, that things took off.

PAUL HUMPHREYS

← Paul and Andy's photo booth passport snaps for the 1981 US tour

↑ Andy and Paul sample lunch in New York 1981

← Andy, Paul and Martin outside the White House in Washington DC

ARCHITECTURE & MORALITY 1981

OMD - ARCHITECTURE & MORALITY 1981

STUART KERSHAW
OMD drummer

Back in 1982 I played drums in a band named The Call. Our regular set-list included a mixture of our own material and covers, including 'Souvenir'. Little did I know some years later I would be playing that live with OMD.

← Andy, Paul and Peter Saville during the 'Souvenir' video shoot at Blenheim Palace

↑ Paul standing and Andy sat in Peter Saville's Karman Ghia

← Andy driving with camera kit on the front of the Karman Ghia

SOUVENIR
WAS RELEASED

4 Aug 1981

↑ *Smash Hits* (in iitalics) show the new OMD lineup with Mike Douglas bottom left

NEIL TENNANT
Pet Shop Boys

When Chris Lowe and I first met in 1981 there were two electro-pop singles we both loved: 'Bedsitter' by Soft Cell and 'Souvenir' by OMD. 'Souvenir' is such a beautiful and wistful song with that sparse early Eighties electronic sound. I still play it sometimes.

OLD WALDORF
27 September 1981, San Francisco, California

ROBIN MACQUARRIE

I've been a fan since 'Enola Gay' hit college station KUSF. I paid $7 for my ticket and when I showed the band my stub at a meet-and-greet years later they signed it and couldn't believe the price: 'Can't even get a pint for that these days!

JOAN OF ARC
WAS RELEASED

9 Oct 1981

ANDY MCCLUSKEY

The release of 'Joan of Arc' was yet another example of my excruciating demo-itis. Standing on stage on *Top of the Pops*, with 'Joan of Arc' at No.5 in the charts, it comes in and the bass drum goes 'boom-cha-cha-boom', I was going, 'God, that bass drum sounds like a cardboard box. I wish we could remix it. But it's too late now. It's in the charts and I'm still hating the mix!' I was such hard work. Only Paul H could have put up with me for all those years. I was so precious, c.
I wasn't arrogant but was difficult because I was bleeding for this stuff and it was never what I imagined it to be. I was living on my nerves. I wish I could go back now, say to my younger self, 'Andy, chill. It's such a great time. You're going to do *Top of the Pops*. You're going to travel the world. Enjoy it.' I didn't really enjoy it at all. I was just so tense all the time. I was a bag of nerves.

→

Andy's hand written lyrics and his critical comments on other songs on *Architecture & Morality*

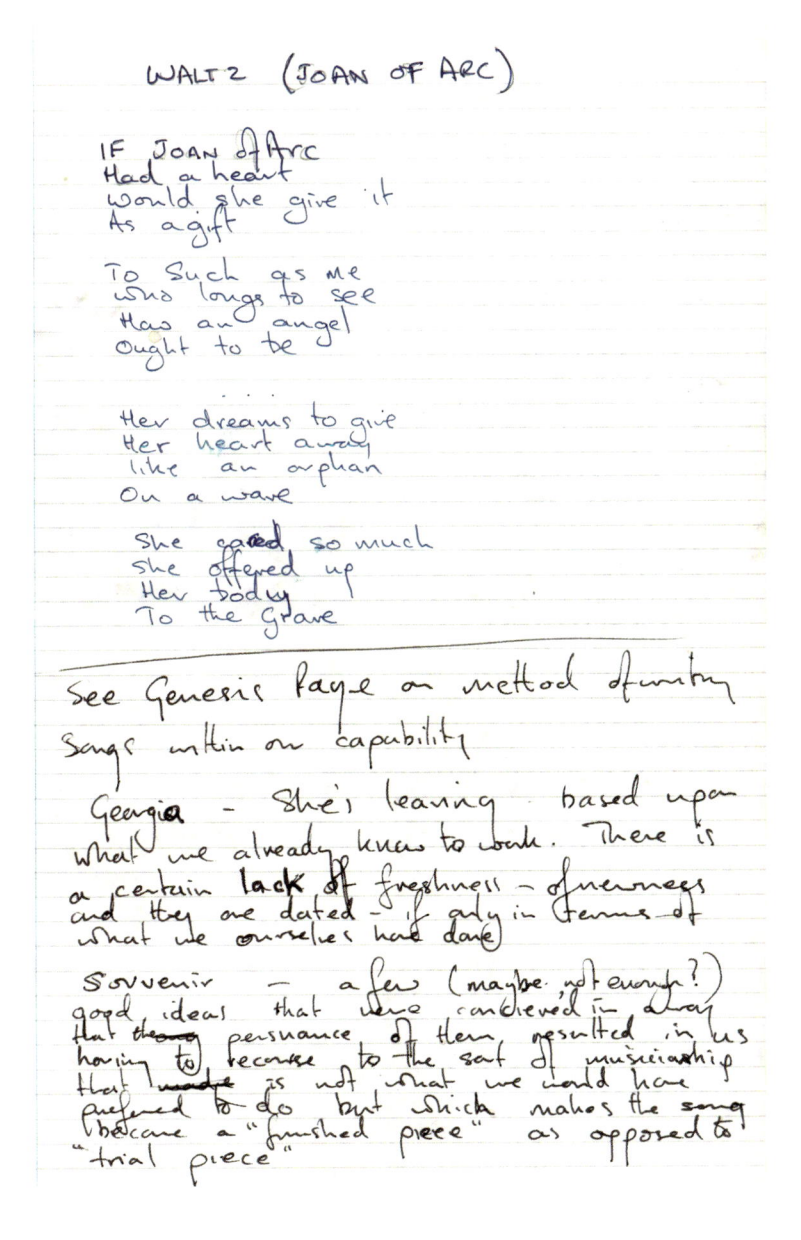

ARCHITECTURE & MORALITY WAS RELEASED

8 Nov 1981

RICHARD PEAT

The first of their records I bought was 'Enola Gay'. I absolutely loved the depth of sound and catchy hooks. Next up I bought 'Souvenir', which was gloriously choral and atmospheric. Then I bought *Architecture & Morality*. When I got home, I told my Dad to come and listen to my new album. I knew he was into classical music so might appreciate it.

The first track 'The New Stone Age' came on with all its dissonant noise and guitars. I was not only highly embarrassed, but Dad probably thought I'd become a punk. He left the room without saying a word. If OMD wanted to take their listeners by surprise with the first song, they definitely achieved it. I never invited him to listen to one of my records again.

PLAYHOUSE
12 November 1981, Edinburgh, UK

GEORGE SCOTT

I was working for a fruit and veg company, a normal 18-year old, and it was pub time on a Friday. There we are at the Cottage Inn on Aberdour Road in Dunfermline and Matty, one of my workmates kept going on about how I was dressed like, 'they two guys fae Orchestral Manoeuvres.' I'm like, 'Who is this? Something yev just made up?'

A week or two later I noticed Lene Lovich was going to be on *Rock Goes to College*. I settled down to watch the programme and who pops up - Orchestral Manoeuvres. I'm like, 'So they are a real band.' I especially enjoyed 'Electricity', so thought I must look for some of their records. I found the debut self-titled album then discovered they had a second, *Organisation*. I liked the thought of being the only guy in Cowdenbeath listening to OMD. Then I saw them at the Playhouse, which really sealed the reason why I became an Orchaholic. To this day my family, friends and workmates think I'm a bit mad, obsessed about OMD.

ANDY MCCLUSKEY

We moved away from the Gothic-y dark sound and got more lush, with choirs and orchestral sounds, we had a mellotron and a set of various tapes that it used. We had a whole new palette of sounds. We'd gone into the studio to do 'Souvenir' with Mike Howlett which was released as a single before the album in the summer of '81. We had no idea we were going to have three top-five singles of that album. It sold over three million and 'Maid of Orleans' would be huge around the north of Europe. But there was a small amount of conflict - Paul didn't really like 'Enola Gay', and I didn't like 'Souvenir', which I thought was drippy. I constantly tried to change the rhythm, saying, 'It's too lush. It's too syrupy.' And I couldn't work out a bass line on it. I was eventually persuaded by Mike Howlett to play the kind of bass-line I absolutely loathed, accompaniment bass, which was just anathema to me. It got to No.3 in the UK, so what did I know? Now I recognise it as an absolutely beautiful piece of romantic, melancholic music. I was determined to write a song about the Maid of Orleans, Joan of Arc. I wrote 'Maid' first and didn't like it. So I wrote 'Joan of Arc' on the anniversary of her death. Malcolm and Paul came into the studio when we were wrapping up to get ready to go down to The Manor, and said, 'What about the other one? The 'boom-cha-cha' one?' I said, 'That doesn't work. That's why I wrote this one.' 'Put it on. Let's have a little play at it.' Malcolm started playing and I thought, 'Well, maybe we'll record it when we're down there, and let's see what happens.' The basic bulk of that song is so short. It's about two minutes, so we came up with this long intro. We just got a load of noises and played chords: 'Turn up the desk. Turn up the Helios until it distorts like a guitar.'

←
George Scott's photo of Andy and Paul outside the Edinburgh Playhouse and his ticket for 12 November 81

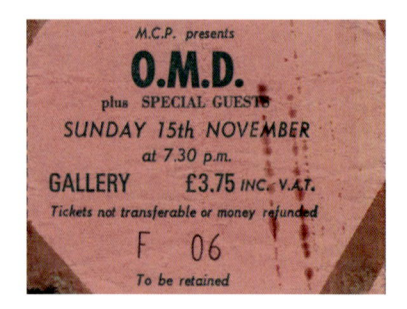

Because we didn't have a guitar. We didn't have a fuzz-box. 'Just distort the desk so it goes 'aaaaahhhhh'.' We just made a load of noise. No hit single should start with that horrible intro, but it does. This is what we loved about being in OMD. We were breaking the rules. We loved the fact that we would have a hit record that started with 30 seconds of distorted choirs. We were definitely changing the world with our music, which was our raison d'être. Or so we thought.

DE MONTFORT HALL

15 November 1981, Leicester, UK

JAN GOULD

I first noticed them on *Top of the Pops* with 'Enola Gay.' I finished my 'O' levels that summer but unemployment was high and I couldn't get a job. I reluctantly started 'A' levels. I was officially studying Maths, Economics and Sociology but it wasn't long before OMD became my fourth subject (fan club card 3255). My best friend Mirelle and I studied together. Boring maths lectures on a Wednesday morning were vastly improved by inserting a fresh copy of *Smash Hits* into my A4 folder. Collecting pictures, posters and lyrics became a weekly ritual. Every folder and textbook was covered with them.

To say I wasn't a natural academic is an understatement. Part of my survival plan was to find ways of integrating my favourite subject, OMD into my school week. Mirelle and I were shipped to school from nearby villages, but luckily my auntie and uncle lived close to our school and considerately gave us the key to their house, use of their hi-fi and storage of our vinyl. The new charts were announced on a Tuesday lunchtime, when I luckily had a free period followed by lunch. I'd escape to my auntie's whilst Mirelle would rush round as the charts were being announced after her chemistry lesson.

Later that year we decided to see both OMD and Depeche Mode live. Depeche was supposed to be my first, but Mum and Dad wouldn't let me go, thinking the students might cause trouble. We had a few heated discussions about that. OMD at Leicester's De Montfort Hall was my first 'proper' concert.

I'll always remember the excitement and energy of that gig. Towards the end we moved to the back of the venue and witnessed the audience going wild as the final 'chug chugs' of 'Stanlow' signalled the end of a great night.

By the time we left school in 1983 Mirelle had her Mini, so our reward for surviving 'A' levels was an OMD road-trip taking in Bristol, Plymouth and Liverpool among others.

↑ Ticket for Leicester's De Montfort Hall

I've seen many great acts such as Bruce Springsteen and Eric Clapton at the Royal Albert Hall, but for me no one has achieved the same level of audience involvement and excitement as OMD. Coincidentally, my most recent OMD gig was also with Mirelle at Leicester De Montfort Hall, 5 November, 2017. 36 years later, we're still best friends and I'm again watching the crowd go wild as another great evening comes to an end.

HAMMERSMITH ODEON
19 & 20 November 1981, London, UK

PAUL CASWELL

My girlfriend and I arrived early and were lucky enough to spend time with the band, them feeding us sandwiches and signing autographs. During the conversation Andy asked what our favourite song was. Lo and behold, in the middle of the gig he announces, 'This song is for two of our friends, Paul and Sandra. This is 'Statues'.' It shows the care for the fans that he remembered our names. I still have the autographs, ticket stub, programme - and the memories.

PETE JENKINS

I was 14 when I bunked off school to go to Hammersmith and get my ticket for the Odeon. I remember queuing afterwards at the stage door, having my programme signed by Andy, Paul, Martin and Mal. Embarrassingly, I also remember telling Paul I'd learnt every OMD song on my Casio keyboard and if he was ever ill to give me a call and I'd gladly step in. I'm still waiting.

PAUL BATTEN

I was 14 when I saw OMD at Hammersmith Odeon. I remember Andy saying, 'Anyone want to dance? Get up on stage.' Most of the stalls invaded the stage.

↑
Andy and Paul signed photo from 1981

ARCHITECTURE & MORALITY 1981 | 141

PETER LOPEMAN

I was a 19-year-old at teacher-training school in Birmingham still stuck in the progressive rock and jazz of the Seventies. My very good friend Babs was a lot cooler. Babs bought tickets for her and her boyfriend but he couldn't make it, so she asked me instead. I was very reluctant, trying to convince her this wasn't my kind of music. But she persisted.

It was the Organisation tour and 'Enola Gay' was in the charts. When the band played those tracks from *Organisation* and the previous album, the superb songs, original sound and the performance blew me away. I was hooked from that day on. As an art student I was into the Russian post-modern and German pre-war Bauhaus movement, and the music and 'feel' of OMD was in that cultural zone.

JOHN KALLEND

Often you discover a band through a friend or older sibling. OMD was my discovery. I first heard what turned out to be 'Electricity' on the radio in late 1980, aged 15, and had never heard anything like it other than my older sister's Tubeway Army cassette, *Replicas*. I rushed out and bought the *Orchestral Manoeuvres in the Dark* album. I was hooked and

Organisation was swiftly bought at the start of 1981, and *Architecture & Morality* later that year. I saw the band twice that year on the A&M tour, including the recorded concert at the Theatre Royal, Drury Lane. I queued on the door for return tickets and got in 10 minutes before the start, four rows from the front.

Still a vinyl enthusiast, all my OMD albums and singles remain with me, despite resting untouched in my loft for a few years when I had no means of playing them, now fully used and joined by vinyl releases of the modern era.

CITY HALL
22 November 1981,
Newcastle, UK

CAPTAIN MICHAEL BARRASS, MNI

As an apprentice officer on a merchant ship in early 1980, I socialised with a young Scouser who made cassettes of Kraftwerk and OMD. I'd heard of Kraftwerk but not OMD. He also recorded a gig in Liverpool on his cassette player (how, I'll never know) and though it was pretty distorted, people talking in the background, the iconic 'Electricity' was a great track. I always remember him telling me, 'OMD will be massive'. I never believed him. How wrong I was. I made a point of getting to see them at Newcastle, while on leave. I only have vague recollections but the next year at City Hall was unbelievable, finding myself drifting from heavy metal to electronic music.

GILL BOWLES

It was 1980 when I first heard 'Enola Gay', buying my first LPs, going to City Hall and enjoying the captivating McCluskey marionette dance, later queuing in anticipation to see Andy and Paul backstage in May 1984. Now for fans it's an even better experience, with gold passes to the soundcheck in Glasgow in November 2017. We were treated to more of the humour of OMD, the great music and mobility aiding heat patches.

EMPIRE THEATRE
24 November 1981, Liverpool, UK

SIMON MAW

'Electricity' was used on Granada TV's news programme as continuity music. No doubt the Tony Wilson/Factory records connection was influential. I'd heard 'Messages' and was hooked. What made the music even more special was that it was local. I bought the albums as and when I could. Then in November 1981 I convinced my mate, Led Zeppelin fan Jay, to come to see OMD at the Empire. He wasn't too keen.

We expected quite a dour affair, given the image. We couldn't have been more mistaken. It was literally electric and lives long in my memory. I've seen OMD many times since. My 21-year old daughter grew up with them, and my wife can't listen to the opening bars of 'If You Leave' without getting emotional.

↑
Rare shot of Andy on keyboards at the Empire, Liverpool, 1981. Photo by Francesco Mellina

OMD - ARCHITECTURE & MORALITY 1981

Paul live at Drury Lane 1981

→ Andy on stage at Drury Lane 1981

MAY HAUGEN

I'd heard them before coming over to live in Formby for a year as an au pair, but hearing 'Souvenir' touched my heart-strings, and seeing Paul sing it on *Top of the Pops* I was lost. He was beautiful, the song was beautiful, and I'd finally found a band I'd love as much as The Beatles.

I got the back-catalogue and loved everything. They were so different to any other band I'd heard or seen. Earning 14 quid a week and working more or less 24/7 meant getting into Liverpool for a gig wasn't an easy task.

I was close to the front and took pictures with a rubbish camera, keeping the ticket stub and a review in my photo album. I kept buying the records, but unfortunately never got to see them live again until Oslo in 2018. That gig blew my mind. They sounded good and looked good, and their humour and banter was a joy to behold. Best part of the night? Paul smiled at me. I think I blushed, and I'm 56. I'd have loved to stay behind, shake his hand and tell him my story. Next time, perhaps.

THEATRE ROYAL DRURY LANE
5 December 1981, London, UK

SUE & ALEX MACDONALD

As first dates go, it was quite something, on our feet from the moment they hit the stage, recalling the electricity of the atmosphere and the way the audience refused to let them go until they'd played the encore twice. But memorable as it was, we didn't realise the significance of what we'd seen. Several decades later we're still enjoying innovative new music as well as all our old favourites from OMD, and with our son, Ed, working for the band's record label, we've got to meet the people whose music has been such a soundtrack to our lives. Congratulations on 40 years of brilliant music and thanks for the many happy hours we've spent singing and dancing along.

WHITLA HALL

20 December 1981, Belfast, UK

ANDY MCCLUSKEY

My abiding memory of this concert was spending the preceding weeks worrying about how the Protestant half of the audience would take to me singing a song about 'a little Catholic girl'. 'The Troubles' were still a violent issue in Northern Ireland. Staying in the Europa Hotel, with the dubious distinction of being the 'most bombed hotel in the world', didn't help my nerves. But my fears were groundless.

MARTIN EDWARDS

It was a Sunday afternoon in 1981 and I was on the bus with my mate. The bus turned onto Whitechapel and Asbi gawped out of the window, 'I saw Paul and Andy.' I stuck my head out of a window and shouted, 'Hey!' I got off the bus and ran, my heart pounding. They were heading into the Gramophone Suite. Paul had a pack of jelly tots. We were invited up and given an autograph on Gramophone-headed paper. I've still got it. After that, every time I went to town I'd take a record with me for you to sign.

1982

Despite reveling in the thought of releasing two different singles with the same name, Andy finally allowed the record label to change the title to avoid confusion with the already released 'Joan of Arc' single.

'Maid of Orleans' would become the biggest selling song of 1982 in Germany and also reached number one in Spain, Belgium, Holland and Austria. It achieved almost 4 million global sales making it the band's second most successful single after 'Enola Gay'.

MAID OF ORLEANS (THE WALTZ JOAN OF ARC)
WAS RELEASED

15 JAN 1982

LEIF WIIK

Living in northern Sweden, aged 15, I'd just discovered artists like Depeche Mode, Yazoo and Fad Gadget. One Sunday night I watched my favourite TV programme, *Sportspegeln*, showing the week's sports highlights, when I heard a great song in a reportage about weightlifting. I never got to know the artist, but what a melody. It wasn't easy to find new music, especially not in my small hometown, Hudiksvall. Sometime after, visiting a friend in Borlänge in Sweden's mid-west, he had a nice stereo system and, when I couldn't get to sleep on his uncomfortable couch, I started listening to his records. After a while, I heard the song I heard on that TV show, 'Maid of Orleans', ending up purchasing all the OMD LPs and singles I could find.

BILBAO
Spain, 1982

TXETXU TORRENTE

One 13-year-old boy, a mono cassette recorder, a radio station, a drum machine, a pumping synthesiser. I'll never forget that moment. Several months are spent waiting for new material, listening to the radio day after day. And then the magic words, 'Orchestral Manoeuvres in the Dark, new single - 'Maid of Orleans.'

Many years later, playing 'Maid of Orleans' on my CD player while my seven-year old son paints a picture, he stops and tells me, 'Dad, that's the prettiest music I've ever heard.' Is it necessary to say anything more?

↑
Another single, another full page in *Smash Hits*

OMD - 1982

THEATRE DE VERDURE
23 January 1982, Nice, France

ANDY MCCLUSKEY

The venue is a lovely outdoor amphitheatre, which we completely fail to fill. Even more memorable is the Sunday morning after when our manager phones to suggest I go out and find some English newspapers. My girlfriend Tracy Dodds had just become Miss Great Britain. Despite telling me she was too old at 22 to compete in beauty pageants, she enters and wins. I'm all over the newspaper headlines. 'Sexy Miss GB dates pop star Andy'. I've turned into Rod Stewart without even trying. The worst part was that she wins a car with her name and title emblazoned across the doors and insists we only go out in her vehicle. Admittedly, mine is a clapped-out Ford Cortina Mark III with a floor leaking so much water that mushrooms are growing in the passenger footwell. Everybody stops and points at us when we're in her car. For a boy who didn't want to be a pop star this is all getting too much!

PALASPORT
28 January 1982, Reggio Emilia, Italy

MARTIN COOPER

In January '82 we undertook a tour of France and Italy in our little Dodge bus, affectionately called the Dazzle Bus, a beautiful mini-bus with tinted windows. Traveling into Reggio Emilia, I was sat in the front seat, the hi-fi blaring, possibly listening to either Grace Jones' 'Nightclubbing' or Marianne Faithful's 'Broken English', both essential listening on that tour.

Steve Baker, our tour manager and driver, parked up in order to get directions. I looked up and in disbelief saw the bus surrounded by men in jeans and leather jackets wielding machine guns. They pulled us from the van, demanded we put our hands in the air and shouted at us in Italian. As I was in the front seat I was singled out for particular abuse and pushed into a nearby black car with a gun in my ribs and whisked away quickly.

We arrived, to my relief, at a police station and I was thrown into a cell to await my fate. What I didn't know then was that the others were following in the bus, desperately trying to explain to the police who we were.

Thankfully I wasn't held for too long. They realised soon enough we weren't a threat or members of the Red Brigade left-wing terrorist organisation active during the Eighties. I was released but not before a thousand scenarios played out in my mind. I must have looked very ill, as one of the policemen took me to a nearby bar and bought me a brandy, which I downed in one.

Apparently that same day, not too far away, Italian police had rescued US Brigadier General James Dozier without firing a single shot after storming a flat in Padua where he was being held by Red Brigade guerrillas. The 50-year-old general and deputy Chief of Staff at Nato's Southern European land forces headquarters at Verona emerged after 42 days in captivity unharmed, but thinner and with a beard. I'm convinced the two episodes were connected, the police on high alert for suspicious-looking individuals and us fitting the bill perfectly!

We couldn't speak Italian and they couldn't speak English. The tour manager and police inspector, a short bald guy not unlike Danny DeVito, talked to each other in very limited French. Fortunately, we had a magazine with us, Paul and I on the front cover, and we started humming 'Enola Gay' to the inspector in his office. In the space of an hour the situation went from potentially all being shot to some comedic rendition of our biggest hit, trying to sing our way out of jail! The police finally realised they'd made an error. They returned us to the venue with a police escort and said, 'Don't tell anybody this happened.'

The concert was shit, a section of the audience who looked like Mods booing and throwing things. Unsurprisingly, we haven't been back to Italy since.

ANDY MCCLUSKEY

Martin was sat in the passenger seat as they opened the door. He went to open the glove compartment to turn the blaring music off, so he could speak to them and they thought he might be reaching for a weapon. They grabbed him, dragged him out and held a gun to the side of his head.

MUSENSAL
2 February 1982, Mannheim, West Germany

GEORG KLUMPP

I was a fan after hearing 'Red Frame/White Light' on German radio, soon buying the first album and hooked by the brilliant melodies and warm synthesiser sounds. I was the only

OMD - 1982

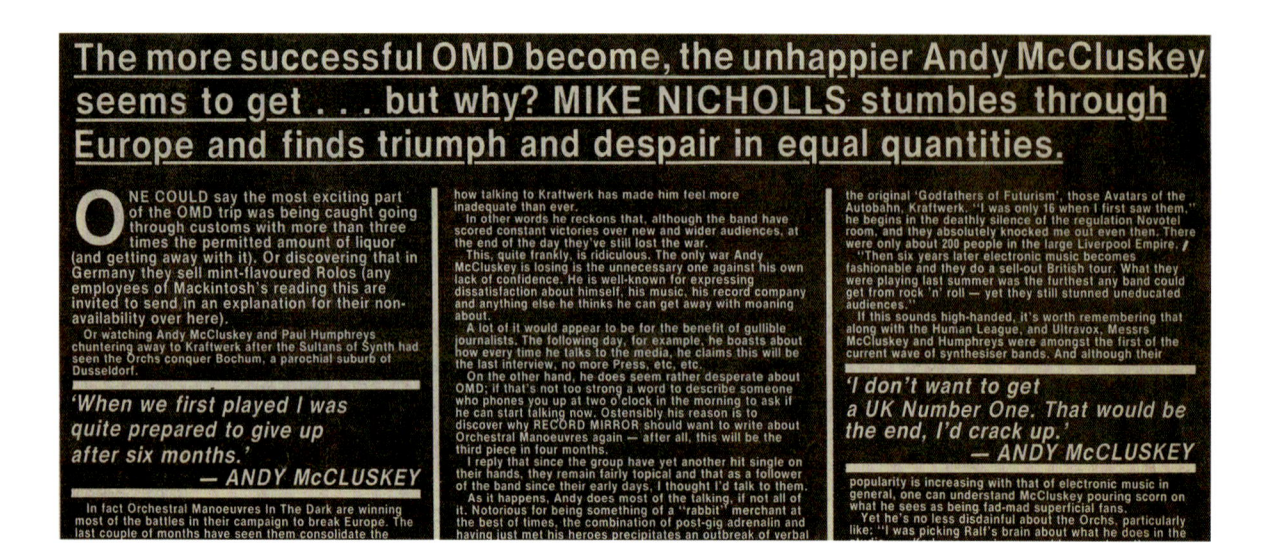

> The more successful OMD become, the unhappier Andy McCluskey seems to get... but why? MIKE NICHOLLS stumbles through Europe and finds triumph and despair in equal quantities.
>
> ONE COULD say the most exciting part of the OMD trip was being caught going through customs with more than three times the permitted amount of liquor (and getting away with it). Or discovering that in Germany they sell mint-flavoured Rolos (any employees of Mackintosh's reading this are invited to send in an explanation for their non-availability over here).
>
> Or watching Andy McCluskey and Paul Humphreys chuntering away to Kraftwerk after the Sultans of Synth had seen the Orchs conquer Bochum, a parochial suburb of Dusseldorf.
>
> **'When we first played I was quite prepared to give up after six months.'**
> — ANDY McCLUSKEY
>
> In fact Orchestral Manoeuvres In The Dark are winning most of the battles in their campaign to break Europe. The last couple of months have seen them consolidate the how talking to Kraftwerk has made him feel more inadequate than ever.
>
> In other words he reckons that, although the band have scored constant victories over new and wider audiences, at the end of the day they've still lost the war.
>
> This, quite frankly, is ridiculous. The only war Andy McCluskey is losing is the unnecessary one against his own lack of confidence. He is well-known for expressing dissatisfaction about himself, his music, his record company and anything else he thinks he can get away with moaning about.
>
> A lot of it would appear to be for the benefit of gullible journalists. The following day, for example, he boasts about how every time he talks to the media, he claims this will be the last interview, no more Press, etc, etc.
>
> On the other hand, he does seem rather desperate about OMD; if that's not too strong a word to describe someone who phones you up at two o'clock in the morning to ask if he can start talking now. Ostensibly his reason is to discover why RECORD MIRROR should want to write about Orchestral Manoeuvres again — after all, this will be the third piece in four months.
>
> I reply that since the group have yet another hit single on their hands, they remain fairly topical and that as a follower of the band since their early days, I thought I'd talk to them. As it happens, Andy does most of the talking, if not all of it. Notorious for being something of a "rabbit" merchant at the best of times, the combination of post-gig adrenalin and having just met his heroes precipitates an outbreak of verbal the original 'Godfathers of Futurism', those Avatars of the Autobahn, Kraftwerk. "I was only 16 when I first saw them," he begins in the deathly silence of the regulation Novotel room, and they absolutely knocked me out even then. There were only about 200 people in the large Liverpool Empire.
>
> "Then six years later electronic music becomes fashionable and they do a sell-out British tour. What they were playing last summer was the furthest any band could get from rock 'n' roll — yet they still stunned uneducated audiences."
>
> If this sounds high-handed, it's worth remembering that along with the Human League, and Ultravox, Messrs McCluskey and Humphreys were amongst the first of the current wave of synthesiser bands. And although their
>
> **'I don't want to get a UK Number One. That would be the end, I'd crack up.'**
> — ANDY McCLUSKEY
>
> popularity is increasing with that of electronic music in general, one can understand McCluskey pouring scorn on what he sees as being fad-mad superficial fans.
>
> Yet he's no less disdainful about the Orchs, particularly like: "I was picking Ralf's brain about what he does in the

↑ *Andy talks rather too honestly to music weekly* Record Mirror

OMD fan in town in early 1982 as 'Maid of Orleans', the song that made them famous all over Germany, was released.

I left my Mum's 44th birthday celebrations early to catch a train from my village to Mannheim, arriving at the venue a few hours early, waiting outside with two or three other fans. I recognised Andy coming out of nowhere, passing by. He stopped and someone asked him a question, but I was too shy to talk except for whispering a silent, 'Hi'. He chatted with us for five or 10 minutes and I remember other electronic bands being discussed. He said he really liked The Human League's *Dare* album. The gig was amazing, a very happy young man taking a train back home that night.

ZECHE CLUB
5 February 1982,
Bochum, West Germany

ANDY McCLUSKEY

Mal and Martin came into the dressing room before the gig to announce that Kraftwerk were in the audience. Paul and I were terrified. The Sorcerers had come to visit the apprentices. I spent the entire concert staring at these black-clad figures on the balcony, wondering what they were thinking. After the show we met them. Karl described me as dancing like a 'Whirling Dervish' and I could think of nothing more interesting to ask my hero Ralph Hutter than what type of speakers they used in their studio. Epic fail!

NEON LIGHTS

'I always loved 'Neon Lights' - the melody is just contagious,' Andy says. He takes another cup of tea and laughs. 'I never thought that one day I would record my own version of it.'

I was pretty surprised to find there really was a version of our song on *Sugar Tax*. Then, less than a year later, Andy and I find ourselves sitting opposite each other in the tiny kitchen of my Düsseldorf studio.

The first time we met was the early Eighties. My former colleagues and I drove to an OMD concert in Bochum (5 February 1982) but only managed to exchange a few words with them after the show. It was a time when our double A-side, 'Computer Love / The Model' was riding high in the charts, right alongside *Architecture & Morality*. It was as if I was hearing 'Souvenir', 'Maid of Orleans' or 'The Model' coming from every speaker I wandered past. That's how it felt, anyway.

KARL BARTOS
KRAFWERK

DAN GALANT

In 1982, my first year in college in California, I became fast friends with a guy called Phillipe, who was looking to improve his language skills. He introduced me to 'Electricity.' I lost touch with Philippe but think of him every time I hear an OMD song. I helped him with his English and he turned me on to an amazing new band.

ALEX CURTIS

My Dad bought a bunch of cassette tapes in a small market in Madrid and brought them to Don Benito in south-western Spain. We were 11 or 12 and just starting to listen to music other than The Beatles and Spanish top-40 songs. Among the tapes was one that caught our eye because of its iconic design and title, *Architecture & Morality*, with odd Spanish translations. We had no idea what it was. Dad had bought it because it was cheap and had the word 'orchestra' in it! We never got to see them live, but they stayed in our hearts.

BOBBY GALE
Canadian DJ & Polydor radio promo plugger

Working with OMD was in my first full year at Polydor. The crux was breaking OMD in the Canadian top-40. The system was much different, with Polydor unlike all the other majors. We rarely relied on America, because they were out to lunch, and we proved capable of taking UK phenomena and

MERLYN'S

16 March 1982,
Madison, Wisconsin

ANDY MCCLUSKEY

As a teenager, my son James was a huge Nirvana fan. I had to drive him on a pilgrimage to Kurt Cobain's house on a family holiday in the Seattle area so he could have his photo taken on the bench outside. He's long gone off my music, but Dad scores big points when James discovers our manager Mirelle knows Butch Vig, who produced the *Nevermind* album, because she worked with Garbage (who Butch plays drums for).

It is kindly arranged for James and I to meet Garbage on July 3, 2012 at a concert in Manchester, Dad proving to be reasonably useful. Shirley Manson was delightful, but Butch knocked it right out of the park for me when he said, "I saw your Dad's band play Merlyn's in Wisconsin in '82. What a great show. Such a cool band!" Instant 10 million 'cool Dad' points! Thank you Butch!

following suit as a way of creating a gateway to the US. I think we did that for OMD, quite remarkably.

CLUB FOOT

21 March 1982,
Austin, Texas

ANDY MCCLUSKEY

On this tour the band has a running joke at our determination not to be rock'n'roll. We ask for a bottle of champagne on the dressing room rider, which we never drink. The irony seems heightened this night as the club is a bit of a dump with corrugated iron walls. After the concert Sting's head appears around the dressing room door to congratulate us on the gig. In a good-natured way he begins taking the mickey out of us for ideas above our station with bubbly on the rider but is cut short by a security man who announces, 'Mr. Sting, your limo has arrived'. He retreats, our cries of 'Mr. Sting, give us a ride in your limo darling. Please Mr. Sting!' ringing in his ears.

DOOLEY'S
23 March 1982,
Tempe, Arizona

JON WILLIAMS

I was introduced to OMD by my friend from Switzerland staying with my family as an exchange student. I was a senior in high school and this was my first concert. I remember vividly the feel of the bass during the show. We went to the back door to get Andy's and Paul's autographs, which we did. While we were waiting, none other than members of U2 came out from backstage.

ANDY McCLUSKEY

U2 came to say 'hello' as they were playing in Phoenix around the same time. We had not seen them since the Talking Heads gig at the Electric Ballroom in December 1979. They were already starting to play bigger venues than us in the USA.

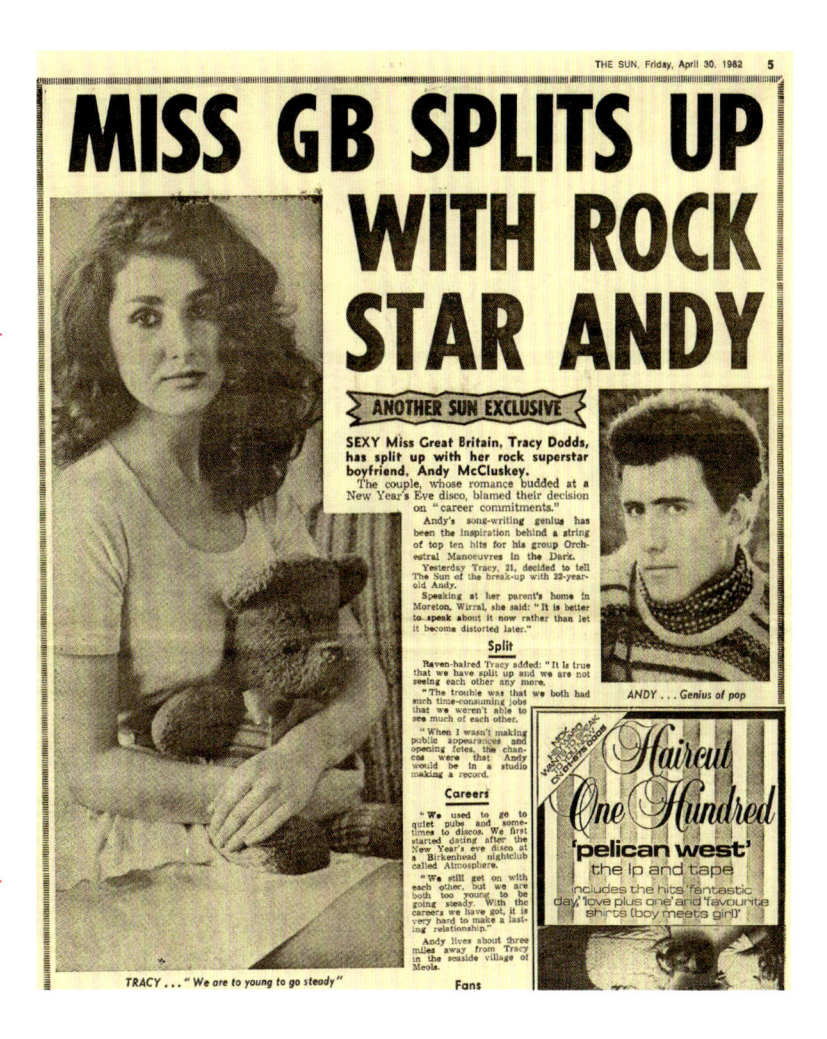

↑ Miss Great Britain Tracy Dodds announces the end of her romance with Andy

1983

With the release of *Dazzle Ships* OMD opted for a major departure shunning any commercial obligation to duplicate their previous LP. The album is noted for its experimental content, and the use of shortwave radio recordings to explore Cold War and Eastern Bloc themes.

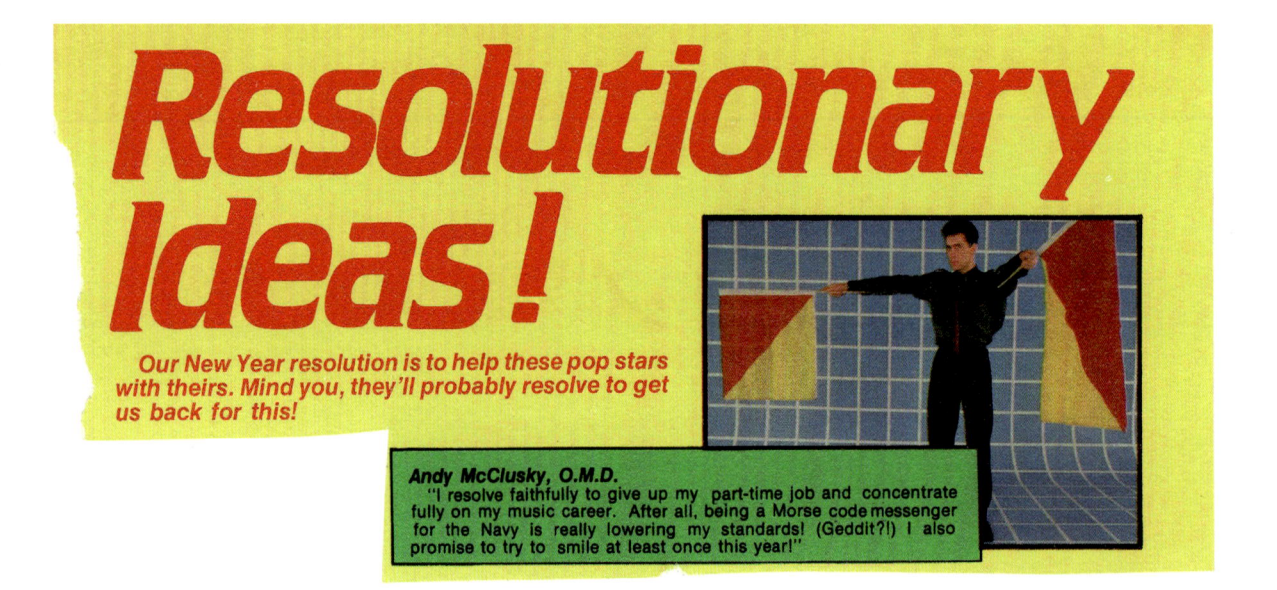

Resolutionary Ideas!

Our New Year resolution is to help these pop stars with theirs. Mind you, they'll probably resolve to get us back for this!

Andy McClusky, O.M.D.
"I resolve faithfully to give up my part-time job and concentrate fully on my music career. After all, being a Morse code messenger for the Navy is really lowering my standards! (Geddit?!) I also promise to try to smile at least once this year!"

GENETIC ENGINEERING WAS RELEASED

11 FEB 1983

DAZZLE SHIPS WAS RELEASED

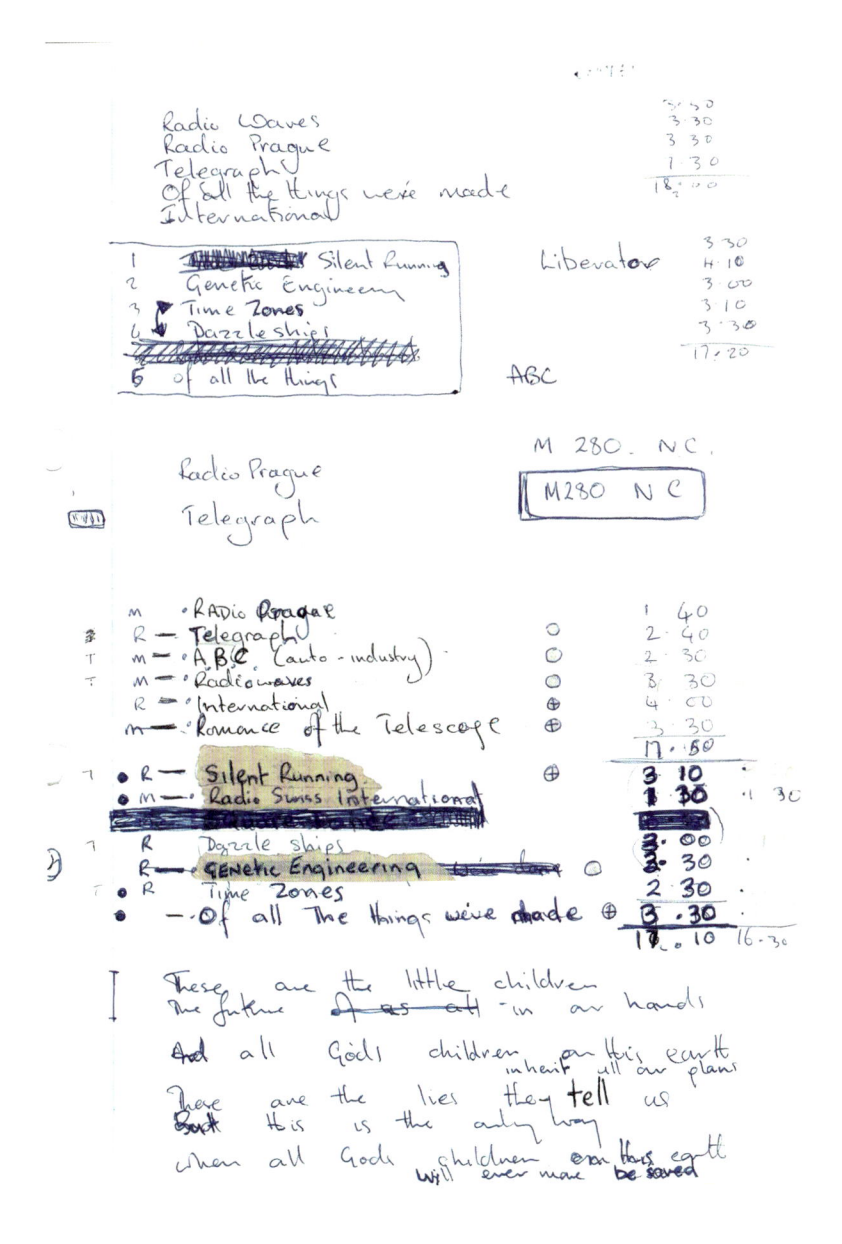

4 MAR 1983

← Andy's notes during the recording of *Dazzle Ships*

OMD display *Dazzle Ships* on another *Smash Hits* cover

PETER SAVILLE

The idea came from me seeing this Edward Wadsworth image in an art catalogue. It was the first time I'd seen this term 'dazzle ship'. It was a woodcut, which was contemporary with the advent of dazzle ships during the First World War. Wadsworth was inspired by seeing these camouflaged battleships in the docks in Liverpool. It's such a great term. 'Wow, dazzle ship! What does it mean?' I had to know more.

Andy is somebody with whom I shared that kind of discovery. He picked up on it and it became the theme for their next album.

I found the cover very difficult. I'm not the best person for doing camouflage. I'm too reductive. Every time I tried there was nothing left by the end of the day. I ended up having to give it to Malcolm Garrett, saying, 'Could you do this again, because there's no camouflage left – I've taken it all away!'

Around that time, I met a couple of young Australian architects who had just graduated and were touring Europe. They were in love with Renaissance Europe. They came to visit me one day, asking, 'Did you do *Architecture and Morality*?' I said, 'Yes, I did', and they said, 'Can we come in?' They were Ken Kennedy and Peter Davidson and were both very familiar with David Watkin's book.

Peter subsequently became a tutor at the Architectural Association, while Ken worked with David Chipperfield and for a while helped me out in the studio. He found the graphics we were doing interesting. As an architect, he was exceptionally good at technical drawing, so I was always very happy for Ken to come over and help out for a few days. He was there when we were doing *Dazzle Ships*. As the need for a stage-set came up, he was able to take the theme and see it three-dimensionally.

Ken took the *Dazzle Ships* aesthetic and combined it with aspects of Italian postmodernism and came up with this extraordinarily set. It was fabulous and I was really thrilled. When I saw it I knew it was something I couldn't have done myself. It was part of our work and it's always great when somebody brings another dimension to the work.

I remember an American newspaper reviewed one of the gigs and the opening paragraph was all about the set, saying, 'This evening was dynamic, electric, dazzling, blah blah – and that was just the set!' I was really thrilled by that.

Andy and I have been friends since 1979. We fell out briefly, when he punched me. I can't exactly remember why he did it. He didn't mean to, but he did. I mean, he did, and he didn't. He playfully punched me and was a bit embarrassed, and I was a bit pissed off. It was a bit of a Clarkson moment. He can be like that. But if you work together with anyone you will fall out from time to time. Other than that, and a few times when my procrastination or lateness probably brought about a lot of stress for him, Andy and I have been friends for 40 years. He's still a friend, and there's been times when he's been a very good friend. He's one of the few people I feel I could turn to if I had a problem. On at least one occasion I've said, 'Andy, can you help?' and he's gone, 'Yes, I suppose so.'

ANDY MCCLUSKEY

Peter came to our production rehearsal before the tour and I playfully tried to smack him on the nose. Unfortunately my boisterous stupidity resulted in a gushing nosebleed and Mr. Saville very unhappy with Mr. McCluskey for a while.

MARILYN WILSON

Certain songs have the power to evoke memories, help me dream away and escape from reality for a moment, lift my mood, help me mourn, or intensify my longing for someone or somewhere. The 'Romance of the Telescope' is a song which triggers feelings of nostalgia and makes me think about the beauty and brevity of life. When I listened to it again recently, it drove me to tears. That moment, I suddenly realised what the only right thing to do would be regarding a major decision I had put off making for over a year: I had to follow my heart. After the decision had been made, everything simply fell into place. I can't predict what the future will bring, but 'The Romance of the Telescope' seems to have steered me into the right direction.

MARC PLAINGUET

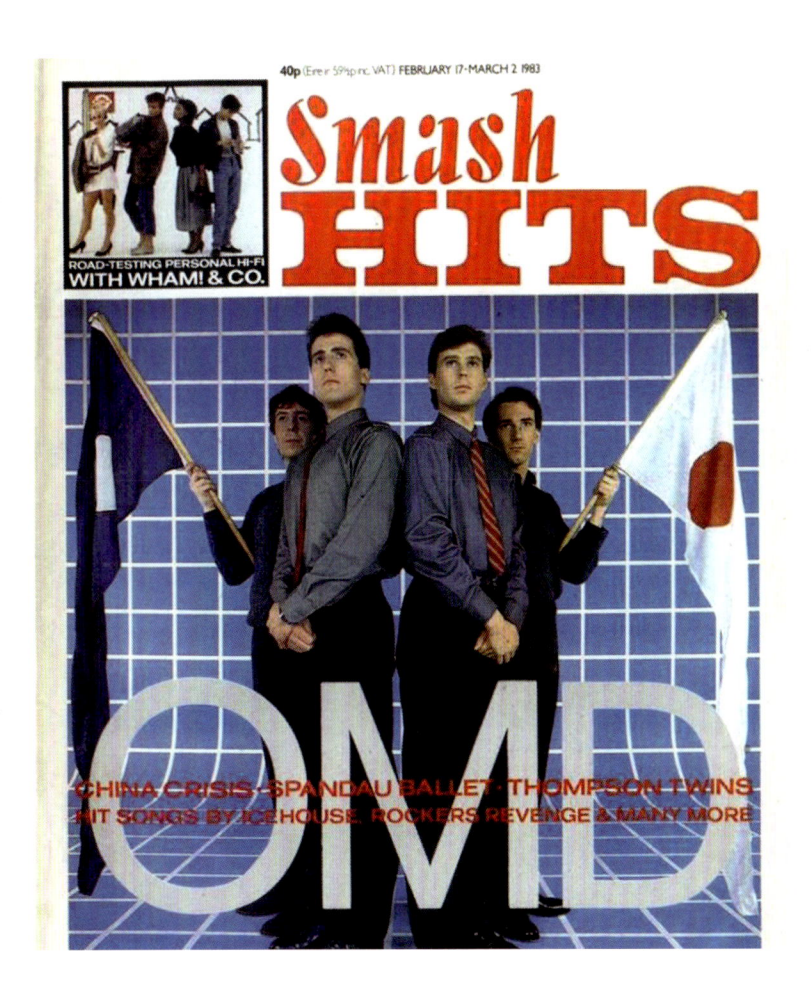

I read in an alternative music press magazine about an album called *Dazzle Ships* and the article deemed on its release it was 'unlistenable'. I instantly knew I must have that album! I scoured every record store in Los Angeles for a copy, found one and instantly fell in love with the experimentation, the lush sounds, the beauty of the balance of poetry, technology and music. I played it for everyone I could. Today, I feel vindicated, seeing people praising the album as the masterpiece it always was.

PAUL HUMPHREYS

Because it was our own art project, Andy and I always, always did whatever we wanted to do. We were lulled into this false sense of security, whereby everything we did, every record we released, just got more and more successful. We thought we had the Midas touch. A lot of the records were quite experimental, but they always had a tune that people latched onto.

Dazzle Ships was linked to a change in the technological landscape of what you could do musically in the electronic music field. New samplers had come out. We'd always done sampling in the past, but it was always very difficult because sampling had to be done in the analogue world.

You would take a sound and sample that. For instance, 'Stanlow' contains tons of samples, but they weren't digital. We took a tape recorder into the oil refinery and recorded the sounds on reels then got them back to the studio and pressed 'play' in the right place, dropping it into the multi-track.

When we got to *Dazzle Ships* there were now these machines called emulators, which meant you could take any sound and play it and not only could you reproduce it at the press of a button, but you could also tune that sample over an octave or two octaves. You could make a tune out of any noise you could imagine. It opened up all these new possibilities.

Architecture & Morality sold five million copies and some stupid person at the record label said, 'Okay, all you have to do is *Architecture & Morality* No.2 and you're the next Genesis.' Andy and I looked at each other and went, 'Well, let's not do *Architecture & Morality* No.2 then. We don't want to be the next Genesis! Let's do something radically different.'

We'd always taken unusual ideas but sweetened them. We sugar-coated them to make them palatable. With *Dazzle Ships* we took the same kind of angular ideas but left off the sugar-coating and thought that would be fine to leave it bare-boned, more experimental.

We should have released 'Telegraph' first but released 'Genetic Engineering' as the first single, on the back of three massive hits - 'Souvenir', 'Joan of Arc' and 'Maid of Orleans'.

Andy and I were together and I remember a call from the manager, saying, 'It's going to get its first play on Radio 1.' We turned on the radio and it sounded like hell. We had this huge bass drum that we insisted had to be the loudest thing in the track. But every time the bass drum hit on the radio, because of the compressors all you could hear was the bass drum. You couldn't really hear the tune. We looked at each other and went, 'Fuck, this isn't going to be a hit, is it?' It crawled up to No.20 then shot out of the charts. We knew we'd basically confused 90 per cent of our audience. It sold 300,000 copies in the end, with about 100,000 returns, whereas we'd sold five million previously.

For a long time I resented the fact that we made that album. It was the start of our struggles. We had all this infrastructure to pay for. We had offices and studios and mortgages and had just bought houses. We had band members and crew to pay, and we'd just done an album that had turkeyed. We went into panic mode, going completely in the other direction, abandoning all our experiments and doing *Junk Culture*, which got us back on track. 'Tesla Girls', 'Locomotion' and 'Talking Loud and Clear' were all massive hits.

We realised we could still write tunes people liked, so we thought, 'Let's concentrate on the tunes and forget the experiments.' We listened to people over *Architecture & Morality* who said, 'You've got this massive audience. Why are you not more political?' And we felt, we are very political in ourselves - we just don't expose it in our music. So we got more political with *Dazzle Ships* as well, and that didn't go down well, us talking about the Cold War.

We had to grow up and think about paying bills, and that affected our music from then on. We were consciously aware of having to be more commercial. We'd switched to the main Virgin label. Virgin inherited us from Dindisc and didn't give us any guidance. They thought, 'They were doing whatever they wanted to on Dindisc and it was all successful, so let them make *Dazzle Ships* even though we don't quite get it. They must know what they're doing.'

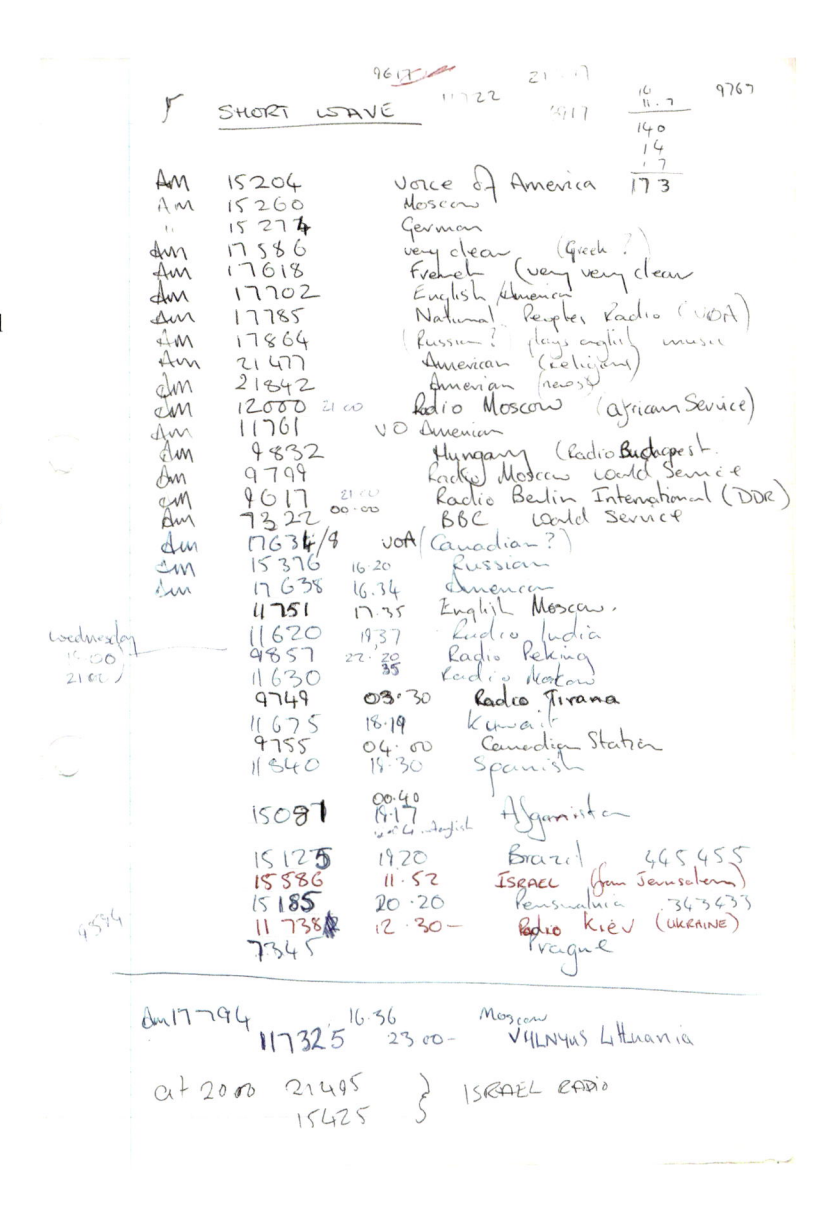

↑
Andy's list of short wave radio stations

I was a little more reluctant to give up Dindisc than Andy. Also, our manager had fallen out with Carol about a few things. We were instrumental in the demise of Dindisc as we were the main act. If they lost us, Dindisc would fail. In hindsight, perhaps it was a bad move, because it wasn't just about the business. Carol was very passionate about the music and she loved OMD.

Jeremy LaSalle, head of A&R at Virgin, was a sweet man and we really liked him, but everything he suggested we would automatically do the opposite of. So we didn't have any guidance and we lost our way.

DEAN COOGAN

I was 15 in 1983 when one of my friends borrowed *Dazzle Ships* from the local library and brought it to my house. I had hi-fi separates, including a decent record deck. I thought the cover was so cool and with anticipation, I put side one on. I was blown away, my life changed forever, starting me on a journey of discovery of OMD. I went on a mission, saving my pocket money so I could scour the record shops, buying all the different coloured versions of die-cut sleeves designed by Peter Saville on the first album, moving on through the catalogue. More than 30 years later, I'm still on that journey and still get the same feeling as I did way back.

ANDY MCCLUSKEY

Architecture & Morality was a big seller, but we never saw a huge amount of money out of it. Virgin Records had a very funny joke, except it was painful at the time. They said *Dazzle Ships* shipped gold and returned platinum.

Dindisc Records folded so we ended up on the parent company. Richard Branson fell out with Carol. We were the only band making any money for Dindisc. Martha and The Muffins didn't make any, The Monochrome Set didn't make any. She got desperate and signed Hot Gossip to a recording deal.

Carol was a control freak. She controlled everything, and in the end Branson said to her, 'It's not working. Your A&R department's not working. We need control.' She said, 'No', and he said, 'Right, you're shut down then. That's it. We'll keep OMD. They'll come to Virgin now.'

For *Dazzle Ships*, we ended up on Virgin but had no relationship with them. They said, 'How does this work?' and we said, 'You let us go to our studio and we write an album. When we're ready, we say, 'We want to work in that studio with that person' and you give us the money, we give you the record and it sells millions. And they said, 'Okay.' Then we delivered *Dazzle Ships* and they thought, 'Well, they must know what they're doing. They sell millions of records.'

Architecture & Morality was beautifully conceived. It was

ORCHESTRAL MANOEUVRES In THE DARK
'Dazzle Ships'
(Virgin Records V2261)***

Have Orchestral Manoeuvres In The Dark nothing better to do with their time?

'Dazzle Ships' is such a contrived package, with no loose ends and nothing that jars the senses, that it is horribly acceptable as that and nothing else. There is a feeling that 'Dazzle' is more of a project than anything else: from the posse of designers who worked on the sleeve to the self-congratulatory listing of all the instruments used — "Sanyo short wave radio, typewriter, 'Speak And Spell' machine used with kind permission of Texas Instruments Ltd". Very clever.

'Safety First' should have been emblazoned all across the LP sleeve, because there is so much caution involved in the simple pop experimentation here — as simple as tiddlywinks, and as exciting. Throughout the record OMD have tossed in, willy-nilly, extra effects and snippets of recording that suggest playtime for the listless instead of adventure for the innovative.

There is a continual stop-start effect as songs rub each other up the wrong way, 'Radio Prague' — a recording of the station call-sign — gives illusions of some constructivist grandeur, but is followed by the mish-mash of old Sparks tunes that comprises 'Genetic Engineering'.

If there was some suggestion that OMD had constructed their LP this way with a deal of wit, it would have solved a few niggling little problems: the patchy contrasting, the relative lack of any new ideas... it is 'less' all the time, sexless, joyless and ultimately it could even be humourless.

In comparison to the new synth burblings of a Depeche Mode, for example, OMD have definitely produced a record of more worth, but it is still shifting itself about at halfway house, not quite sure which way it should be headed.

Having stepped away from the more grandiose sweeps of sound on 'Architecture And Morality' to the sweeter and simpler songs of 'Dazzle', OMD are still not that sure of themselves as purely pop artistes. The clever-clever trickery is like a salve to their conscience — to give the impression that here is something of lasting quality.

'Dazzle' isn't just plain bad, it is just not that outstanding or special. 'Time Zones', which comprises solely of speaking clocks from around the world, is an amusing idea and that is all, suggesting that OMD have had a surfeit of inspiration but have not been too canny about the way they have utilised it.

'Time Zones', and 'Radio Prague' would have been better suited to being a part of another song rather than existing as entities. In fact the weak construction of the more "straight ahead" synth-pop could only have benefited from the inclusion of some constrasting shapes within the actual song.

As it is, the possibilities of both the experimental and the populist are wasted, they don't have the strength to stand out on their own.

It would seem that OMD have squandered the chances they had with 'Dazzle', perhaps because they themselves cannot be that sure about exactly what direction they shold now take. The project that is 'Dazzle' is too sketchy, too unsure and wobbly to be worth much.

What it does provide, though, are some interesting clues about what OMD could turn up with next — something a bit more inspired and surefooted, I hope.

CHRIS BURKHAM.

conceptual music with aesthetic, sugar-coated songs on it. Even the title track's a very listenable piece of experimental music. For *Dazzle Ships*, I decided we needed to be more experimental, more radical. We hadn't changed the world and people were saying, 'The world is listening to you now. What the hell are you singing about bloody saints for? Why aren't you doing something really positive and political and powerful?'

My reaction was, 'Yeah, that's

↑
Chris Burkham thought *Dazzle Ships* not that outstanding

OMD - 1983

what we need to do', so I got my shortwave radio out and started recording eastern European communist radio stations. The war was on in the Lebanon, and it seemed that the Cold War a very dark place.

People who liked 'Souvenir' and 'Joan of Arc' bought *Dazzle Ships* and went, 'What is this?' We hadn't coated the conceptual ideas in a beautiful veneer. We were saying 'Here's an idea. Speaking clocks, synchronised. Isn't it great?' Sadly, most of our audience replied, 'Maybe, but it's not what I call music.'

Some people who like the conceptual elements just think, 'How radical. How amazing that a pop group would dare to do something like that.' But it sold about one tenth of what *Architecture & Morality* sold.

We went from thinking, 'We don't care about selling records because we're going to change the world', to, 'Oh shit, we've done something wrong.' The realisation was, Paul's just bought a house. I've just bought a house. Paul's married. If we can't sell records, we don't get to make any *more* records. Shit, we're in trouble.'

KUPPELSAAL
25 March 1983, Hamburg, West Germany

ILKA WEGNER

Our seats were high up, very far away from the stage, but after the break my friend and I followed others and ended right in front of one of the massive loudspeakers by the stage. Wow, what an experience! I also introduced my partner to OMD and 35 years and many concerts later, he made me the proud owner of my very own OMD number plate, which can be seen on the streets in and around Weston-super-Mare.

TELEGRAPH
WAS RELEASED

1 APR 1983

KRISTIAN YNGVESSON

Living in the village of Fristad in Sweden, I began to listen to pop music on the radio. In 1984, aged 12, I remember hearing 'Tesla Girls', which I grew very fond of. Later that year I bought my first two OMD records, 'Talking Loud and Clear' and the picture disc of 'Telegraph.'

In our secondary school music class, our teacher spoke of sounds and modern music like Stockhausen, and we discussed the differences between real and synthetic strings. After the lesson I told her I thought synthetic strings existed in their own right and had an ideal example to show the class. The following

Andy's sketch for ideas for the 'Telegraph' video

The 'Telegraph' girls, Loraine, Cia and Susie, rehearsing for the video

Models of the Dazzle Ships stage set

week I brought 'Telegraph' into school to play the B-side, '66 and Fading.' It was interesting to hear the diverse opinions about whether the recorded strings were real or synthetic.

In the end, our teacher told the class it was made by a synth-pop group named OMD and played the A-side as well. When I picked up my record afterwards, my teacher told me her daughter was a big OMD fan.

GREG MORGAN

My discovery of OMD came in the unlikely city of Lubbock, Texas. I'd only caught a glimpse of an amazing video clip on *MTV's 120 Minutes*, which I had to sneak into my living room to watch at 2am on a school night. But I missed the title so didn't catch the name of the band. A week later I was at my local record shop, University Records, where the owner had records that shouldn't have been in Lubbock, a town with a healthy appetite for Country and Metal. I did my usual round of the bins with no special moments. My last bin was always the clearance and a black sleeve caught my eye. A strange machine and the word 'Telegraph' were on the cover and I realised I'd found an interesting 12-inch. I asked to put it on the turntable, the owner cued it up and hit the volume. The voice and xylophone-tinged synth filled the store. The track lit up the place, everyone grinning and beginning to dance as they flipped through the racks. The last smile of this sunny day was me, at the checkout. The disc had been marked down to 99¢.

ANDY MCCLUSKEY

We used a custom-designed stage-set for *Architecture and Morality*, but this tour saw us with the greatest stage design we'd ever had. Peter Saville had suggested the whole Dazzle Ships concept and now he and his assistant Ken Kennedy delivered an incredible, almost Russian Constructivist meets Futurist creation for us. The set was a huge hit. Persuading Martin, Paul and Mal to wave flags, count building blocks and turn a word box handle in a mime didn't make me very popular with the other band members.

COLSTON HALL
14 April 1983, Bristol, UK

ALI SMITH
Founding member of The Barmy Army

I first got into OMD listening to late night Radio 1. Then, in 1979, a schoolfriend who was a huge Gary Numan fan wanted to go and see him at the Southampton Gaumont. She was only allowed to go if she had someone to go with and I jumped at the chance - not to see Numan, but the support band, OMD. After that, every time they played on the South Coast, I'd go. In spring 1983 they announced the Dazzle Ships tour. I'd left school and it seemed obvious I should go to as many gigs as I could. I hung around outside to meet the band when they turned up for the soundcheck. Andy and Paul signed a few things and asked me the deal with the rucksack and sleeping bag. 'I'm coming on tour with you,' was my answer, taking everyone a bit by surprise. 'What, every gig?' 'Yep, every gig.' After the show, I slept on a bench in Bristol Temple Meads station, waiting for my train to the next town. Every day I'd be waiting, and soon I was sitting watching the soundcheck most afternoons. Outside, I met other fans and it wasn't long before I got to know people from all over the country. This also meant the station benches were sometimes replaced by people's floors as overnight accommodation.

By the time the tour reached Brighton, it felt like second nature, and as I sat watching the soundcheck, Steve the tour manager said he 'wanted a word'. I wasn't sure what I'd done, but it didn't look good. He said, 'We didn't believe you in Bristol, but you're still here, so we might as well make it official.' With that, he handed me a laminated Access All Areas pass. The rules were set out, and I'd been accepted. By the end of the tour, I had met Hugh, Carmel and Wendy and when the band came back to the UK later that year, I wasn't alone on my travels any more. Andy called us the 'Barmy Army' and our ranks grew each tour. When we

OMD - 1983

weren't on tour, we were planning the next, and not just in the UK. OMD had sort of taken over, and my year was all about the tours. I will never forget, though, the looks on Andy and Paul's faces when I told them they'd better get used to me being around on that grey day in Bristol.

ANDY MCCLUSKEY

I clearly remember meeting Alison when we arrived at the Colston Hall and her telling us she planned to follow the entire tour. She was the first to ever do this, but not the last. We were terribly flattered, and that's why we usually let the Barmy Army into soundchecks, especially if it was raining.

DE MONTFORT HALL
15 April 1983, Leicester, UK

ANDREW LIDDLE
OMD lighting designer since 2009

Instead of staying in Leicester city centre, they decided to stay in a little village outside, at the Quorn Country Hotel, where my girlfriend was a chambermaid. Entering one of the keyboard player's rooms in the morning, she was enticed to get into bed. Bearing in mind they've got two keyboard players, I couldn't possibly comment which one.

They turned up later in my local for a pint, where I first met McCluskey and got told to, 'Fuck off, Andrew.' Years later, being interviewed for my job, he asked, 'Is there anything else?' I said, 'Yeah, you're allowed one, "Fuck off, Andrew" a day.' I'm Andrew and he's Andy. He explained this to me on our first meeting, saying, 'There's only room for one Andy around here.' So I said, 'Right, fuck it. I'll be Andrew from now on.'

CITY HALL
17 April 1983, Sheffield, UK

TONY NEUL

Me, my late wife Alison (nee Pacey) and our friends Phil and Biddy travelled to the Sheffield gig in a car with a hole in the passenger footwell. I was sat over the hole and couldn't put my feet down properly, as you could see

→
OMD on stage with the Dazzle Ships set

the road beneath the car. The police stopped us on the way home, telling my friend his rear light wasn't working.

HAMMERSMITH ODEON
19 & 20 April 1983, London, UK

JOHN OWENS

I first saw OMD at the Hammersmith Odeon, supported by the Cocteau Twins, who moaned about having to rewire their synths between numbers. I've followed OMD in all their incarnations and really loved *Sugar Tax* and *Liberator* from the 'Andy only' phase, with 'Call My Name' the stand-out of that period. I was heartbroken when Andy called it a day in 1996. However, I kept the faith and continued to play the back-catalogue. May 2007 found me back at a rammed Apollo for the *Architecture & Morality* restaging. It was a triumphal return.

OMD - 1983

OMD performing Dazzle Ships live

What is it about the music that keeps me coming back? I love the syncopation, the offbeat and the fact you just have to dance. There's nothing like OMD, never has been and never will be. Oh, and Andy, I've almost (but not quite) forgiven you for Atomic Kitten.

KATHRYN HOOPER

Where to start? I guess in 1981 with the release of 'Joan of Arc.' At 15 I couldn't get enough of that. It was lonely being a fan of a group seen as 'boring bank clerks', dressing the part. At the time I wasn't into buying singles when you could spend a few more pounds and get an album. *Architecture & Morality* went onto my Christmas list, Mum and Dad kindly buying it for me. It was promptly put onto my vertical Amstrad. My initial thoughts on hearing 'The New Stone Age' was that my record was badly damaged. I was a bit annoyed before I realised this was how it was meant to sound. The rest of that album was just superb and was played non-stop in my room. The pleasure of turning it over to listen to side two is something almost forgotten. I was so concerned this fantastic album would be worn out that I recorded it onto tape.

One week, 'Joan of Arc' made it onto the Dial-a-Disc playlist. I phoned up to hear what in reality was an awful recording just to get a kick out of OMD playing. I expect my parents' bill went up that quarter. I didn't own up.

I eagerly awaited news of the Dazzle Ships tour. My first concert was at Hammersmith Odeon and I almost had to bribe a friend along. Hearing the music live for the first time was exhilarating and the energy from the band was something I still value today. *English Electric* will always be a memorable album for me, released on my birthday, with a cheeky request to Andy for an interview via the fan forum to my utter amazement accepted. With only a few days to prep questions I spent a delightful hour chatting to him. My initial nervousness eventually left me and I was able to have more of a 'normal' chat, while almost constantly pinching myself, talking to a person who had been a constant since my teenage years, whose pictures had adorned my bedroom walls and whose music and lyrics had touched me in a way no other music had.

ARTS CENTRE
22 April 1983, Poole, UK

LISA HAWKINS

I loved 'Joan of Arc' as soon as I heard it on the radio. I bought the 12", my first, and played it continually. The cover still shows signs of over-handling. From there I went back to *Organisation* and *OMITD* and loved every track, while *Architecture & Morality* was highly anticipated and didn't disappoint. I knew every word within days.

Then, more excitement - OMD were actually going to play Poole Arts Centre. None of my friends were interested but I went anyway. I was only 13 and fairly nervous about my first concert and I'm sure Dad waited outside for me, although he never said.

I got there early to get close to the stage but stayed to the side so there was plenty of room for dancing. The songs sounded so much better live, plus Andy and Paul really were there in the flesh. I remember being impressed with how well the band played and how seriously they seemed to take the performance, even wearing ties. It was such a great night and went by far too quickly.

I didn't get to see OMD live again until the Royal Albert Hall in May 2016. I went alone but was surrounded by the amazing fans that chatted and encouraged me to go again in 2017. I did - to Guildford - and with my daughter to Manchester. She agreed that OMD really are the best live band.

BRIGHTON CENTRE

23 April 1983, Brighton, UK

MARK SIMMONDS

In 1981, I was given a copy of *Architecture & Morality* by a schoolfriend who wasn't sure if he liked it or not. I never gave it back. I first saw OMD live during the Dazzle Ships tour. It was the largest venue I'd been to and the set alone was something I still vividly recall. I'm not sure you'd get away with a set like that now.

The album and concert stand out because neither conformed to the norm. I mean, what other band could get away with standing still for three minutes doing semaphore? *Dazzle Ships* remains my favourite album for that reason. Many more concerts followed. I often remember the album tracks played live more than the hit singles. 'White Trash', 'Crush', 'Was It Something I Said' all sounded so much better live. 'Sugar Tax' the album track that never was; the perfect way to open that show.

LAURENCE COLEMAN

I got into OMD when 'Souvenir' was released and *Architecture & Morality* is still one of my all-time favourite albums. I just had to see them, but how was I going to be able to afford it when I was at college with no money apart from the paltry amount received for my paper-round? Not all was lost. The Evening Argus held a competition for Brighton Centre tickets and I only bloody won!

I remember walking five miles from my village to Hastings to get my copy of 'Locomotion' on the day of release. I almost ran all the way home, just to slap that lovely piece of vinyl on my deck, blasting my parents' eardrums for many weeks after.

ODEON

25 April 1983, Birmingham, UK

STEWART CRANER

My journey as an OMD fan began at age 14 when a schoolfriend asked to swap my copy of 7" Gary Numan record for his 10" copy of OMD's 'Messages.'

My friend, Kenny Owen, and I

travelled to Birmingham and stood near the main entrance where all the trucks were parked to watch the equipment being loaded in. To our surprise, Andy came out to have a cigarette. He waved us over, so we chatted. We were pretty nervous, but he put us at ease.

If I could write a book about my experiences of seeing OMD live, it would also be about the friends I've made over the years, the gatherings, and getting to DJ at OMD parties. At one event I got to pick up a copy of 'Sister Marie Says' from Andy at his studio and play it exclusively for the fans.

ODEON
26 April 1983,
Birmingham, UK

KEVIN BRUERTON

It was my first concert. I'd just turned 16. I borrowed my Dad's flasher mac to look cool, or so I thought. Schoolfriends from Codsall High, Steve Sellick and Mark Bason, and I had heard everything that had been released. Nothing, however prepared me for my first Dazzle Ships tour show. That album still means so much to me, as does the visual display I saw that evening.

On 14 June 2007 at Wolverhampton Civic, the hall was set out for seating downstairs. No one was going to use that. We rushed to the front and spent the whole concert looking up at the band, front row standing! I still remember Andy looking around towards the end; he couldn't believe the reaction. Then he said, 'I suppose we'd better not leave it as long next time'.

PLAYHOUSE THEATRE
27 April 1983,
Edinburgh, UK

MARTIN WEST

I first came across OMD when I heard 'Enola Gay' on the radio, then saw the band perform on *Top of the Pops*. The attraction was instantaneous and I needed to find out more.

The first LP I ever bought was *Dazzle Ships* and from the first track to the last I loved every minute. I still do. It was just so different from the first three albums, sounded so raw and not polished as *Architecture & Morality*, fractured but at the same time with a beautiful quality so hard to explain.

My first ever concert was on the

↑
OMD concert ticket,
Odeon Theatre,
Birmingham, 1983

1983 | 171

OMD - 1983

We receive quite a lot of really good pictures and drawings from people.
We always enjoy looking at them and keep them all.
We've decided to start printing some in the newsletters from now on.
Here is one, not necessarily the best, but it makes a good start.

Gail Harrison

Dazzle Ships tour. I had to go with my older sister. The support act was The Cocteau Twins. I can't remember a lot apart from I was now well and truly hooked. Each time they came to Edinburgh I was there. Last time I saw them in Edinburgh was July 1991 on the Sugar Tax tour. A month later I was on a plane starting a new life in Australia.

It was a long time before I'd see the band again. A gift from my partner Deb was a ticket to see OMD play the Sommergarten in Berlin in September 2011 on the History of Modern tour. Bearing in mind I still lived in Western Australia, it wasn't like going on a train to a venue.

The next was again a gift from Deb, a gold ticket to the Royal Albert Hall in May 2016, but I was unable to attend - Deb was recovering from breast cancer and with two young boys to look after it was just impossible to go. I couldn't sell my ticket but Ed at 100% music very kindly sent out my gold package items and some extra goodies, for which I was very grateful.

The same sister that took me to the Dazzle Ships concert once told me her ex-partner managed Edinburgh nightclub Valentino's, where OMD played in March 1980, leaving behind a piece of equipment that found its way into the attic of a house they shared. I wonder if it still is?

APOLLO
28 April 1983, Glasgow, UK

JOHN GRANT

A fan since I was 14, the first single I bought was 'Joan of Arc' and my first gig was at the Apollo. I had a C90 cassette filled on both sides with 'Maid of Orleans', recorded from the radio every time it was played. The 1991 Sugar Tax gig was inconveniently scheduled for the week of my wedding. Two years later, my wife gave birth to our twin boys five days before what proved to be their last gig in Glasgow for over a decade.

Discharged on the day of the gig she could hardly walk following childbirth. I found a win-win solution and went along with her twin sister, while her Mum stayed with my wife and the babies. Then, 20 years later, we had VIP tickets to a pre-gig Glasgow meet-and-greet, and the first thing my wife said to Mr McCluskey was, 'Aye, he missed the first night with our sons to attend an OMD concert in 1993.' Long memories, eh?

←

The rear cover of the 1983 *OMD Fanclub* magazine with a drawing by Gail Harrison

APOLLO

1 May 1983, Manchester, UK

DARYN BUCKLEY

They were supported by a band with a loud drum machine, a miserable guitarist and a singer who kept on thumping herself in the chest every time she sang. They were, in equal parts, brilliant and strange and the Cocteau Twins were to become one of my favourite bands.

As the lights dropped and the ear-splitting strains of 'Dazzle Ships' rang out through the darkness, I held my breath. This was incredible. Then the band came on. Oh, they seem to be waving flags around. Is this right? Surely, they're not just going to mime the whole gig.

Of course, they didn't. I was treated to a gig that changed my life. In many ways and for many years, it ruined gigs for me. No other band could get as close visually, musically or emotionally as Orchestral Manoeuvres in the Dark did that night.

EMPIRE THEATRE

3 May 1983, Liverpool, UK

SIMON GARLAND

In 1979, Jim Brown, Head of Music at Calday Grange Grammar School, played us a record by recent old boy, Andy McCluskey. It was called 'Electricity' and during the end-of-year exams we were required to identify it for one mark. In 1980, I spent my £5 Christmas record token buying my first ever non-parentally approved cassette from Dins Records, Heswall, *Organisation*. It got played to death. In 1982, my mother enrolled as a mature student nurse and was intrigued by the number of her class claiming intimate knowledge of a certain curly-haired bassist. In 1983, the night before my German O-level oral examination, I attended the Dazzle Ships tour at the Empire. Not enjoying The Cocteau Twins, I wondered if it was a mistake. But by the end of the night I was blown away.

MARK PHILLIPS

My wife was expecting our first child and we laughed when 'ABC Auto Industry' was sung, saying at least our child would be able to say, 'ABC 123.'

NEW THEATRE

7 May 1983, Oxford, UK

LUCY FREEMAN

Andy was very serious and barely spoke, apart from introducing the songs. How times change. He's now full of humour and great banter.

HAMMERSMITH ODEON

9 May 1983, London, UK

PAUL BROWNE
founder of Telegraph fanzine & long-time moderator on the original OMD website

The release of *Architecture & Morality* established OMD as a band that could deliver smart electronic music - yet also with a sense of style. They demonstrated that they could tackle difficult subjects in surprising ways, as 'Enola Gay' proved. The arrival of *Dazzle Ships*, however, featured their most pointed political commentary and combined it with their most challenging musical approach to date.

I became so used to the warm tonal approach OMD employed on the likes of 'Souvenir' and 'Maid Of Orleans', that the arrival of 'Genetic Engineering' in February 1983 was a shock to the senses. The cold, chittering melodies and odd nursery rhyme intro sounded like a completely different band.

Introducing the album with a Czechoslovak radio interval signal was strange enough, but the album was peppered with unusual experimental compositions, such as 'Time Zones' or the disconcerting qualities of 'Dazzle Ships (Parts II, III & VII).'

Despite the challenging approach, it was an album I fell in love with for many reasons. Peter Saville's design concept had an abstract quality unlike any other album sleeve from OMD's contemporaries.

But outside of the experimental and musique concrète elements, there were other gems to be savoured. Few songs have an intro as shocking as the one that precedes 'International'. The dispassionate news reading introducing a statement from '...a young girl from Nicaragua whose hands had been cut off at the wrists' revealed a darker mood than the group had approached before.

Much of *Dazzle Ships* had this intriguing quality in which song lyrics could be interpreted in different ways. It was a coded language that the listener could impose their own meaning on. It was something OMD managed to cultivate across their career and led to fans forever quizzing the band on the actual meaning behind these strange titles - and often-stranger lyrics.

The album's conceptual qualities, however, took on a new life when the band rolled out the set design on tour. For an electronic band, OMD had always been conscious of the limitations on stage that beset bands whose primary sound was generated by synthesisers. But even their early efforts to overcome these restrictions (which included fluorescent tubing and Andy's unique dance moves) were dwarfed by the sheer scale of *Dazzle Ships* on stage.

For a start, they decided to utilise the vertical space on stage by elevating band members, giving Mal Holmes a powerful visual focus at the centre. Meanwhile, painted screens that took elements from the album sleeve were presented as large-scale pieces of artwork bolted against the stage scaffolding. The end-result was less a stage-set, more installation art.

It provided a backdrop for a live performance at Hammersmith Odeon that's seared itself into my memory as one of OMD's finest concerts. Even the odd performance art elements that preceded the main concert, such as band members holding aloft large flags in a semaphore routine - or Paul Humphreys dropping blocks into a basket with a mechanical claw - seemed to give the concert a distinct theatrical flourish.

Despite the commercial failure of *Dazzle Ships*, there was no denying the sheer power of its songs in a live setting. The likes of 'Genetic Engineering' and 'Radio Waves' seemed to seamlessly slot in with classic tunes such as 'Messages' and 'Souvenir.'

As with any formative moment, it would be a natural course of action that the euphoria of these live shows would fade over time. Yet somehow the sheer bravado of *Dazzle Ships* managed to grip me in a way that not even the classic *Architecture & Morality* could eclipse. It was the consummate musical package that displaced other contenders as the actual soundtrack of this 20-something's life at the time.

↑

Since 1983 Dazzle camouflage has become ubiquitous. Dazzle Ships socks, promotional image and a Dazzle Ship at Canning Graving Dock, Liverpool

1983 | 177

PABELLON DE DEPORTES
12 May 1983, Bilbao, Spain

ANDY MCCLUSKEY

After I suffer the most appalling seasickness on a ferry to northern Spain, things don't improve when the promoter expresses concern about us using red and yellow semaphore flags in 'ABC Auto Industry'. He explains that the Basque region is undergoing a very violent separatist campaign and he can't promise us that someone supporting ETA would not try to shoot us if we waved flags in the national colours. No-one can source flags in an alternative hue, so we start the set with a different song. Paul, Mal and Martin are silently delighted!

Unsurprisingly, we didn't take the Dazzle Ships tour to North America. We were straight back into the studio then out on the road to try some new material live with a support act that was about to be bigger than we were on the other side of the Atlantic.

ROCK CITY
6 September 1983, Nottingham, UK

HOWARD JONES

I couldn't believe it when I was asked to play five support gigs with OMD in September 1983. I was a huge fan, so much that the only cover I played in my early Eighties set was 'Enola Gay', but I didn't perform it in Nottingham, Cardiff, Bradford, Manchester's Hacienda and Liverpool. I seem to remember it was the first time I'd seen or heard an Emulator I sampling keyboard, and keyboard lust took a hold of me, having to wait until the Emulator II came out in 1984.

It was the first time I played Liverpool Royal Court and I got a traditional good-natured roasting from the audience. It was a big deal for me to open for Andy and Paul, and watching their set inspired me to go for it, at the time my first single 'New Song' was about to be released. I've enjoyed following their career ever since.

That classy British Minimalist Synth Music still does it for me.

THE VIRGIN DEAL

ANDY MCCLUSKEY

I don't remember us having a conversation with Richard Branson. I don't think I'd have wanted us to have a conversation, because I really felt like we'd been ripped off. I felt angry. I was glad we were able to make music and had an audience and he gave us the opportunity, but the contract we signed was just this side of criminal. A couple of years later, after a few hits, somewhere in London I bumped into a guy who came sheepishly over and introduced himself, saying 'I need to say hello to you. I'm the lawyer who let you sign your contract with Virgin and Dindisc.' 'Oh, are you?' 'In my defence,' he said, 'I looked at the name of the band and thought, 'Sheesh', and I met your manager and went, 'Oh yeah'.' Paul Collister at that time had long greasy hair, never washed, green teeth, pumps that the soles were coming away from, so they looked like the mouth of a dog or something, and he never bathed. The lawyer said, 'I'm really sorry, but I looked at your manager, looked at the name of the band, and just thought, 'They should just take what they get given, because they're going nowhere'. And I said, 'Can I have that in writing please, because I'm going to sue you, you bastard.'

Our record deal was terrible. We were on six per cent of retail price for singles. So if a single sold for a pound, we got 6p. On international sales we were on two-thirds royalties, so we were on 4p for most of the sales for, say, 'Enola Gay.' The producer, Mike Howlett, negotiated three points that came out of our royalty. So we were on one penny, out of which we had to pay back the advance, the recording costs and half of any video costs. You can imagine why, for all the many millions of records we sold, we were permanently skint.

1984

After the lack of sales for the *Dazzle Ships* album we were conscious we needed hit singles on the follow up. However, it was strange that the very next single choice had originally been intended as a song about the problems of mobility for disabled people. Not the usual subject for a pop song, but typical that we could consider it. In the long process of trying to make 'Locomotion' work musically, the lyric lost most of its original intention.
Andy McCluskey

| **LOCOMOTION** | 2 APR 1984 |
| WAS RELEASED | |

→ Andy during the 'Locomotion' video shoot in Belgium

ORCHESTRAL MANOEUVRES IN THE DARK
LOCOMOTION
7 INCH & EXTENDED 12 INCH SINGLE

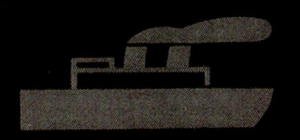

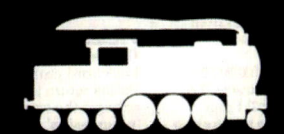

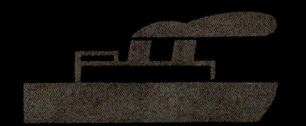

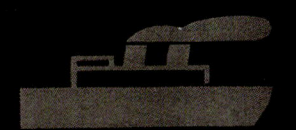

WIN A SONY COMPACT DISC PLAYER OR ONE OF 500 SIGNED COPIES OF THE NEW O.M.D. ALBUM "JUNK CULTURE". SEE 7 INCH SINGLES BAG FOR DETAILS.

OMD – 1984

> Andy's notes to 'Locomotion'

> Photo shoot for *Junk Culture* at the Brighton Pavilion

JUNK CULTURE WAS RELEASED

30 APR 1984

JUNK CULTURE

Junk Culture took a very long time to complete. Regrettably, we decided to leave our own studio. We became bored of working in the same environment after four years. Now we were nomadic, and it cost a fortune wandering from studio to studio. We couldn't even finish in Montserrat. We went to Brussels and were still adding and writing in Wisseloord in Hilversum, Holland.

ANDY MCCLUSKEY

SAM O'DANIEL

I bought *Junk Culture* on cassette after hearing it over the speakers in Rocky Mountain Records & Tapes in the 16th Street Mall, Denver. I had money burning a hole in my pocket, was looking for something to buy and wanted something new, something different. I must have been looking around for 15 to 30 minutes before I realised I really liked what I was hearing over the store system.

OMD – 1984

Andy in Montserrat at the end of the Junk Culture sessions at Air Studios

MONTSERRAT

PETER SAVILLE

I have fond memories of Andy and I having a week together in Montserrat at the end of the recording of *Junk Culture* at AIR Studios. I was always envious of groups going there, and rarely had a holiday, so Andy dreamt up an urgency for us to meet at the studio.

The album was finished and the group had left, but Andy stayed on four or five days in a house he rented. It was fantastic. There was a beach we would go to that was quite remote. You had to drive for half an hour to get there, and when you arrived there was no one there. Anything you needed, like Coca-Cola or water, you had to take with you.

One afternoon the two of us were sat on this little beach looking at the sea, thinking, 'This is nice', when a shoal of flying fish went by within 20 or 30 yards of where we were. It's not until you see it that you really believe such things exist, and it's quite a shock when it happens, because they are flying fish.

Andy and I instinctively turned to each other and I think we were both thinking the same thing. From a pub in Rochdale to flying fish in the Caribbean - how did that happen? It was one of those strangely idyllic and cosmic moments. We didn't have to say anything. We were both having the same feeling of wonder. It happened. We were there, and fish flew!

ASSEMBLY ROOMS

31 May 1984, Derby, UK

CHRIS INNS

Having discussed with my next-door neighbour, two years above me at secondary school, how good *Architecture & Morality* was, I then obtained an autographed *Dazzle Ships* tour booklet from my maths teacher. Then in 1984, I saw OMD for the first time in Derby, going to the stage door beforehand and getting tour bus driver Dave's autograph. And that concert was closely followed by one at De Montfort Hall, where Paul's keyboards broke down.

A 1985 gig at Loughborough Students' Union was also special. At the end – with my train back to Derby not until the early hours - I went to a fire door at the side, casually knocked and Andy opened it. He welcomed me in, where they were chilling, and Paul and Martin walked in. They signed my tour programme and I thanked them for their hospitality and left. Walking back through the main building I bumped into Malcolm, who also signed the programme.

APOLLO

26 May 1984, Glasgow, UK

LINSEY PITHERS

We met all the band at the stage door, except for a briefly glimpsed,

↑ Paul in the control room at Air Studios, Montserrat

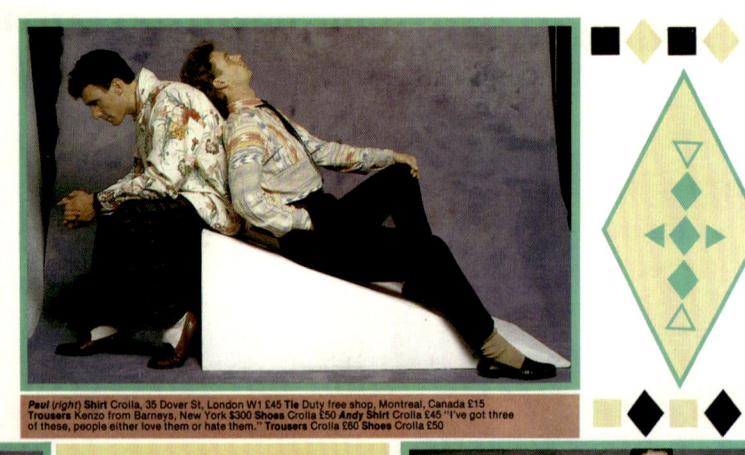

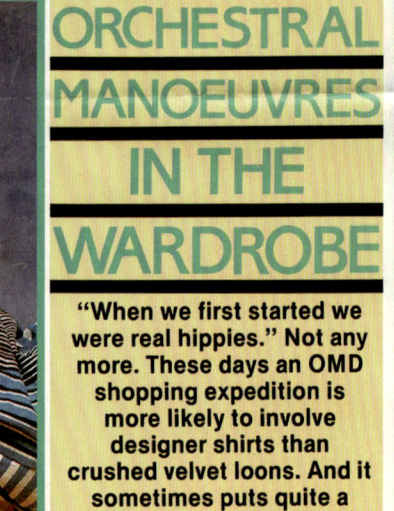

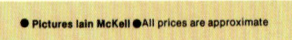

OMD - 1984

Paul and Andy pose for a Smash Hits fashion shoot

Chris Oaten from Hull asks Smash Hits where he can buy OMD's Crolla shirts

stressed-looking Andy. It turned out that the band's emulator synths had broken down in the soundcheck. Fortunately, they were sorted for the gig. Fast forward 33 years and an equipment breakdown at Glasgow's Royal Concert Hall that saw the show temporarily suspended. Pure coincidence, I'm sure.

EMPIRE
27 May 1984, Liverpool, UK

GRAHAM MORRIS

The first time I met OMD was when they stayed back to sign autographs at the Empire. I had my original braille-sleeved copy of 'Electricity', which they signed in silver and gold pens, genuinely knocked out to see it.

ODEON
30 May 1984, Birmingham, UK

ROY BONEHAM

I was 15 and in boarding school in 1980 when I kept hearing this song every morning, 'Enola Gay.' It was 1984 before I could afford a ticket. Before the encore, Andy came on stage and announced that Liverpool had won the European Cup. Two good reasons why that night was special.

| TALKING LOUD AND CLEAR | 4 JUN 1984 |
| WAS RELEASED | |

PARADISE THEATRE

26 July 1984, Boston, Massachusetts

ANDY MCCLUSKEY

The one and only time I was ever stoned on stage. I'd not even started smoking cigarettes until the year before. I'd take the mickey out of the others who smoked, but pressure of *Dazzle Ships* disasters saw me join them. Malcolm had a habit of 'front-loading' his joints - putting the dope in the part he smoked, then passing around the tobacco. I didn't smoke dope but knowing Mal's rolling habit I took a few tokes when the joint arrived. Ten minutes later I was in trouble. It was an American pure grass joint. I spent the entire gig in a paranoid state, asking Paul or Martin which verse was next and if my bass was in tune. Never again!

Andy McCluskey's shirt – an artist's impression.

Please help me find out where Andy McCluskey of OMD bought his red, white and black shirt, as worn recently on TOTP. I have enclosed a drawing but it's not 100% accurate.
Chris Oater, Hull.
● But it is *very* artistic. The shirts came from *Crolla Menswear*, based at: 35 Dower Street, London W1. Both Andy and Paul opted for the medium size, selling at around £55. However, hot news has just filtered through that *Crolla's* have started to sell matching boxer shorts at £11 from the underwear department. Game, 'fellas'?

AUSTRALIA 1984

I recall several interesting incidents on the Australian tour in 1984. First, almost getting the gig cancelled at RSL Balmain because I was wearing a Chinese communist hat with a red star. The veterans who fought in Korea were very angry. Second, having a continuous conversation with someone in the front row at Canberra University who insisted the psoriasis scars on my arms were proof that I was shooting heroin. Third, our backline crewmember Nick Sizer going missing after too many tequilas in Perth, fortunately discovered passed out in the gutter at the back door of the Red Parrot venue the next morning, in time for the load-in!

ANDY MCCLUSKEY

ANDY McCLUSKEY (OMD): MY FIVE OBSESSIONS

Japanese food. It's actually the only food I'd kill for. I desperately adore it, particularly the *Sushi* food — that's the raw fish and so on. I really like *Kappa Maki*, which is seaweed rolls with rice, cucumber and green mustard in them, and *Tempura*, which is a battered dish with shrimps and vegetables — brilliant!

Speed. I love going fast, almost to the point of death and destruction, in my car. I have a Cortina 2-litre which goes like a bat out of hell but isn't really my ideal car. I had quite a bad smash in it once. I also love the moment where a plane gathers speed before taking off and you get flung back in your seat. I could definitely handle going up in a rocket.

Liverpool FC. It's something I've kept quiet — mainly because everyone you meet claims to have been a Liverpool supporter since they were three — but nothing cheers me up more on a Saturday than if they win. Funny, because I never go to the games or anything.

Fossils. I collect them. Anything from shells to bones to fossilized tree trunks. My mum's attic is so full of them it'll probably collapse one day. When I was a kid it got really ridiculous with me digging up main roads and pulling down people's garden walls because there were fossils in them. My favourite is one of the first I found when I was about eight. It's a piece of fossilized sponge I found in the quarry of the local brickworks.

Buying new clothes. You spend so long living out of two suitcases that when you stop you shop desperately to get a new outfit. I recently got this *Versace* jacket which is leather and rubber with these *enormous* shoulders. It's my pride and joy at the moment and everyone wants to steal it off me.

JET CLUB
15 August 1984,
Coolangatta, Australia

CLAIRE TEARE

I moved to Australia in 1982 with my family, and back then it was like travelling back in time, especially the Australian music scene. OMD were considered alternative and their music did not receive a lot of airplay. I managed to see them at Coolangatta, about an hour's drive from where we were living. It was my first concert.

Three years later, in January '87, OMD toured again and, now having a driver's licence, I was able to go to all three Queensland concerts. Each night I stood in the same spot at the front, next to the same tall guy to my right. After the show I was invited backstage to meet the boys. I was quite overwhelmed and rather shy and quiet, but Andy took the lead, making me feel comfortable and welcome. It was the best night ever. I'd seen my idols three times and I'd got to meet them.

But something was missing in my life. I wanted someone to 'hold me, love me, see me smile at the break of day', and it just wasn't happening for me.

Three weeks later I was on a deserted beach when I noticed a gorgeous guy walking towards me. He stopped nearby and after a while, came over. I had butterflies as he approached, and he then asked me the time. As soon as he spoke I recognised his accent, asking which part of England he was from. He replied, 'Liverpool, most people think of The Beatles when I tell them.' I replied, 'No, I think of OMD.' His gorgeous blue eyes popped open and he said, 'Really. You're into OMD?' Well, that was it. We had so much in common, even emigrating around the same time. We talked for hours and loved all the same OMD songs. He'd also gone to the concerts each night … and he was the tall guy standing to my right each night. We were both too entranced to pay attention to each other, even if he was really cute. It was love at first sight.

We moved in together, got a cat, named him Winston. Three years later, Mark and I married, dancing to OMD at our wedding. We were so in love and 30 years on still are, with two beautiful grown-up daughters. And we still enjoy the music of OMD. We'd love to see them in concert again, but it's just too far. Maybe one day?

NATIONAL PALACE OF CATALONIA

23 June 1984, Barcelona, Spain

ANDY MCCLUSKEY

The 1984 tour of Spain was remarkable for two standout reasons.

On June 20th in Madrid I met the girl that I would ultimately marry.

On June 23rd the band played in front of what remains to this day as the largest crowd we have ever performed for. 250,000 on the Piazza in front of the Palace in Barcelona. The view from the stage was unbelievable. A mass of faces as far as the eye could see down the long avenue. The crowd were in a very boisterous mood throwing fireworks at each other and empty bottles at the stage. I could see them coming - unfortunately Paul could not and received a direct hit to the forehead during 'Joan of Arc.' Glass shattered all over him and his keyboard. I was in full swing and only realised that something was wrong because the sound grew weaker as one by one the other band members were ushered off stage by our manager.

↑
Andy tells the press 'they never wanted to be the biggest thing since sliced Boy George'

←
Andy kept quiet his love for Liverpool FC

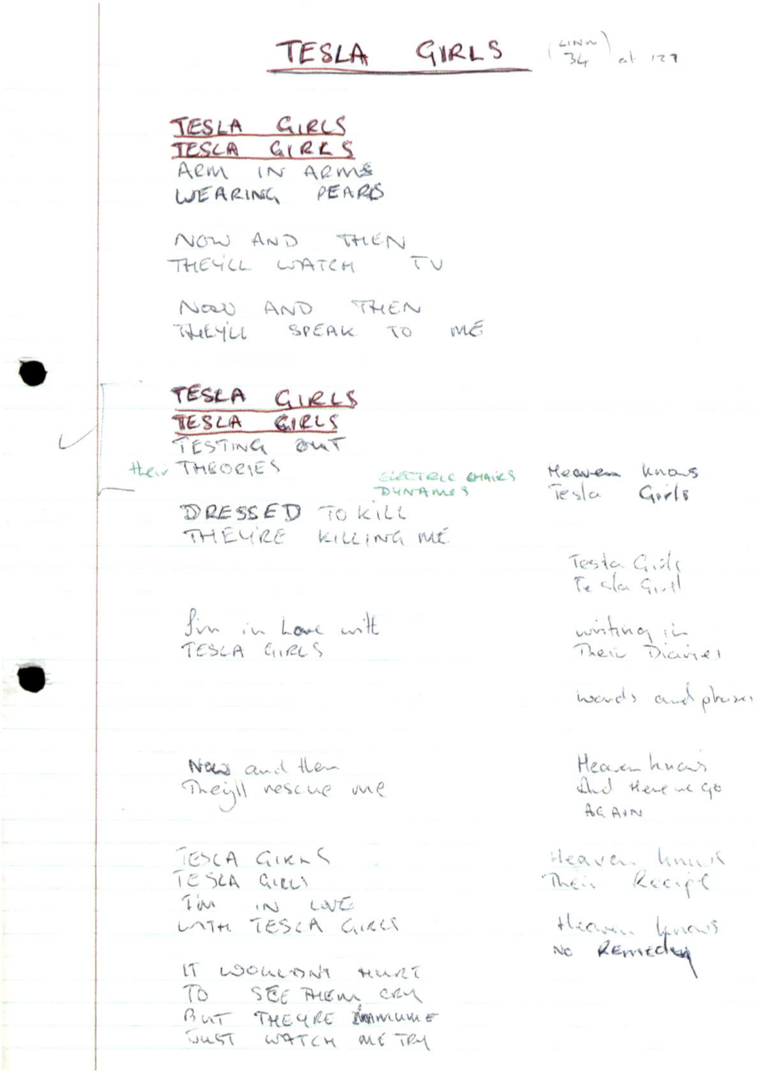

OMD – 1984

Handwritten notes:

TESLA GIRLS (LINN 34 at 127)

TESLA GIRLS
TESLA GIRLS
ARM IN ARMS
WEARING PEARS

NOW AND THEN
THEY'LL WATCH TV

NOW AND THEN
THEY'LL SPEAK TO ME

TESLA GIRLS
TESLA GIRLS
TESTING OUT
their THEORIES   ELECTRIC CHAIRS   Heaven knows
                     DYNAMOS   Tesla Girls
DRESSED TO KILL
THEY'RE KILLING ME
                                        Tesla Girls
                                        Tesla Girls
I'm in Love with
TESLA GIRLS   writing in
                                        Their Diaries

                                        words and phrases

Now and then   Heaven knows
They'll rescue me   And there we go
                                        Again

TESLA GIRLS   Heaven knows
TESLA GIRLS   Their Recipe
I'M IN LOVE
WITH TESLA GIRLS   Heaven knows
                                        No Remedy
IT WOULDN'T HURT
TO SEE THEM CRY
BUT THEY'RE IMMUNE
JUST WATCH ME TRY

We did resume playing and I recall Paul calling out that he knew who the culprit was. Not the best plan, I thought, to offer out quarter of a million Catalans for a fight! Despite the bottle incident the concert was an utterly amazing experience. It was filmed but sadly the footage has since been lost.

The surreality of the whole event culminated in a girl from the record label offering me sex for my birthday present. As she did seem a little drunk and I had met a lovely girl a few days earlier, I politely declined her generous offer.

↑
Andy's notes on 'Tesla Girls'

TESLA GIRLS
WAS RELEASED

28 AUG 1984

UK TOUR SEPTEMBER 1984

DUNCAN LEWIS
The Reverb Brothers front of house & tour manager

When they put the full band together, they really did put it together from mates who had played in the bands back home. I thought that was great. They invited us onto the Junk Culture tour. I was doing out-front sound, helping a band called the Reverb Brothers, really good but stylistically the most unlikely support band for OMD. It was really kind of them to offer that slot when they were doing sold-out gigs, reaching back and helping another friend's band from the area.

When we went on that tour, the proverbial jaw hit the floor. You grew up pretty quickly and saw how far they'd gone and were still going. As individuals they'd be very grown up in the industry whereas we were seeing the real magic properly for the first time. I was also struck by the number of people on the tour from Meols, Hoylake or West Kirby. That was brilliant.

We hired a motorhome because we couldn't afford hotels, living in that for three or four weeks. We told the motorhome company we were using it to go fishing. When we gave it back they looked at the mileage and said, 'Some fish, that!'

Then they asked us to join them on the European dates and we did that tour on InterRail cards. They moved the equipment for us and we existed on sleeper trains or in various bed and breakfasts across Europe. We got to meet all the guys in the 'barmy army' and some of them travelled with us on trains across Europe. They were an amazing bunch and it was a wonderful experience.

OMD - 1984

Mirelle Davis meets Andy during the '84 UK tour not knowing that one day she will manage OMD

DE MONTFORT HALL
19 September 1984, Leicester, UK

LEE MCNULTY

One of my lasting memories is from the 1984 Junk Culture tour. The band was going to play 'Locomotion' next and the Fairlight computer crashed. They didn't panic. Paul went to work, trying to get it back up and running. It seemed to take a long time, but I guess it was only a few minutes.

ROYAL CONCERT HALL
22 September 1984, Nottingham, UK

MIRELLE DAVIS
OMD manager since 2010

This will always be a special gig for me, as it was outside the Royal Theatre that I met one of my very best friends, Pauline. She and her then-boyfriend Paul came by train from Southampton and were standing outside the stage door surrounded by what appeared to be every possession they owned to be signed by the band. Paul, Pauline and I became part of the so-called

'Barmy Army' who followed OMD from venue to venue. The band split, as did Paul and Pauline, and that's when she and I discovered we had way more in common than a liking for OMD.

There was our love of food and travel and our ability to be happy in our own and each other's company. Most of all, a shared sense of humour that has kept us laughing to this day … and many more things I couldn't possibly write here. My love of OMD has lasted more than 35 years but I'm sure my friendship with Pauline will last even longer.

HAMMERSMITH ODEON

2 October 1984, London, UK

CLIFF BOWNES

Lucky enough to get seats in the first few rows, I took one of my favourite pictures of Paul, surrounded by all his technology. That particular show has special memories for my wife Sharon and me, as it was just before we married. The first time I saw the band was as a teenager in 1980 at Hammersmith on the Organisation tour. I have this vivid recollection of 'Stanlow', one of my top OMD tracks, performed with blue lights and enough dry ice to fill Wembley Stadium.

HAMMERSMITH ODEON

3 October 1984, London, UK

JIMMY RAE
Ex-Reverb Brothers

We were all at school together on the Wirral, with Andy a year ahead at Calday Grange, very much a larger-than-life figure, with crazy corkscrew hair and eccentric style of dress. He really stood out, was a really nice guy, and we got on very well.

They took off very quickly on becoming Orchestral Manoeuvres in the Dark. I remember buying 'Electricity', at Probe Records, Liverpool, then seeing them at Eric's a few days later.

I was more into rockabilly and 60s stuff but saw straight away they were going to do well. There was something very different and engaging about them, Andy is such a powerful front-man, and they had great songs. We watched them heading towards *Top of the Pops* and big tours of their own.

also ex-Calday School, and we were starting to get attention on the local circuit, playing universities and bigger venues.

Although we weren't musically like OMD, we had a similar sort of slightly eccentric approach, using backing tracks for our fusion of drum machine technology, 50s and 60s rockabilly and Beatles-type influences. We were a bit of an odd support band for that tour.

We got into an after-show party and I chatted to Andy over a beer and said, 'Next time you're touring, if you want a band that'll get your audience warmed up, give us a shout. We'd love to do it.' Not really thinking he would. A month or so later he rang and said, 'We're doing some dates, do you fancy opening for us?'

It was a fantastic opportunity. We'd never played before crowds much bigger than about 300 people. To suddenly play venues like Hammersmith Odeon was tremendously exciting. It was Andy's generosity that led to that. Very often support bands had to pay the bigger bands for the privilege of playing. We had no money. We were completely self-financing, and unsigned. We couldn't afford to 'buy on', so they very kindly agreed to pay us, another lovely gesture.

We travelled from gig to gig in a motorhome, which seemed the most sensible way of getting five guys and various equipment around. We did all the UK gigs on the cheap, sleeping in our smelly 'The Cheese on Wheels' motorhome (nicknamed by OMD's road-crew), getting to play some fantastic venues.

↑ Supporting OMD The Reverb Brothers travelled from gig to gig in a motorhome

I had a real sense of pride that these Hoylake and Meols guys had done so well. I stayed in touch with Andy, seeing him every now and then around Hoylake when he was home. By then I'd formed the Reverb Brothers with Colin Free,

On the final night at Hammersmith Odeon, we had a lot of record companies in. It wasn't our best performance, but led to RCA signing us. I have Andy directly to thank for that. That chance might never have come along had we not been playing that gig.

We thought it was all over and came home full of tales on the road, then got another call from their then-manager, saying, 'Do you want to do some European dates?' We jumped at that chance and then wondered how we were going to be able to afford it, ending up getting student EuroRail tickets and doing that tour by train with a mixture of taxis and buses, OMD's crew carrying our gear. I'm eternally grateful for that opportunity.

We ended up at RCA with David Van Day of Dollar as our manager, releasing a couple of singles that sadly didn't chart. Now I'm a solo artist with my own band, Jimmy Rea and the Moonshine Girls, an independent country rock band, with two albums behind me.

PHILIPS HALLE

12 October 1984, Düsseldorf, West Germany

ULRICH POHL

Today is the day. At 18 I'm seeing OMD live for the first time. Nervous, I stand out front and wait to enter. After what feels like an eternity, we are allowed in but the huge hall is empty with no stage. At the other end is a curtain. I look behind and see multi-storey scaffolding, musical instruments and Winston the legendary tape recorder. After just over an hour, musicians enter the colourful back-lit scaffolding - the four members of OMD. The rest is history.

HAMMERSMITH ODEON

16 October 1984,
London, UK

TRACY SCHOFIELD

I was 14 when *Dazzle Ships* came out. Robert, a sixth-former I had a crush on, was carrying the LP and I liked the cover, so went out and bought it. My first concert was on the Junk Culture tour and I've never looked back. I haven't converted my children, but my 18-year old bought me *The Punishment of Luxury* at Christmas.

NEVER TURN AWAY WAS RELEASED

29 OCT 1984

ANDY MCCLUSKEY

Our raison d'etre was always to keep doing something different, so when we got the Fairlight for the *Junk Culture* album it had brass samples on it. We did 'Locomotion' with a real brass section in Holland, which Tony Visconti scored for us. It was the only thing he did for us before he left, because he didn't like the mess the tapes were in.

Our manager at the time also managed Fiction Factory, from Scotland, who had friends who played brass with them. The manager said, 'If you want a real brass section on tour, these guys play other instruments. You've got so much on tape and they'd give you spare hands for keyboards and bass', so we got the Weir brothers in, Graham and Neil.

'Locomotion' was the first single from the *Junk Culture* album and the Weir brothers were brought in to add a bit of colour on TV. There was brass on the record and we wanted brass with us on screen. We didn't get to hear them play at first. When we did, we realised, 'Shit, these guys are actually quite good.'

The Weir brothers were different to the rest of us. Paul and I were totally self-taught and can only play our own songs. We can't sit down and jam and we've never tried to play other people's songs. Whereas Neil and Graham were trained musicians and like Stuart Kershaw, they could read sheet music and play anything. They can go into a bar with other people and go, 'Play a 12-bar blues? No problem' 'Jumpin' Jack Flash'? No problem' and get up and play while we'd sit and watch. I wouldn't even know the words to 'Jumpin' Jack Flash.'

We didn't audition them. We didn't hear them play until we went off to De Haan in Belgium to rehearse, because we were tax exiles and couldn't be based in the UK. We stayed in an L-shaped farmhouse. In the corner of the 'L', one room had drapes visible through the keyhole. We thought it was the owner's stuff in storage while the house was rented out. The day we were leaving, the girl behind the bar in town said, 'I think you're so brave to have stayed in that house all this time.' When we asked why, she said, 'Because of the murder.' The woman who lived there murdered her family and got out of jail not long ago. I said, 'I'm glad you

← Paul on stage at the Hammersmith Odeon 1984. Photo by Cliff Bownes didn't tell us that while we were living here!'

We were there several months, through the whole summer doing TV shows, and used to rehearse the band in the school hall round the corner. We were rehearsing one day, I started playing the bass-line to 'Julia's Song', Malcolm played along, Paul started, and the Weir brothers joined in, and I went, 'That's fucking great. Why don't we do this as a B side?' The Weirs said, 'What do you mean?' 'Your brass solos were good on 'Julia's Song.' 'That was a song? We thought you were jamming. We were just joining in, in that key.' So there's a version of 'Julia's Song' with brass on, all these little phrases they knew off by heart. That's how good they were as musicians. The dangerous thing was that really well trained musicians can lead you down the dark roads to compromise and convention.

Initially you go, 'that's new, that's different. We haven't heard that sound before.' Then you look back and go, 'we shouldn't have done that. It's not Orchestral Manoeuvres in the Dark anymore.' A lot of people stopped listening to OMD when we got a brass section.

That was part of the band degenerating into a very conventional mid-80s electro-funk pop band, and in hindsight I wish we hadn't. Once they were in the band they started to influence the musical direction and the way we sounded on stage. We went further and further away from our minimal, clear-thinking electronic roots. It wasn't their fault. It was ours, but we lost direction.

Having the Weir brothers in the band created new tensions. Every band has politics. There was Paul and me, then there was me, Paul, Malcolm and Martin … and the Weir brothers. You could divide it into several different ways. The Weir brothers weren't earning much money. They were very good jobbing musicians looking to maximise their earning potential. They thought they could get more out of being more involved in the song writing. We never made money on tour until a few years ago. In trying to take care of business and keep costs down, management at the time were treating the Weir brothers like session musicians, and unfortunately Martin and Malcolm sometimes got treated like session musicians too. Martin and Malcolm were employees and sometimes were treated less well than Paul and I by managers and record labels.

Neil's memory of going on strike at Christmas in Australia was the management saying, 'We're not going to pay you today, because you're not working. If we do, we're going to lose money. You've got to go home.'

There were these pay gradations. Management's position was, 'Paul and Andy signed the contract, you two (Mal and Martin) have been in the band for five years and you two (the Weirs) are definitely session musicians. You're not in the band.' Except they were photographed with the rest of us as being in the band, so yeah, it was a bit messy. And because it was messy, people had concerns and frustrations over the way they were perceived.

NEIL WEIR
musician

My whole family have been musicians for a long time. And from our parents telling us all our lives to avoid music as a career, we all ended up doing it. My brother Graham and I had been playing together as a brass section. For three or four years we'd been establishing ourselves, primarily around Edinburgh, building up a lot of session work. We got a session to do an album with Fiction Factory, who had the same management as OMD. I had a particularly virulent strain of glandular fever during the recording of that album. Very shortly after, we got the call to go and audition with OMD for a two-week tour of Spain.

They were living in Belgium at the time, a place called De Haan.

Graham and I met them at Heathrow to catch a flight to Brussels on 1 April, 1984. The band were staying in a farmhouse and using the village hall for rehearsals. We went out to do the audition but spent most of the next 12 weeks travelling around Europe, city by city, doing promo stuff for 'Locomotion.' We never auditioned. The band didn't see us play a note for a long period. We were in a bar in Madrid or Barcelona after doing a TV show, Graham and I around the piano playing, jamming and doing songs and stuff before Andy and Paul had heard us. I said to Andy, 'You don't even know if we can play.' He said, 'If you can play a few notes that's a damn sight better than we can do.'

Eventually, in downtime between promo stuff, we went to the village hall and rehearsed. Graham and I were trying to push them away from backing tapes and programmed synths, saying, 'Let's do more live playing, because we can play keys and everything else as well.' It started as a two-week tour of Spain, and four years later I found myself in the Rose Bowl, LA, thinking, 'How the hell did we get here?'

It was magnificent fun. I was 22. We were young boys really. We'd been doing session work with Hue and Cry, Love and Money, Wet Wet Wet, all these kinds of bands, pretty much the only horn players in Scotland at the time,

↑
Graham and Neil Weir

with a lot of work around. It was very carefree. We were just doing whatever came along.

Playing places like the Fillmore in San Francisco and Red Rocks in Colorado with OMD was phenomenal. We were in the States for such long periods, round and round America, over and over and backwards and forwards, gradually doing a bigger gig each time. Dearborn, Illinois was great, playing in an outdoor amphitheatre, lazing around in the sun, pre-sound check, totally chilled.

Everybody was pals, so we were all goosed up to do it. On the first big tour of America, the crew and band shared the one bus. Eventually, as productions got bigger there was more crew and more money to pay for the buses and we'd get a band bus and a crew bus, or a couple of crew buses.

We did mammoth drives from Vancouver right down to Texas, a two and a half, three-day drive. It meant hours and hours of backgammon, Pass the Pigs, liar dice and so on for days on end, staring at the scenery going by.

Playing in Japan was memorable. Where they're all so polite and they'd barely even clap at the end of a tune. That was an interesting experience. Glasgow Apollo was a phenomenal gig. I'd seen people like Slade and The Boomtown Rats, always thinking to myself I'd love to be up on that stage. Hammersmith Odeon, Liverpool and Manchester were always memorable.

Whenever there was any downtime and days off between gigs, Martin, Mal, Graham and I would look for something to do that was different and exciting. One time we had a couple of days off in Chicago in an absolute shithole of a motel. The floors were flooded from a burst ice machine. It was rotten, in the middle of nowhere. Across the road was a camping shop. Mal and myself wandered over and thought 'Bugger it, let's buy a tent.' We bought a tent, a camping light, a stove and fishing rods, sleeping bags, the works. We went to the tour manager, Gus, 'Don't pay for our hotel rooms. We're not going to use them. Give us the money to pay for the tent.'

We hired a car and went to Bear Lake, a big forest area just outside Chicago, went wild camping with all this gear that we abandoned after two days. Mal was, and still is, an avid fisherman, which I've always teased him about mercilessly as I never saw him catch a fish, despite us going fishing together dozens of times. On this occasion, we were out rowing in a small fishing boat we'd hired. Graham tied a bit of fishing line round his toe with a hook on it and a worm dangling in the water. He was lying back with a beer can in his hand and was the only one of us that caught a fish that whole afternoon. Which was great to wind Mal up.

I remember one time flying to the Bahamas for a day, hiring a yacht, sailing around for a day and having a nice meal at night. We then had to drive from Miami to Texas in the back of the swag truck with all the merchandise.

Wherever we were, we'd find out what the best restaurant was and Graham, Martin, Mal and myself would go somewhere nice for dinner, to experience something different and not have another hangover. Well, we might still have a hangover but at least we'd had a good dinner beforehand!

We did a little four-seater seaplane trip once. You had to row out to it and clamber on. That flew us up the coast north of Sydney to a place called Whale Beach, where there was a restaurant on top of the cliff. It was phenomenal, with dolphins leaping in and out of the surf. We all ate lobster.

Sometimes you'd just sit back and think, 'Is this really happening?'

We were in San Francisco and Graham and I decided to go for a helicopter trip round Alcatraz. It was a horrible, windy day and the trip was cut short because it was so windy they couldn't land the helicopter. The next one that loaded up crashed in the sea, with everybody killed. We saw it on the news later, thinking, 'Shit, that was the one straight after us.'

Shortly after, we flew into Heathrow, with a bomb in Terminal 3. We narrowly missed that as well, having got the bags and off we went. We missed that by a few hours.

Another time we flew to Amsterdam, and as we were leaving the Sonesta Hotel in the morning we had a couple of hire cars we were driving. Martin, Mal and myself were parked at the front of the hotel and were just loading the bags in at the revolving doors. It was a big glass-fronted hotel and, as I was coming through the revolving doors, a bunch of skinheads in paramilitary gear were coming in. I came out and said to Mal and Martin, 'I'm sure those guys just said something about a bomb. Let's shift.' Mally and I ran up behind the nearest wall at the side of the hotel. Martin decides to go and have a quick look to see what's going on. He began sauntering back towards the revolving doors. I grabbed him by the scruff of the neck, hauled him away and said, 'Martin – shift!' and we dived behind this wall just before the whole frontage was blown out by a paint, bolts and ball-bearing bomb. They were protesting against mass tourism in Amsterdam. I remember sitting down afterwards, thinking, 'What the hell's going on here? We're dodging fate an awful lot. This can only go on for so long before something catches up with us.'

We went on strike in Hawaii. That was me, Graham, Mal and Martin again. We refused to get on stage and refused to leave the hotel in Hawaii because we were going for a few gigs and were going to be in Australia over Christmas but management wouldn't pay for flying us back home or for accommodation there. We were just going to be dumped there. We said, 'We're on strike. Until this is sorted there's no more gigs. We're not going anywhere. We're staying in Hawaii at this hotel, at the band's expense. Simple as that.' It was quickly sorted out.

Ten per cent of your day is spent on stage and the rest of it's spent hanging around, busy doing nothing. One of the ways we'd amuse ourselves was that we made puppet shows on the tour bus at night. Andy and Paul had these enormous video cameras,

↑ Andy meeting fans in his Versace jacket (with massive rubber shoulders)

and Martin bought a slightly smaller version. We'd get cuddly toys thrown on the stage all the time and they were distributed to hospitals and children's homes, but the odd one or two bizarre ones we'd keep. There was a toy shrunken head made of leather, 'Shrinky', and we designed a whole puppet show around him, a Johnny Carson-type show. We spent hours filming and making sets for this puppet show. The toaster from the bus was his desk he used to sit behind. We had a clockwork-dancing penguin too. It was stop-frame animation and we spent hours shifting stuff around slightly to get each shot. I think Martin still has all that. We did it out of sheer boredom.

AVONIEL LEISURE CENTRE

19 October 1984, Belfast, UK

MARION MURPHY

I grew up in Belfast and this was the first year I was allowed to start going to concerts because of security concerns. There were many exciting bands to go and see that year, but my favourite was OMD. It was my 19th birthday and I managed to get quite close to the stage. They always come to Belfast in October to help me celebrate my birthday!

DARYN BUCKLEY

In the summer of 1984, having done well in my O-levels, I visited my school's sixth-form common room, wearing my *Junk Culture* T-shirt. I heard a shout from the back that sounded something like 'Love OMD' and then the sound of 'Telegraph' from the record player. It made my mind up - further education wouldn't be so bad.

Once I started sixth-form, I learned that the voice behind that shout was Vikki McMenemie, from the year above. We became friends, then boyfriend and girlfriend. We bought a house together and even got married.

And in 1985, she did the ultimate thing for me: writing to the Orchestral Manoeuvres in the Dark fan club asking to transfer her membership over to me because she loved me so much.

The fan club were so impressed by this amazing show of love that they sent us a bundle of goodies, including a Telegraph scarf each, a copy of 'Messages' each, and some badges. They also kept both of us as members. Whilst, ultimately, it didn't quite work out with Vikki, we remain friends and both still love OMD.

LEISURE LAND

20 October 1984, Galway, Ireland

MIRELLE DAVIS
OMD manager

There was a show in Ireland and we decided we were going. That's Alison, Wendy, Paul and Pauline and myself. What's the big deal? I told my family I was going to Ireland and to say they were furious was an understatement. My brother, also a student in Manchester at the time, tried to stop me. It was pistols at dawn, or in this case in the middle of the night. Nice Jewish girls didn't follow bands. They did not approve of my actions.

I left anyway. I was alone and took a late train from Manchester to Holyhead, then an overnight ferry to Dublin. I was terrified, sat bolt upright all night, surrounded by singing drunks. I can't remember what time I arrived in Dun Laoghaire, but I got a bus to the train station and sat there in the waiting room with a book, waiting for the others. Boy, was I happy to see them arrive. We took a train to Galway and I think it was then that 'Locomotion' truly became our song, having taken just about every form of transport to get there.

Galway became the start of my international travels. As the band's manager I've subsequently seen them all over the world and no one bats an eyelid if I say now I'm off to LA for an OMD gig.

ANDY MCCLUSKEY

Galway was a real party atmosphere, '84 had been a very successful year. However, the drive back to Dublin was most unpleasant. A crew member decided to adorn the band's hire car engine with various pieces of rotting fish found on the beach. It slowly cooked during the journey and the stench was utterly sickening!

1985

OMD spent most of 1985 touring the UK, Europe and North America

SO IN LOVE	
WAS RELEASED	**13 MAY 1985**

LIVE AND IN LOVE

■ OMD ARE back with their single 'So In Love' on May 13. Not only is it available in the regular size, 'So In Love' also comes in seven inch doublepack and 12 inch formats.

'So In Love' is taken from their forthcoming album 'Crush' but the B-side 'Concrete' will be unavailable elsewhere. The 12 inch version features extended versions of both songs, while the double pack has a bonus record featuring Maria Galiante and a live version of 'White Trash'.

OMD will be playing a few live dates to warm themselves up for foreign parts and you can see them at Oxford Polytechnic June 8, Guildford Civic Hall 9, Warrington Spectrum Arena 10, Norwich East Anglia University 11, Chippenham Goldiggers 12, Loughborough University 13.

OMD look likely to be playing an anti racist festival with Culture Club in Wembley sometime during the summer, but nothing has been definitely confirmed.

An action packed OMD feature will be in next week's RECORD MIRROR.

ROCK AGAINST RACISM

15 June 1985, Place de Concorde, Paris, France

ANDY MCCLUSKEY

We were honoured to be asked to perform at such a prestigious gig for a great cause. But we never played. I had stupidly eaten steak tartar for my dinner, immediately contracted food poisoning and began throwing up. The whole event was so badly organised that the stage times were being pushed back later and later. I decided I would hang on in there and do it despite feeling terrible. The massive crowd were very patient, and our crew finally got our equipment onstage three hours late at 1am. Just as we are climbing the steps to start, the band Telephone jump the queue and start performing before us on the other stage. I just walked off saying 'Fuck it!'

CRUSH
WAS RELEASED

17 JUN 1985

CRUSH

Junk Culture saw us having hits again, but album sales did not really recapture *Architecture and Morality* levels. We finally succumbed to record company pressure and allowed a producer back into the studio with us. Stephen Hague had been very successful with New Order and the Pet Shop Boys but there were personality and musical clashes on the *Crush* album recordings.

ANDY MCCLUSKEY

PAUL HUMPHREYS

We got more and more conventional, particularly as we tried to break America, and we got Stephen Hague in, who's an American producer, to help shape our sound for America and American radio. Stephen's a great producer and he's made some amazing records and he's done some great things for us, but he was always a bit of a control freak in the studio. It had to be Steve's way, which is probably the way he works and it might have been a good thing or it might not, but Andy and I always resented Steve's input into everything. It was almost like we'd lost control. Andy and I are control freaks also when it comes to our music, and that's why after our experience with Steve Hague we never used a producer ever again.

For the last three albums, in the newly reincarnated OMD, Andy and I produce everything. We rarely allow another voice to come in. We allowed it in the 80s, because we were convinced that the way out of our financial hole was to break America so we allowed Stephen Hague to produce us. And credit to him, he got us big trans Atlantic hits with 'So in Love' and '(Forever) Live and Die', and they still sounds great now. Although you could argue that I produced most of 'Forever (Live & Die)' and he just recorded it well. But whether it was his input in our sound or not, we did break America after working with Steve. And I can't leave out the contribution of Grammy Award winning engineer/producer Tom Lord Alge in us breaking America, as he co-produced 'If You leave' with us.

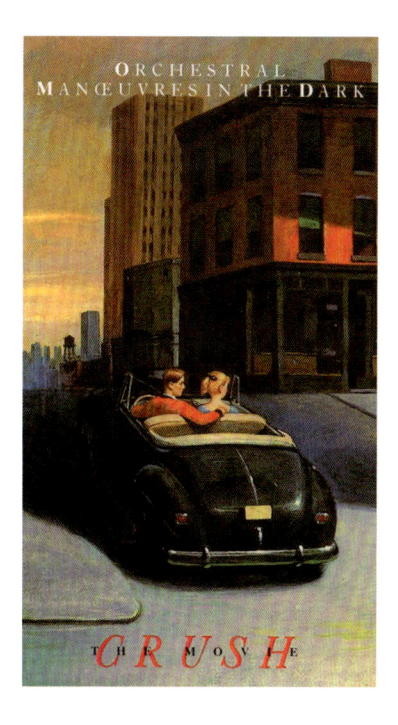

←
Record Mirror announces news of OMD's latest single 'So In Love'

OMD – 1985

> OMD will be doing a few warm up concerts, without their full production. The shows will feature some or all of the songs from the new album 'CRUSH'.
> The venues are as follows:
>
> Saturday 8th June — Oxford Polytechnic
> Sunday 9th June — Guilford Civic Hall
> Monday 10th June — Warrington Spectrum
> Tuesday 11th June — Norwich University East Anglia
> Wednesday 12th June — Chippenham Golddiggers
> Thursday 13th June — Loughborough University

Press release announcing the Crush *album warm-up shows*

PAUL ABUNDIS

The year 1985 saw my discovery of OMD. *Crush* seemed to hold true to the synth music I had grown so fond of. Any chance I got, I'd go to the record store and buy another OMD release, eventually searching for a copy of every 12" release. I was drunk on OMD, wanted everything and never disappointed.

STADT GARDEN

29 June 1985, Hamburg, West Germany

FRANK JASCHKE & ANDREW

I was 13 when my father bought the *Architecture & Morality* LP, as the single 'Souvenir' was already sold out. He found the album too weird and gave it to me. There was born a new OMD fan.

In the 80s the Cold War was still on-going. In West Berlin we were surrounded by a wall. That's when Andrew and I became friends at school. We had one thing in common: a passion for OMD. We were allowed to see them in concert in October 1984 at the Berlin Metropol and it was an overwhelming, unforgettable experience. We even picked up an autograph from Andy and Paul. We were looking forward to many more. But then the autumn 1985 tour in Germany was cancelled other than an open-air show in Hamburg. We had to go.

We were not of legal age, only had a little pocket money, and between Berlin and Hamburg was the GDR. That wasn't going to stop us. We played the old trick, telling our parents we'd stay overnight at each other's. We made it to the border and thumbed a lift to Hamburg in a rickety car. The car broke down

← Two photos Frank Jaschke took of OMD at the Stadtgarden, Hamburg in 1985

on the way, so it was very late when we arrived, the hostels closed. It was cold. The central station was warm, but the floor next to the lockers was hard. The police asked if our parents knew where we are. Luckily, our 'yes' was convincing.

Next morning, we still had to get concert tickets. Again, we were lucky. We then went quickly to the Stadtpark. We were in the front row, only a small wall and patch of grass separating us from our heroes: Andy, Paul, Mal, Martin, and the Weir brothers.

Then came the encores. The singer of China Crisis, the opening act, came up to us and pulled us and other fans onto the stage to dance - so we were dancing right next to Andy and Paul. We were so close! Did we get into trouble when we made it back to West Berlin? No! Our parents hadn't noticed anything wrong.

GLC JOBS FOR A CHANGE FESTIVAL BATTERSEA PARK

7 July 1985, London, UK

NEIL HOLLIDAY

Me, an Aswad fan and two girls went, parking miles away and following the crowds. It was a fantastic day and a chance to see OMD front a big festival. I was worried the odd mix of bands would mean a lot of people would loathe their music (Aswad to OMD was a bit of a jump) but you can't keep Andy McCluskey down and within five minutes everyone was dancing.

I had one of the girls, who I was hopelessly hooked on, sat on my shoulders, when McCluskey buzzed across the stage, gave her a grin and mouthed, 'You having a good time?' I wanted to yell out, 'Ask me, I buy the bloody records, she's a Culture Club fan,' but by the time I'd thought of it he was about a mile away on the other side of the stage.

STEVE CAVEY

In 1981 I heard a strange bagpipe-type sound from my twin brother's latest album purchase on the music centre. I fell down the stairs in my rush to find out what this strange music was. 'Maid of Orleans' was on the deck and a 37-year love affair started. I've been to 40-odd concerts since, most post-2007 due to finance being more available as an adult, from Battersea Park in 1985 to Las Vegas in 2011 and taking in Brighton, Liverpool, London, New York, Paris, and Bognor Regis.

STEWART CRANER

Our parents said it was okay for us to go, but we didn't realise OMD were headlining, consequently missing our train home and having to wait overnight in the National Express depot for the next bus home, terrifying our parents. We survived.

MIKA RONKAINEN

I was in love for the very first time. A new girl joined our class at school, different from all the others. But I was too shy to approach her. That summer I heard 'Secret' on the radio. It was like part of my life. I found my story in it. The following spring, school ended and our paths separated. Still, every time I heard 'Secret', the memories came back.

Some 30 years later I met her again. We talked over and over again. The old feelings came back, grew even stronger. I realised what real love is. We both did. Now we share each day together, living the best days of our lives. It is no surprise that I have listened to 'Secret' and the whole *Crush* album a lot lately.

AMY UNSWORTH

I was born in 1989 but brought up with 80s music. When I was younger, my family and I had days out in the North West of England or Wales in the car, listening to 80s hits. OMD were always on the playlist and I grew to love them. One song in particular is always there, 'Secret.' Every time it comes on, I can't help but smile, thinking of those precious memories with my family. It never fails to cheer me up when I'm sad. Now, the words resonate with me in another way. A longing need to hold someone's hand but having to keep it secret. The song has so much meaning to me in different ways. It has become so special to me.

GARY HODGSON
The Id guitarist & OMD keyboard tech

It was '85 when I started as a tech. Mal Holmes spoke to the tour manager about me. I was a friend of his and had the electronics experience as a civilian working for the RAF. I don't know how much Andy and Paul had to do with it. The keyboards they were using were very unreliable, breaking down virtually every day on tour, and they needed someone to look after them.

Some techs held it against me a little bit because I'd gone straight

OMD – 1985

into the big time. I did three tours with OMD and remember a gig in New York where I started the tape machine halfway through the first song. Paul knew, but I don't know how much Andy knew about that. I held my hands up straight away and said, 'Sorry about that!' We had a slot supporting The Power Station. Support slots were really good. You'd be on stage at 7.30 or eight and doing a half-hour set, so you'd be packed away by nine. It was great fun. You'd get on the tour bus in the States and get off it 30 hours later.

We were travelling from a West Coast city to Salt Lake City and had to cross the Rockies. We got stuck halfway up a mountain in a snowstorm. It was horrendous.

The rear ventilation hatch on the roof of the bus blew off, leaving just a hole, and it was freezing. We all moved to the front of the bus and then the front hatch blew off. Then the bus got stuck and we all got out because we didn't know if it was safe or if it could slide back down the mountain. Remember that scene from *Fawlty Towers*, where John Cleese attacks his car with a tree branch? Gus the tour manager, the same tour manager who also superglued his hands together, had two hands on the back of the bus and was attempting to push it up the hill. I was looking at him, thinking, 'What the hell are you doing, you idiot?' Those things are absolutely enormous. He was asking us to help. 'Come on, if we all push …'

SECRET
WAS RELEASED

8 JUL 1985

REUNION ARENA
21 July 1985, Dallas, Texas

COLLEEN THEIS
The Orchard, OMD's current US distributor

I first saw OMD live supporting The Power Station at Reunion Arena. I was obsessed with British new wave, Duran Duran in particular. So when John and Andy Taylor formed their side-project, I had to be there, and with OMD on the bill too ... event of the summer.

This was before OMD's big US breakthrough with 'If You Leave'. But I knew about them from the guys who worked at Bill's Records, Dallas' epicentre of cool music discovery in the 80s, where I spent thousands of hours and dollars getting my music education. I'd also read about them in import mags like *NME* and heard them on DJ George Gimarc's radio show, *The Rock and Roll Alternative*.

I bought *Crush* on cassette and LP, memorising every lyric in preparation. I especially loved 'So in Love.' Both 'Secret' and 'Enola Gay' were club staples at Dallas 80s era hotspots, Starck Club, Mistral, and Trax - all of which I frequented, putting my fake ID, radical fashion and beauty skills to good use.

That steamy hot night in July, my 16-year-old self headed downtown with a concert-frequenting gang of alterna-types: goths, skaters, new wavers, glams. Most of my friends only wanted to see OMD, such cool electro-pioneers.

After that show I was truly hooked. Power Station were OK too. We headed to Starck Club from there, continuing to dance the night away.

More than 30 years on, I've seen the band countless times. And since meeting them via their manager Mirelle in 2012, I'm now lucky enough to work with Paul and Andy as OMD continues to release new music and tour the world. The experience of working with people whose talent you truly admire and finding they are gracious and wonderful has been utterly rewarding and totally fucking awesome.

COW PALACE
29 July 1985, San Francisco, California

KRISTA HAMBY

My first experience with OMD was seeing them open for Power Station at the Cow Palace. I was 15. I really had no idea who they were, but instantly loved them. I went out and purchased *Crush* the next day. Soon, I had their entire back-catalogue on vinyl. I became obsessed with *Dazzle Ships*, playing it constantly. Later that year, I bought a ticket to The Thompson Twins at Oakland Coliseum Arena just because OMD were opening. In December '86 I saw my first headlining OMD show at the Warfield Theater, San Francisco, a 100-mile round-trip the night before my SATs, the band inspiring me, passing the tests at a high enough level to get into college.

And whenever I went out to a club or concert I made sure

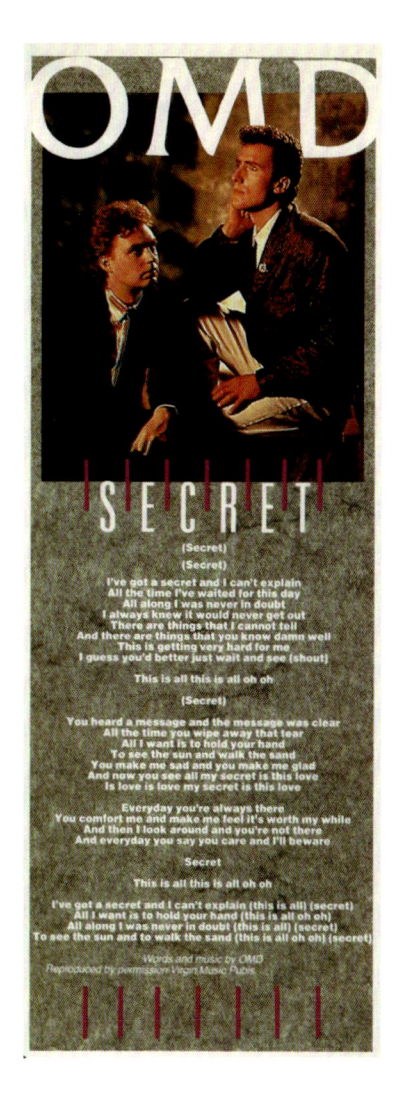

OMD - 1985

everyone knew I considered myself a graduate of the Andy McCluskey School of Dance.

SEATTLE CENTER COLISEUM

1 August 1985, Seattle, Washington

SUSANNE SWANSON

In 1980 I was 10-years-old, unhappy at my parents moving me from the city of Seattle to a middle-of-nowhere town called Belfair on Hood Canal. We didn't have stoplights and to get to a mall you had to drive 30 minutes. I was stranded. I didn't fit in. I was a city girl into music, movies and fashion.

By the time I was 13 I was a huge Duran Duran fan, dreaming of getting out of the town I was stuck in. I felt I should have been born in England, so when The Power Station came through Seattle I was there ready to get it on. I adored John Taylor. Who didn't?

Durannies were out in full force, but the opener was a band called OMD and I knew really nothing of who they were. The only thing I remember was Andy dancing all over the place, but I loved the music and knew they would be one of my favourites. I found them fascinating. My love for OMD started here.

In 1986, *Pretty in Pink* came out and I could so relate to the movie. It has a special place in my heart and remains my favourite. The soundtrack was amazing, ohn Hughes was brilliant and wrote for my generation, and a piece of my childhood crumbled when he passed. 'If You Leave' became my favourite song, the movie and this song keeping me going.

MEMORIAL COLISEUM

2 August 1985, Portland, Oregon

CHRISTINE MAIR

My sister Kristi and I were so excited to be attending our second-ever concert, seeing The Power Station. We learned from our first that getting up early wasn't enough to ensure decent seats, so we queued overnight, sleeping on the sidewalk at GI Joe's in Gresham, Oregon. Staying up all night, we listened to music, ate junk food, and talked with others about bands we liked. So much fun at 14. Sadly, our seats were still at the back of the arena.

On the day we all dressed up in our best new wave 80s outfits, made our hair super big, and headed downtown. We went down early because they were having a poster contest, the winner set to meet the band. After hanging around a couple of hours, we really had to go to the bathroom. We tried every single door in the hope of finding something open, finally finding an unlocked door on the main concourse, visiting the women's room. Deciding to then mill around, these two guys in suits approached and we knew we were totally busted. But instead of saying, 'What are you doing in here?' they said 'We're the opening band! Have you ever heard of us?' We were like, 'Uh, no.' Andy and Paul then took a few minutes to tell us about their music and the tour and we took a bunch of pictures together on my Kodak Ektralite 110mm camera. We were ecstatic because we had just met our very first band.

We made our way back outside and joined the crowd assembling. When the concert started we decided this opening band was our kind of music and pretty flippin' good! I took a bunch of pictures, but later my camera was stolen and I was devastated.

FOX THEATER

6 August 1985,
St. Louis, Missouri

ANGELA ROGERS

I was 14 and attending a Power Station concert with my sister and three of her schoolfriends. All I knew about the opening act was that they were also English. The lights went down, OMD took the stage, and music as I knew it changed forever.

We danced and danced. I loved every single song. Their set ended and we began our wait for the main course. But I'd been won over. OMD had left me energised.

When the lights went down for the main act, I noticed that my sister and one of her friends had raced out of our row and up the side-aisle, next to the backstage door. Maybe two songs in, they came back and my sister blurted, 'We just met Andy McCluskey!' Tears instantly welled up. Come on, I was 14. 'I wanna meet Andy!' I cried. She took my hand and led me to the lobby where a tall man in a black trench coat was chatting. My sister walked up and after he'd finished his conversation, said, 'Excuse me

OMD - 1985

↑
Studio photo of Paul

→
Paul filming the 'So in Love' video

FILMING IN SPAIN

↑
Andy in Almeria

←
Mart, Mal and Paul applaud Andy (out of shot) being hung western style with a noose around his neck

1985

Andy, my sister really wanted to meet you.' He smiled and said, 'Hello.' I threw my arms around him and yelled, 'I love you guys!' Something I've never done before or since. He laughed, said, 'Thank you,' and I pried myself away, feeling sorry/not sorry for acting like a weirdo.

RICHFIELD COLISEUM

17 August 1985, Cleveland, Ohio

PAUL M. LYREN

I first heard OMD in early 1983 at my friend John Isham's house. It was their eponymous first album. We hunkered down in his basement bedroom in Akron, Ohio and the world changed. We'd recently discovered David Bowie, Kraftwerk, Roxy Music and Brian Eno, but OMD were something else altogether.

We spent hours deciphering and deconstructing 'Electricity', 'Julia's Song' and 'Messages' and calling the number for 'Red Frame/White Light', which in 1983 was rather expensive. We got in a lot of trouble from John's Mom when she saw the charges as someone actually picked up the phone but had no time for American teenagers being music nerds! 'Stanlow' rewired our concept of what a song could be and how it should be structured.

Within a few months of this epiphany we declared to our families that we wanted synthesisers and drum machines for all foreseeable birthdays and Christmases. We got summer jobs and bought a four-track Fostex tape recorder, a Korg Poly 61 (no midi) and Korg DDM-110 and 220s drum machines. We were on our way to being the US version of OMD, as Edelweiss! That was until *Dazzle Ships* blew our minds.

'The Romance of the Telescope' and 'Of All the Things We Made' had a level of pathos and beauty we had a hard time understanding. So sad and beautiful. 'ABC Auto Industry', 'Time Zones', 'Genetic Engineering' and 'Radio Prague' stretched our outlook of what pop music was. We'd already accepted that songs like 'Enola Gay' could have levels of meaning and that nothing was off the table metaphorically, but these sound sculptures messed with our heads in the best possible way.

In the summer of '85 I had tickets for The Power Station at Richfield. The opener was supposed to be Go West and I couldn't have cared less, but that changed a week before when OMD were announced. John came, as did my semi-girlfriend, only there to see John Taylor. Before the show started John and I roamed around. They closed off the back of the arena oval to accommodate the stage and stood there in plain view but utterly unmolested were Paul and Andy. John and I were about 20 feet away and snuck into a closed seat area for a better view. There was no way to traverse the set-up and get closer. We just yelled their names, freaking out. I think we scared them. Andy looked pensive, but saw us, waved and smiled, tapping Paul, who also waved and smiled. This went on a tad too long, but we were over the moon to have made contact with our heroes. They then went out to support *Crush* and destroyed a complacent, bored, Michael Des Barres-led Power Station, although Tony Thompson on drums was kind of awesome.

OMD returned that same year, playing a small venue in Cleveland with local band Home and Garden opening. They played a ton of older stuff to about 250 people in an 800-person theatre. Everyone mashed up front and Andy came out and sat at the edge to play 'Julia's Song', seemingly genuinely amazed at everyone singing along. They played two encores and security had to kick us all out amid a mini-riot. It was amazing, and I met my next girlfriend there. It was one of the best nights of my young life.

OMD showed a whole swathe of young technocratic kids yearning for the promise of the future that there was a way forward, and it could be equal parts sad and beautiful, danceable and ambient, experimental and pop, real and imagined. They wanted to change the world. They changed mine.

THE ICE BUCKET

There was a tour. I can't even remember which tour it was. Andy had been in a bad mood for weeks and weeks, and we'd all been fighting on the bus. The previous night he'd had a go at Mal on stage in front of the audience. Mal used drum sticks like telegraph poles because he used to hit them so hard, and because he used to break a lot of sticks he had a bucket of sticks. Andy said something derogatory to Mal in front of the crowd and Mal had had enough and emptied his sticks at Andy on stage. Andy was dodging these sticks and the crew were running around trying to pick them up. These kinds of things happen! The next night Andy said something derogatory about me, so I don't know how I picked up the ice bucket back stage but I managed to, and it was 'whoosh' and I tipped the contents over his head! I don't even know if he remembers it, but I do. I feel really bad about it now. But this is what happens on tour. You live in each other's pockets 24/7 and even the tiniest thing can rub you the wrong way and you obsess about it all day and it boils and boils and boils until you blow. Maybe Andy said something derogatory about me because I'd done something to wind him up. There could have been a reason why he did. I'm sure it wasn't all Andy's fault. You're sleeping on the same bus. You never get away from each other. And the tiniest little comment can be construed as an affront to your complete being.

PAUL HUMPHREYS

OMD - 1985

The 1985 Crush tour saw OMD playing over 150 shows

CIVIC CENTER

20 August 1985, Hartford, Connecticut

CHRISTINE SCHINELLA

I first fell in love with OMD when I heard 'Talking Loud and Clear' in 1984 on college radio station, WXCI. My favourite memory of the band was them replacing Go West last minute, supporting The Power Station. I was ecstatic. I begged and begged Dad to postpone our vacation plans. I was so grateful he did. During the concert, my friend and I were screaming so loud that

WARSAW STADIUM

21 September 1985, Warsaw, Poland

NEIL WEIR

We went to Warsaw when it was still behind the Iron Curtain, to a Greenpeace benefit gig. A plane was chartered for all these pop stars – including The Communards and Roger Daltrey - and we were in Warsaw for four or five days. You couldn't buy anything in the shops. You would walk into the supermarket and there would literally be six products on the shelf; a tin of tuna, a loaf of bread. Living this life of indulgence, we were seeing these lives where people had nothing.

We had the Polish secret police follow us everywhere, but one night were with Poland's top jazz pianist and he invited us back to his apartment for a party. He managed to get hold of a black market bottle of Johnnie Walker whisky. Some of the crew and some of the band went backs, drinking all his whisky, which probably cost him a year's wages. He'd never heard of a CD or CD player. You looked out the window and everything was grey and concrete.

We'd all been given the equivalent of six to eight months' zlotys to spend during the few days we were there. But there was absolutely nothing to spend it on and you couldn't take it out of the country. So while we were at his house, all of us were stuffing money into album sleeves and down the back of a couch and anywhere we could, rather than just handing it to him and embarrassing him. By the end of the night he must have had about 10 years' wages saved around his flat waiting to be found. I'd have loved to have seen his reaction when he started to find it all.

ANDY MCCLUSKEY

We filmed the video for 'La Femme Accident' in London on the day of the European Cup final at the Heysel Stadium. I returned to my hotel room for a break between shooting delighted to be able to watch Liverpool on the TV. The horror that unfolded with 39 dead made returning to filming that night seem utterly trivial!

Andy acknowledged us, saying something like, 'Some people know us.' We weren't so close to the stage, so must have been loud!

OMD – 1985

LA FEMME ACCIDENT	12 OCT 1985
WAS RELEASED	

TOM BAILEY
The Thompson Twins

Pop music often forces itself on to our awareness with some gimmick or other. I remember all the fuss about OMD when they first caught the attention of the British music press and fans.

Finally, we all thought, a great band from the UK who can show us the way to pop innovation with technology at the core of their ideas. What an edgy and futuristic sound! And the cool, not to say bleak, world-view of their songs was all part of the appeal. But it was sometime later, touring together in the USA, that I realised a profoundly universal musicality, especially in their melodies, surpassed all the hipness: I found myself singing along backstage every night. To this day, listening to 'Souvenir' or 'Enola Gay' and other songs transports me to a powerfully nostalgic place, with all the associations of that great time. I expect we'll be enjoying them well into the future. Could all this be any better? Yes: they're great people, too!

IRVINE MEADOWS AMPHI THEATER
2 November 1985, Laguna Hills, California

DARREN ROSS
Magic Castle Hotel
Los Angeles, California

On a Saturday morning in 1984, I saw the video for 'Locomotion.' I was 13 that first time I heard OMD and was immediately drawn to Andy's voice. I thought it was incredible. Mom bought me the Junk Culture album and I listened to it constantly then started listening to the earlier releases, thinking it the best music I'd ever heard.

From seeing them for the first time supporting The Thompson Twins at Irvine Meadows, to the second row at the Rose Bowl in June 1988 and many times since, they're without a doubt one of the best live bands ever.

Come 2011, operating a hotel in Hollywood, California, I receive an email from a travel agent I know in New York. A band called OMD are going on tour and need rooms. I called right away, saying, 'Joe, you have to get them here. You don't understand. I want them at our hotel.'

While OMD was still in planning mode, I emailed Joe letting him know I wouldn't charge the four band members and offered the crew and management ridiculously low rates. It worked, and they stayed. I found out their favourite drinks and had them waiting for them. In Andy and Paul's rooms I included copies of a picture taken of the two of them with me and my cousin in the mid-80s. On their copies, it read, 'Your Hotel General Manager. Thanks for all the great music' With a Sharpie marker I drew an arrow pointing to my face as a teenager, writing, 'A long time ago'.

They thought this was funny, and we developed a great rapport. They offered tickets to the show and invited me to the sound check. What a great experience. Hearing Andy sing without a crowd is pretty surreal and cool. The next year they came back and did it all over again and have done many times since.

Andy and Paul often return to the hotel between tours on personal trips, as has Martin. Now I don't think I'm overstepping by calling them my friends. At first it was really weird getting texts from Andy, letting me know they're arrived, etc. The weirdest part is how completely comfortable and normal it is.

↑
The photo Darren Ross left in the rooms for Andy and Paul

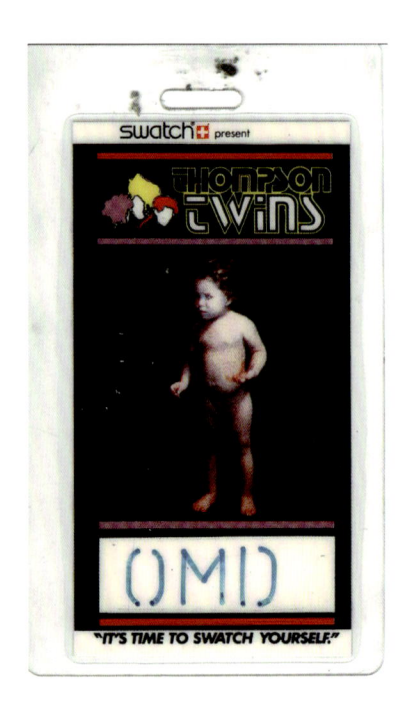

UNIVERSAL AMPHI THEATER

4 November 1985, Hollywood, California

BRANDON PATTERSON

I lived in Southern California. My favourite band was The Thompson Twins, who I had the opportunity to see in 1985. Friends told me OMD, the openers, would surprise me - I was familiar with *Junk Culture* and earlier stuff. The band launched into 'Electricity' and mid-song Andy jumped off stage and danced up the aisle and back. Just as he was about to climb on stage again I saw a rather large woman moving down the aisle towards him. She jumped on him like she was planning on taking him home as a souvenir! He was struggling to get free and a stage-hand had to step in and get him back on stage.

I had a special female friend who I tried to get to notice me as something more. We sat for hours in her front yard, chatting about life. We listened to OMD and talked about the songs. Some scream her name when I hear them. One is 'Hold You' from *Crush*, a perfect song for a perfect memory.

CITY HALL

11 November 1985, Sheffield, UK

STEVE TOWNSLEY

Returning home from school one afternoon I heard a melody emanate from a neighbour's window. Who the hell was that? The girl across the road from my house revealed the music I'd heard was OMD.

I had a piano lesson that evening. However, two things changed that week; my discovery of a new band and the arrival of my first synthesiser. Formal piano training and ordinary music would have to wait. I spent weeks trying to emulate 'Messages' on a keyboard and stereo cassette machine with limited success. My mother was furious, not because I was listening to OMD at full blast in my bedroom but because I was picking out riffs and melodies on a monophonic keyboard from every single song from the debut album instead of practicing piano. But I'd discovered real music, the moody, haunting, thought-provoking stuff that would transport me through my adolescence and maturing years.

I saw them at Sheffield City Hall, a gig televised for a BBC documentary and the most emotional and sweaty concert I've ever attended. The atmosphere seemed charged and the band, especially Andy, loved every minute. The whole place was throbbing to the rhythm. Andy specifically addressed my group of friends, exclaiming, 'I'm glad to see the people in the balcony persist in standing up even when the bouncers want to make them sit down'.

By the way, the morse code signal running through 'Telegraph' is exactly the same pitch as the proximity sensor on my car. I found this out to my peril as I reversed into a wall while listening to it.

UNIVERSITY OF WISCONSIN

25 November 1985, Madison, Wisconsin

JEFF LIPSCHULTZ

I didn't go to any concerts in high school, but when I got to the University of Wisconsin, I had a friend who insisted we go see The Thompson Twins. When the lights came on, there was this band on stage with a huge brass section. The energy in the room skyrocketed. OMD started playing awesome songs and I was immediately hooked. In 2018, I saw them at the House of Blues in Dallas. They had the audience in a frenzy. I was in the front row, soaking it all in.

COBO HALL

29 November 1985, Detroit, Michigan

CHRIS BARTON

Andy and Paul's melodies and lyrics have been with me in the deepest of valleys and in the highest of mountains. It was a cold November day in 1985 when I was putting on my multiple Swatch watches and doing my hair, short on the sides with a long floppy top, getting ready for The Thompson Twins concert.

My brother Ken, cousin Stacey and I had upper bowl tickets - shit seats, really. But when the opening act hit the stage I was awestruck. Who were these guys? Orchestral what? Their sound was new, like nothing I'd ever heard. They played with emotion and style and Andy danced … really danced. Orchestral Manoeuvres in the Dark, I did hear that right. I bought *Crush* the next day.

Fast forward to July 2016, introducing my 16-year old son, Bailey, to OMD at White River

State Park, Indianapolis. I got to chat with Paul after the show about our kids and his love of 80s festivals. My son has fallen in love with the sound of OMD. Like I did.

FOX THEATER
8 December 1985, Atlanta, Georgia

JIM DONATO

My first exposure to OMD was on the *Import Hour*, a weekly programme on FM rock radio station WORJ-FM. My ears perked up when 'Electricity' and 'The Messerschmitt Twins' got played.

When I found out about the OMD/Thompson Twins date at the Fox Theater, I called my college friend Jim Ivy to tell him. The band was touring in a six-man formation, the Weir Brothers on horns and guitar augmenting the classic OMD line-up. They performed a fantastic opening set. I recall a smattering of *Crush* tracks and as many OMD classic singles as they could pack into the remainder. We left three songs into the Thompson Twins set.

HAMPTON COLISEUM
10 December 1985, Hampton Roads, Virginia

SUSAN SHRODE

I was 21, still at home with my parents in Richmond, Virginia, working at a record store for Christmas, printing the tickets myself for two friends and me. Nowhere on any of the store information or on the tickets did it mention OMD as the support. It said, 'To be announced.'

We noticed two things when we arrived and took our seats. One was that the venue hadn't sold very well (it was a large venue in a military town where country rock or heavy metal ruled), the second was that it wasn't the Thompson Twins' gear set up on stage. One of my friends became curious so asked the people near us who was opening. Four rows away, a woman yelled back, 'Its Orchestral Manoeuvres in the Dark.' The whoop and happy dance I spontaneously did right then and there turned heads. Five minutes to showtime and a wonderful surprise!

The show started, and there was Andy dancing. I was mesmerised. I remember thinking, 'I don't want to stay in this seat. I don't want to try to dance in this space. I want to go dance with Andy.'

The first song was 'Tesla Girls'. Andy then stopped, said hello and then called for the crew to turn the lights on the audience. He said, 'I thought so. Didn't sell. Well, okay. Here's what we're going to do - everybody move up front. Forget about your seats. Come to the front and we'll make a party out of this.'

The show converted into a small club dance party. Just about everyone moved forward and started jumping and dancing. The connection between audience and stage was amazing. For the next hour, I danced and danced. I had so much fun. By the time The Thompson Twins came on stage, I was exhausted.

I'm 53 now. The most fun I've ever had at a concert was that night. I think I shot up a beam of happy that could be seen from space.

METRO CENTER

26 December 1985, Halifax, Nova Scotia, Canada

KIRK FERGUSON

I was front row at the Halifax, Nova Scotia and Moncton, New Brunswick dates. I never thought either band would ever tour Atlantic Canada. I remember the reel-to-reel machine running on stage during OMD's set. Was it still Winston then? 25 years later I saw them again in London at the Hammersmith Apollo. I managed to get passes for the after-show meet-and-greet. It was cool to meet Paul. We chatted about the new record and me seeing them back in 1985 in Canada and he kindly signed my copy of the *History of Modern* CD. I also scored a tour poster on the way out from a nice worker at the venue.

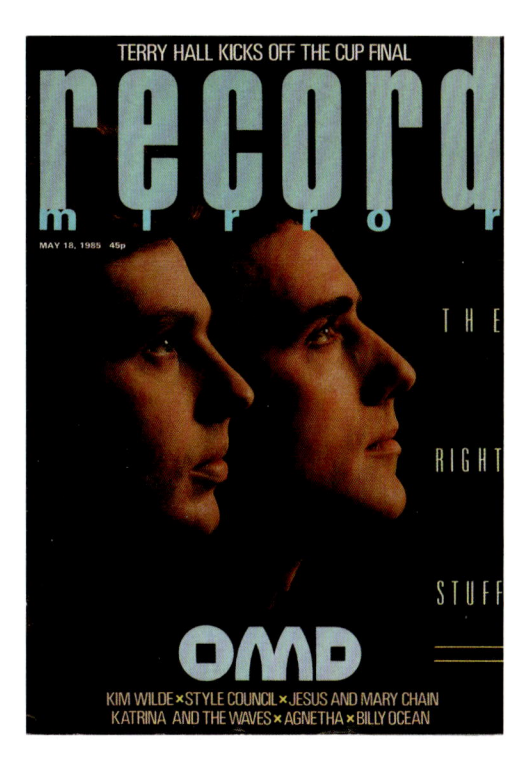

1986

OMD released their seventh album *The Pacific Age* along with the singles, 'If You Leave,' '(Forever) Live and Die' and 'We Love You'

PETER POWELL (SHANKS)
OMD lighting rigger on the *Crush* UK Tour, February 1986

OMD had a reputation for looking after their crew, with good hotels, good tour catering and comfortable tour coaches. Mutual respect meant a crew would go the extra mile. There was a good sense of fun, which included a mixed-sex sauna session at a venue that was part of a sports complex (Crawley Leisure Centre, I believe). We had homemade Bloody Marys among other naughties. I remember it getting real rock'n'roll in the heat, although I don't think the band were in on that one.

One of my favourite examples of the band's sense of humour involved one of the lighting crew, Nick Bruce-Smith – sorry, Nick. He's a brilliant monitor engineer but had taken a lighting position because he wanted to be on the tour. During a sound check, he was up in the lighting rig fixing a plug. Unfortunately, he slipped and dropped the screwdriver. I can't remember which keyboard it was, Paul or Martin, but it became embedded in the keys between the musician's hands! This didn't go down well with Rob Mackenzie, production manager and lighting designer, who immediately banned anyone from being in the rig during sound check. Nick was mortified.

At the next gig the crew was a bit tentative and subdued before sound check, but then the band walked on stage wearing Tonka Toy hard hats, presenting Nick with a plastic toy tool kit. Nick went a bit red; the rest of the crew pissed themselves, an example of how OMD put people around them at ease.

OMD tours were always feelgood tours. That's why people wanted to be on them. The fact I loved their music was a bonus. I sometimes wonder what they would have worn if they'd been invited to the sauna.

EMPIRE
2 February 1986, Liverpool, UK

MARTIN NEESON

My friend Siobhan and I were teenagers growing up in Northern Ireland. Siobhan got to see the band first, on the Architecture & Morality tour. I didn't get to see them until 1984. Many bands didn't want to come to Belfast in the 80s because of the perceived dangers. In 1985 the Crush tour dates were announced, Siobhan and I having just started at the University of Belfast. Undeterred by our favourite band not heading over, we bought tickets for Liverpool Empire. It was a whole new experience for us. We got to Liverpool by overnight ferry, the gig was fantastic and they played our favourite song, 'Romance of the Telescope'. We waited for Paul and Andy after the gig and spoke to them for several minutes. It got to the point where there was just me, Siobhan and Andy outside.

ORCHESTRATING MANOEUVRES

JAN 86

THOMPSON TWINS/OMD
Madison Square Garden, New York

HYMNS to future days aside, this evening ended up nothing more than a remembrance of things past. A few jolly minutes with a long-lost love cut short by an overbearing spinster aunt. A postcard and a post-mortem, in that order.

OMD, who have a future, don't seem all that worried about it. Intent on not flogging "Crush" they screen a brilliant travelogue covering half a decade of places and phases. "Enola Gay", however, is not the ideal opener. Its dizzy heights leave nowhere to go but down. "Tesla Girls" creaks at the corners, but Andy McCluskey's "Ferry-Cross-The-Mersey" croon gives way to genuinely excited shouting on a horn-driven "Julie". "This is very old," they confess, "but don't worry – it's brilliant."

Bashing and bonking happily, the OMDies just want their friends here to know they are alive and well. The souvenirs are nice; the current events more electric.

Looking back just as often, but a lot more furtively, are the Glimmer Triplets. Not so much sexy as sleepy, they droop lazily from "Here's To Future Days" to "Sister Of Mercy" to "Doctor Dream", the latter starting off like a malfunctioning helicopter and briefly threatening to become Depeche Mode's "Master And Servant" before lapsing into a coma. None of the new Twins material inspires interest much less movement. Everyone's standing, but nervous foot-shuffling outnumbers swaying three to one.

There is nothing remotely involving about this event, merely a big emptiness. Big empty videoscreens, big empty gestures, big empty heads. And big meninblack mainly preoccupied with making sure Alannah Currie has enough gew-gaws to bang on, although she usually can only be bothered to give a few random thwacks before flouncing off to stage left to share a joke with Joe Leeway.

The odd Twins out are more expendable than usual, playing clothes-horse assistants to Tom Bailey, the bumbling magician. Parading around in his hospital-issue Merlin robe, he stammers through some over-rehearsed ad libs. He looks out with a glazed stare, as if the headset he's wearing is no mere microphone, but some alien communicator. The result is still babble.

Precisely 90 minutes after traipsing on, the Three Blind Mice dutifully depart. Possibly it's a tribute to their tour sponsor, Swatch, or perhaps that's why the Twins can't see that their time has run out.

DAVID SPRAGUE

← A&M records promo still for the '(Forever) Live and Die' video shoot

↑ Thompson Twins and OMD Madison Square Garden press review

1986 | 227

OMD – 1986

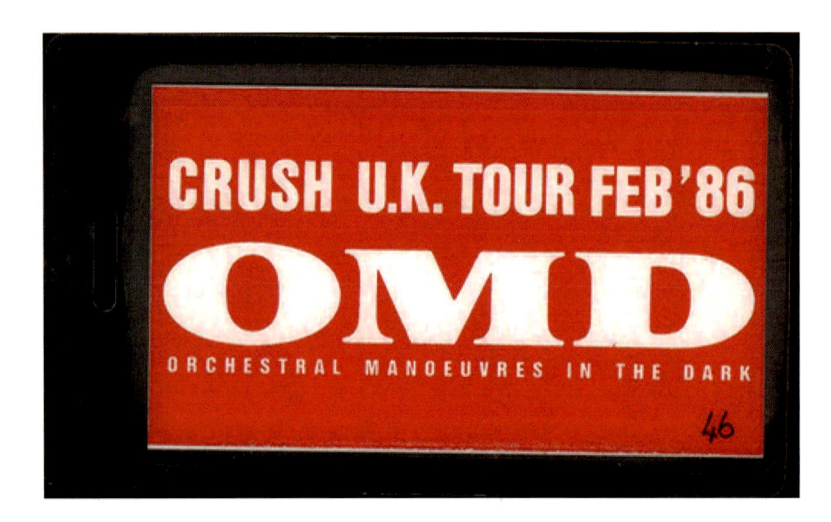

We wanted to talk longer so he invited us on the short walk round to the Adelphi Hotel. We were starstruck! Once we arrived, Andy said he couldn't invite us in. We didn't mind. He'd made our year already. I vividly recall Siobhan finding the nearest call box to tell her parents what had happened.

BARROW LANDS

3 February 1986, Glasgow, UK

MIRELLE DAVIS
OMD manager

I'm pretty sure I've been to more OMD concerts than anyone other than the band, including the crew, so picking individual shows is more of a challenge for me. The first time was 15 January 1981 at Leicester's de Montfort Hall on the Architecture & Morality tour. My best friend Jan said she would come and see Depeche Mode with me if I went to OMD with her. I kept my side of the bargain and Depeche Mode became my first live concert and OMD my second. The rest is history. Something happened to me that night and I just couldn't stop. Three concerts on the next tour - one in Nottingham, two in Birmingham. I'll never forget my embarrassment, having my Dad march down the corridor backstage at Nottingham University to drag me home, having dutifully waited in the car outside long enough. Soon three concerts became five, then eight and very quickly I was going to every UK and European show, part of the infamous 'Barmy Army'. I made a lot of new friends, including Pauline, one of my dearest friends to this day. Politics aside, we had a huge amount of fun too.

It was my final year at Manchester University, the phone rang late at night in my student digs and my life changed for ever. My Dad had died in a sudden, tragic accident. My world literally stopped that night and it became, 'It's one day since Dad died', 'It's two', 'It's a week'. I didn't know how I'd get through each day, let alone my final exams. I did, and a lot of that was down to OMD.

It might sound crass but OMD were touring and suddenly I felt myself counting towards something good instead of away from something bad. I never thought I'd enjoy anything again and yet instead of saying, 'It's seven weeks since Dad died', here I am saying, 'It's seven weeks until I see OMD'.

Following OMD was always my escape from the real world, my place to hide. Just being able to forget that pain for 90 minutes every night kept me going. But that night in Glasgow for some reason, I didn't want to forget it. I wanted to embrace it. I found myself alone and started to cry. An older man came up and looked after me. I think that night was the only time I truly let my guard down about Dad and I know I needed it. Later Andy introduced me to his father backstage, and needless to say we'd already met.

I carried on, did the whole tour, sitting on the floor in sound checks with my books on my knee, revising for my finals. I passed those exams, moved to London and got on with my life. I almost definitely ended up following a career in the music industry because of OMD and 25 years later I wound up managing them. I'm pretty sure my father would have been proud of me and would also have seen the funny side.

CITY HALL
5 February 1986,
Newcastle, UK

GAIL CAVANAGH

I'd just started secondary school and discovered *Top of the Pops*, and at school we'd chat about

↑
Paul and Andy press shot from '86

the bands we saw and what was going up and down the charts. I remember the first time I saw OMD on *Top of the Pops*, playing 'Enola Gay.' It was so removed from anything I'd heard before and the mix of synthesised sounds was hypnotic, beautiful and exciting. Also, it was refreshing to have a pop song with a serious message behind it. That Christmas I got a little red plastic Fidelity HF42 portable record player and my quest to buy records began.

Back then, Hula Hoops would send you a free record if you collected 10 empty packets, so for several months I ate cheese Hula Hoops for lunch every day. I've never wanted to eat them since. That, along with birthday and Christmas money, meant I was able to buy singles and albums.

By the time I was 14, I was allowed to get a bus to Newcastle, usually with school friends Julia and Helen, and we discovered an amazing basement record shop, Pet Sounds. Unlike Woolie's, which tended to have only chart music and a few easy listening titles, Pet Sounds was a deep underground cave filled with every genre of music and huge back-catalogues. There I bought *Orchestral Manoeuvres in the Dark, Organisation, Dazzle Ships, Architecture & Morality* and *Junk Culture*. I couldn't wait to get the bus home, so I could listen to the tracks repeatedly, some familiar, some new. Other bands released albums containing a few hits and lots of filler. Not OMD.

I also joined the fan club, whose early magazines were called *OMITD*. Getting fan club letters was very exciting, giving access to exclusive posters, information and badges. Mine are hidden away in a box in my Mam's loft.

For my 17th birthday, Julia and Helen clubbed together to buy me a ticket to see OMD in concert. We had tea then set off across Newcastle in the dark to get to the venue. Then it started to snow. The whole experience was ethereal and wonderful. The music I so enjoyed on my scratchy little record player was being played live. It was breath-taking. I felt like every single nerve was tingling. When Dad picked me up to drive us home I felt so alive, never wanting the evening to end.

In 2016, Andy McCluskey was on Vintage TV. They played some new OMD tracks and there was an advert for a weekend at Butlin's at which they were playing. I booked straight away. A few days later, helping one of the eight-year olds I teach put on their boots, he was humming a song. It sounded familiar. I asked what it was and he said, 'You won't have heard of it. It's called 'Dresden' and it's by a group called OMD'. Of course, I had to tell him who my favourite group was. As luck would have it, our next topic in class was called Playlist and involved listening to music of different styles and cultures. This child brought his iPod so all the children could listen to 'Dresden.' I showed the children the 'Enola Gay' video and they loved it. I'm sure part of my role as a teacher is to give children an opportunity to listen to exceptional music and introduce

OMD to the next generation.

Butlin's was amazing. I felt like a teenager again. Andy and Paul's friendly banter made us feel welcome and part of the experience rather than spectators coming to be entertained.

ODEON

6 February 1986,
Birmingham, UK

DEAN CALEY

When I heard 'Messages' for the first time on radio it was a moment that told me there and then I was going to be a fan of this band forever. And 38 years on, I have too many great times to talk about. However, I remember with fondness bumping into Martin Cooper at the Royal show in 1985 and my first concert for *Junk Culture*, still my favourite album, the year before.

Another highlight was the Pacific Age concert in 1986 at Birmingham Odeon, being in the crowd for the 'We Love You' video. However, my all-time favourite moment was meeting Andy and Paul on the Architecture & Morality tour at Wolverhampton Civic Hall, having been on the front row.

HEXAGON THEATRE

13 February 1986,
Reading, UK

RICHARD MORRIS

It was the summer of 1986 and I was on holiday with my parents in Majorca. It was a quiet hotel with not much for a 17-year old boy to do other than sunbathe. Earlier that year I saw my first gig, OMD at the Reading Hexagon. By chance, a work friend was arriving at the next-door hotel a few days later and we arranged to meet. Tim's hotel was busier, and by the time I found him he'd made friends. I was immediately drawn to one of the girls, Kerry, and romance followed. We spent time sunbathing and listening to tapes. Kerry introduced me to 'Come Back to Me' by Big Country and in return I played 'If You Leave.' The words were particularly poignant given that Kerry was going home a few days before me. As the days passed, 'If You Leave' became 'our' tune, until the inevitable parting with hugs, tears and promises to keep in touch.

Every time I hear 'If You Leave' I'm reminded of that romance.

COLSTON HALL

19 February 1986, Bristol, UK

CAROLINE LEECH

In April 1983, on my 15th birthday, I bought my first *Smash Hits* magazine as The Thompson Twins were on the front. On page two was a photo of OMD and lyrics for 'Telegraph.' I thought, 'Who are these guys and how come I haven't heard this song on Radio 1?' Most of my friends were Durannies, but OMD looked cool in shirts, ties and sensible haircuts. My Thompson Twins phase fizzled out, while my OMD phase has lasted 35 years so far.

I took a complete punt and invested £2.44 in *Dazzle Ships* as it was half price in a Woolworth's bargain bin. 'Radio Waves' and 'Telegraph' got me hooked and I bought the first three albums. 'Joan of Arc' became my favourite song - and still is. And at Colston Hall in 1986 my sister and I were in the front row and got to shake hands with Mr McCluskey.

I loved 'Walking on the Milky Way', and when I took up skiing a couple of years later and people said, 'Sing while you ski, it'll help you relax', I sang 'Milky Way'. It did the trick and now a ski-trip wouldn't be the same without a head full of OMD songs. On our latest trip, it was 'Isotype' and 'Robot Man.'

CORNWALL COLISEUM

22 February 1986, St Austell, UK

STUART JOHNSON

I hadn't taken any interest in pop music until I saw OMD perform 'Maid of Orleans' on *Top of the Pops* with my parents, my Dad commenting that he loved the sound of the bagpipes and thought the track was rather good compared to the crap on that night. Well, if it was good enough for Dad, it was good enough for me. I've only just found out it was a synthesiser, not bagpipes.

Hardly anyone turned up at the Coliseum as snow caused chaos everywhere in Cornwall. Only locals could make it. The band was staying in Fowey so I was surprised even they got there. Halfway through, they all went outside and came back to throw snowballs into the crowd, one of which I caught and threw back to a very surprised lead singer.

After the concert Andy came into Quasars, the local nightclub, with a couple of bouncers in tow. He had a quick look around and hit the dancefloor, going straight up to the best-looking girl, who was wearing a red polka-dot dress, dancing with her for one song. I caught up with him later and got my copy of *Junk Culture* signed, which I'd just won from the DJ by answering a quiz question.

PRETTY IN PINK

In 1985, John Hughes - the American writer/director/producer of a wave of successful teen-movies, *Sixteen Candles*, *The Breakfast Club*, *Weird Science* - was preparing his next film, *Pretty in Pink*, and wanted one of his favourite new wave acts, Orchestral Manoeuvres in the Dark to write a new song for the end of the film.

In the summer of '85, I accompanied Andy and Paul, as their manager, to the set of the movie to see Molly Ringwald (playing main character, Andie Walsh) and Jon Cryer ('Duckie' Dale) film a scene directed by Howard Deutch, and we discussed how the film needed a song to reflect the ending. Andy and Paul wrote the excellent, 'Goddess of Love', with that in mind, and we submitted it with great optimism. Everyone seemed to agree. However, once the editing was finished and the studio tested the film on audiences, those audiences indicated that while they loved most of the film, they almost unanimously wanted to see a different ending involving Blane McDonough (played by Andrew McCarthy) and not Duckie. John Hughes agreed to film a new ending and suddenly the OMD song didn't fit. However, he wanted to keep his word about a new song by Andy and Paul at the close.

This news was broken to us just two days before OMD were booked to start their biggest US tour yet, with The Thompson Twins, and the deadline for the soundtrack looming. After a short, fairly tense discussion, Andy stood up and said, 'Let's get into a studio and see if we can get something.'

Within two hours, we'd booked a small studio in West Hollywood and they immediately got to work. About five hours later David Anderle, the A&M music supervisor, and I decided to drop by to see how things were going and were highly surprised to be told, 'We've got a rough idea, it needs a lot of work, but see what you think'. Even at this rough stage, the emotional power of 'If You Leave' was easily apparent, Andy had sung the entire lyric and the music was already fully structured. We were so shocked at the quality that had been achieved so quickly, that I forget exactly what we said, beyond, 'It's great, can you finish it tomorrow?' The guys worked through the night, Martin Cooper adding a beautiful, wistful sax solo, and by the next day they were able to play a mix for the stunned, delighted studio executives.

In some ways, my fondest moment came after the film-makers departed, Andy looking me straight in the eye, with a 'there's many a true word said in jest' grin, saying, 'The worst thing is, now you're going to think we can always write a song this way, aren't you?'

'If You Leave' was OMD's biggest US hit, hitting the Top-5 in May 1986, and became 'the' prom song for an entire generation of Americans.

MARTIN KIRKUP
FORMER OMD MANAGER

OMD – 1986

'If You Leave' was played prominently during the final scene in the film Pretty in Pink

IF YOU LEAVE

PAUL HUMPHREYS

I'm very proud of 'If You Leave'. It divides our fans. Some people hate it. Some people think it's cheesy. Some people hate it because it was a hit in America. Making it was just mad. We'd contributed to a John Hughes movie before *Pretty in Pink*. He'd used 'Tesla Girls' in *Weird Science*. John was a massive fan of all British bands and he was a big fan of OMD.

And after he'd used 'Tesla Girls' he was making *Pretty in Pink* and thought there was a slot at the end of the film that needed a song. It was the culmination of the movie, ending up at the prom, and it had to be a really great song and he asked us to write it. We were flattered that he asked us and so we wrote the song 'Goddess of Love' for him. He liked it and thought it was going to work, so we recorded it.

We were just about to start a tour of America and decided to go over early to LA. We had three or four days before the American tour started and went over with the multi track of 'Goddess of Love' to simply mix it. We landed to an urgent message from John, 'You've gotta get in touch asap' was the message. This was before mobile phones. So we got in touch with John and he said, 'Really, really sorry guys but I've changed the whole end of the film. I've reshot it and your song just doesn't work. I'm really sorry.' And we were like. 'Oh shit', because A&M Records had put together a whole campaign being linked with this film in order to really break us in America.

And all of a sudden we didn't have a song for the end of the film. We were about to start a two month tour and it was a case of, 'What the hell do we do now?' We didn't have any other songs that we knew would work. So we said, 'John, we don't know what to do. We don't have anything.'

And he said, 'Look, I believe in you guys. I'm going to book you into Lrabee Studios, which is one of the best studios in LA. Hire anything you want – I'll pay for it.' Because we didn't have any of our instruments, all our gear was in transit to San Francisco. He said, 'Hire anything you need and write something.' And we were like, 'You've gotta be fucking kidding me!'

So, here we were, jet lagged to hell, now under extreme pressure to deliver something in just a few days. What to do? Well, lets just say we managed to find something that really stopped us sleeping, and we stayed up for almost 24 hours straight. It's the only song that we've ever written where I'm at the piano and Andy's on his notepad writing the words. We only ever write songs starting from an abstract idea. That's the only thing we've ever known. We'll start with something completely bonkers, and by the end of the process we've got a tune on and a vocal on. But we've never sat down and gone, 'Okay, I'll play some chords and you hum along until we have a tune.' We'd never, ever done that. Until this moment.

So we hadn't got any equipment and the stuff we'd hired hadn't arrived yet. But we saw a piano out in the room and I said, 'Andy, come on', and so we just stayed up and thrashed out this song! And then the hire gear arrived and we tried to translate it onto the Fairlight and did a very rough version of it. It was absolutely the first thing that came into our heads.

It's very interesting when musicians analyse that song, because several have said to me, 'How on earth did you do that, because each verse and each chorus is in a different key? That was absolute genius. How did you do it? That's so clever.' And I say, 'The thing was, we had

24 hours to write it and we got into the chorus in a nice key but I could never work out how get back out of the chorus and back into the verse and it not be an uncomfortable chord change.' We were basically in a musical corner so I thought the only way to do it is to change key. So it was just to make sure the song worked in 24 hours. I couldn't physically get back to the key it started in otherwise I would have done it. I thought the quick way out of this is to change key. It keeps changing all the way through. I couldn't work it out musically any other way.

Our engineer and co-producer Tom Lord Alge joined us and after 24 hours we'd roughed it out. It was five or six in the morning and we sent it over in a cab to John Hughes at Paramount Pictures. Andy and I went to bed because we hadn't slept. We'd just got off a plane and so we'd been up for two days. We had a couple of hours sleep and about eight or nine in the morning we got a phone call from John: 'Love it. Get back in the studio now and finish it!' So within two and a half or three days we had it finished. Martin and Mal arrived and Mal played some drums on it. Martin wrote the middle eight and blasted a beautiful sax over it and - hey presto! - it was a finished track. We hadn't mixed it but we had a working version. The tour began but soon we had two days off on the tour and so we flew back to LA to do the final mix with Tom at *Giorgio Moroder's private studio in LA*. Nine times out of ten when you write a song under pressure it doesn't work and you write a piece of shit. We were just very lucky that we nailed it in one, because everything was hinging on that. It turned out to be a monster hit in America, which was a huge relief!

It's still popular now. Over the years I've gone to visit my daughter Madeline, who lived in LA and now in New York, and I'll hear it at the supermarket. It's still on high rotation on all the 80s stations and it's a staple at high school proms. The movie *Pretty in Pink* has become a bit of a cult classic over the decades, and now younger generations are watching it and liking it, so that's contributed to a lot of younger people in America coming to see us. A lot of younger bands in America have covered it on TV shows as well.

We noticed a few years ago in America that the fans were getting younger and younger, and we've noticed it now in Britain and Europe, that we're getting a lot of younger people coming to see us. We don't know quite why that is. Is it the internet? Is it a lot of younger bands citing OMD as an influence? Is it the algorithms on line? 'If you like this you might like that.'

Are we on Spotify playlists? I'm not sure why, but we do have a lot of younger fans now, which is great.

ANDY MCCLUSKEY

The engineer, Tom Lord-Alge, was there. He'd flown in to mix 'Goddess of Love' with us as we'd worked with him in New York on a B-side, 'Firegun', and we really liked the sound Tom got. He only worked with us because his brother, Chris Lord-Alge, had been arrested that morning. All the Lord-Alge brothers drove suped-up decommissioned police cars and were always getting arrested for speeding then pretending to be one of the other brothers. Chris hadn't got away with it that morning, so Tom had to come in.

We flew out for the premiere of the film in LA on the same flight as New Order, who also had a song in the film. Peter Hook likes to tell the story that we corrupted him and Paul and I got him into cocaine. My memory is that they had their own supply. OMD and New Order each had their own bags of cocaine and we were all chopping them out for each other in the toilets in the smoking section at the back of the plane. We got off that plane in LA grinning like idiots.

We took limos onto the red carpet for the premiere, at the Chinese

↑
Invite for the world premiere of *Pretty In Pink*

New Hollywood

LOS ANGELES — The invitation said dress was a "matter of individual expression," but most who attended the recent premiere of Paramount's new film "Pretty in Pink," and the party at the Palace afterward, appeared to have collaborated on the dress code.

O.M.D., a hot L.A. band

↑ The members of OMD dressed for the *Pretty in Pink* premiere

→ 'If You Leave' at No.4 on the *Billboard* charts

Theatre on Hollywood Boulevard. We knew our song was at the end of the movie, so sat there watching the movie thinking, 'There's the scene in the bedroom that they shot which we were at. God, that's amazing' and, 'Here we go, big ending.' However, we were so disappointed when our track finally arrived! 'Who edited this crap? There's not one person dancing on the beat'. It looked awful. The only instruction we'd been given was that it must be 120 beats per minute. But it hadn't mattered at all. It was a proper Hollywood premiere. It was amazing. But whoever edited it …

We went to the party afterwards and George Michael said to me, 'Oh, my God. Best gig Andrew Ridgley and I ever went to was you guys at Aylesbury Friars.' I said, 'That's cool! By the way, could you give me an autograph for Tiffany? It's my girlfriends best friend.' He went, 'What?' I went, 'Yeah, she's 18.' My girlfriend Toni was still at school when I met her.

For the next six months, we spent a lot of time in America. By that stage I was dating a Californian girl and Paul was married to a Californian girl. We would be driving round LA, on would come 'If You Leave' on the radio and we were bored of it: 'Oh God, not that.' We'd change the channel and there it was again on another channel. We'd change the channel and hear it again: 'God, it's on three radio stations at the same time. How boring! Ha ha!' It was a monster. We'd never experienced anything like that.

PETER HOOK

Hooky had to babysit my girlfriend, because I had an interview to do and she was only 18 at the time. When Hooky's autobiography came out in 2016, my son James went to see him at a book signing in a record store in San Diego. When James got to the front of the queue, he put the book down
  and Hooky said, 'That's the English version'. James replied, 'Yeah, I go backwards and forwards to England. By the way, my mum said to say 'hello'.' And Hooky went, 'Oh, do I know her?' James explained, 'Yeah, you baby sat her at the premiere of Pretty in Pink.' Hooky said, 'So I babysat your mother?' And this look of sheer horror came over his face as he thought, 'Oh Christ, this isn't my kid is it?' James later told me, 'I could see him thinking, 'How old is this kid? Oh, fucking hell.' James had done this specifically to wind him up. 'No, I'm Andy McCluskey's son.' 'Phew! Yes, of course I'll sign!' In hindsight, I can't imagine a worse person than Hooky to ask to babysit your attractive 18 year old blonde Californian girlfriend!

ANDY MCCLUSKEY

IF YOU LEAVE WAS RELEASED

21 APR 1986

ANDY MCCLUSKEY

The big tours with The Power Station and Thompson Twins and the success of 'If You Leave' had certainly brought us to the attention of a wide audience in North America. We were persuaded to go back into the studio with Stephen Hague producing again and Tom Lord-Alge engineering at Studio de la Grande Armée in Paris. We had not had time to really write enough new material and had to leave mid recording to play as a two piece in Manchester as a favour to Tony Wilson.

G-MEX

19 July 1986, Manchester, UK

ANDREW LIDDLE
OMD lighting engineer

I remember OMD did the Festival of the Tenth Summer at G-Mex, one of Tony Wilson's ideas, a celebration of the 10th summer

Here are this week's top-selling records, as compiled by *Billboard* magazine:

Top albums
1. WHITNEY HOUSTON. Whitney Houston.
2. 5150. Van Halen.
3. LIKE A ROCK. Bob Seger & the Silver Bullet Band.
4. RAISED ON RADIO. Journey.
5. PARADE. Prince & the Revolution.
6. CONTROL. Janet Jackson.
7. PRETTY IN PINK. Various artists.
8. WINNER IN YOU. Patti Labelle.
9. PLEASE. Pet Shop Boys.
10. PLAY DEEP. The Outfield.

Top singles
1. GREATEST LOVE OF ALL. Whitney Houston.
2. LIVE TO TELL. Madonna.
3. ON MY OWN. Patti LaBelle and Michael McDonald.
4. IF YOU LEAVE. Orchestral Manoeuvres in the Dark.
5. I CAN'T WAIT. Nu Shooz.
6. ALL I NEED IS A MIRACLE. Mike & the Mechanics.
7. SOMETHING ABOUT YOU. Level 42.
8. IS IT LOVE. Mr. Mister.
9. BE GOOD TO YOURSELF. Journey.
10. WHAT HAVE YOU DONE FOR ME LATELY. Janet Jackson.

OMD – 1986

Direct Management Group
213 945A LOS ANGELES CALIFORNIA 90069
854 NORTH LA CIENEGA BLVD
3535

PO Box 314
London SW2 5AX

7th August 1986
SJ/fmp

White Noise Ltd.,
Sloane & Co.,
112a & b Westbourne Grove,
London, W2 5RU.

TO:

The following expenses incurred in July 1986:

Lunch with Gemma Corfield & Caroline True/ Virgin Records	$ 73.00
Lunch with Willie Smax ref video	$ 36.00
Lunch with Mick Haggerty - Art Director/ The Pacific Age	$ 50.00
Various Taxis	$ 146.11
Hotel in Paris for Steve Jensen	$ 165.12
Hotel in Paris for Steve Jensen	$ 97.50
Hotel in London for Steve Jensen	$ 565.36
Federal Express Charges	$ 44.00
Airfare: Paris to London (Steve Jensen)	$ 125.58
Airfare: Los Angeles-Paris London-Los Angeles (Martin Kirkup)	$ 928.00
Airfare: Paris-London (Martin Kirkup)	$ 126.83
Lunch with Andy Wooliscroft -Station Agency	$ 38.01
Airfare: Los Angeles-New York-London-Los Angeles (Steve Jensen)	$1769.00
Taxi: LHR - Hotel	$ 31.40
TOTAL DUE:	$4195.91

Please arrange for immediate payment by bank wire to Direct Management account in LA.

c.c. Steve Jensen & Martin Kirkup
Andy McCluskey

↑
Management expenses on behalf of the band. $4,195 spent on lunch, hotels and flights and they wondered why they never had any money!

→
Malcolm and Martin on a train to Plymouth for a TV show promoting '(Forever) Live and Die'

since 1976, when 2,500 people were at the Free Trade Hall watching the Sex Pistols, four times the capacity of the venue! It was before I worked for them. Peter Saville designed the branding. The Saturday afternoon was quite surreal. I remember the sun coming in and OMD being on stage in the afternoon. I think Winston was still with them. And they had a stage invader. The Smiths were on the bill and The Fall, A Certain Ratio and I think Happy Mondays might have been too. I think they felt slightly out of place.

ANDY MCCLUSKEY

I suffer from stage fright. I'm much calmer than I was, because it finally dawned on me that if people have bought a ticket to see us they probably already like the music so we're onto a winner.

I think the most terrified I've ever been was playing the Festival of the Tenth Summer. We were recording the *Pacific Age* in Paris with Stephen Hague and Tom Lord-Alge when we got asked.

We thought, as a 'thank you' to Factory, and because we wanted to remember that we'd started 10 years previously, we'd do it, with a tape recorder and just me and Paul. What we hadn't factored in was that we'd be playing in front of 8,000 Smiths fans. I was more and more frightened as the day went on. I was in bits, really anxious. I was so nervous I threw up before I went on.

Matters were made worse by being introduced on stage by Paul Morley as, 'And now, two rich bastards from Los Angeles', which hurt like hell. About 30 years later, he hosted a Factory thing at the South Bank when Ray Davies curated Meltdown, he interviewed us and we played, and he took the opportunity to apologise for that introduction.

(FOREVER) LIVE AND DIE

WAS RELEASED

26 AUG 1986

OMD – 1986

THE PACIFIC AGE
WAS RELEASED

29 SEP 1986

Handwritten lyrics:

The Pacific age
has no regrets
it feeds on dreams
it ~~counts~~ wins its bets

A new dawn breaks
from the east to the west
and the plans we made
stop making sense

like a wave that breaks
over foreign shores
~~its~~ begs for mercy
and ~~it~~ takes some more
and more and more

The Pacific age
it calls our name
it bites our hand
you ~~but~~ ~~or~~ feel no pain
~~and~~ racing home
~~you~~ run in vain
as your heart slows down
and you loose the game

The Pacific ~~Age~~
can tell no lies

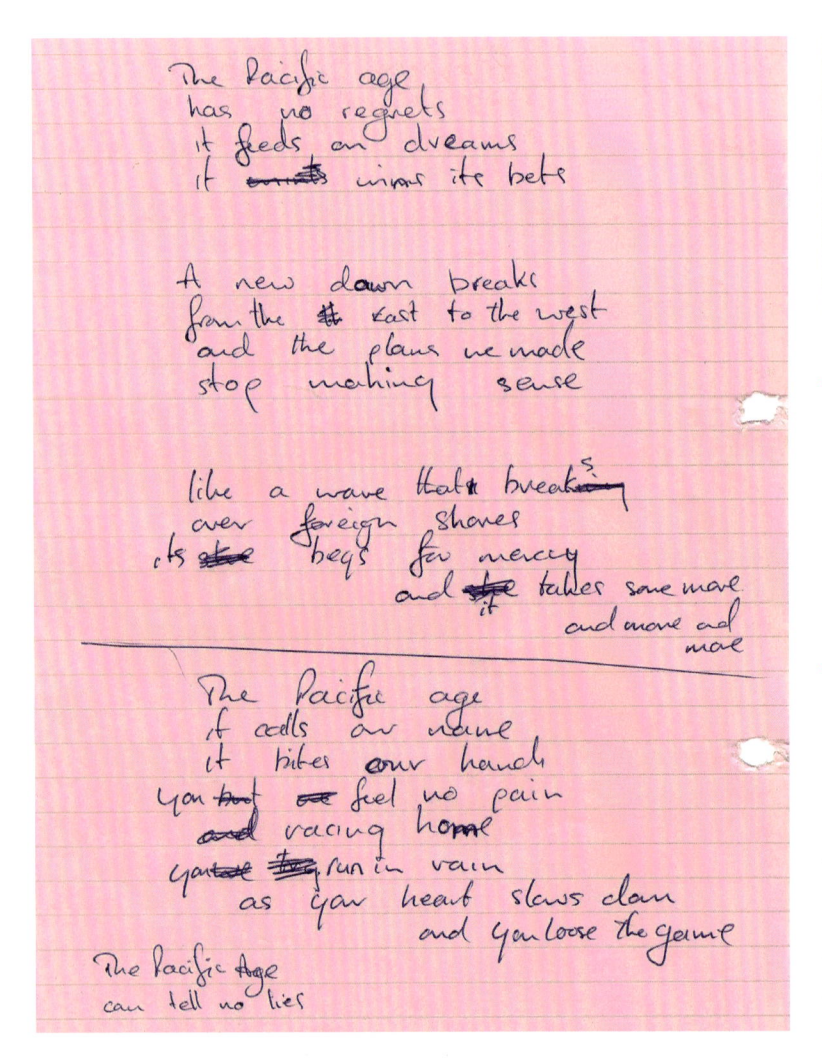

↑ Hand written lyrics to 'Pacific Age'

ODEON
21 October 1986, Birmingham, UK

NEAL MCCLIMON

Sitting at the table at home in Telford on a Friday night, watching TV while eating dinner, I was suddenly aware of some music. I looked up and saw the video to 'Enola Gay' on *Central News*. I was instantly gripped. After the video both Andy and Paul were interviewed. They were funny, comparing themselves to bank-tellers.

I was never a big radio listener. All my time went on football. Yet

I found myself starting to listen to Radio 1's chart show to try and hear 'Enola Gay' again. Thing is, I never actually caught the band's name. A while later I heard another song I fell instantly in love with. 'Maid of Orleans.'

About six months later, a friend asked if I'd sell him my Jean-Michel Jarre *Oxygen* album. Instead I swapped it for the LP that had 'Maid of Orleans' on. So I discovered the band I liked was Orchestral Manoeuvres in the Dark and the LP was *Architecture & Morality*. I drove my mother crazy, playing it on repeat on my deck, the arm left up. Five times side A, then repeat for side B.

At the time, Telford had no railway station and my mother no car, so trying to see the band was impossible on my pocket money. But following the release of *The Pacific Age*, my girlfriend (who hated OMD) got me a ticket to see them at the Birmingham Odeon, three days after my 21st birthday. She wouldn't be going, it was just me.

I was on a Government training scheme, earning £25 a week. Thankfully, as it was my 21st, Mother told me to keep all my wages to myself. Yet I still had to save like crazy.

It was my first concert and I was in awe of the atmosphere. When the band came on, the crowd surged towards centre-stage, I was around 15 rows back to the left side. The energy was fantastic. Everyone was jumping, sweating, singing out loud.

Watching Mal belt out 'Maid of Orleans' was the highlight. The 90 minutes flew by, but it wasn't over. They were going to film the video for the next single, 'We Love You.' I had to watch the time, as there was one late train back to Wolverhampton. Twice the band lip-synced the song, the crowd bouncing like lunatics, Andy somehow still having the energy to throw himself around like a whirling dervish.

A look at the watch and I had to run. I sprinted to New Street station and made the train with minutes to spare. The only way back to Telford was a black taxi. The cost? Just over a week's wages, £27 to be exact. I felt sorry for the driver. He asked where I'd been and got a full review. I bet he wished he never asked.

COLSTON HALL

27 October 1986,
Bristol, UK

STEVE NASH

My first gig. I remember going to C&A in the afternoon and buying a new shirt, white with thin peppermint green vertical stripes - very 80s.

OMD took the stage and opened with the instrumental, 'Southern.' The brass was so powerful and

OMD – 1986

OMD — Dead Or Alive meets Iron Maiden?!?

Andy McCluskey tells ROBERT PALMER about his latest Orchestral Manoeuvre in the Dark.

OMD have been gracing the charts wince Enola Gay way back in '79. Since then practically all their releases have reached the top 40.

Their consistency has been rivalled only by the now-defunct Madness.

Early this year they released If You Leave from the film Pretty In Pink. The song had already climbed to number three in America but this feat was not repeated here. Surely this disappointed singer Andy McCluskey?

"The lack of success disappointed me but I wasn't surprised," he said. "Since we first became successful the charts have baffled me. Singles which I like or expect to do well usually don't — songs I don't like do. People say that fans are fickle, well basically they just confuse me."

Still OMD are back in the upper reaches of the chart. (Forever) Live And Die is just tickling the top ten at present.

"The singles success comes as a surprise to me but hopefully the album will prove just as popular. Singles-wise we do very well but our albums sell erratically to say the least.

"Architecture And Morality sold well, then came Dazzle Ships which was a disaster. The last album, Crush, was satisfactory but The Pacific Age should be our most successful yet."

A very strange name for the album and title track, so how did it come about?

"Last year I was watching a documentary called The Pacific Age and thought it would make a good title. The album has already received a few reviews and for some reason people compare it to a Howard Jones-type song, singing about peace and vegetarians.

"Things like that annoy me because what we are trying to convey is something completely different. The songs depict the decline of the European economy and the gradual rise of countries in the Pacific."

Certainly a strange subject to sing about, but then OMD have written songs on topics ranging from nuclear war to burning saints.

Their concerts too are usually strange affairs — for Andy McCluskey's dancing if nothing else. This tour promises a few changes

"We haven't used projections for a long time but they might make a reappearance

"The other big difference is that our concerts have been rapidly turning into greatest hits affairs. This time a lot more new material will be played.

"I think for once we have a lot of confidence in it. Also the style of music has reverted back to a much more orchestral sound but at the same time is much harder. For instance the next single called We Love You is very fast and dance-orientated — Dead Or Alive meets Iron Maiden you could say."

They play the Colston Hall on October 27

Andy McClusky... "The next single is very fast and dance-orientated."

↑ Preview for the Bristol show

crisp, Andy's bass really thudding. It was sheer magic. So many of my favourite songs were played that night, including 'So in Love', 'If You Leave', 'Julia's Song' and 'White Trash.' It was the perfect way to open my gigging account. Over 300 gigs later, I'll never forget that first one.

APOLLO THEATRE

28 October 1986, Oxford, UK

ANDY MYHILL

My Dad was a keen Airfix model-maker and had recently made a kit of the aircraft, Enola Gay. He told me some group had made a song about the airplane that dropped the first atomic weapon and thought it was quite good and very catchy. I listened to it myself and thought, 'Wow'. How different it was to other sounds around. I saved and saved, bought *Organisation*, and was hooked. Any pocket money and any money from Christmas and birthdays was saved. I now have a sizeable collection, including obscure imports and remixes from around the world. I even painted my bedroom wall like the *Dazzle Ships* LP cover, not appreciated by my parents.

I took my *Architecture & Morality* album into school for a music lesson and when it was played I received some funny looks and comments. My music teacher said, 'Well, each to their own. It's not really music, just people fiddling with knobs and electrical gadgets.' I was branded a bit of a weirdo. Most of my schoolfriends were either into Madness or heavy metal, but I didn't care.

I first saw OMD on the Pacific Age tour and have now seen them many times, most recently in 2018 in Orlando. I didn't even know about this until the morning of the concert. It was a brilliant end to our holiday in the area and I got to meet the lads after, spending a good few minutes talking football with Andy and Paul. Andy's team had just knocked my team out of the European Champions League and Paul's team had beaten my team the previous weekend. They both rubbed it in.

HAMMERSMITH ODEON

29 & 30 October 1986, London, UK

MARTIN DAY

Born in 1968, I missed the early tours and had only just started going to gigs when I finally saw OMD at Hammersmith Odeon.

It was my first time hearing my favourite band run through their hits, and they threw 'Telegraph' and 'Julia's Song' into the mix for good measure. Over the next few years I'd stop taking myself quite so seriously, studying Andy McCluskey's lyrics with the same fevered intensity that I did TS Eliot and Sylvia Plath. But if you can't be obsessed to the point of near mania in your teens, when can you?

I didn't have an opportunity to see OMD again until the Liberator tour in December 1993, at the NEC, Birmingham. I went with my wife, who was pregnant with our first child, so my daughter's first musical experience involved OMD, maybe explaining her abiding love of good music in general, and Sigur Rós in particular. After all, who knows what 'King of Stone' might sound like in the womb?

REV. DAVID DOWNING

I went to my first concert aged 16: OMD, The Pacific Age, at Hammersmith Odeon. Not living in London, my parents were concerned I would miss the last train home. I had to prove I had enough money to get a taxi. I went with a friend, Tom, and remember discussing what songs would be played. We both went with great excitement, and from the moment 'Southern' started I was having the time of my life. We both made the last train home. Which was good, because having bought a programme, a t-shirt and a poster, I'd spent my taxi money.

JAY SIDPARA

Born in West London in November 1968, I was raised on a healthy cocktail of post-punk and new wave bands such as The Associates, Echo and the Bunnymen, The Human League, Joy Division, Kraftwerk, Magazine and XTC. The synthesiser broke free from the guitar rock machismo, producing an infinite array of musical soundscapes that perfectly synchronised with a visual awareness.

Orchestral Manoeuvres in the Dark was a ridiculous name and a bit of a tongue-twister, but the quality of the sounds and lyrics formed the backdrop to my musical outlook. *The Pacific Age* was a watershed moment as, at 17, I was invited to see them at Hammersmith Odeon, my first ever concert. Witnessing McCluskey's madcap romp through 'Maid of Orleans' from the front row, I left the venue ecstatic, overwhelmed at the quality of execution.

EMPIRE
2 November 1986, Liverpool, UK

SIMON GARLAND

Longest-standing friend Mark and I both made an aborted attempt at procuring a degree from the University of Birmingham. Friends since the age of three who attended the same primary and secondary schools and about a dozen OMD tours, we even went out with the same girl at one point. Mark brought our femme fatale to the Empire for The Pacific Age tour and I sang the chorus of 'So in Love' to the back of her head.

NICK WHITFIELD

My best mate Johno was already into OMD. We were both about 13. I went to his house and he said, 'Listen to this', putting 'Dancing' on. His parents were out so it was full blast. I thought, 'This is weird but different.' Then he turned the record over and 'Bunker Soldiers' came out of the speakers. I was awestruck, the bass-line seeming to hit me right in the stomach.

A few years later, working on a cash till in W.H. Smith, Nantwich, Cheshire, Andy and his girlfriend entered the shop, which was busy, so I just couldn't jump off the till. As luck had it he came to my till to buy a copy of *Smash Hits*. I said, 'I'm sorry to bother you while you're shopping, but can I have an autograph?' By now I was grinning like an idiot and felt like a nervous schoolgirl. Andy asked, 'What name shall I put on the autograph?' and I said 'Mine!' It took me a moment to realise what I'd done but we all laughed and I just said, 'Oh, err, err, umm, it's Nick.' How uncool was I?

My friend and I got to the Liverpool gig early and were around the back of the venue in the car park. The tour bus was there and my friend, into lorries and HGVs, was shouting, 'Nick, look at the size of the wheel nuts on this.' While he was doing that, Andy and Martin Cooper walked past, so I said, 'Hi gents, I'm looking forward to the gig.' My friend was still bent over the wheel of the bus, shouting, 'Nick, these are like the biggest tyres ever!' I was shouting, 'Johnno, come over here quick, look behind you!' But he was ignoring me. Andy and Martin were laughing, and I shouted, 'Johnno, here now!' He turned around, saw what was happening and ran over, the guys good enough to chat to him for a bit too.

↑
Andy with Paul in his garage studio with converted first tour keyboard panel as a wall light and the Fairlight computer

WE LOVE YOU WAS RELEASED

3 NOV 1986

PLAYHOUSE

4 November 1986, Edinburgh, UK

LESLEY O'TOOLE

Mirelle Davis and I met at an OMD gig at Edinburgh's Playhouse in 1986. I was a newly-minted music journalist reviewing the show for *Record Mirror*. We became fast friends, sharing a love of bands (especially those from Liverpool or Glasgow it seemed) and often travelling together. New research suggests gig-goers live 21% longer than those who've never thrilled to the ineffable joy of experiencing their favourite artists live. We're both good there.

In the same way Messrs. McCluskey and Humphreys parted ways for more than 20 years, so too did Mirelle and I. The teenager I met in Edinburgh was clearly ahead of her time, so I wasn't surprised when she told me two decades later she was now OMD's manager and would be on tour with them in Los Angeles.

Their show at The Fonda that night in 2011 was joyous, and not just for the still-loved songs and new ones from *The History of Modern*. Each song from the pair's first recording collaboration in 24 years seemed more rapidly brain-ingrained than the last. And there was something reassuring about the still-bonkers McCluskey dance moves/lyrical interpretations. But it was extra joyous because I was there as the guest of my friend of so long, no longer the fan but the extremely capable woman in charge.

I was working as an entertainment journalist in London, LA and Sydney for the same time span, fleetingly a band manager too. But I'd never stood on the stage during a show until 29 July 2017 when OMD headlined 80s Weekend #4 at LA's Microsoft Theatre. Given a bill also featuring The Psychedelic Furs, Colin Hay from Men at Work, The FIXX, Berlin, and Belinda Carlisle, plus former KROQ radio DJ Richard Blade as host, sets were curtailed. And while there was a certain thrill at being so close to the action -limited as it was to 11 songs - there was a more immediate realisation. Years of being at soundchecks, waiting to interview bands, should have yielded an innate sense of this, but apparently didn't - the sound onstage is horrid. A fan's view is always best.

Fast forward to March 31, 2018: 60th birthday of one of my dearest friends, Colin Howe, OMD promoting *The Punishment of Luxury*, making a Saturday stop in San Diego, Mirelle with them.

The show, from the House of Blues balcony, was mesmerising, ample compensation for the previous stage-side sound-bath. While they played only one new song at the 80s Weekend outing ('The History of Modern'), they neatly slotted in songs galore from *The Punishment of Luxury* ('Ghost Star' as opener, 'Isotype', 'One More Time', 'What Have We Done', and the title track). *History of Modern* bookending new and older hits, all blending seamlessly.

An intimate venue at which people sat upstairs stood and danced (LA audiences like to sit), San Diego bore witness to an energized, at times overcome band. So rapturous was the response to 'Secret' that Paul forgot the words, but acquitted himself perfectly on 'Souvenir', for which Andy slunk around the block-based set, guitar slung low, as if determined to give Paul as much time in the spotlight as possible.

The night concluded, as now seemingly the norm, with 'Electricity.' The spark remains in all four band members - McCluskey, Humphreys, Stuart Kershaw and Martin Cooper, the latter a balancing act to the 'front' men. They stood together on stage, looking for all the world like they'd had the time of their lives.

Afterwards, a friend of the band's hyper-efficient tour manager Ryan Westbrook handed me a copy of a poster for the concert. He didn't know about my friend's birthday, but I knew this was a gift, metaphorical and otherwise (almost) worthy of my other great friend. The universe being aligned as it was, Ryan produced a silver sharpie, and Andy and Paul signed it.

↑
Photos taken from the *Pacific Age* tour programme

1986 | 249

A night - and a Souvenir - to remember. Even better when the birthday boy saw his present, noting, 'I used to know Paul Humphreys to say hello to and met Andy once, with Paul, in 1980 in the queue at the Nat West bank on Whitechapel, Liverpool, as their rehearsal studio was nearby.'

Long may OMD's pulsating electricity stay connected. Old friends too.

UNIVERSITY OF WESTERN ONTARIO

10 November 1986, London, Ontario, Canada

COLAN LANCASTER

Growing up in Northern Ontario, contributed to a sense of isolation. Long, cold, dark winters didn't help, the outdoor night scenes in *A Charlie Brown Christmas* capturing the vastness of the night skies. My father was a young teen when his family emigrated, leaving post-war England. Later, as a young father and land surveyor, he moved his family to North Bay, Ontario, setting up the remote English colony that was our household, with meticulous lawn, flower garden and borders.

The local AM music station and church supplied the music of my early youth, while at friends' houses we could listen to elder siblings' stereos. Early favourites were The Beatles and The Beach Boys. The station played 70s pop and rock, but nothing experimental. But in the early 80s, listening to the Canadian Broadcasting Corporation's *90 Minutes with a Bullet*, I began to hear UK acts such as Elvis Costello and Gary Numan. My thirst for new music grew, graduating from Kiss to The Clash.

It was in 1984 that I first heard OMD. My elder brother had been in Toronto and recorded some songs off new music station CFNY 102.1. 'Talking Loud and Clear' wasn't something I'd have heard anywhere else. It combined melody and electronica beautifully. In the fall that year I was off to university. I remember my brother buying *Crush*, then I went out and bought the extended mix of 'So in Love.' I started mining the older OMD albums, with *Dazzle Ships* the sound I really appreciated.

I was so fortunate when OMD were on the Pacific Age tour and came to my university in London, Ontario. I was able to get floor tickets and danced most of the show. I recall the back-projected art and large reel-to-reel tape machines. Visually the most I saw of OMD was the video for 'Forever Live and Die', going out and getting Clubmaster-style sunglasses so I could be cool in the film version of my life.

I saw OMD open for Depeche Mode in Toronto in 1988 and then on 1991's Sugar Tax tour. Miracles happen and OMD released *History of Modern* and the even better *English Electric*, which for me encapsulated all the best elements of OMD into one album.

I saw OMD twice at Danforth Music Hall, including the infamous heatwave concert. On this latest tour I saw them twice more. A highlight was the soundcheck and a chance to meet the band. It was a true privilege to meet them in person, saying thanks for all the enjoyment they've given me. They seem to me a band you could have an enjoyable intelligent conversation with over a couple glasses of wine. I am available for dinner.

Growing up in North Bay, an old oil painting hung in our living room. With my father's passing in 2011, the painting eventually wound up on my living room wall. I can't make out the artist but the title appears to be 'Lighthouse on the Mersey.' I believe it's of the lighthouse that exists in Wirral. I just connected the dots this year. A beacon of light from Liverpool shining on my youth.

▲ Andy McCluskey (left) and Paul Humphreys – no fresh clothing and only the cemetery to snooze in...

ORPHEUM THEATER

25 November 1986, Minneapolis, Minnesota

MATTHEW DAHLQUIST

OMD gave the crowd everything and the crowd gave it right back. I can't say for sure whether the show was sold out, but the balcony of the Orpheum Theater, at the time owned by Bob Dylan, was busy.

My friends and I camped out before tickets went on sale, scoring spectacular seats dead-centre on the sixth row. Once OMD took the stage, it was only seconds before the crowd was on their feet and moving. At the end, 'Locomotion' happened and fans closest to the stage noticed the band look toward the balcony with expressions of concern. Row by

↑ Filming *Crush The Movie*

row, people turned to see what was happening then adopted similar expressions. Some started pointing up with mouths open. When we turned around and looked up, the cause for concern was obvious. The crowd jumping up and down in time to 'Locomotion' made the balcony flex by a couple of feet. We were certain the whole thing was going to collapse onto the main floor seats. Fortunately, the balcony and fans survived.

Shortly after, Bob Dylan sold the venue to the city of Minneapolis and it was closed for a renovation. It might be a coincidence, but I always suspected OMD's show had something to do with it.

LAURIE AUDITORIUM

1 December 1986,
San Antonio, Texas

SCOTT SCHUMAKER
Bright Antenna Records

The first OMD song I heard was 'So In Love' in 1985. I was 15 and living in San Antonio, Texas, then heavy metal capital of America, so OMD wasn't being played on radio, but the video found its way onto *MTV*. This was before *120 Minutes* or 'If You Leave,' and the band hadn't really broken through in the States. Maybe it was the weird synth sounds, the saxophone during the bridge (I was playing sax then), or the Día de los Muertos skulls in the video, but it stuck with me.

A few months later Andy, Paul, Malcolm and Martin came through San Antonio. Graham and Neil Weir were on stage too. The Models supported. The show was at a theatre meant for symphonies and I'd say only a third full as *Pretty in Pink* hadn't come out yet. The room was all weird angles and too brightly lit, but it sounded great. And there was Andy, with his whirling dervish dancing.

I bought the picture-disc vinyl with 'So in Love' (extended) on side A and 'Concrete Hands' (extended) and 'Maria Gallante' on side B. The picture on side A was a neon Día de los Muertes skull, which I thought was the coolest thing I'd ever seen. I hung around after the show hoping the band could sign it, but I couldn't find them.

Never in my wildest dreams did I imagine I'd meet them someday, much less work with them. Yet, fast-forward to 2009 and a label I co-founded, Bright Antenna Records, licensed *History of Modern* to release it in North America. It was the first record featuring the original Andy-Paul-Malcolm-Martin line up in 20 years. The band was gracious, approachable, super-professional and worked harder than most bands we knew in their early 20s. We joked that they should give a class: 'What it Really Takes to Succeed as a Band'.

They sold out shows across the US. Gwen Stefani and Tony Kanal of No Doubt reached out to get on the guest-list. The live shows were still on-point, probably even more so. These guys had decades of performing under their belts, Andy still dervishing his whirl, no substance enhancement needed. The joy I saw in the crowd during those shows is something I'll never forget. Some weird mystical kismet led to that point and I'll always be grateful for it. Somehow, I still managed to fail getting my 'So In Love' disc signed though.

PARAMOUNT THEATER

3 December 1986, Denver, Colorado

TODD CHRISTOPHER MCMAHON

I was a big synth-loving nerd, growing up listening to electronic pioneers like Wendy Carlos, Tomita, Vangelis, Jean-Michel Jarre and Kraftwerk. It was the 80s when we first heard British synth-pop and I listened to all the new wave acts I could. This included tuning into Andy Dean's *London Calling* on KBCO 97.3 FM from Boulder, Colorado, a British graduate exchange student at the University of Colorado convincing the station to give him a one-hour show every Monday night. Unscripted but insightful, through Andy I heard Depeche Mode, The Human League, then in 1984, 'Locomotion', and later 'Souvenir' and 'Talking Loud and Clear.' I decided to buy their current LP first chance I got. Back then, it was really hard to buy UK music in America.

I was into my high school senior year that year when my father suddenly got sick and passed away. My mother and sister decided we needed time away and we spent a few weeks in Hawaii. Not feeling great I went into a record store in Honolulu and purchased *Junk Culture*. I was impressed. What made me a greater fan was the release of *Crush*, heard while I was a first year at university in Tempe, Arizona, far from home. I was hooked after hearing OMD again on the radio with 'So in Love.' I thought, 'Wow, this band really is talented.' They were like The Beatles of the 80s!

Back in Denver, I purchased the back-catalogue, spending my extra dollars at our hip Wax Trax record store. Until I rented *Crush the Movie*, I'd never actually seen what they looked like, but I found out we had much in common, not just electronic music, but also a great love of history and archaeology. They even inspired me to purchase my own synth, a Sequential Circuits Six-Trak, creating music of my own, labelling myself

More Than a Pretty Face
OMD brings substance to British pop

BY JOEL SELVIN

Hit British rock groups have been so guilty of ridiculously shallow trendiness in the past that it almost comes as a surprise to encounter so musically solid and intellectually sound a band as Orchestral Manoeuvres in the Dark, who appeared Friday at the Warfield Theater.

"If You Leave," OMD's major hit from last year's "Pretty in Pink" soundtrack, earned the Liverpudlian synth-popsters an enthusiastic teenage constituency, but the group displayed a healthy reluctance to pander to such appeal, cheerily downgrading the song's impact before playing the smash single at the Warfield.

"We used to have tons of credibility," said lead singer Andy McCluskey, "before we released this track."

Indeed, the band carved out a minor niche for itself, crafting sleek microchip-driven dance tracks for an artsy British record label beginning seven years ago, and notching a series of electro-pop U.K. dance hits that never broke into the mainstream on this side of the Atlantic. The "Pretty in Pink" soundtrack may have changed all that — "The Pacific Age," the band's seventh album, is currently ascending the charts steadily, courtesy the hit single "(Forever) Live and Die" — but OMD clearly refuses to tailor its act to assure American success.

In front of an audience composed largely of overexcited teens, OMD opened the scintillating show with "Southern," a track from the new album that combines excerpts of speeches by Martin Luther King with a throbbing dance groove for a pointed, provocative effect. This kind of thoughtful social comment is not customarily the province of teenybopper faves.

OMD founders McCluskey and his partner Paul Humphries were aided and abetted greatly by four accomplished musicians, the band changing instrumental formations on virtually every song. McCluskey delivered an inspired, charismatic performance, singing in clear, resonant tones and driving home the sound with dance moves that fell somewhere between James Brown and an acidhead at a Dead concert.

Humphries remained largely behind his Emulator, singing through a headphone microphone, and producing a cornucopia of exotic sounds from his keyboard, ranging from rude, rumbling belches to delicate, tinkling figures that sounded like a music box from outer space.

The group seems to delight in contrasting the mechanical thumping of synthesizers with regulation acoustic instruments, dropping a trumpet solo in the middle of one instrumental passage or using an honest-to-god old-fashioned drum kit, along with the inevitable drum machines.

The songs showed real flair at wit and empathy, at times verging on friendly pop fluff, but never succumbing to empty-headed platitudes that mark so much of popular British synth-pop. The performance drew from the full range of the OMD songbook, with early pieces like "Julia's Song" and "Electricity" (undoubtedly unfamiliar to their recently acquired "Pretty in Pink" fans) jauntily juxtaposed with later, more successful pieces.

But the snappy, irresistible dance grooves the band can seemingly fashion endlessly served as the main feature of the evening. "Don't you dare sit down," ordered McCluskey at one point, as he launched yet another crackling, driving track. The audience happily complied, swaying and bobbing in front of their seats, mesmerized by the entrancing sounds.

Paul Humphries brought a cornucopia of exotic sounds from his synthesizer

↑ Live review from the *San Francisco Chronicle*

Euphonic Sound, or ES.

My first OMD concert was in 1986. Not only were they enthusiastic but also turned the concert venue into a dance hall. Everyone was dancing. There was no turning back. They met all my criteria as the greatest band ever. I've kept up since, seeing them perform with Depeche Mode, who they upstaged, buying all Paul and Andy's side-project releases through to later OMD releases, my wife Heidi joining me at Denver's Bluebird Theater in 2011 for the History of Modern, the whole family now fans.

KURT IVERSON

Before I even knew who OMD were, they were helping shape my night-owl habits. In middle school, I'd stay up late to watch movies in the basement. One intro to a show featured a lone taxi-cab driving through the night lights of a city. In the background I heard what I later discovered was 'Messages.'

Several years later, my sister dated a guy she nicknamed 'Otto Tendon Plaids'. He introduced us to the fact that people actually bought $150 leather shoes while travelling in Europe, as well as the one thing of value he brought back with him, a copy of *Crush*. I wore that tape out.

They came to Boulder, Colorado, opening for The Thompson Twins, my first concert. I was amazed at the energy and melody of every song. My sister took me for my birthday. This was the first time I saw Andy dance. I based all my perceptions of how I should be on the dancefloor around his energy. My moves eventually got way better over time.

WARFIELD THEATRE

5 December 1986, San Francisco, California

NOREEN CHWEE

It was the name that drew me first: an evocative, artistic, moody, slightly pretentious moniker with weird British spelling that my teenage soul truly appreciated. My first glimpse was on *MTV*, seeing these pale English gentlemen in pristine white shirts and cool leather jackets roaming exotic Mexican cities and driving across empty deserts, drawn in by Andy's deeply passionate voice.

San Francisco radio station, KITS, were playing 'So in Love', so I'd call religiously to request it. I couldn't afford to buy the album at the time. This was the best I could do. One day, they had a contest to win tickets to their show. I planted myself by the radio all day, and with perseverance and sore fingers from dialling, won a pair.

I found a friend willing to see a band she'd never heard of, and my Dad reluctantly dropped us off in an unsavoury part of town, so I could attend my first concert. I naively expected good seats, but they were right at the back - folding chairs placed last minute in an undesirable location. But I cheered myself up by thinking I'd finally see my favourite band.

Once they were on stage I was in heaven, singing along to all the songs I knew and appreciating the unfamiliar. It was such a tremendous and unforgettable evening, seeing Andy prance around the stage with boundless energy and hearing Paul's sweet voice live. Near the end, I wasn't sure what to expect. After the last song, no one seemed to be leaving. After minutes of rapturous applause, they returned, and I knew I had to leave my place of exile in the back and rush to the front, experiencing the last songs in ecstatic, euphoric union with the band. It was the best night of my teenage life and one that will stay with me always.

ONE OF THE BEST NEW BANDS IN AMERICA

↑ During '86 OMD played another 36 shows in North America

1987-1988

OMD toured Australia, Japan, Canada and the US and the start of 1988 saw the release of the group's twenty-first single, 'Dreaming'

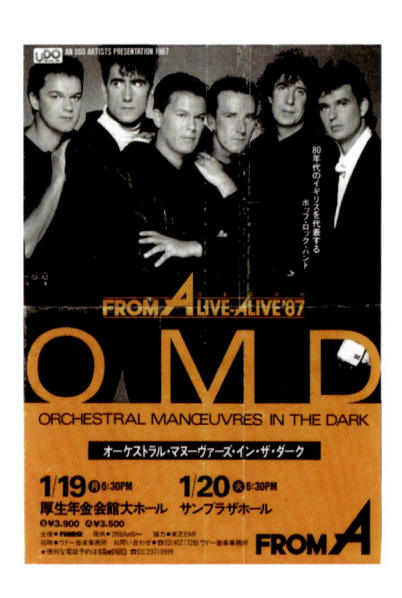

OMD played five nights in Japan in January 1987

A doll of Andy made by a Japanese fan

ANDY MCCLUSKEY

Our first time in Japan was a remarkable cultural experience. The audiences were polite but their silence between songs was rather disturbing. I recall Malcolm, Martin and I standing behind the curtain screening us on the back riser as the house lights went down in Osaka. Rapturous applause followed by an eerie noiseless still. So quiet that not only could we not hear Paul's footsteps as he crossed the stage to his keyboards, but also the 'click' of the tape machine as he started the tape for 'Junk Culture'.

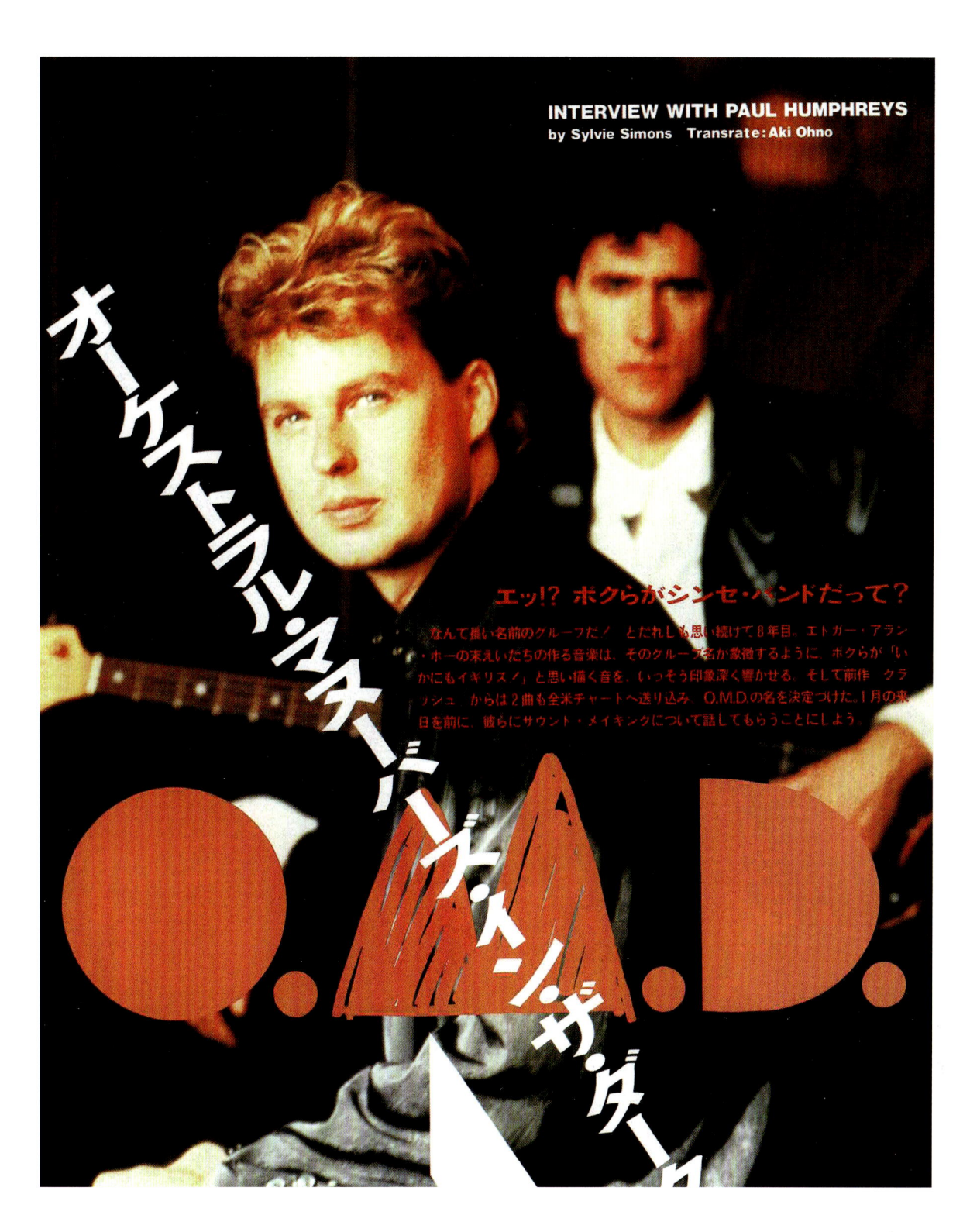

INTERVIEW WITH PAUL HUMPHREYS
by Sylvie Simons　Transrate:Aki Ohno

オーケストラル・マヌーヴァーズ・イン・ザ・ダーク

O.M.D.

エッ!? ボクらがシンセ・バンドだって?

なんて暗い名前のグループだ!とだれしも思い続けて8年目。エドガー・アラン・ポーの末えいたちの作る音楽は、そのグループ名が象徴するように、ボクらが「いかにもイギリス!」と思い描く音を、いっそう印象深く響かせる。そして前作『クラッシュ』からは2曲も全米チャートへ送り込み、O.M.D.の名を決定づけた。1月の来日を前に、彼らにサウンド・メイキングについて話してもらうことにしよう。

OMD - 1987-1988

I bought a new Sony Professional Walkman. Such a technology treat. A portable tape player that also recorded. I remember sitting in my hotel room recording endless Japanese TV commercials, just because I loved the crazy tones and voices. I had no idea that they would become a staple in our sample library for the next few years.

SHAME
WAS RELEASED

13 APR 1987

→
Andy with record company rep January 1987

→
Paul and Andy arrive at Tokyo Airport January 1987

MALTE WERNING

In the 80s, my local German radio station WDR had a chart show called Schlagerrallye. Every Saturday a top-15 was played and the audience voted for their favourite. Each week five new singles were played, giving them a chance to enter the chart, and every month five volunteers were invited to go to Cologne to select the best new singles for the show.

A friend's brother bought the *Junk Culture* album and we played that disc up and down. I wasn't a huge fan of 'Locomotion', but 'Tesla Girls' thrilled me – it was so different. I became a devotee, loved *Crush*, and especially *The Pacific Age*.

In February 1988 it was time for me to join the Schlagerrallye show's jury. I was nervous since I knew OMD had a new single,

'Dreaming.' The guys at the station presented us with new singles, but no OMD. I asked for 'Dreaming' but the jury had rejected it. I was disappointed - the radio guy made an exception and presented me with the single, giving it another chance to be accepted.

A week later I was asked to present the track in the show. The audience loved it, even though, looking back, it wasn't their best.

DREAMING
WAS RELEASED

25 JAN 1988

Orchestral dreaming

Has OMD done a pop OD?

"Dreaming" is the 22nd single in the 10-years-and-counting career of England's Orchestral Manoeuvres in the Dark, the band that set the standard for the post-punk synth pop duo. OMD's visibility (videos and tours) and proliferation (7 albums) paved the way for a new kind of band with no drummer or guitar players.

Originally inspired by Brian Eno and German bands (especially Kraftwerk), the early sound of Paul Humphreys and Andy McCluskey is computers, radios, electronics and ambience. Each new album differed so dramatically from its predecessor that OMD eluded commercial success and confused listeners. For the better part of their career, the band (now six members) worked a grueling album-tour-album-tour routine. Last year they took off time and listened to their accomplishments, putting together their latest lp, *The Best of OMD*.

Laurie Pike: Were you ever encouraged before now to make a greatest hits record?
Andy McCluskey: For a long time, we thought of a compilation album as a bit of a cop out, a bit of a cheat. I suppose we've mellowed with age.
Paul Humphreys: I think with 21 singles we sort of merit one.
A.M.: It was a useful thing to have around. We'd taken time off last year and we're not a band who can afford to disappear for any great period of time.
L.P.: Why?
P.H.: We're not a highly visual band when we don't have records out.
L.P.: But you've always had videos of your song from an early time on, and you had that film *Crush* to go with that album (1985).
P.H.: The record company (Virgin) really messed that up. By the time they got it together, we were working on the next album.
A.M.: The electronic and experimental side of you isn't very well represented on the *Best of* album. You didn't include any songs from *Dazzle Ships* (1983), though there were two singles from it.
P.H.: We didn't want to go with a double album and all the songs that are on this album we thought are important. But "Telegraph" and "Genetic Engineering" weren't really hits anyway. They were singles, but they weren't big hits.
A.M.: "Telegraph" and "Genetic Engineering" are on the European CD. I don't know why they aren't on the U.S. CD.
L.P.: What do you think of the spate of cover versions on the charts?
A.M.: Cover versions are symptomatic of the retreat of the music business back to conservative attitudes. I think it's proof positive—especially in Britain from people you expected *not* to be doing them—that people want so much to be pop stars, but they don't have anything to say for themselves, they're not able to write new songs anymore. The '80s seem to be about constant rehashing of old ideas, not just in music, but in film, fashion . . . this sort of a collaging together of older ideas, it's a conservativeness and a scaredness that people are retreating from the future.
L.P.: And sampling?
P.H.: It's really going down a cul-de-sac. By the end of the year, everybody's going to be so sick of these pieces. That's all they are, just collages of samples without any song content. We've sampled for six or seven years, but we've always managed to use samples as building blocks to larger things.
L.P.: Are there regrets in your career?
P.H.: Plenty. Not in the music, but I think commercially we've made some wrong moves.
A.M.: We could be a lot richer now.
P.H.: We should have gotten a good lawyer from day one.
A.M.: I do sometimes wonder about *Dazzle Ships*. Commercially, we murdered ourselves for about three years. *Junk Culture* (1984) followed and—without sounding unnecessarily big-headed—was a fantastic pop music album, and it didn't get as much of a positive reception as it should have. It wasn't as big commercially as it should have been.
A.H.: It would have been if it would have followed *Architecture and Morality* (1981). We changed too radically for most people.
L.P.: Your lyrics and music are much more consistently pop than before.
P.H.: Musically we're still doing whatever we feel like doing.
A.M.: In comparison to the musical environment we're in, we probably appear more conservative. We're not as far ahead of the pack as we used to be, but how long can you keep yourself ahead of people? The world catches you up. We haven't consciously manipulated our music in order to appeal to a broader audience.
P.H.: To a certain extent, we have compromised, but it's not in the music, it's in spending an immense amount of time in America.
A.M.: The only conscious compromise comes in after the songs have been written. What's going to be the single, and how are we going to sell this, because, yes, we want to sell our records. ★ Laurie Pike

Head maneuverers: Andy McCluskey (L) and Paul Humphreys

OMD Dreaming

Once upon a time OMD only had to burp and they had a mega-hit. But then Andy McCluskey and Paul Humphreys decided a rest was the order of the day.

"Paul went home and his wife didn't even recognise him," japed Andy. "No, seriously folks, we needed a break."

"I spent some time in the States with my wife," burped Paul. "I love it there because the TV has 35 channels and I'm a TV addict."

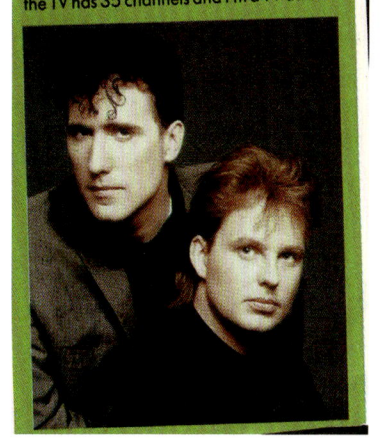

↑ 1988 press interview with Paul and Andy

OMD - 1987-1988

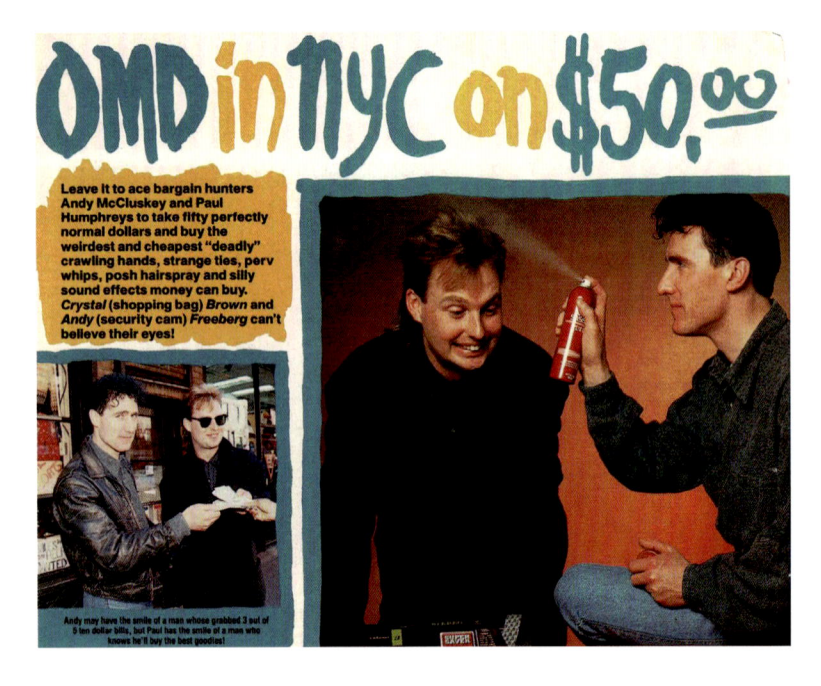

OMD in NYC on $50.00

Leave it to ace bargain hunters Andy McCluskey and Paul Humphreys to take fifty perfectly normal dollars and buy the weirdest and cheapest "deadly" crawling hands, strange ties, perv whips, posh hairspray and silly sound effects money can buy. *Crystal* (shopping bag) *Brown* and *Andy* (security cam) *Freeberg* can't believe their eyes!

Andy may have the smile of a man whose grabbed 3 out of 5 ten dollar bills, but Paul has the smile of a man who knows he'll buy the best goodies!

↑ Paul and Andy are asked to buy the weirdest things they can for $50

ANDY MCCLUSKEY

The *Pacific Age* album had sold reasonably well and 'Forever Live and Die' had been a hit, but we were still not reaching the success that we had experienced earlier in the decade. The massive world tours were actually losing money and we had no funds in the bank. We didn't care about money, but you can't run a band on fresh air!

The only quick way out of the hole was to release a compilation album. But we needed a new single to promote this. Easier said that done.

By this stage Paul and I were working at the studio in the converted garage at his house, living a nocturnal life. We would work until 7am. I would go home, sleep, have breakfast and return to Paul's after it had already gone dark. We never saw daylight. Vampire musicians trying desperately to write a single for the 'Best of' release. The song we finally created was 'Dreaming'. Don't ask me what the lyrics are about. They mean nothing; I just wrote some words - I had to have something to sing. To promote the *Best Of OMD* we went straight on tour with Depeche Mode.

CALIFORNIA EXPO

30 April 1988, Sacramento, California

JAMES LAROT

They were the surprise opening act for Depeche Mode during the Music for the Masses performance in Sacramento. A mostly-conservative Christian audience was preparing to boo and hiss at Depeche Mode for the song 'Blasphemous Rumours' and many of the concert-goers hissed and threw shoes at OMD, one hitting Andy in the chest mid-song. A strange night indeed.

260 | 1987-1988

> **ROCKPIX**
>
> OMD seem to be following in the vein of bands like INXS or XTC who based their names on letters that sound like a word. Actually, this is far from the truth! OMD is short for Orchestral Manoeuvres In The Dark, whereas INXS stands for "In Excess" and XTC stood for "Ecstasy." But if you wanna hear some real ecstasy, just check out the glorious pop melodies of OMD. Formed by Andy McCluskey and Paul Humphreys six and a half years ago, the dynamic duo have incorporated other instruments into their "band" over the years, but they've never forsaken what many consider to be the best synth pop to ever come out of England. No tales of alienation here. Just melodies like you wouldn't believe! And *Pretty In Pink* made 'em a household name! OMD—they're great!
>
> Anastasia Pantsios/Kaleyedoscope
>
> 13

SEATTLE CENTER COLISEUM

2 May 1988, Seattle, Washington

STACY LYNCH

I grew up outside Seattle, Washington. When I was 12, I started to discover new wave and punk. We had a Canadian TV station that had a great music video show and was introduced to OMD via that seeing the video for 'Secret.'

↑
The dynamic duo!

In 1988, OMD opened for my favourite band, Depeche Mode, and 30 years later I still remember that first time. So much energy, so much fun.

OMD were also a very important and special band to my friend, Missy Van Slyke, a super-fan who travelled around the States to see them live. She surprised me with a copy of *English Electric* when it came out. She passed away in February 2017. I know wherever OMD are Missy is, with the best seat in the house, enjoying the music she held so dear.

SIX FLAGS
13 May 1988, Arlington, Texas

JONATHAN PROUGH

I played my *Crush* cassette over and over on my Walkman as I delivered newspapers around my town of Ponca City, Oklahoma. It was a rural cowboy town and OMD weren't known beyond a few new wave friends. I saw them open for Depeche Mode on the Music for the Masses tour at Six Flags. As I grew up, got married and had kids, my entire family fell in love with OMD. On Friday nights we'd let the kids DJ, with OMD always top of their setlist, all of us dancing in the front room.

In 2011 they announced they'd be playing Cain's Ballroom in Tulsa, Oklahoma. There was no age restriction, so Cait, five, and Crewe, seven, came along. During the concert, Andy said he wanted to thank the two kids who had been dancing all night, waving at Crewe while he was singing. Crewe thought he was waving at someone else and turned around to see who the lucky person was. As soon as the concert was over, Cait said, 'Can we try to meet the band?' We tracked them down and they were beyond nice to the kids and took the time to take a picture with them.

The concert was on a school night. The kids didn't get to bed until almost 2am as we had to drive two hours to get home!

UNIONDALE
3 June 1988, Jones Beach, New York

STEPHANIE ALLEY

I first heard OMD on WLIR, the Long Island radio station that played new wave music. In 1988 they toured with Depeche Mode and I asked my Mom if I could go see them at Jones Beach. I was only 15, a freshman in high school, and having a rough time. Music seemed to be one of the only things bringing me joy, so my mother said I could go. It was my first concert and I was beyond excited. At some point they announced that OMD would be signing autographs at Tower Records in Roosevelt Field Mall. Again, I asked Mom if I could go. Not only did she say yes, but she offered to pick me and a friend of mine up at school and drive us.

My friend and I were both dressed in school uniforms: green blazers, plaid skirts and penny-loafers. We stuck out so bad but must have caught the attention of people from the radio station, and they came over to talk to us. When we got to the front of the line the people in charge let us stay a long while. We got to ask questions, talk and take a bunch of pictures. Andy and Paul were so nice and charming. I brought a picture from a magazine for them to sign. The concert was truly amazing and it's one of my greatest memories.

A few weeks after I wrote Andy and Paul a letter, thanking them for talking to us at the record store, telling them how much we enjoyed the concert and asking them about the inspiration for 'Tesla Girls.' I never expected a response. One afternoon I headed out to our mailbox and found an envelope from an address I didn't know, my name and address written with unfamiliar handwriting. When I opened the letter, I was shocked.

I screamed and ran back in. Andy had answered the letter himself. It had been such a rough year, but that letter made me forget all my teenage problems. For years the letter hung, framed, on my bedroom wall. It always made me smile and reminded me just how lucky I was. I call 'If You Leave' my lucky song. Whenever I hear it, it reminds me just how lucky I am.

COMPTON TERRACE

15 June 1988, Phoenix, Arizona

JAY DEWITT

My friends and I loaded into an old Econoline van that evening to see OMD. It reached 108°F that summer day. At one point, Andy asked the crowd why we weren't dancing more, then answered his own question, saying it was 'too fucking hot!' The heat kept OMD away from Phoenix until April 2018. It was only 89°F when the same group of friends and I went to an indoor, air-conditioned venue to see them again and danced like crazy. They played a great mix of old and new songs in what is our favourite concert ever.

OMD – 1987-1988

OMD cricket team vs Depeche Mode. Back (left to right) Wob Roberts, bus driver, Stuart Kerrison (FOH), Martin, Malcolm, Andy, Graham Weir, Eddie Butler (drum roadie). Front (left to right) Neil Weir, Donna (wardrobe), Paul, Richard 'six dinners' Carter (merchandise), Rob McKenzie (lights), unknown

ROSEBOWL
18 June 1988, Pasadena, California

ANDY MCCLUSKEY

I was so nervous for the last concert of the Music for the Masses tour (in front of 70,000), that I crawled behind the sofa in the dressing room so no-one could find me, falling asleep until 15 minutes before stage-time. It was a trick I'd developed when facing severe stage-fright. The walk down the long ramp to the stage looking at all those faces seemed to be miles and the fear grew almost unbearable before we finally started playing. Twenty seconds into 'Enola Gay', a momentary power-spike stopped both Emulator keyboards and they began reloading the sound discs. Mal and I were left doing a drum and bass-only version for 40 seconds. Not a great way to start a show. But we recovered, and the concert was truly amazing.

CHAD HUEBNER

Everyone booed Thomas Dolby off, but OMD came on, electrifying the crowd. A food-fight started and all you saw was the sky filled with edibles. Depeche Mode were headlining, and they couldn't have had a better support band to get the Rose Bowl jumping.

RICHARD BLADE
US-based British DJ/radio broadcaster

My earliest memory of Orchestral Manoeuvres in the Dark was in 1980 when I was DJing at a hard rock station in Bakersfield, California. The staples of our playlist were Ted Nugent, Black Sabbath, AC/DC and Motorhead. As program director of Magic 98 I introduced two weekend 'specialty' programs aired on Sunday nights. One, *Reggae Revolution*, allowed me to bust out Bob Marley, Peter

Tosh, Toots and the Maytals, etc. The other was *The English Invasion*, spotlighting a music renaissance happening in the UK.

Among the mix of The Police, The Jam and Elvis Costello was one band I was playing that had a radically different sound; their music had an incredible beat, but it seemed that electronic drums were generating the rhythm, matched with haunting melodies played on synthesisers and topped off with incredible vocals, the songs catchy and unforgettable.

It wasn't just me who felt that way. I got calls from listeners asking who was making this incredible music. My answer was always the same, 'They're from England and they've got a strange name, Orchestral Manoeuvres in the Dark.' The words coming back to me down the line were inevitably, 'Who?'

As 'Messages', 'Enola Gay', 'Souvenir' and 'Joan of Arc' followed 'Electricity' and made our playlist; the band's name became more and more familiar to listeners and was quickly shortened to OMD. Many a night I played an OMD song and talked on the air about their

↑
Richard Blade with Paul, Andy and competition winners

OMD - 1987-1988

↑
OMD fan club newsletters often carried cartoons drawn by a young Greek fan called Alex Machairas

heritage, hailing from a city with such a legendary music history, Liverpool, wondering to myself what they'd be like in person - untouchable pop stars or down-to-earth guys? Little did I know that in the years to follow not only would I get to meet them but that we would become friends.

At KROQ in Los Angeles, and on my *MV3* and *Video One* TV shows, OMD became a mainstay of any musical playlist, and when I finally get to know them after Andy and Paul came to our Pasadena studio for a live interview, I was blown away at how down to earth, open and funny they were. And the live concerts didn't disappoint. With Malcolm Holmes and Martin Cooper behind them, Andy and Paul put on an amazing series of shows in California, winning the hearts and souls of fans.

When my radio station was in the planning stages of bringing Depeche Mode to California to play the Rosebowl and put on the single biggest new wave show in US history, there was no doubt in the minds of anyone in those early meetings just who we wanted and needed to open. When we received the OK from OMD's management we breathed a collective sigh of relief. With those guys on stage we knew the show would be a night to remember, and it was, with 18 June 1988 looked upon as a defining moment for UK music in America. More than 70,000 fans packed every seat in that famed stadium for what became known as *Concert 101*. But none of those seats were needed when OMD took to the stage. Everyone was on their feet dancing and singing for every second of a brilliant set.

When I heard they had a new album out, *The Punishment of Luxury*, I waited eagerly for a copy, hoping there'd be something on it I could play on my Sirius XM *1st Wave* show. I was stunned when I listened. The problem was not finding something to play but deciding which track to put on first. It was that good. Here was a band after 40 years continuing to not only reinvent themselves but pushing for new heights.

Vince Clarke told me in a 2014 interview how OMD influenced him. Asked what got him into music, he paused, then said, 'I was into guitar big time, then heard this song, 'Electricity'. I couldn't believe it. Everything changed for me. I sold my guitar and went out, bought a synthesiser, because I knew that was the kind of music I wanted to make.'

That's the kind of influence OMD has had. Without them perhaps Vince Clarke – and countless others – might never have turned to music or synthesisers, and there would have been no Depeche Mode, Yazoo, Erasure, etc. Without them we'd have not only missed out on the amazing songs they brought us, but who knows where the genre we call alternative music would be today without the enormous impact OMD had on it.

THE BREAK-UP YEARS

I needed the break that I always wanted. I had a house in California that I hadn't really been living in so I spent more and more time in California. But I wanted to do something. My daughter was born there in '91, and I wanted to be a dad for a while. Then I thought, 'I need to do something'. Martin and Mal and I had always wanted to have a Liverpool label. Also, there were a lot of Liverpool artists that couldn't find record labels. So we started Telegraph Records. We signed China Crisis, we signed Pete Coyle's The Lotus Eaters, and we had various other new bands that were developing. We needed to launch the label, so Martin, Mal and I decided to put a band together. We had some songs kicking around anyway so we thought, 'Why don't we just launch a band, the three of us, as the opening release on Telegraph Records?'

We released The Listening Pool album. The idea was never for it to be long term or take over from OMD. It was more to launch the label. But then I lost the plot because I got divorced. It was a very difficult time. I had to move back permanently from California. I was commuting back anyway because of the label, and then I spent more and more time in the UK. It got quite ugly. I became depressed. I didn't have any energy or focus left and didn't want to do the label any more. Fortunately I had enough money, because when the band stopped we actually started making money. We did a greatest hits album which paid off the million pound debt - the royalties came in without them having to go to pay for recording, videos, crew and touring. I was quite well off and didn't need to work. Then I started a band with Claudia Brücken, Onetwo, and we made an album and toured the world.

PAUL HUMPHREYS

PAUL HUMPHREYS

It wasn't until *Crush* that we actually got onto A&M, and 'So in Love' was a minor hit - all of a sudden things took off. 'Secret' was a radio hit, but it was pulled because 'If You Leave' was coming through, with the might of the movie industry as it was the lead single from 'Pretty in Pink'.

We did end up breaking America, but we toured and toured. There was one time when we spent nearly six months in America. We toured with Depeche on their 1988 Music for the Masses 101 tour. And before that, we toured with The Thompson Twins and also with The Power Station.

You shower at the venues and you live on a bus. We were all in each other's pockets. Towards the end of those tours, we'd really had enough. We were stressed about the money because we kept taking more advances from Virgin. It was costing us thousands a day to be on the road in America, and the financial pressures were building. At the end of the 80s, we had sold I don't know how many millions of records and yet ended up owing Virgin £1million.

Andy and I started not getting along. We weren't happy with the records we were making. *Pacific Age* particularly we weren't happy with. We had no time at all to make the record, we had no time to write. And the well of ideas was completely dry. Until *The Pacific Age*, there was always a well of ideas that Andy and I had built up which we could go to when we needed some songs: 'Remember that idea we had? That tune?' But we got to *The Pacific Age* and we looked in the well and it was, 'There's nothing there, is there?'

Plus we were taking too many drugs to keep us awake and drinking too much. We got into this cycle, particularly Andy and I, where we were so busy we didn't even sleep. We had no time off. We barely had a holiday in the whole of the 80s. I remember two holidays.

On tour we'd get into the cycle of leaving a gig at 2am, driving to the next gig, partying all night on the bus and going to sleep at 6am. The tour manager would wake us up at 7am saying, 'You've got to do the drive time radios. We're in the next town and you're live on air.' And you'd have this over-the-top American deejay going, 'Hiiii, and here we have – let me read who we have – OMD!', all after one hour's sleep. We just used to have a powder breakfast and get on with it.

But that takes its toll. I think it made us both paranoid about each other, about everything. The worries were all accentuated. And at the end of the 80s, Andy and I just wanted to kill each other.

We compared the differences between us and Depeche Mode sometimes. Depeche had a deal with Mute where they were on a 50/50 profit share. They probably sold the same amount of records as us during the 80s, but they were making fortunes and we were making pennies. They had good guidance from Daniel Miller on what to do next, and when to do something and when not to do something. They could take a step back and make good decisions whereas we had to keep doing things just to pay the bills. Depeche modified their sound when electronic music went temporarily out of fashion with the arrival of Britpop and Grunge. They got the guitars out and went Gothic and dark. That helped them ride out the 90s and project them into the massive band that they are now, whereas we fell apart because we had no guidance and no money, which made things very difficult.

By the end of the 80s I said, 'Either we take two years off to catch our breath and reinvent ourselves or I'm done with this.' Andy agreed at the time. He was also threatening to do it. But management didn't want that to happen. There were contracts with Virgin and they were saying, 'You've got to make a new album.' And I said, 'Well fuck that. I'm not doing that.' Then management and Virgin got to Andy's ear and said, 'If Paul doesn't want to do it you must continue without him.'

We ended up arguing over the name. I got a call from the managers saying, 'Andy's going to take the name, like it or lump it.' And it rubbed me totally the wrong way, it was completely the wrong strategy really, so I said, 'Over my dead body.' I pretended to want the name, which I never really did, just as a negotiation strategy, basically just to fuck with the managers.

I didn't mean to fuck with Andy. We didn't fall out initially but then we fell out because the lawyers were arguing over rights. It was like a divorce. Andy and I owned the OMD brand together so I wasn't just going to let it go and let him have it without any kind of financial deal. So to get the deal that I felt was right I had to pretend to want the name.

ANDY MCCLUSKEY

We were so damned broke in the late 80s we were constantly living hand to mouth, constantly taking more advances and having to deliver albums to pay for the advances.

We did renegotiate but had to give them more albums. We ended up on a 10-album deal instead of the original seven, because they grudgingly gave us a couple more points. But it was still peanuts. We were still paying back vast amounts of money and then, when we started to try and break America, we were losing money hand over fist, even in 1988 when we did the Depeche Mode tour, which culminated in 70,000 people seeing us at the Pasadena Rose Bowl. We were being paid $5,000 a gig while they were earning enough money to retire. And that $5,000 a gig was losing us money. It was no surprise that by the time we got to 1988 our accountant said to us, 'Not only are you skint but you owe Virgin a million pounds.'

It's not that we had castles or yachts. We just kept giving it back to the record company. They would give money to us with one hand and take it back with the other. They made tens of millions of pounds out of us, but I was driving a second-hand car and Paul was driving a car he'd bought in 1980 that was on its last legs. Paul had a three-bedroomed house and I had a cottage, with both of us mortgaged up to the eyeballs.

When we were touring and, particularly when you're the support band, it's us and the crew all on one bus. You come off stage, full of adrenaline, and have to go 500 miles. We'd climb on the bus and everybody had a load of cocaine. There was nothing else to do.

The front lounge was the dope lounge and the back lounge was the coke lounge. The front was comatose by midnight while the back were talking broken biscuits until eight in the morning. I was invariably in the back lounge. We only had to perform 30 or 40 minutes, so I could stay up all night. My voice wasn't getting that hammered. We didn't have sleeping pills or anything like that, and I didn't smoke dope. I was utterly wired, trying to get to sleep at eight in the morning. I'd drink a bottle of Jack Daniels or a bottle of brandy and feel like death the next day. But you could stay in your bunk until four then get up, have breakfast, do a sound check, do the gig, get back on the bus, and do it all again!

I'm not proud of it. It wasn't big or clever. It's just that everybody was doing it. There was no band not doing that in the 80s.

Had we had money and a management company with a more constructive overview, they'd have said, 'Guys, you've done your *Best of*, you've toured with Depeche Mode, you've now paid off your debt.'

What they should have said was, 'The quality of your music has suffered. Take some time, walk away from it, smell the roses and do what you do best, which is write some weird music that isn't designed to sell but is just what you like and what you find interesting. They didn't do that, and again there was a difference of opinion. Paul said we should come off the road and take time out. The management and I were saying, 'No, we've done all this work to get here. We must keep going. We've got to keep delivering. We rushed back in. But we didn't have any good ideas between us and there was also divisive stuff going on within the band.

Malcolm and Martin, understandably, were fed up with just being on a wage. They wanted to be more involved, creatively and financially. I think they saw me as a block to them, because I was saying to Paul,

'No, we write the songs, not them. They're great musicians and we love them, they're really good friends, but they're not the creative element of the band. It's you and me, Paul.'

Paul, I think, was starting to feel like he was getting marginalised. His wife certainly felt that. I remember Maureen kicking off at a TV programme, going ballistic. We came back from a camera rehearsal and she was just effing and blinding, going, 'I'm going to talk to that effing director. Who the eff does he think he is? He didn't show Paul's face at all. It was just his fingers.'

Paul said, 'Yeah, but Andy's singing. It doesn't matter. It's promoting the song.' 'Yeah, but you're equal to him. I'm tired of it. You don't earn as much money as him. You're not on the TV as much. He's not the lead singer in OMD. It's equal!' She was raging, and Paul was just trying to put the fire out. She wanted Paul to get more money, and Martin and Malcolm realised Paul might open the door for them while I wouldn't. Then the brass section, the Weir brothers, who were now part of the band - however the hell we allowed that to happen I don't know, I love them but – thought,

'Yeah, well, we could start writing now. We could become part of the band and get royalties, not just get a wage.'

Everybody was angling to change the dynamics. What was then happening was that Paul and the others were writing and I was on my own. We wrote for a few months, then got together in the studio and they played their demos and I played my demos, and it was, 'It sounds like two different bands'. First of all, we said, 'Well, you have one side of the album and I'll have the other.' Then we said, 'No, we can't do that. That's desperate. That's sad. It's over. It's finished. The end.'

Then, a few months later, Paul came back to me with a proposition, saying, 'My accountant says the name of the band has a value, and there's three of us.'

The Weir brothers hadn't really joined properly but Paul, Malcolm and Martin wanted to be OMD. I went to Virgin and said, 'Can they do this?' And Virgin said, 'Well, we still own the rights to release things under the name of OMD and would like to see what you do as OMD on your own. Virgin put this idea in my head: 'You're the lead singer. You're the recognisable face.' Which just made Maureen's point for her! And they said to Paul, 'We have the rights to OMD. We're not sure. Why don't you write music and Andy write music?'

By that stage I'd met Stuart Kershaw and Lloyd Masset, because I was asked by their manager to produce some of their stuff. It didn't work out, but I liked them and they started to do some writing with me. We created a few tracks, going back into Virgin with the demos around 1990, and Virgin said, 'Yeah, we think this could be

OMD music.'

I had to go back to Paul and say, 'Actually, I want to keep the name.' You can imagine how painful that was for Paul, because a) he'd worked with me since we were 16, and b) he'd been in OMD since we were teenagers and made millions for Virgin Records over the last 11 years and didn't have much to show for it. Then Virgin said, 'Actually, cheerio, get lost. We want Andy to be OMD. You can go and do your own thing. We'll release you from your contract.' That had to hurt a lot. I'd have been destroyed if I were him.

Then you have to get lawyers. We were okay with each other up to that point. We weren't angry with each other. We were just fed up, and exhausted. But when you get lawyers involved, it's in their interests to make it confrontational in order to run the meter up. So it got messy.

By the time *Sugar Tax* was released I was un-recouped at Virgin by another £450,000! *Sugar Tax* sold over three million copies, but I wasn't to know that at the time.

Instead of celebrating Virgin supporting me to continue, I had the nearest to a nervous breakdown that I ever wish to experience. Paralysed by many psychosomatic pains and illnesses, that at the age of 30, I felt the need to move back to my parents house for a month. I would lose my voice when I was in a loud environment due to tensing up all my throat and neck muscles. I found the Alexander Technique to help me overcome that problem or I never could have sung live again. I was a total emotional and physical wreck… but I was determined to make music again.

1990-1991

SUGAR TAX

ANDY MCCLUSKEY

Recording *Sugar Tax* took a long time. I had so much riding on the outcome. I worked relentlessly in my rehearsal room writing on my own and with Stuart and Lloyd. Several recording studios, different producers and finally mixed at Roundhouse studios by Jeremy Allom.

I was so nervous that I would not be accepted without the other original band members that my name does not appear anywhere in the album credits. I was hiding behind the 'corporate logo' of OMD. The first single was 'Sailing on the Seven Seas' and it's initial chart position had me worried. Fortunately, it just kept climbing higher and when the album was released it became my first UK platinum studio album since *Architecture & Morality*.

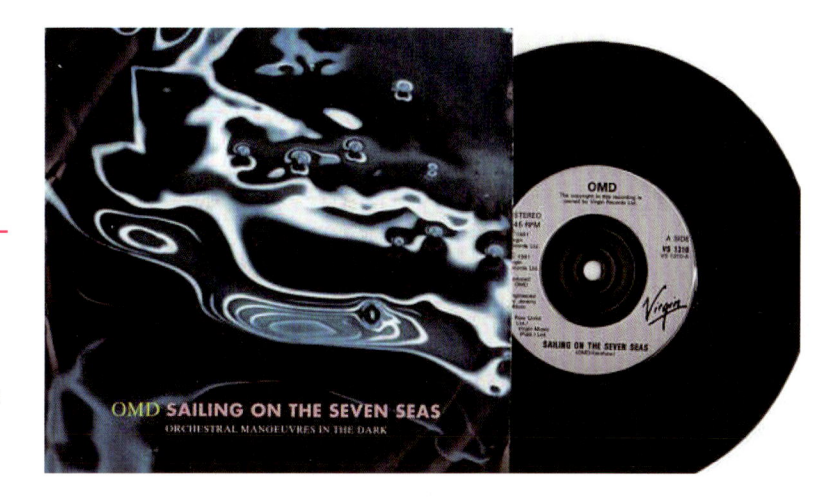

↑
Andy working in his rehearsal studio in Liverpool '91

OMD - 1990-1991

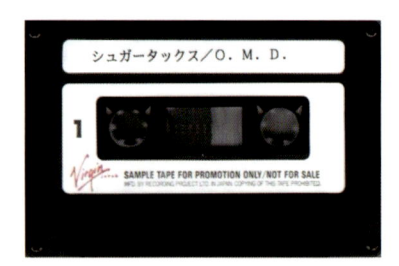

SAILING ON THE SEVEN SEAS	18 MAR 1991
WAS RELEASED	

SUGAR TAX	7 MAY 1991
WAS RELEASED	

PANDORA'S BOX
WAS RELEASED

24 JUN 1991

ABE JUCKES
OMD drummer

The Liverpool music scene is a very small village, and everyone knows each other. My Dad and I knew Hambi Haralambous (Hambi owned the recording studio where Andy had been demoing) and my dad also owned a recording studio, and Hambi knew I played drums.

At this point *Sugar Tax* had been recorded, but Stuart and Lloyd, who helped Andy write the songs, had themselves been signed to Virgin and were wanting to go out on their own rather than be members of Andy's band. So I got a phone call from Hambi, saying, 'Would you be interested in meeting Andy? He's looking for a drummer.'

I was in a band called The Preachers then, and we'd spent the last 18 months trying to get signed and doing showcases. We were getting close but at that time there was no cigar. I went and met Andy and we just had a chat. I was at Art College and Andy's always been into his Flemish paintings, so we talked about art.

Andy said, 'All I can offer you at the moment is a video (for 'Sailing on the Seven Seas') and a couple of TV shows in Germany. Are you interested?' I said, 'I've never been to Germany before. Sounds great fun.'

When the album came out, the German market was doing the biggest push on the band and we started going out there, doing TV

OMD - 1990-1991

OMD drummer Abe Jukes liked to shake his hair

shows. You'd go and mime for three and a half minutes, then the record company took you out for dinner. It was great fun.

The first TV we did in the UK was *Pebble Mill at One*, broadcast live every weekday lunchtime on BBC1. I learnt a very valuable lesson as a drummer on that show, which is to always have a third drumstick. No offence to keyboard players, but the only two animated people on stage in a keyboard band are the singer and the drummer. For everyone else, it's their fingers doing all the work. Nothing else is moving, so there were lots of cameramen coming in for close-ups of me.

The pattern for 'Sailing on the Seven Seas' is all on the toms, and I was doing that when the drumstick jumped out of my hand. One drumstick was bouncing around the toms and I had to grab it and carry on with the song. It's the scariest thing in the world to know a cameraman's going to be legging it up to you, going for a close-up when you're pretty much playing the drums one-handed. From that day on, a pair of drumsticks was shoved under my drum stool just in case it happened again. Which it did, when we did an awards' show in Germany and I snapped a drumstick straight off. Luckily, this time I had one under my seat so was able to carry on.

After that, the album was becoming popular, we were climbing the charts, and Andy said, 'We need to do a British tour.' I remember being in rehearsals and whenever I said, 'I play drums for OMD', people would say, 'Oh, it's a drum machine, surely? You don't do anything.' Andy even came to me and said, 'You know, we can put all these extra bits on tape. You can just play along'. But I said, 'No, no, no. I need to play everything, because that's the part.' You have to justify yourself. I was adamant that I would play everything.

We went to London to shoot the video for 'Sailing on the Seven Seas.' I remember the director had this really long puffer-coat that went to the floor and she smoked a cigarette all the time. She was incredibly aloof. She called 'Action!' and I started playing along with the track and she shouted 'Cut!' She came over to me and said, 'Darling, we all know you can play drums. Just shake your head!' At the time I had all this long hair. I was thinking, 'I've been playing drums since I was 10. Are you telling me now all I have to do is shake my head?'

Andy and I had a really great relationship. After we'd finished the European tour in 1991, the record company put us up in Paris for nearly a month, so we could just do TV shows here, there and everywhere. It was great because Andy and I would just go to the Louvre to look at art. It's not exactly rock'n'roll, but it was what we did. One day in Paris we got chased through the streets like The Beatles. It was ridiculous. Don't get me wrong. It's every young boy's dream. But you go, 'Hold on a minute. This is off its head!'

I had a drum-riser that was quite high and made of steel. Andy was climbing up on it. During 'Talking Loud and Clear' he gouged this massive hole into his hand. But your blood's pumping when you're on stage and he didn't really take much notice. Andy wore a white shirt on stage. Suddenly this white shirt was turning redder and redder. Blood started to pour everywhere. I was shouting to the monitor guy, saying, 'Andy's bleeding, Andy's bleeding!'

He finished the gig and we went backstage. We were in Bradford and there was this strange little doctor, a real Dr Crippen type, all Tweeded up with a leather briefcase, all his equipment in it. He said it needed sewing up, saying, 'We can either do it here, backstage, or you can go to A&E.' Andy had a bottle of J&B on his rider and said to me, 'Pass us the whisky.' He told the doctor, 'Do it here.' The doctor started sewing and Andy just necked this bottle of whisky, one of the most rock'n'roll things I've ever seen anyone do. Proper Keith Richards-style stuff. Normally backstage, all we ever did was drink tea!

We played a Miss Belgium competition at Spa, where the racetrack is. We were standing on the side of the stage looking at all these women changing into costumes and it was like 'bingo!' We, as young men, are going, 'Oh, 25 … 25!' and 'Oh, 15 … 15!'

The people in charge of the girls had taken over one hotel and none of them were allowed to leave. After the show we got invited to the party downstairs at this hotel, so we went - but really wanted to party. We sneaked some of the girls out, went to the club in the village. We bumped into Andy there, with the record company guy. Andy sensibly left to go back to the hotel, but we stayed out.

Then this guy started coming over to the table, saying, 'You're OMD. I'm your biggest fan, let me

OMD - 1990-1991

Andy featured in the German music magazine *Bravo*

buy you a drink.' Obviously, you let people buy you a drink because you don't want to offend them. He kept coming over, saying, 'I'm your biggest fan,' and talked us into going to his house in the middle of nowhere at five in the morning to sign his CDs.

We drove to his house, then we all start sobering up. The guy goes, 'I will wake my parents.' We're thinking, 'Whoah, what's going on here?' The guy goes and wakes up his pensioner parents and this old couple appear in pyjamas. There are four Miss Belgium contestants and a rock band in his living room in the middle of nowhere and the guy opens this cupboard which is a shrine to OMD. That's when we thought, 'Oh shit. We need to get out right now.' We signed what we needed to, made our excuses and left.

The little village hotel we were staying in was run by this grumpy French guy. We get back to the hotel, by then carrying one of the keyboard players because he was totally, totally drunk, and knocked on the door at 5.30am. There's no answer. We rang the doorbell and eventually this guy came downstairs and opened the front door, wearing suspenders, a see-through negligee and really badly put on make-up. We're thinking, 'What the fucking hell have we walked into here?' And he's really pissed off with us. We've obviously interrupted him at the wrong point. Nigel the keyboard player looked at this guy and just burst out laughing.

After *Sugar Tax* it all went a bit quiet. There was difficulty within the band and I wasn't getting on with a certain person, so decided to leave the band and go to pastures new, which was difficult for me because Andy and I were such good mates. It disappointed me that I had to leave, because I enjoyed playing with Andy.

I didn't want to become damaged goods, but somehow I survived the rock'n'roll business. Before I went out on the road with OMD I'd never seen drug-taking. I'd never seen vast amounts of alcohol abuse. You see a lot of car crashes. To get through the other side is quite commendable.

I was 19 when I did OMD, loving every minute of it. I could never understand why people wanted my autograph. I'd be nice, and I'd chat with them. Now I think there must be people looking at their autograph collections, saying, 'Who the fucking hell is this Abe Juckes guy?'

But it was a real privilege to play drums in OMD. It gave me the chance to meet fans from all over the world, and I hoped they liked my drumming as much as I enjoyed playing their favourite songs.

NIGEL IPINSON-FLEMING
OMD keyboard player 1991

I was born in 1970 and in 1978 my grandfather took my sister and myself to go and live in the Caribbean, so I was on a beach in 1979 when OMD were first having hits!

I was playing keyboards for a rap artist, the Rebel MC. but whenever I had time off I'd come back home to Liverpool and go down to the music stores. That's where we hung out. There were three music shops in Liverpool then - Rushworth's, Hessy's and Curly's.

On one particular visit, the guys behind the counter at Rushworth's said someone had been in the shop asking how they could get in touch with me. Rushworth's gave me the number. It was the number for the Pink Museum and it's etched on my brain - 727 7557. I rang the number, spoke to Hambi, and he gave me a bit of background in terms of the band.

I went and met Andy. *Sugar Tax* was already a completed body of work and the idea was that I'd participate in the TV promotions for it in Europe. The idea of a tour then started to solidify.

Technology had moved on from the early days of OMD and it was easier to replicate the sounds on the *Sugar Tax* album because it had just been made

↑ Nigel Ipinson on stage with Andy

and the synths used on it were very current. It was harder work to recreate the sounds from older material and we spent a lot of time in the rehearsal studio at the Ministry doing that and sourcing the equipment we were going to use on tour. It was exciting, but quite a whirlwind.

The tour started in July 1991 and the first gig was at the Oxford Apollo. Then we did an arena tour with Simple Minds, finishing in December at Wembley.

It was brilliant. It was fresh in the sense that the band was making its comeback, Andy back on his own with a re-formed band. I was the musical director and a lot of the parts I was playing were the parts played by Paul. That was interesting, because Paul wasn't just a keyboard player. He and Andy were the entity. You can be a little apprehensive as to how a band's going to be received in a situation like that - you're mindful of the fact that people are attached to the personalities that have been there before and the body of work they've done. I felt that responsibility. I was 21 and at that age you have a certain level of naivety and don't necessarily over-think things too much. You just do it.

I could only really be myself. The way I play as a performer, the way I get a crowd moving, the way I articulate music, are all things that come naturally to me. In 'Talking Loud and Clear', I had a portable keyboard I could strap on, so when it came to the melody line I'd put the keyboard on then I'd be down alongside Andy at the front. People's hands would be waving in the air and I'd be getting the crowd moving. That was what I knew I could naturally bring to OMD.

Liberator came about in 1993. We did the Liberator tour around the UK and Europe, then a tour of South Africa, and then went our separate ways.

Then I got together with Andy in 1994 and we collaborated on 'Walking on the Milky Way.' I wrote that song with Andy, so for me it's a very personal connection with the band, in particular with Andy. After *Liberator*, relationships were challenging. It was tough, and we hadn't seen or spoken to one another for a little while. I was living in a flat on Linnet Lane, just around the corner from Lark Lane and the Pink Museum. I knew Andy was there recording, and one day I decided to go down to the studio. He was in the control room and we talked for a while. He played me what he was working on. He started talking about that particular piece of music and asked me what I would do with it. We cycled around a few bits and he left the room for a bit, went up to the reception area and came back down. Out of that conversation, came 'Walking on the Milky Way.'

I didn't write the lyrics. I only contributed to the music. But from a lyrical perspective, when I first heard the lyrics, 'When I was only 17, my heart was full of brilliant dreams, a heart would call and I

→
Andy photographed on Hoylake Promenade, Wirral peninsula

would gladly go', from a personal perspective relates very much to when I was 17, when I won BBC's *Saturday Superstore*'s 'Search for a Superstar' with a band. The lyric, '21, the world was mine'? Well, I was 21 when I joined OMD, so whether that's by accident or design, whenever I hear that piece of music it feels like a personal narrative. Contributing to that was really cool.

When the song was released I didn't get the chance to perform it. By then I was in the Stone Roses. It was weird, being in another band, hearing a song you'd written being performed elsewhere, knowing how well that was doing.

In October 2017, I took my teenagers to see the band at the Colston Hall, Bristol. Being there with my children, knowing the history of the band and watching the band do those tunes, then seeing them come back on for an encore and do 'Walking on the Milky Way', I don't think it gets much better really.

ANDY MCCLUSKEY

'Sailing on the Seven Seas' had been a huge hit, the *Sugar Tax* album was doing very well, but could I possibly dare to play live with a totally new band? We had rehearsed more than I had ever done before, because Nigel, Abe and Phil had to start from scratch. I was petrified as to how the audience would react. As we exited the stage into the corridor, with the encores complete, the screaming started. All four of us were yelling our heads off in relief. Nigel and I were wrestling each other in exuberant delight. We'd been accepted.

APOLLO
2 July 1991, Manchester, UK

STUART KERSHAW
OMD drummer

Having worked with Andy on the *Sugar Tax* album and written so many songs with him, it was a massive shock when I saw him in his element on stage for the first time. He commanded the audience in that iconic theatre and between songs I knew so well from the album, he slipped in tunes I'd forgotten, those OMD classics whipping the crowd into a frenzy all around me.

I stood silently as massive cheers greeted the opening bars of 'Sailing on the Seven Seas', the hairs on the back of my neck on end as the crowd sang along with every word. I felt such a mixture of pride and waves of surprise as I watched them all dance and sing, with the knowledge that nobody in the room knew it was my song.

CITY HALL
4 July 1991, Sheffield, UK

DECLAN SHIELS

In the late 80s, when I was a young teenager, UK chart music went through a low point. In those days, the simplest, cheapest way of discovering music was to go to your local library, hiring cassettes for just 20p a week. Having seen the film *Pretty in Pink*, enjoying the music, I noticed one of my favourite tracks was by Orchestral Manoeuvres in the Dark. Those next few weeks and months I listened to all the OMD back-catalogue the library had, a real love of their music growing.

When I heard they had a new track, 'Dreaming', I saved my pocket money and was so excited when I had that new 12" in my hands. Unfortunately, news soon followed that OMD were splitting. This was their last single. I thought OMD would be a thing of the past.

In 1990 I went to Sheffield Hallam University where I met a wonderful girl named Juliet. She was older than me, but also loved early 80s music. We'd listen to OMD and seemed to like the same tracks. We put different bands in our respective top-10s, but OMD was the only band we both loved. How excited were we when we heard they were set to release some new music? *Sugar Tax* was an amazing album and we soon found out they were to play Sheffield's City Hall, managing to get seats in the third row.

They let us run to the front, so we managed to get right by the stage, reach up and touch

Andy's hand. We danced and jumped throughout, seeing Andy's enjoyment, sweat and crazy dancing, up close for the first time.

In 1994 I graduated, and we left Sheffield to start a new life in the Midlands. We married in 1996, and our wedding song had to be an OMD track. We didn't really think about having to dance in front of hundreds of family and friends, just picked our favourite song, agreeing on 'Maid of Orleans.' It was only when the DJ started playing the track that we remembered it had a long introduction. We stood there like lemons.

In 2000, we moved to the village of Bredon, outside Tewkesbury, and one new friend, a lady called Helena, soon decided to hold a 40th birthday party at her house. I had a reputation for good party music and made up CDs full of tracks. Instead of putting personal favourites on, I chose ones I thought would get everyone dancing. OMD weren't the most popular band, so I left them off, but at the party someone asked if I had any. I replied, 'Sorry, I didn't

↑
Juliet and Declan Shiels take a photo with Martin

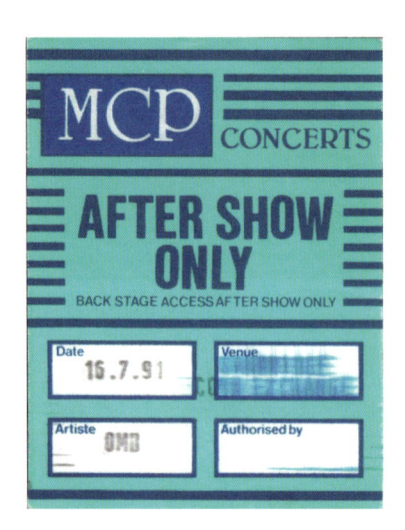

think anyone would ask for them.' They replied, 'You can't say that. Helena's brother-in-law is from the band, Martin Cooper.' I was quite drunk and not sure if they were winding me up. Juliet, my wife, went to ask Helena, who said, 'Yes, he is, and has just left. Come back in the morning and meet him.'

The following day, with a slight hangover, we sheepishly returned to Helena's house, finding Martin, broom in hand, sweeping rubbish off the kitchen floor. We were both quite embarrassed, but he was very friendly and kind. That's when our two-member 'Martin Cooper Fan Club' started.

When OMD reformed in 2007 and were touring again, our children were eight and six, and we hadn't been to a gig since they were born. But we booked for the Hammersmith Apollo, organising sleepovers for the kids and booking a first night away as parents. It felt strange going without them, but we were excited. During the concert, we noticed Helena in the audience with her family. It was a fantastic show, and afterwards Helena asked if we wanted to go backstage. Martin was very kind again and chatted to us. Andy and Paul had to rush off, but we spoke to Mal and Martin, getting our photo taken with Martin. From then on, Helena would try to get us backstage passes, and we'd often been seen holding up a 'Martin Cooper Fan Club' poster at gigs during his sax solos. The first time, Andy took a double-take, saying, 'Where's my poster?'

CITY HALL
6 July 1991, Newcastle, UK

SEAN CHURCHILL

The Sugar Tax concert at Newcastle City Hall was unbelievable. I'm not sure Andy had any idea just how the new album and band would be, but it was a tremendous concert on a red hot summer's evening.

CORN EXCHANGE
16 July 1991, Cambridge, UK

MARK CROUCH

My parents saw Andy and Paul support Gary Numan in 1979 and have followed the band since, although not to my obsessive levels. I remember liking what I heard on a TV advert for *The Best of OMD* in 1988 and that was the first album I ever bought.

I played the first four albums from my Dad's extensive vinyl collection, but in reverse because of how they were stored, so my first album experience was *Dazzle Ships*. I loved the sounds, the words, the melodies and radio samples. I loved all four LPs, and guess some of that was from hearing Dad play them years before.

I then 'borrowed' any missing records from my aunt (I still haven't given them back). It was 1991 by then, *Sugar Tax* coming out, and hearing 'Sailing on the Seven Seas' takes me back being at school that summer.

Cambridge Corn Exchange was my first OMD gig. An awkward 15-year-old, I sat in the balcony with Dad, who was up and dancing along with everyone else, the balcony moving. What a show. I assumed this was the standard for all gigs, only to discover in later years that most bands don't put in a 10th of that effort on stage.

At the Ipswich show that October, I saw someone reading a fanzine and remember seeing the 7" discography near the back, listing B-sides I'd never heard. My obsessiveness went into overdrive. I went to as many record fairs as I could to track down these records, spending years buying everything I could get my hands on.

In 1997 at a fan convention in Liverpool I was amazed to find people from other countries. I still thought only I listened to OMD. And I'll never forget meeting Andy for the first time at the Motor Museum. Surreal.

Back at the hotel, I got talking with others who had a passion for collecting the records, and my collection exploded. It sits currently at over 500 records, CDs, tapes and more as I started to lean towards live albums. I was too young to attend any shows in the 80s so the only way I could hear them was to buy live recordings. My obsessiveness kicked in once more, deciding I needed to find a way to identify the different shows. So I started a log of the gigs with set-list details, using comments from Andy to identify whether they were new recordings.

What started out as a list of live recordings grew into documenting every show played, to help identify the gigs but also include other information to help provide statistics on the years of touring. I now have more than 200 live recordings from around the world and host the www.omd-live.com website.

DOME
17 July 1991, Brighton, UK

BARRY PAGE

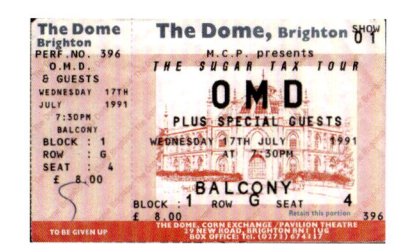

My introduction to OMD and many of their contemporaries came via *Top of the Pops*, *Smash Hits*, *Number One*, *Look-in*, and the iconic *Now That's What I Call Music!* series. I was 11 when I first heard the Caribbean-flavoured 'Locomotion', coinciding with a time when my father introduced me to the marvels of recording the Top-40 show off the radio. Every Sunday I dutifully tuned in, not only recording my favoured tracks, but also writing down the top-10 in an exercise book. 'Locomotion' was an early entry, and perhaps unsurprisingly, the band's sprawling name was spelt incorrectly.

I remember 'Secret' entering the Top-40 in the summer of 1985 as I was on my way back from a family holiday to Lincoln. My Nan kindly gave me an old wireless and I had the chart show playing in our carriage. A fellow passenger took offence and, after much huffing and puffing, headed to another compartment.

After audio-bingeing on the back-catalogue at my friend's house, I started building a substantial OMD collection. By then I'd started a part-time job at a fish and chip shop (prophetically the Seven Seas Fish Buffet). I took regular trips to the south coast, attending large record fairs at Brighton Centre when it was easy to pick up rarities such as the FAC6 'Electricity.' I also blew a fair percentage of my lowly wages on mail order records, gleaned from the back pages of my new favourite magazine, *Record Collector*. My parents frowned on such frivolous spending and I eventually resorted to having my parcels shipped to the chippy.

What I didn't realise was that the band was imploding. As far as I was aware they were working on a new album (evidenced by a *Record Mirror* article in 1988, Paul Humphreys mentioning work on new song, 'Wild Strawberries')

but I did have suspicions about the band's status when Andy McCluskey turned up on Arthur Baker's 1989 LP, *Merge*. In early 1991, word eventually filtered through that OMD had split into two camps. I vividly recall my surprise at the sound of comeback record, 'Sailing on the Seven Seas' and its huge drums, but it remains one of my favourite songs.

With the band back in the public eye, I sent *Record Collector's* features department a letter suggesting an OMD article to capitalise on their new-found fame. I cobbled together notes and sent those in. I didn't expect a reply suggesting I wrote the article, for which they'd pay me £100. I gleefully accepted, marking the start of a writing career that endures to this day. Problem was, it coincided with the last few months of college studies and I had to balance that lengthy seven-page article with exam revision.

Facing an uncertain future on leaving college, I still had an OMD show to look forward to in the summer of 1991. The personnel had changed, but I was excited to see OMD live for the first time for a Brighton date on the Sugar Tax tour, Andy and his new band playing a mixture of old and new songs.

That night I emerged with signed CDs and a poster but was far too star-struck - and hopelessly shy - to say anything of real relevance to Andy. I remember having my picture taken with him, mumbling something about my *Record Collector* article, but felt sure there would be more opportunities to meet the band.

DOUGLAS WILSON

I was 10 when my big brother came home with 'Enola Gay.' I heard him playing it in his bedroom and when he was out, I'd sneak into his room and play it on his record player. I played it so much I wore it out, and ditto for *Architecture & Morality*. I got caught a few times and he'd get angry with me.

My first OMD concert experience was at Brighton Dome. I remember vividly the opening song, 'Apollo XI', which I instantly fell in love with, leaving the show that night bursting with excitement at finally getting to see my beloved OMD.

A sudden illness struck me in 2011 and I ended up in end-stage renal failure. My wife, Alison, put herself forward as a donor and after rigorous testing was confirmed as a suitable kidney donor for me. The transplant went ahead in February 2013 at Edinburgh Royal Infirmary. We'd already bought tickets for the English Electric tour in Glasgow in May. It was touch and go whether I was going to be able to attend. However, my consultant reluctantly agreed to let me go on the understanding that I stayed at the back of the theatre, away from the crowd. I don't think so. Row C in the stalls. To top it off, we met Andy and Paul at the sound check, the icing on the cake and a moment I'll always treasure.

EMPIRE THEATRE
20 July 1991, Liverpool, UK

ERIK SMALBRUGGE

25 October 1985 was one of the most memorable days of my life. A Dutch TV station was broadcasting *Veronica's Rocknight for Greenpeace* and I decided to watch it in bed. The headliners were OMD, a band I knew from the radio. I taped the broadcast in case I wanted to listen to it again. They started with 'Enola Gay' and my heart started beating faster and faster. Goosebumps kept coming due to the overwhelming flood of great tunes. When 'Secret' was played I was in shock. I started buying all their albums, singles, interviews in magazines, etc. But when they split my dream of being able to see them play live was crushed.

I had to wait until 1991, when Andy reformed OMD and played the Liverpool Empire. I flew to London to meet a friend, but he was late and I worried he might have forgotten me. Fearful of missing out, I made my way to the taxi-stand, asking a driver if he could take me to Liverpool. 'You mean Liverpool Street?' he said. 'No, 'I said, 'Liverpool, the one up north.' You should have seen his face, knowing I wasn't joking! A

OMD - 1990-1991

Andy on stage during the '91 Sugar Tax tour

450km, four-hour drive cost me a lot, but my sacrifice and dedication were rewarded as I arrived sooner than the others, seeing Andy walk into the venue. Overwhelmed, I had a chat with him and had my photo taken.

RADIO 1 ROADSHOW
July 1991, Swansea, UK

DOM TOLLER

I first heard OMD when John Peel played 'Electricity' on the radio and was captivated once I heard 'Messages.' I didn't see them live until 1981. For me it was as much about their sensibility as the sound, post-punk with a non-conformist attitude. I've seen them 40 or 50 times over the years. In 1991, I met the then-line-up backstage in Swansea after the Radio 1 roadshow. I half-jokingly mentioned to Andy that, 'having played piano since the age of six', I was available if he needed a keyboard player. At which point Nigel Ipinson trumped me, saying he got the gig because he'd been playing since he was four. My parents had the foresight to name me as an anagram of OMD. If only they'd encouraged me to take up piano from the age of three.

GATESHEAD INTERNATIONAL STADIUM
17 August 1991, Newcastle, UK

SEAN CHURCHILL

OMD were performing on a bill with Simple Minds, The Stranglers and Roachford. I got married that morning, and the gig was so good, despite electrical problems and Andy hurting his knee or ankle. I was two hours late for the evening reception. I thought I'd got away with it until I got to Newcastle Airport that night to fly out to Zante on the honeymoon. Several of the people at the concert were on the plane. My wife didn't speak to me for a week.

MILTON KEYNES BOWL
24 August 1991, Milton Keynes, UK

STEWART CRANER

The band appeared to blow the generator, but in good OMD style, Andy came out and said, 'I think it's rather appropriate we play 'Electricity' now.'

ANDY McCLUSKEY

Live on Radio 1, some fool forgot to put diesel in the only generator! I couldn't even announce that we would come back soon until the problem was fixed. The entire system was down!

STUART KERRISON
OMD front of house engineer, 1984–2008

I worked with the band for 24 years. I'm English but grew up in

Australia. I started singing in bands but was always really into sound and the whole production and engineering idea. I was working in Australia with a successful band and we toured Europe with ZZ Top and Bryan Adams around '83. Then in '84 I moved to England, sleeping on friends' couches and calling around to PA rental companies, saying, 'This is me. You've never heard of me, but this is what I do. Give me a chance.'

Three or four weeks before I left Australia, I saw a video of OMD doing 'Souvenir' on a music show, thinking, 'I'd love to do sound for a band like that'. A couple of months after I arrived in England I got a call from a PA company saying, 'We've got this band called Orchestral Manoeuvres in the Dark and they need a sound guy, would you be interested?'

I met them at the airport when they were flying somewhere. They said, 'We're doing a gig next week in the Netherlands. Come and have a look at us.' I went over there and saw the band play live and thought, 'This is right up my alley, exactly what I should be doing.'

We did some production rehearsals for the Junk Culture tour. I was a real perfectionist. I was really into studio sound. I was very particular about keyboard levels and different sounds in different songs rather than having a basic mix and going for it. We'd have a different approach to the levels from one song to the next. It required a lot of work and a lot of rehearsals, but the band were fantastic, so into it. They had so much patience with me and were just brilliant to work for.

I wasn't available for the 1985 US tour but in 1986 went to see INXS at the Albert Hall and met Nick Sizer, a back-line tech who'd worked on the Junk Culture tour. He said, 'The OMD boys are trying to get in touch with you. They've got a tour going on'.

I did the Pacific Age tour, then did everything with them until 2008, when we were playing with Simple Minds. After that I got a little too old to tour, so stopped working because of my bad back. With the exception of the US tour, I worked with them for 24 years and we did hundreds of gigs together.

They were fantastic to work with, their performances were full on and they gave everything every night. They really made me look good. I was very fortunate. They really got my career going.

I remember the Milton Keynes Bowl gig. I think it was live on the radio. When we came on all the power went out. The generators backstage had run out of fuel, so everything stopped. There wasn't much the band could do, so they went off stage for five or 10 minutes while the generators were fixed. When the band came back they did 'Electricity'. The place went bananas.

The gig at the NEC in Birmingham on the Sugar Tax tour was just phenomenal, a mega-gig. And we did a gig at Wembley Arena, notoriously with shit sound, where loads of people came up after - not just punters, but agents and managers and people who've seen hundreds and hundreds of gigs - and said they'd never, ever, heard a gig like that there.

I live in Norway now. I was in a packed pub at the end of the Junk Culture tour when in walked this woman, a Norwegian acupuncture student. I looked at her and thought, 'I'm going to spend the rest of my life with that person'. Lene's a huge OMD fan and has been to lots of shows and always been really supportive and understanding of what I was doing. We've been together ever since.

WESEREMS HALLE

27 August 1991, Oldenburg, Germany

GUNNAR SCHOLZ

In 1981 I accidentally recorded the single remix of 'Messages' on tape from the radio. I was 14 and liked what I heard but had absolutely no idea about the band behind this song. I only knew they had this strange long name and had a hit single in the UK with a song called 'Enola Gay.'

When 'Maid of Orleans' became the biggest-selling single of 1982 in Germany, one couldn't escape from it turning on the radio. Having grown up with German 'Schlager' music, that song opened a whole new world to me, musically. Even my mother liked it. I bought *Architecture & Morality* to see what else they had to offer.

When OMD stopped recording in 1996, I'd lost interest and they became one of many bands I once listened to but then vanished in my vast musical memories of the 80s. Who would have known that 20 years later I'd have a seat in a stall at the Royal Albert Hall in London, watching OMD in their (almost) original line-up and having one of the greatest concert experiences of my life.

I went to Liverpool to see them live and got a ticket for the Hamburg show. I got to know so many nice people and made new friends, for example on Phone Box Sunday in Meols in August 2017. Being able to stay in contact with all fans in many different countries is one of the joys of the Internet.

THEN YOU TURN AWAY
WAS RELEASED

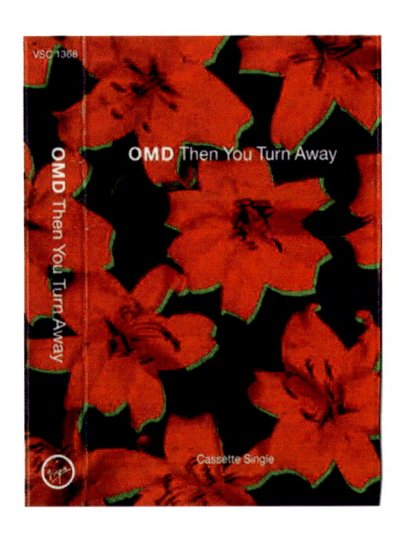

2 SEP 1991

CONCERT HALL
15 September 1991, Toronto, Canada

IOANNIS SKOUFARIDES

I was hanging around the side of the building after the show and lied to security to get myself backstage. Security had just let in a young girl. I didn't know her but said it was my girlfriend. Without hesitation, he opened the door and allowed me in. Andy was great when I confessed I wasn't supposed to be there. I told him he needed better stage-door security and he thanked me for the tip and my honesty.

KINGSBURY HALL
1 October 1991, Salt Lake City, Utah

KURT IVERSON

I was at a fairly-strict Mormon college, Brigham Young University, with no direction. I rode my bike everywhere after midnight when the town was lifeless, blaring *Architecture & Morality* through my headphones to find some escape. OMD came to perform at our little town at an old church, the venue small enough for me to feel I was in the front row. I stayed outside all night for those tickets.

CLUB IGUANAS

5 October 1991, Tijuana, Mexico

JOEL RAMIREZ NEGRETE

As my father worked on a Mexican radio station just south of the US border, he'd bring home all kinds of promotional vinyl the station wouldn't play. Among them I found *Architecture & Morality*, playing 'Georgia' over and over.

When OMD came to Tijuana, a good friend and I were driving back from San Diego and decided to stop by Club Iguanas to see if tickets were still available. We arrived in time for the sound check. We sneaked inside so we could listen. We were allowed to stay but asked to leave immediately after.

We then ran to our houses, changed clothes and rushed back to get a good spot. As we arrived we saw a couple of disclaimers stating there was going to be some filming for the single, 'Call My Name.' We all tried to push our faces to the front to be in at least one scene. Taking advantage of the dancing and jumping I squeezed myself into a little opening at the front and there I was, finally enjoying the band I waited so long to see live. At the front of the stage was a series of bars covering a ventilation system, where you could grab hold so you wouldn't get pulled back into the crowd. As I was doing this Andy came in jumping and dancing and, as he approached our side of the stage, he stepped on my hand and twisted one of my fingers. I looked up, screamed a bit (it did hurt) and he turned and said sorry, then carried on singing and dancing.

The next day my finger was swollen, but I paid no attention. As the years passed I noticed my finger twisted a bit to the left and said to myself, 'There's a permanent memento from my favourite band.'

Then, 18 years on during the History of Modern tour, I bought a VIP package and during the meet-and-greet, showed Andy my twisted finger. He offered a kiss from Mal as compensation. As they performed 'Talking Loud and Clear' that night he told the crowd, 'I broke his finger 18 years ago in Club Iguanas in Tijuana.'

PAVILIONS

14 October 1991,
Plymouth, UK

ANDY MCCLUSKEY

My daughter Charlotte was only 10 days old when she attended this concert, strapped to her mother in a papoose, her ears bandaged to reduce the sound. Crazy!

NEWPORT CENTRE

15 October 1991,
Newport, UK

PAULA MACKEY

My elder sister introduce me to OMD when I was nine. She bought the *Best of OMD* and played it constantly. I remember hearing 'Messages' and fell in love with the song. Over 30 years later, it still gives me the same goosebumps. In tough times, it is one of my few 'go-to' songs. Corny as it sounds, it takes me away from real life, just for a few minutes, calming me.

My first live concert was on the Sugar Tax tour. I was so excited to see the concert but disappointed there would be no Paul. Needless to say, the concert was amazing and blew me away.

When I heard that the original members were reuniting, I was straight in touch with my sister. We managed to get tickets for Birmingham Symphony Hall, and from the second they appeared on stage, I was a kid again!

LEANNE GILES

In March 1991, I heard 'Sailing on the Seven Seas' for the first time and absolutely loved it. I became obsessed with trying to record the MTV video and every live performance. I also adored 'Pandora's Box.' One of the first CDs I bought was *Sugar Tax*. I listened to it non-stop. That summer, hearing OMD perform live on Radio 1 I realised how many of the songs were in my childhood memories. The words and tunes to 'Joan of Arc', 'Enola Gay' and 'Souvenir' came flooding back. I particularly remembered 'Tesla Girls'. I'd always wanted to be able to switch on lights by clicking my fingers like the girls in the video.

The gig at Newport Centre in Wales was my very first gig. In November 2017, my sister and I got tickets to see the original line-up perform at Birmingham Symphony Hall. It was well worth a 26-year wait. 'Maid of Orleans/Joan of Arc Waltz' had me in floods of tears. It was just so emotionally charged.

SANDS CENTRE
25 October 1991, Carlisle, UK

SEAN CHURCHILL

I was right at the front when the dry ice set off the fire alarms. We had to evacuate to the car park. All those at the front ended up at the back for the rest of show.

METROPOLE
6 November 1991, Berlin, Germany

MELANIE MESSOW

Aged 13, watching a VHS tape of German TV show *Bananas* while babysitting at a neighbour's house, I found they'd recorded the video for 'Talking Loud and Clear.' And that was the beginning of a very long connection with OMD.

In 1986 I took my '(Forever) Live and Die' and 'We Love You' 12" records to the ice-skating disco every week, lots of people having to suffer/discover OMD. And in '91 I visited Liverpool and the Wirral for the first time, spending a night in London before hiring a car, ending at Hoylake police station, where they helped me find a B&B (four houses from Jan and Mike Humphreys, I later realised).

While away I discovered Kraftwerk were playing Liverpool, buying a ticket. Waiting to enter, people told me OMD were playing Manchester that night, so I sold my ticket and drove there, only to discover I was a day late.

In 1996 *Universal* helped me through the hardest time of my life. I lost my boyfriend, my home and my job within a month. I jumped in my car and drove the west coast from Land's End to Carlisle, listening to *Universal*. I found a nice holiday flat at North Parade in Hoylake and I've returned to the Wirral several times since. I love the peninsula and being a short distance from North Wales and the Lake District. My favourite music allows me the joy of discovering parts of Europe, driving from Berlin to North West England. Leipzig in 2018 marks my 50th OMD concert. I look forward to many more.

OMD - 1990-1991

↑ OMD celebrate selling one million copies of *Sugar Tax* in Germany with Dirk Hohmeyer and Sylvia Bell of Virgin Records Germany

BILL LAWSON

I have been a fan of OMD since their earliest days as can be testified by family, friends and colleagues. We have the vinyls, multiple copies of CDs, t-shirts, mugs and box sets to prove it. Their music has been with me for the major part of my life. We have songs on the common themes of love and relationships but who else can give phone boxes, aeroplanes, Joan of Arc and a refinery? This is just to say thank you to the gents for their music, which has been a profound and valued companion on my life journey. I still haven't mastered Andy's dance style yet but it's still early days.

KONGRESS HALLE

9 November 1991, Frankfurt, Germany

TATJANA MEINL

In the 80s the music of OMD was my life. It was electric but also hand-made and lovingly detailed, and I like Andy McCluskey's expressive sensitive voice so much. I was delighted when they came back in the 90s.

I saw them in Essen and again in Düsseldorf in 2017. They are true to themselves and still in the moment, with new songs and sometimes delicate lyrics peppered with British humour.

DAVID RICHARDSON

In the early 90s I owned a bakery in Windermere, Cumbria. One day, a chap wearing jeans and polo shirt walked in to order a sandwich. Nothing unusual there, but what stopped me in my tracks was his *Crush* polo shirt. I'd never seen one before. I also vaguely recognised the wearer but was distracted by another customer before I could apprehend him and find out more.

That night I waded through a treasure trove of OMD memorabilia to see if I could shed any light. Lo and behold, in a *Telegraph* magazine was a picture of said man in said shirt, Paul's brother, Mike Humphreys.

It turned out that Mike and his wife Jan had a static caravan in the Lakes. It also turned out that they loved the bakery's many goodies and, sure enough, a few days later they returned. This time I wasn't letting Mike escape so easily. Not only did I get the lowdown on his polo shirt, but glimpsing that shirt was the start of an enduring friendship. I'm now very lucky to count Mike and Jan among my best friends.

Sometime in the early 90s, staying with them in Hoylake, after dinner one night, Jan needed to go to Paul's to check everything was okay as he was away. Did I want to come? I had my coat on before Jan finished the sentence.

I was struck by two things. First, it was an ordinary house on an ordinary street. Where was the sweeping drive, 10 bedrooms, the pool, the vintage Jag? Second, in the dining room was an open box stuffed to the brim with copies of the original 'Electricity' with black on black thermographic sleeve, the single I paid a king's ransom for some years earlier.

We'd been there 10 minutes when the door swung open and in walked one of my all-time heroes, large as life, back early. This was surreal, in a strange house with *the* Paul Humphreys shaking my hand. He and Jan caught up while my mind raced with questions and thoughts that would no doubt impress upon Paul the breadth of my OMD knowledge and general all-round intelligence.

However, when my moment came, it was all I could do to muster lame platitudes followed closely by inept mumbling. Then came a 'duh!' moment I've regretted ever since. Paul had been working on new tracks. Did we want to come into the studio and have a listen? Jan looked at me, and while every fibre in my body said, 'Oh my God, yes please', a small, stupid part of my brain said, 'Play it cool' and I heard the words, 'Nah, that's okay' come out of my mouth.

Having the opportunity to meet Paul several times since, I now believe I'm ready to go into the studio and listen to any new tracks he's working on.

CALL MY NAME
WAS RELEASED

18 NOV 1991

↑ 'Call My Name' lyrics in English and German

JONNY PETTERSSON

In Summer 1992, as a wild 11-year old Swedish kid trying to climb our balcony, I fell and broke my arm. But my sister recorded a four-hour VHS-tape off *MTV* for me to watch while I convalesced, and 'Enola Gay' blew me away. I've been a fan ever since.

ANDY CARTER

I used to work near Alder Hey children's hospital. A charity auction was being held at the police social club in Fairfield in Liverpool in aid of the Alder Centre which offers bereavement care and support to those affected by the death of a child. Mr McCluskey had very kindly donated his platinum disc of the *Sugar Tax* album. It was a great cause but a chance to win a great item. On the night, I heard people had travelled from Bolton and other parts of the North West so I felt a bit of pressure. The disc was the last lot of the night and when the bidding started my heart was racing. I tried to disguise my interest but soon joined in. It evolved into a battle between myself and the Bolton contingent and the bid went up by £10 and £20 to reach £200. I blurted out, '£250!' and, with no response from the room, the day was won. I couldn't believe it. My happiness was slightly tempered after the event because I didn't have the cash on me and had to knacker my hand writing five separate cheques as I only had a £50 cheque guarantee card. The disc hangs on my wall to this day

MARTIN DAVIES

My older brother was a massive fan and I soaked up all of his influences, as I didn't have a stereo at the time. When he got married, left home and took all his records with him, I started to build my own OMD collection. OMD were one of the bands that turned me into a synthesiser obsessive. Quite a few years later I actually got to release my own Neu! inspired album on Elefant records with ex-members of the 80s Creation Records band, Felt. I eventually ended up working in music management, representing Wolverhampton based singer/songwriter, Scott Matthews, who was signed to Island Records. I no longer work in music, but last year self-published a book about my experiences of working in the music industry. OMD get a few name checks. They helped influence the course of my life. For that, I will be forever grateful.

1993-1995

1993 saw **OMD** release *Liberator*, three singles and play shows in the UK, Germany, Sweden, Norway, Denmark, France, Holland and their first ever dates in South Africa

STAND ABOVE ME

WAS RELEASED

4 MAY 1993

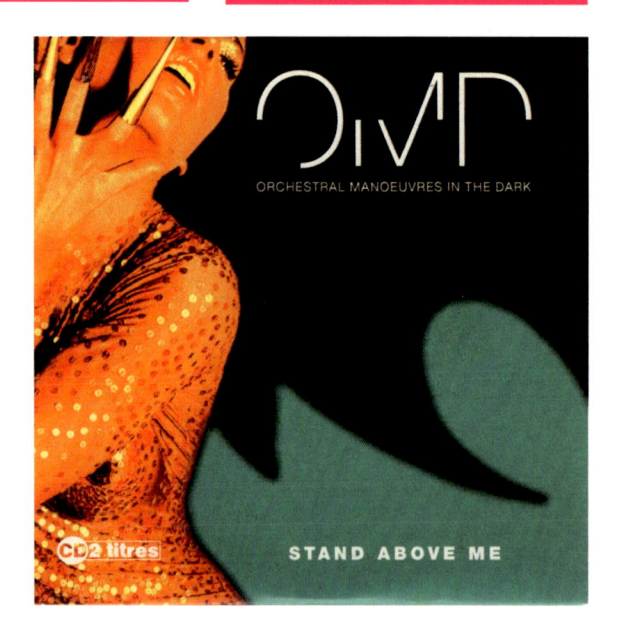

LIBERATOR
WAS RELEASED

14 JUN 1993

→ Andy by the Mersey with Liverpool in the background

ANDY MCCLUSKEY

I then made *Liberator*, where I completely forgot all the things I re-learned about being true to myself and not rushing, making an album that didn't do terribly well.

OMD – 1993-1995

| DREAM OF ME | 5 |
| WAS RELEASED | JUL 1993 |

Andy, Stuart Kershaw and Nigel Ipinson on stage

ROYAL COURT THEATRE

25 August 1993,
Liverpool, UK

STUART KERSHAW

This was my first OMD gig playing drums. I remember a sick feeling at the pit of my stomach. A boiling, bubbling blend of raw nerves, excitement and outright fear as I stepped out to play 'Agnus Dei' for the first time live, the first gig of the Liberator tour in front of friends and family in my hometown.

It went pretty well though, and during final encore, 'Best Years of our Lives', I looked up with tears streaming down my face as I spotted my mother up in the circle, waving and smiling down on me. It was a glorious night.

Two days later we went to Germany to play Rock Over Wildenrath supporting Prince. Straight on stage with no soundcheck, we had no idea what our stage monitoring would be like. It was in front of 100,000 people and we just started the 'Enola Gay' drum machine and went headlong - straight in. The sound on stage was terrible, but the crowd was all jumping, a sea of heads all the way to the horizon. It was an incredible feeling, the crowd still shouting 'OMD' when Prince came on stage.

| EVERYDAY WAS RELEASED | 6 SEP 1993 |

LA CIGALE
2 November 1993, Paris, France

HERVÉ CHABOT

As a teenager, I listened to OMD all day long, but a lack of money and living far from Paris made it impossible to get to live shows. I loved *Architecture & Morality*, the innovative sounds and melodies of *Dazzle Ships*, and all the other albums.

My first OMD live show was at La Cigale in 1993, albeit without Paul. I was so happy when I was at the live show in L'Olympia concert hall, Paris, on 25 May 2007 for the Architecture & Morality tour though. All my youth came back in my mind and in my body.

BUISKUIT HALLE
16 November 1993, Bonn, Germany

KERSTIN KAUSSEN

My OMD story started in 1991 when 'Pandora's Box' was released. At 15, I loved that song. I bought all the CDs and waited two years for my first OMD concert. At 17, I got tickets for my Mama too (I needed a driver) and a passion for OMD concerts was born. Beginning with Bonn in 1993, we saw every tour that came to Germany, other than in 2011 when I was pregnant with triplets, Julius, Laurin and Tom. Surprise, surprise, they all love to dance to OMD's music, with Julius really good at dancing 'Andy' style. A very special thanks to my Mama, who still comes along with me to see OMD (now I'm the driver).

↑ Andy graces the cover of *Future Music* magazine September 1993 edition

SECC ARENA

4 December 1993, Glasgow, UK

ANDY MCCLUSKEY

Our first headline UK arena tour and to make things more surreal, Gary Numan is supporting. I'd not met him for 14 years but remembered just what a genuinely lovely guy he is. I enjoy a few evening chats with him in hotel bars after gigs. That is, when you can get to him through a throng of Numanoids. He continued to have a real hardcore following, even when he was on his long journey back to being accepted properly by the wider public and press for just how important his music was and still is.

GARY NUMAN

I believe it was late '93. I'd just finished yet another UK tour when I received a most interesting and unexpected offer. OMD were about to go out on another arena tour and wondered if I wanted to go along.

It was perfect timing, on many levels. First, I hate it when tours end. Life feels slow and boring until you eventually adapt back into normal life, so the idea of going back out again straight away was very appealing. My own career was struggling at that time, one of its many up and downs, so the idea of playing arenas and being seen by large numbers of people was also very appealing. Mostly though, it would be good to be touring again with OMD.

The roles were reversed this time though. I'd be opening for them. It was a unique experience for me not to be headlining my own shows and I found that change to be a glorious shedding of anxieties and pressure. It was probably the most easy, stress-free tour I've ever been involved in. Attendance? Not my problem. Production nightmares? Not my problem. Every little hiccup or worry that usually drops firmly on my shoulders? Not my problem, not on that tour anyway. It was a fantastic experience. Both times.

G-MEX

8 December 1993, Manchester, UK

BEN SOUTHWOOD

It was *Top of the Pops* night. My ears pricked up as an insanely catchy and bizarre drum-beat introduced an even catchier and quirky synth melody. I confidently announced after the song had finished that 'Sailing on the Seven Seas' was the best song I'd ever heard. I was 12, and that moment started a lifelong obsession with OMD.

As I perused the music aisles of Woolie's not long after *Sugar Tax* was released, I was astounded to find they had a 'Best Of'. I just assumed they were a new band. I bought all the CDs, proudly wore their t-shirts and attended a couple of fan meetings in Liverpool, despite being alone as a painfully shy 16-year old.

I saw them at G-Mex. They were the best band ever to me, even though no-one my own age seemed to agree. On the Punishment of Luxury tour, as a treat for the year I turned 40, I bought VIP tickets and met my idols. It was short and sweet, but they were all lovely.

ANDY MCCLUSKEY

My parents attended the Manchester concert, as there isn't an arena in Liverpool. Afterwards, my father told me, 'You always say your band is top of the second league. All I can say after that performance is that you're in the top division now, son.' I realised he finally felt I had a 'proper job', after 15 years in Orchestral Manoeuvres in the Dark.

BOURNEMOUTH INTERNATIONAL CENTRE

11 December 1993, Bournemouth, UK

SARA PAGE

In the summer of 1990 I was staying with my gran and uncle in Sark, working in a tearoom. When the weather was bad and ferries bringing the day trippers over didn't run, my colleagues and I hung out at the Mermaid Tavern, which had a pool table and a jukebox. It was the day before I was due to return home to Guernsey that the fates threw torrential rainstorms and high winds, me feeding hard-earned pound coins into the jukebox. The CD I selected didn't come on, but the memory recalled tracks that remained prior to it being switched off the previous night. 'Enola Gay' came on. Then I heard a tune I didn't know yet was so familiar, the haunting keyboard melody of 'Souvenir.'

Returning to Guernsey the following day I went into

↑ Sara Page meets Paul at an OMD event

independent record store Number 19 and bought *The Best of OMD* on cassette, surprised how many songs I recognised. I was playing it when family friend Mark recognised it. He said he'd lend me his OMD albums. I put them and his B-sides on cassette, never having heard anything quite like the distorted yet melodic sounds emanating from my tape recorder.

Through *Record Collector* I found a 10" copy of 'Messages', my favourite track, for £3.49 and sent away for it. While trying to obtain as much vinyl as possible, I was also attempting to amass the back-catalogue on cassette. At Christmas, Aunty Belle kindly sent a Woolworth's voucher for £3 and I discovered a copy of *Organisation* on cassette that same afternoon – for £3. It was to become and remains my favourite album.

By December 1993 I'd left home, got myself a flat, and a ticket to the Liberator gig in Bournemouth for £12.50. I bought a spare in case anyone wanted to come but ended up going alone. Arriving at my hotel, I heard fellow fans saying Gary Numan was supporting, a bonus for me.

I was too shy to push my way to the front so loitered four rows back to watch Gary. The moment OMD came on, I was shameless, pushing to the front. I even threw my hat on stage, Andy picking it up, putting it on Stuart Kershaw while he was drumming. I was reunited with it at the end. I was buzzing, couldn't stop smiling, unable to sleep until 3am.

On returning to Guernsey I took my disposable camera to be developed. My Gary Numan pictures were a little dark, but I discovered a perfect photograph of Stuart wearing my hat.

In 2000 I attended a fan event in Burnley, meeting Paul Humphreys and Malcolm Holmes for a first time. Other events followed, and at one in 2001 I met fellow fan, Barry, who, although I didn't realise for another four years, would change my life.

In March 2005, Paul Browne and Neil Taylor organised an event in Manchester with Paul Humphreys and Claudia Brücken, including a premiere of a new OMD song and full fan tour followed by a Q&A session with Andy and Paul at The Pink Museum.

Hearing the unreleased 'Sister Marie Says' was like going back in time – that same exultant emotion of something new from my favourite band, with added excitement being surrounded by others who felt the same.

About six months later, Barry and I got together and now have a wonderful daughter. Parenthood put paid to our stalking the band around the UK for a few years, but in 2011 we attended an intimate gig at Eric's in Liverpool, and in May 2016 got tickets for the Royal Albert Hall. I remember hairs on the back of my neck standing up hearing 'Of All the Things We've Made', Andy, Paul, Martin and Stuart Kershaw all lined up playing on stage.

PLETTEN BURG BAY BEACH

30 December 1993, Plettenburg, South Africa

MICK COOPER

My first concert was aged 12 in Derby, 38 years ago, and my last in 2016 in Florida. Working overseas all my life, I've seen OMD in various places, the best in 1993 when we took a two-day drive from Swaziland in our Opel Kadett to Plettenburg Bay. We were right at the front on a beautiful beach, surrounded by thousands of South Africans who didn't really know the songs but loved that a British band had come out to play there. A few days later we drove up to Jo'burg and were in the video of that concert, singing and clapping away. On the English Electric tour in Philadelphia, my wife Beth was throwing up during the concert due to the heat, Andy giving her his water bottle. Getting to take my kids to see them in St Augustine, just a 30-minute drive away, was another high-point.

ANDY MCCLUSKEY

We'd been treated like The Beatles when we arrived at the airport in South Africa. VIP

Mick Cooper and his wife Beth get a photo with the band

OMD - 1993-1995

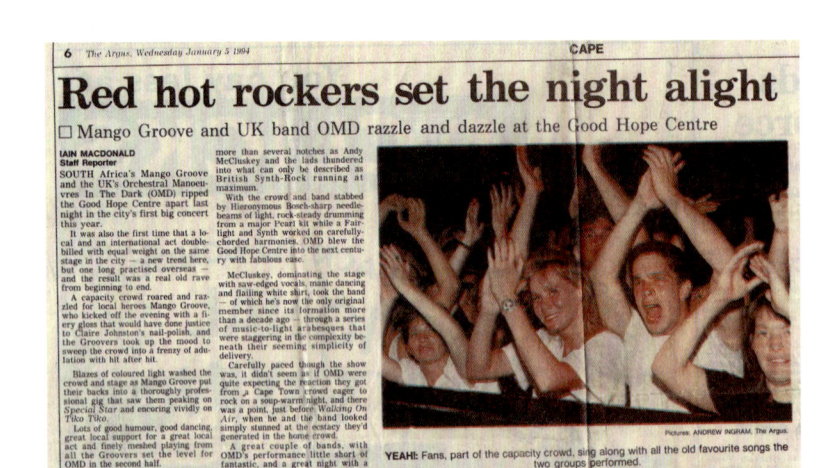

Red hot rockers set the night alight
Mango Groove and UK band OMD razzle and dazzle at the Good Hope Centre

IAIN MACDONALD
Staff Reporter

SOUTH Africa's Mango Groove and the UK's Orchestral Manoeuvres In The Dark (OMD) ripped the Good Hope Centre apart last night in the city's first big concert this year.

It was also the first time that a local and an international act double-billed with equal weight on the same stage in the city — a new trend here, but one long practised overseas — and the result was a real old rave from beginning to end.

A capacity crowd roared and razzled for local heroes Mango Groove, who kicked off the evening with a fiery gloss that would have done justice to Claire Johnston's nail-polish, and the Groovers took up the mood to sweep the crowd into a frenzy of adulation with hit after hit.

Blazes of coloured light washed the crowd and stage as Mango Groove put their backs into a thoroughly professional gig that saw them peaking on *Special Star* and encoring vividly on *Tiko Tiko*.

Lots of good humour, good dancing, great local support for a great local act and finely meshed playing from all the Groovers set the level for OMD in the second half.

OMD, however, raised that level more than several notches as Andy McCluskey and the lads thundered into what can only be described as British Synth-Rock running at maximum.

With the crowd and band stabbed by Hieronymous Bosch-sharp needle-beams of light, rock-steady drumming from a major Pearl kit while a Fairlight and Synth worked on carefully-chorded harmonies, OMD blew the Good Hope Centre into the next century with fabulous ease.

McCluskey, dominating the stage with saw-edged vocals, manic dancing and flailing white shirt, took the band — of which he's now the only original member since its formation more than a decade ago — through a series of music-to-light arabesques that were staggering in the complexity beneath their seeming simplicity of delivery.

Carefully paced though the show was, it didn't seem as if OMD were quite expecting the reaction they got from a Cape Town crowd eager to rock on a soup-warm night, and there was a point, just before *Walking On Air*, when he and the band looked simply stunned at the ecstacy they'd generated in the home crowd.

A great couple of bands, with OMD's performance little short of fantastic, and a great night with a wonderful crowd.

YEAH! Fans, part of the capacity crowd, sing along with all the old favourite songs the two groups performed.

---

treatment, paparazzi thronging for photos. It was our first time in the country after the Musician's Union had lifted the embargo on playing, apartheid having finally ended. OMD were just about the first UK band to tour, with audiences so starved of modern entertainment that I remember them applauding the vari-lights when the excellent support band Mango Groove were on stage.

The gig was on the beach. We hadn't played for three weeks and our stage sound was terrible. The experience was made even more difficult by realising the ticket price meant no black people could afford to attend. We could see them behind the fences in the distance. I was delighted when they broke down the barriers and joined an exclusively white crowd.

STUART KERSHAW
Drummer

We were playing on the beach and had a huge PA set-up. I can't remember whether it was Phil or Nigel but one of them had samples of whales singing, so we played them through the PA across the ocean, hoping to attract marine life. Unfortunately, whilst there are blue whales off the coast of South Africa, the only samples we had were of humpback whales.

An hour before showtime, Andy passed me a CD Walkman

with a Best Of and said, 'We're playing 'If You Leave' tonight, so get learning it fast'. I sat there, learning the song for the first time, knowing we had to go out and play it without rehearsal in front of 5,000 people.

STANDARD BANK ARENA

11 & 12 January 1994, Johannesburg, South Africa

DAVID CARR

My parents emigrated from Scotland to South Africa in 1972 when I was two. Television only started there in 1976 and there wasn't the same level of music journalism or programmes on the telly as in the UK. First time I heard OMD was when I was 10, seeing the video of 'Maid of Orleans'. I wasn't really into music but that stood out for me as different to everything else. Next time I heard OMD was a couple of years later, hearing 'Telegraph.'

When *Junk Culture* came out, OMD became the favourite band for me and my friends. We managed to get copies of all the previous albums and every new one that came out after that.

We never thought we'd ever see OMD live. Bands never came over in the 80s, so it was absolutely brilliant when they came out for 1993's Liberator tour. We went to the show in Jo'burg and had a great time. Although I really enjoyed the show as I never thought I'd see OMD live, it was a little bittersweet – I'd been disappointed by the split and it wasn't the original line-up. I was so happy when OMD announced they were getting back together and touring.

I moved back to Scotland in 2006 and was able to go to the first reunion gig in Glasgow for the Architecture & Morality anniversary tour. For me, it was as exciting as that first gig in SA. I never thought I'd get to see the original band line-up play live. I feel lucky to have experienced the thrill of seeing OMD for the first time twice, not something many people can say.

Andy McLuskey (left) and Stuart Kershaw, two of the members of rock group OMD which played to thousands of fans at the Village Green on Friday night, took a break from watching Zimbabwean Highlanders Football Club beat Amazulu yesterday to prepare for Red Nose Day later this month. Picture by ANTHONY McMILLAN

↑ Andy and Stuart Kershaw take part in Red Nose Day while on tour in South Africa

← Press reviews from OMD's show at the Good Hope Centre, South Africa

Like most parents, my Dad thought the music I listened to as a teenager was rubbish. The only records I played that he thought were good were OMD. He loved 'Talking Loud and Clear' and, after hearing it for the first time, said he thought it was a great tune. He'd never enjoyed any of my other music, so that was a first, and it's a nice memory when I listen to it today, as Dad passed away only a couple of years after.

ANDY MCCLUSKEY

I lived in Dublin for almost 10 months in 1994. I was unhappy, temporarily separated from my girlfriend, frustrated with some of the new band members and basically running away from myself and OMD. I lived just around the corner from Lansdowne Road stadium, rented a room at the Factory studio/rehearsal building and began writing again after a long break. I also found a new wonderful friend in Tony O'Donoghue, one-time Cork band manager and gig promoter, who had moved to the capital to become a TV sports presenter.

TONY O'DONOGHUE
football correspondent for RTÉ

When Andy was living and writing in Dublin during a particularly creative period in 1994 his tour manager and my friend, Tom Mullally, offered me strict instructions on taking care of his boss. 'He doesn't know anyone here, just look after him, hang out with him and make sure he's alright.'

On Monday nights my journalist mates played football at University College Dublin, and with the World Cup in full swing we were all keen to show off our silky samba skills. Andy arrived in pristine retro Liverpool FC shirt, the deep red one with the white V-neck collar and simple Liver Bird crest. As ever he looked the part. It wasn't long however before the red bird had its wings clipped. A dreadfully mistimed tackle on yours truly took Andy out and the next move was directly to St. Vincent's Hospital A&E department. 'I'm afraid we're going to have to cut the jersey off,' said a sympathetic casualty nurse.

'But it's a perfect Liverpool 1960s' replica kit,' I argued. 'Just cut the fucking thing off!' wailed the OMD frontman, in surprisingly shrill tones. His broken collarbone resulted in several tour dates being cancelled.

It wasn't that the 'Maid of Orleans' couldn't sing, it just never occurred to me that his back-to-front bass-playing style required Andy to sling a leather guitar strap around his shoulder while playing. He wasn't going to be able to do that for a while.

When I think of the many memorable OMD shows I've seen in Dublin at The Olympia and Vicar Street and The Point Depot (where, of course, they blew Simple Minds clean away) the amazing night of 'Electricity' in Liverpool with the Royal Liverpool Philharmonic Orchestra, I always get a shiver, remembering, guiltily, I could never pick a favourite gig because I was responsible for so many OMD gigs that never were.

ANDY MCCLUSKEY

I spent the next three weeks parked in front of my TV in Serpentine Road watching every subsequent World Cup game, morphined off my face due to a very kind doctor (who shall remain nameless) giving me way more painkiller than was normally allowed. The related drug hangover may explain some of the more psychedelic songs on the *Universal* album. It certainly resulted in me being so off my face that I insisted the doctors file down a bone spur that remained in my shoulder because I was so worried it would interfere with my bass playing. Long after the drugs wore off, I remembered my strap was on the other shoulder! My lovely friend Mr. O'Donoghue, who I had failed to tackle but had tried to save my replica jersey, could barely contain his delight when unsympathetically regaling all who would listen to the story of the surgery - with the gloriously untrue ending… 'And, they had to use a 'bastard' file on him!'

CHELSEA
August 1995, London, UK

ANDY MCCLUSKEY

I was awoken by the telephone in the middle of the night. Toni was going to the hospital. She was still four weeks before full-term, but her waters had broken and the baby was on its way. I waited until 7am, a reasonable time to call our management assistant in London. 'Kim, sorry to wake you, I need you to book me a flight to Los Angeles immediately. I'll call you from Heathrow to find out what plane I'm on.' Programming sessions for the *Universal* album were postponed and I flew to California. I missed James' birth by a few hours. He'd been delivered by emergency caesarean section, because the umbilical cord was tight around his neck.

After four weeks doing the night feeds I returned to London, straight into the recording with no pre-programming. Every Friday night I'd take the train to Liverpool and paint the new house our expanded family was going to move into when Toni returned to England with James. Back to the Townhouse Studio on Monday morning. Everything was going to be different now. My domestic situation would become based around a family and my performing career was nearing its end. At least for a decade.

OMD – 1996

WALKING ON THE MILKY WAY	5 AUG 1996
WAS RELEASED	

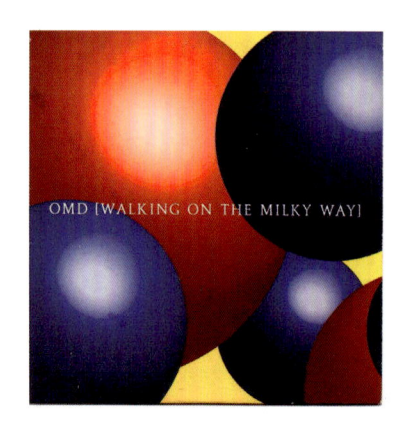

UNIVERSAL	2 SEP 1996
WAS RELEASED	

↑ *'Walking on the Milky Way'* and OMD's 10th album *Universal*

312 | 1996

		WORKED	TO DO	VOX	DRUM BASS	READY TO MIX
1	UNIVERSAL	●	KEYBOARDS	○	●	2 DAYS
2	THAT WAS THEN	●	Revising	○	●	1 DAY
3	NEW HEAD	●		○	●	2 DAY
4	OBOE SONG	●	ORCHESTRATION + STRINGS	○	●	2 DAYS
5	VICTORY WALTZ	●	✓	●	●	½ DAY
6	IF YOU'RE STILL					2 DAYS
7	MOON AND SUN					
8	GTR 9	●		○ THANKS	●	2 DAY
9	NEW DARK AGE					
10	GOSPEL	●	✓	●	●	½ DAY
11	THANK YOU	●		●	●	1 DAY
12	WALKING ON THE GREEN / FLOYD	●		○ BV	●	3 DAY
13	TOO LATE					
	VERY CLOSE	●			○	½ DAY
	CHOSEN ONE	●			○	1½ DAY

UNIVERSAL

It Doesn't matter
If you're black or white,
or which creator made you

It doesn't matter
Bout the clothes you wear
or which god you choose to pray to

Br We all bleed the same blood
    We all need the same love
    And when we die there's no Heaven Above

Cu Its universal
    Its universal

It doesn't matter
Who you think you are
You are living
And you know you feel it

Its not important
As to why were here
You know
There is no reason

↑ Andy's studio notes for the *Universal* album

← Andy's handwritten lyrics to 'Universal'

1996

ANDY MCCLUSKEY

I stopped in 1996. The *Universal* album came out, and 'Walking on the Milky Way' was released and got to No.17, yet Radio 1 wouldn't play it – they felt it didn't fit their target audience. And because they weren't playing it, Woolworth's refused to stock it, and 40 per cent of singles sales on a Saturday were through them. To get to No.17 with both arms tied behind your back was pretty amazing, but I thought, 'You know what? I can't write a better song than this. 'Walking on the Milky Way' is a great song. It's not electronic pop music and it's not going to change the world, but it's a bloody great, well-crafted song.

The album didn't do very well. A lot of the subsidiaries of Virgin paid lip service to promoting it. They got me in for a day to do a bit of PR, but we weren't getting TV shows and I chose not to tour. It was excruciating. It was painful. It really felt like I was past my sell-by date. I was 36 and I was no longer wanted. It was very depressing, having to still go through the motions: 'Well, we've booked the press, so I've got to go to Paris, got to go to Germany, got to do these interviews.' I just wanted to go home and cry. My son James had just been born, and having a stiff of an album, a record company that didn't seem to care anymore, and feeling I was old, I thought, 'I don't want to do this anymore. I think I'll stay at home, be a Dad, and not make records that break my heart because nobody wants to buy them.' I stopped at the beginning of '96. That was the end of OMD. For eternity. Or so it seemed

KARL BARTOS
Kraftwerk

After our first meeting in Bochum it took over 10 years to get together again and have the time to talk plans. It came after a long period of stagnation and solitude for me. Andy suggested we write a song together. Back then, I recorded almost everything I played or wrote, so I played him rough mixes and improvisations I had on cassette. How prehistoric! Then, after we finally stopped ourselves from talking, we hooked up with Wolfgang and Emil for dinner.

I visited Andy a little later in Liverpool; he showed me Penny Lane, Strawberry Fields, and the Cavern Club. This was followed by more trips to Dublin and L.A. 'We threw a few ideas into the computer,' is how Andy once described our method, but we still managed to gradually write three songs this way; 'Kissing The Machine', 'The Moon And The Sun' and 'Mathew Street.' Then, when it looked like we might be able to add Paul Humphreys to the mix, something in my head clicked – I should finally write my autobiography and tell my story.

When I was asked if I'd like to contribute to a book on OMD, I was stuck for words. What could I say about a music group whose songs have become so much part of our fabric? What could I possibly add? Have you ever been to Torre del Lago Puccini, on the north coast of Tuscany? Well, since 1930, very close to the villa of the late Italian composer, the annual Puccini Festival takes place, on a floating stage no less. Some time ago, I was lucky enough to see a performance of Manon Lescaut, one of the greatest Giacomo Puccini operas. The next day, as I drove to Lucca - birthplace of the composer - I happened to hear 'Enoly Gay' on the radio. In that instant I realised the magnificent melodies of Andy and Paul are actually very much reminiscent of Italian folk music, the very music Puccini absorbed.

Andy's always insisted that a certain German band heavily influenced him and Paul. That may well be right, but I've always felt all music is kind of interrelated anyway. Since the dawn of time we've been subjected to, and have experienced, a kind of miraculous transfer of cultures. European music, with its Italian traditions, mixes with the soul and rhythms of African Americans, then returns to Europe in the early 20th Century as jazz. Then, music transforms again, combining the sounds of the European continent with the sounds beyond it.

Human beings just can't stop making it. It's in our blood. No surprise, then, that it's able to touch us inside. For many, music is an escape from reality. For others, it has the power to fulfil. If we listen closely enough, we'll learn something about life. So perhaps it's not so hard for me to say something meaningful about Orchestral Manoeuvres in the Dark after all. The world's a better place with their music in it!

PAUL HUMPHREYS

I toured America in 2000, taking Claudia Brücken with me, performing as 'Paul from OMD', playing OMD songs because OMD wasn't active. I did a festival and took Claudia as a backing singer as we were together as a couple. It was just a bit of fun. I put a band together and thought, 'Whilst I'm

↑
Andy and Karl Bartos at the Pink Museum studio in 1996 shortly before both electronic music pioneers got refused entry to The State techno club in Liverpool for the dress code violation of wearing (white) jeans!

out there and spending all this money I may as well do some other gigs.' So I played Hollywood and Texas and Chicago, put a bit of a tour together. I sold out all the shows, because people wanted to hear those songs again, and at that point thought, 'I'm going to call Andy.'

Andy had stopped OMD and was doing Atomic Kitten. This was round about the turn of 2000. I contacted him and said, 'I did that tour because I got a call saying there's a real demand to hear OMD songs live again, so thought I'd see what happened and do a few shows. I'm getting calls from promoters, people want to hear us live. Do you fancy doing something?' And he said, 'I'll think about it, but I've joined the manufactured pop world now and want to do this for a while. And to be honest I'm happy to be home with the family and not go on the road again'. So it took a bit of convincing for Andy to get back into it again.

It was around 2006 and it was Andy who got the call. A German TV show were putting together the ultimate chart show of all the best-selling records in Germany. They wanted us involved as 'Maid of Orleans' was featured. Andy phoned me and said, 'Look, we've been offered this show. It's kind of cool that it's one of the best-selling songs of all time.'

At that point, we'd both been thinking there had been all these documentaries about bands of the 80s and we were being included less and less. It was all about the New Romantics, Duran Duran and Spandau Ballet. We were one of the biggest-selling bands of the 80s, yet we were getting forgotten, barely even mentioned. We were starting to get a bit worried about our legacy. I said to Andy, 'I'm getting a bit annoyed. We wrote some great songs and sold millions and millions of records, yet people are just forgetting about us. Maybe we should start thinking about doing something.'

We did the TV show. We hadn't seen each other for so long, so it was great to spend a whole weekend together. We all met in Cologne and only needed to do four minutes work performing 'Maid of Orleans'. The rest of the weekend was ours. We had such a good laugh.

At that time, offers were coming in to do things and we said, 'Shall we just dare to put a few shows on sale and see what happens?' We decided to do nine shows. And nine shows turned into 49 shows, because those shows sold out really fast, and all of a sudden, we were back doing it again.

We did that for a few years, just playing our old stuff, which was great, we had loads of fun doing it. Then one day Andy and I said to each other, 'Well, is this it? Are we just going to be trading on our former glories, or are we going to be an active band again?' We'd stuck our toes in the water and were actually liking it, but thought, 'We can't just keep doing retro gigs. If we're going to be a real band, go forward from here and have a future, we've got to back into the studio and see whether we've still got anything to offer, song-wise.'

→

Paul with Alex Machairas

→

Andy's press interview for the release of the album *The OMD Singles*

1998-2010

ALEX MACHAIRAS

A fan since the 80s, I somehow ended up friends with Andy and Paul on a personal level. It was surreal how I met them in person for the first time over 20 years ago, when one morning Paul buzzed my door at 8am in Athens in Greece. That was a surprise, and then we drove together to meet Andy, after changing a flat tyre. Between my closest friend and I, we believe we have one of the biggest OMD collections. I have about 30 imports of *Dazzle Ships* on vinyl, for example, not to mention the cassettes, two-inch reels, and more.

ANDY MCCLUSKEY

Alex had been a fan since he was very young. He contributed amazing OMD cartoons to our fan club newsletters. I couldn't believe it when he and his friend George turned up at the airport to collect Paul and I in 1998 for a promotional visit to Athens for the *Singles* album. George was working for our record label in Greece. Once we were captive in the car, the two of them proceeded to ask us every question they ever wanted answering. I'm sure that flat tyre was all part of the plan. They played 'Navigation' and wanted to know about the vocal. I don't think they believed that there are no vocals. I never had time to write real words, just made sounds like words. George also happens to be in the band Fotonovella, who wrote the music for our song 'Helen of Troy'.

OMD - 1998-2010

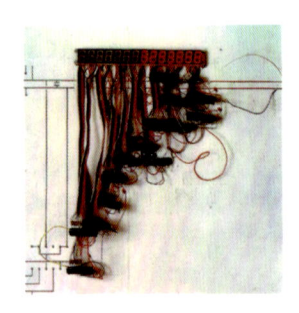

↑
Four alternative ideas for cover artwork for *The OMD Singles* album

THE SUN THEATRE

20 Sept 2000, Ananhiem, California

MADDY HUMPHREYS

First time I remember seeing Dad in concert was when I was really young, maybe eight. We'd lived on opposite continents from when I was five, so when he finally came to play a show in L.A., it was really special to be able to see him for the very first time in my hometown.

As I got older, I'd round up a different friend each summer to bring out to the UK to see him, touring around with him. It was really cool to see Dad at work, in his element, something I hadn't really understood as a child - he was always on the road, so I didn't and couldn't see or spend time with him.

I've always looked up to Andy, Martin, and Mal as uncles, and they'll always be family to me (sorry, Uncle Andy, for always hoarding the vodka backstage). I love them very much. They also don't know this yet, but I'm making them play at my wedding, and one day probably my kid's bat mitzvah. Thanks in advance, guys.

MARKUS HARTMANN
Vice-president
RCA GSA Sony Music Entertainment Germany

I got into OMD when I discovered 'Genetic Engineering', I must have been 14 or so and found that sound life-changing. My memory says 'Joan Of Arc' followed, but that might be wrong.

Decades later, managing Norwegian electro-act Apoptygma Berzerk, I ran into Paul Humphreys, who was in a relationship with Düsseldorf's Claudia Brücken, famous as the vocalist in Propaganda, since we wanted her for guest vocals.

Later, when OMD were appearing in Hamburg, Apoptygma mastermind Stephan Groth, a really big fan, brought all the vinyl he owned for Paul and Andy to sign after the show. That was something like 50 or so, which felt a bit embarrassing to ask for. Also, by the time we were supposed to meet after the show, we were seriously drunk. Usually that doesn't make things better when it's already awkward.

Anyway, Paul and Andy are among the finest people to work with. Being from the Electric City of Düsseldorf I always carry that sound in my heart, and adore OMD as godfathers of electronic pop.

NAVIGATION: THE OMD B-SIDES
WAS RELEASED

14 MAY 2001

SIMON CULLWICK
engineer at The Motor Museum Studio

One of the things I most enjoyed during my time working with OMD at the Motor Museum was the process of restoring and transferring their multi-track tapes.

When I became Andy's studio engineer in 2005 he was mostly focused on writing, producing and developing new acts. But when ideas started to emerge about OMD going back on the road, the process of restoring and digitally archiving the OMD catalogue became a full-time project.

A lot of tape used for OMD recordings was produced when manufacturers were trying out new adhesives, which it turned out, had a tendency to break down to a sticky mush over time.

ANDY MCCLUSKEY

In the 70s recording tape manufacturers decided to be more moral and stopped using glue made from whale product. Unfortunately, the new synthetic adhesive tended to accumulate moisture. After a few years the magnetic oxide would start to come off, ruining tape machines and stripping the recording from the tape. The only solution is to bake the tapes and transfer the recordings.

SIMON CULLWICK

In order to avoid losing the recordings irretrievably on to the playback head and studio floor, each tape had to be slowly baked in a laboratory oven to drive out the moisture before it could be safely transferred. Then we'd follow the session notes to set up the playback exactly as it had been during the recording - to accurately reproduce the performances and transfer them into digital Pro Tools.

One of the first tapes I processed was 'Enola Gay'. I remember having a 'lightbulb moment' when I heard that famous synth melody coming through the studio monitors. I wasn't too familiar with OMD's repertoire then, but instantly recognised it as a tune I'd been taught to play on keyboard as a kid. I was a little awestruck to find myself, nearly 20 years later, playing back the original recording - made before I was born, in a studio that no longer existed.

It was a privilege to be given a window into OMD's early recording sessions. You never knew quite what you might find. We rediscovered unused vocal takes, parts that didn't make the final cut, discussions between the producer and musicians (usually with only one side of the conversation recorded). I remember a few tracks sounded so far removed from what you hear on the record that we were left wondering whether we had the right version, until we managed to reverse-engineer the processes that had been applied in the mix.

When OMD started putting together the live show, the transferred tapes were an invaluable resource, the band putting a great deal of time and effort into translating the parts and sounds for use with their modern backline. When you see OMD perform those classic songs today, often the sounds you hear from Paul or Martin's state-of-the-art keyboard are literally those that were produced by a much more primitive synthesiser and committed to tape back in 1979.

The original Korg Micro Preset synth bought by Andy and Paul from Kays Catalogue

WIRRAL
1 July 2006, Liverpool, UK

SIMON GARLAND

I have two OMD encounters. On the day a winking Ronaldo's Portugal knocked England out of the World Cup on penalties, I spotted Andy McCluskey touring the stalls at my son's school fair, so went over and bothered him. The reunion had been announced and we were both excited by the prospect of the monster coming back to life. Our chat was fleetingly interrupted by a call from Kerry Katona, but once off the phone he had a question for me. 'I'm wondering about the dancing,' he said, 'Do you think I should still go for it?' My reply was that if he didn't do the dance, the army of the faithful would go home a little disappointed. He seemed reassured. The dance stayed.

The previous year, collecting my son from his first half-term football camp in 2005, he wanted to know why I was behaving strangely around his team-mate's Dad. It was Martin Cooper. After standing in many a post-gig queue to get his autograph, it felt odd at first to find ourselves at the school gates, the football pitch respect tape or cross-country finishing line, both of us waiting for our kids. We've since developed one of those nodding parental relationships where he knows I'm a fan, but after so much band/sport/painting/parental gossip, he's too polite to ask me what my name is again. It's Simon, Martin. Don't worry about it. Later I explained to other parents that I met one of OMD last week. 'Isn't the lead singer called Andy? He goes to my gym,' said the Dad. 'I think the drummer's my cousin,' said the Mum. This exchange perfectly sums up Wirral.

EBAY

When we got back together in 2006 we realised we didn't have many of those old sounds anymore that we used on the early albums, so we thought, 'Right, let's just buy the synths we used to have.' We needed to buy that Korg Micro Preset synth again, because the one we still owned didn't work anymore. We were scouring the internet trying to find it, because it's quite a rare synth. One came up and we lost it. Someone out-bid us. So we thought, 'We don't care how much it costs - we need to get this one.' One came up on eBay, but we saw this individually and stupidly didn't let each other know we'd spotted it. We were basically bidding against each other and paid far over the odds to get this one synth. We really should have spoken. I phoned him the next day and said, 'I lost another Micro Preset'. And he said, 'You idiot! That was me you were bidding against!'

PAUL HUMPHREYS

SAP-ARENA
19 December 2006, Mannheim, Germany

ALEXANDER SCHILL

I was 14 when I discovered the single '(Forever) Live and Die' in my Dad's record collection. I didn't have my own record player so always had to ask if I could listen. When I heard the song for the first time it was like magic for me.

I got my first OMD CD a year later. I bought albums in different places - *Sugar Tax* in Hamburg, *The Best of OMD* in New York, *Crush* in Hamburg, *Junk Culture* in Paris. So those albums bring back lots of memories. It's a crazy feeling to be able to combine events from life with music and special songs.

History of Modern was a fantastic return. Seeing them live in 2006 at the Nokia Night of the Proms, together with my other favourite musician, Mike Oldfield, was unbelievable. I never thought I'd see OMD live again.

GRAEME COOPER
OMD tour manager, 2007, 2010, & 2011

When I was at school I wanted to be a musician but wasn't any good on drums so in 1977, with the help of an old schoolfriend, I got into theatre, working for a sound and light company based in London's Covent Garden. I worked on a couple of musicals, including Jesus Christ Superstar at the Palace Theatre before moving into lighting. During the early 80s, as a lighting tech, I was asked by a band if I could tour-manage them

1998-2010 | 323

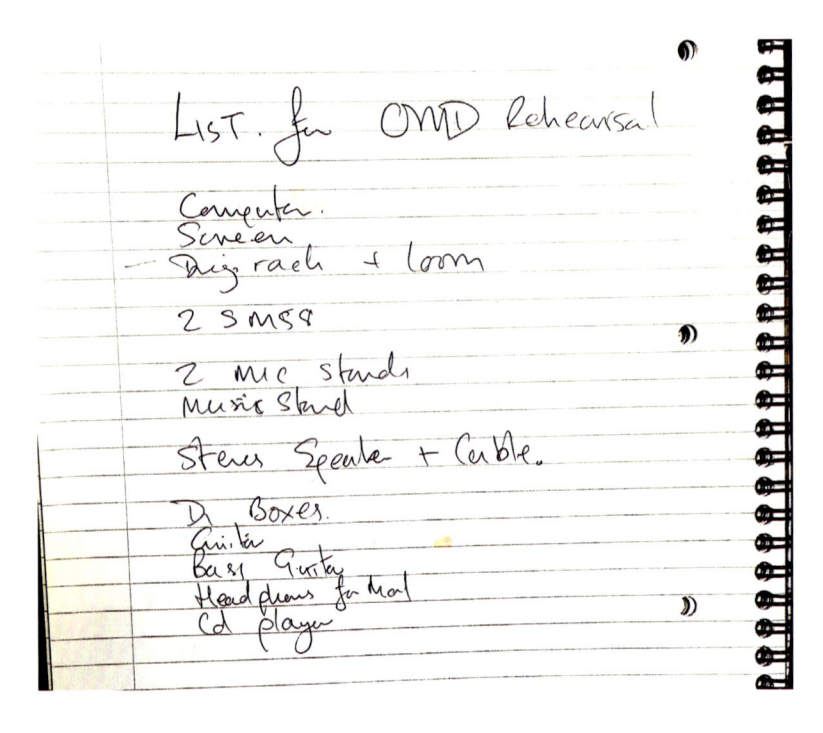

Hand written list Andy's list of equipment for the first reformed OMD rehearsal in 2006. Note the last item is a CD player for the band to listen to and relearn their own songs!

as well as do their lights, the start of my career as a tour manager. Over time I worked with various bands and management companies, including Direct Management, who were managing OMD. I was on board in 2007 for the 25th anniversary of Architecture & Morality and long-awaited comeback, going on to do two further tours in 2010/11 in Europe and the US.

I clearly remember meeting the band in Liverpool at the rehearsal studio prior to the tour. It was a surreal experience, Andy, Paul, Mal and Martin and I in a small studio. I sat and listened to them bang out hit after hit, knowing the songs and amazed at having a private show for an audience of one.

For the 2007 Architecture & Morality tour, it was important to keep costs down. The production Andy wanted was great but wasn't cheap and there was much discussion about how to proceed. But Andy was very focused on what he wanted. The tour itself was a great success and proved to many people the band was still relevant, but it lost money largely due to the films and screen.

One of my tasks was to launder Andy's shirts. As you can imagine he perspires no end with the lights, the jumping around and the windmilling. I'd swap shirts with him during the show then wash them afterwards, soaked in sweat. That along with wiping sweat out of his shoes was a daily chore. Never let anyone tell you this job is glamorous.

ROBANNAS STUDIOS
6 May 2007,
Birmingham, UK

BARRY PAGE

Prior to the Architecture & Morality shows in 2007, just 100 fans were present to witness the classic four-piece line up perform for the first time since 1988. It was a genuine thrill to see this in such an intimate setting.

OLYMPIA THEATRE

13 May 2007, Dublin, Ireland

MARK WARRINER

The first night of the comeback tour was held in a small venue and made for a fantastic atmosphere. I saw them a further three times on this tour, with the highlight seeing my name appear on the big screen during 'Messages.' Fans had been asked to send in envelopes with names and addresses to be used during the song.

ANDY MCCLUSKEY

A hundred die-hard fans in Birmingham had been one thing. What would a full gig be like? I'd been so fearful of a negative audience response to a bunch of old guys that I insisted we commissioned films for every song. My nerves were terrible as we walked out on stage. I could see the faces of the crowd illuminated by the light from the LED screen behind us. They looked nervous too. As the song 'Sealand' unfolded, their countenance changed. A definite appearance of relief on those faces. Yes, we could still play, and sounded good. We would be accepted back! The band and audience were reconnecting.

AIDAN CROSS

Aged nine, I spent a lot of time watching *The Chart Show* and *Top of the Pops*, starting to wake up to pop music, mainly into stuff like MC Hammer and Vanilla Ice. The more music TV I watched, the more real music I was exposed to. 'Sailing on the Seven Seas' was insanely catchy. I loved it immediately. I remember dancing to it at a disco for kids from my school. That night I flirted heavily with my 'girlfriend' at the time and was violently sick when I got home, a bug going around. But that night I got my first taste of the 'club culture' that would become the norm for me a decade later, and associate OMD heavily with that memory.

'Pandora's Box' came out a few months later and was played frequently at the nightly disco at a Cornish campsite my family took me to that summer. When I hear that song I still recall my nine-year-old self, dancing to it each night.

Not long after came 'Then You Turn Away'. I saw it on *The Chart Show* and was disappointed. It was a lot slower and more downbeat than the two OMD songs I knew and loved and didn't connect with me. I began to have doubts about buying *Sugar Tax*. But I recorded that particular edition of *The Chart Show*, watched it again and second time around it blew me away. OMD could also have been my first gig, but tickets for Chester's Northgate Arena sold out before I could get them.

On my 10th birthday that November, *Sugar Tax* was by far the present I was most excited about. Alone in my bedroom, I put it in my new ghetto blaster, another present - and had my first OMD album experience. I was totally lost in it, which at my young age struck me as particularly dark and emotional. It was a voyage into a strange, almost gothic, often surreal world, full of introspective lyrics about love, loss and the city, a few outright weird songs like 'Apollo XI', and 'Neon Lights', particularly weird but extremely atmospheric and romantic.

Sugar Tax became my soundtrack to the winter of '91/'92 and I had it on repeat play during those cold, dark months. I knew OMD already had a long history and Andy was the sole survivor of the classic line-up and became intrigued to hear their back-catalogue. As the 90s progressed and I entered my teens, the *Liberator* and *Universal* albums were added to my collection. I particularly loved the latter. When the singles album came out in 1998 I finally acquainted myself more directly with vintage OMD.

When I joined the fan community on the official website in 2005, there was an announcement. Not only were OMD returning, but it was with the classic line-up of Andy, Paul, Mal and Martin. Better still, they'd be releasing new material. Getting excited and emotional about an impending reunion, I bought old VHS tapes from eBay of *The Best of OMD* and *Crush: the Movie*.

I finally saw OMD live for the first time on the first show of their reunion tour. I went to four different shows on that tour, making lifelong friendships through the fan-base.

I first met Andy McCluskey at an album launch party for *History of Modern* in September 2010 in London. Although thrilled to finally meet one of my main musical inspirations after 19 years loving his music, I've never been the type to have 'heroes' or get star-struck, so it was refreshing how 'normal' that meeting was. Andy knew who I was from the web forums and seeing me in the audience and shook my hand and said 'hello' like we'd known each other for years. I've met the whole band since, recalling a lovely chat with Paul at the after-party of the *Dazzle Ships* gig at Liverpool Museum on my birthday in November 2014. A month later I ran into Paul by pure chance, standing next to him at a Gary Numan gig in London.

EMPIRE

16 May 2007,
Liverpool, UK

PAT FETTY
creator of the first
OMD website

I first heard OMD sat on the back-seat of a friend's car heading to a volleyball match in Berkeley, California, in 1985. He put on the *Crush* tape and fast forwarded to 'So in Love.' None of us knew the lyrics, and although we later read the liner notes, we couldn't believe it was actually, 'Heaven is cold, without any soul, it's hard to believe….' We were singing something totally different and, after hearing the lyrics, still sang our version.

I would be a casual fan and listener during the 80s. The *Best Of* got me through college and *Sugar Tax* got me back into the band, when I started to buy their earlier stuff. By 1995, I was a hardcore collector.

When I first got connected to the web, the very first thing I searched for was OMD, and practically nothing came up. There weren't any websites, official or otherwise, and the only thing I found where people were talking about the band was in a newsgroup. I quickly jumped in and started chatting almost every evening.

It finally dawned on me that instead of waiting for someone else to create a fan-site, I could do it myself with the help of friends I knew in the industry, one being my father. The first step was to find a domain name. I asked around and the one that stuck was omdweb.com and, with that, in 1995 Pat's World of OMD became an official project.

Cut to many long nights of writing HTML, trying to find pictures I could scan so the site had material and, more importantly, people had a reason to visit.

In 1997 a couple of friends met via the site, Neil Taylor and Paul Browne, were putting together a fan party in Liverpool. I was able to make it over to the UK and talk with real OMD fans face-to-face for the first time. During that session, I asked Andy a question, mentioned how I'd come all the way from America, and he shook my hand and said, 'It is a pleasure to meet you finally, Pat,' then told everyone about Pat's World of OMD.

I was finally fortunate enough to see OMD live for the first time in 2007 in Liverpool, and it was brilliant. I ended up catching at least five others in the UK during the reunion tour, had a chance to catch up with all my old friends and meet a bunch of great new ones. I honestly don't know how many shows I've now seen since 2007, but I would guess it's approaching 50.

To date, my site has been visited roughly 13 million times and is also host to other OMD-related properties such as the world's

OMD

Featuring the original band line-up performing their classic album Architecture & Morality

May 2007
13 Olympia, Dublin
15 Clyde Auditorium, Glasgow
16 Liverpool Empire, Liverpool
18 Hammersmith Apollo, London
21 Theaterhaus, Stuttgart
22 Ancienne Belgique, Brussels
23 Grosse Freiheit 36, Hamburg
25 Olympia, Paris
26 E-Werk, Cologne
27 MCV, Utrecht

www.omd.uk.com

largest German OMD site www.germanmanoeuvres.com and ultimate OMD Collector's site Compiled www.omdweb.com/compiled

Those late nights at the keyboard writing HTML also helped me land a job at Microsoft. So OMD not just brought me new friends but gave me a very fruitful career.

HAMMERSMITH APOLLO

18 & 19 May 2007, London, UK

BRADLEY ROGERS

Both my parents are to thank … or blame. There would always be OMD albums in the car and my first memory of their songs was thinking 'Tesla Girls' was 'taz the girls'.

I was only 10 when I attended my first OMD gig. I met Andy at the stage entrance, where he kindly signed my ticket and chatted with my parents, as I wasn't really aware of who he was. I also had a friendly chat with Martin Cooper, who was genuinely nice.

I then saw the *Dazzle Ships* anniversary tour at Birmingham Symphony Hall and got to hear 'Stanlow' live. During 'Locomotion' I had a 'fan girl' moment when Andy shook my hand where I was stood in awe in the second row. At the end of the gig a chap called Pat Fetty handed me Andy's water bottle, which he had rolled off stage. I still have that bottle.

GARY ARNDT

In the spring of 2007 I stood in the front row of the Hammersmith Apollo, thousands of miles away from my home in Oregon in the US, Mr McCluskey standing directly in front, singing 'If You Leave'. 20 years ago, this had been the first song I'd heard by OMD and now this was the first concert where I had heard my favourite band live… and in England. I clearly remember hearing it for the first time in 1986, aged 14, recording songs off the radio in my brother's room.

Dazzle Ships really caught my attention. I bought it at the same time as U2's *Zooropa*. Listening to both of these experimental albums, I wondered if I'd made two of the worst purchases ever, or two of the best. It took a few more listens to realise it was the latter; both became favourites, and *Dazzle Ships* remains my favourite OMD album.

After I ran out of OMD albums to buy, I started collecting vinyl singles with various B-sides and mixes. In my quest for old vinyl, I spent a lot of time in record shops. I have a particularly strong memory of the day I found a store with several particularly unusual OMD treasures, including a floppy-blue record with an alternate recording of 'Pretending to See the Future', and a four-track EP called 'Introducing Radios.'

When OMD decided to play all of *Architecture & Morality* in 2007, my wife and I built vacation plans around their two concerts in London. She managed to score front-row tickets for the first night, with those concerts at the end of our first trip to Europe and the pinnacle of that experience.

Since 2013, I've struggled with health problems and can't go to concerts now. A bright spot has been OMD, as they continue their commitment to the fans. I've been thrilled by the CD and DVD recordings of their concerts and would like to thank the band for bringing so much joy into my life over more than 30 years, something particularly important to me in the struggles of recent years.

CLIFF BOWNES

OMD came back together to perform *Architecture & Morality* in its entirety. As the lights went down, you could cut the air with a knife. The tension was that great. If that wasn't enough, when Andy walked on stage for 'Sealand', the emotion was unbelievable.

MARTIN DAY

When OMD reformed and announced they'd be playing the entire *Architecture & Morality* at Hammersmith Apollo in 2007, I pretty much beat down the door to the place. I can barely describe how much I loved that evening – all those songs I thought I'd never experience in a live setting – Beginning and the End', and 'The Romance of the Telescope' usurping 'Electricity' from its traditional position at the end of the encore. On the DVD release of that incredible evening, I'm there in about row three, jumping up and down in a red Labour Party/World Cup t-shirt.

BARRY HEATHER

In early 1982 my best mate, Gary Hobdell and I were 15. 'Maid of Orleans' had been released and we were both mesmerised by the strange noises in the intro, the drumming and searing synth hook. We worked out the melody on piano and were intrigued to find that most of the notes were from the black keys. We tasked ourselves with trying to find out more about this band with a strange name. The nearby Our Price and Venus record stores, together with *Smash Hits*, helped us find 'Electricity' and the first two albums.

We didn't get to see OMD live until the Junk Culture tour in 1984, and it's fantastic that Andy still has the same energy on stage now as he did back then. Gary passed away suddenly in early 2009. He never got to hear the new material, but we saw the first comeback gig at Hammersmith Odeon in May 2007 and the atmosphere that night was absolutely electric. Often at gigs over the years a seated audience would take time to get up and dance, but Gary was always up and at it from the first song. Here's to Gary, and long may OMD keep adding to the memories of my life.

JEREMY VINE
BBC TV presenter & broadcaster

I was a teenager who loved his music. I was switched on to music around the age of 14, most powerfully by David Bowie's album *Lodger*. Bowie had versioned himself to avoid the car crash of the late 70s when punk basically took out everything and put himself in a position where he was leading what became the New Romantics. I'd started listening to John Peel, who obviously had amazing music on. He also flipped totally into punk and new wave. There was Theatre of Hate and Joy Division and The Fall and all that, and then suddenly there was OMD as well.

OMD did this brilliant switch from being quite cult-y to being on *Top of the Pops*. They did it very quickly, a bit like Tears for Fears. And it was clear that there were brilliant songwriting minds behind it.

The first thing I remember hearing was 'Electricity' on the first album, before they were really big or famous. Everyone who knows them loved that track. It seems incredible that it can be an original composition by them, but it is. Also from that first album, 'Messages' is a great song and 'Julia's Song' is fantastic. I just played and played and played that album on vinyl in my teenage bedroom.

I didn't see them in concert until I was 42. I was very square as a teenager. Concerts weren't as available as they are now. They cost a lot of money and travel. None of us would really travel anywhere to go and see anybody, and that was all really crap. We had no social media, so couldn't find out anything about the bands we liked. So OMD became very mysterious, particularly when their first album had that weird fluorescent perforated cover. And they had a strange band name as well. It was an incredible band with the word 'orchestra' in the title. The Yellow Magic Orchestra was also around at the time, so for all I knew OMD could have been 85 people with drum kits. I didn't know who or what they were. It was a complete mystery to me. And then of course they broke through.

My memory was that they broke through with 'Enola

Gay', another great song, and I saw them of *Top of the Pops* and thought, 'Oh, this is only two people. How does that work?'

It was the liberating force of the synthesiser in those days that allowed two people to sound like 20. I saw them and just thought, 'They're brilliant!' And I remember 'Joan of Arc.'

They were obviously highly creative and more serious than a pop single necessarily allowed them to be, and the seriousness caused them to topple over a bit in the early years with *Dazzle Ships*, when they went a bit off-track. Then when they came back to pop they just about stabilised it.

The early albums were absolutely stunning. I used to watch them and think, 'I can't believe all this music is coming out of these two brains.' It was similar with Blancmange, where they had just two guys writing incredible stuff and sounding like a 10-piece band.

McCluskey and Humphreys are complete geniuses of the pop world. In the end I think they possibly weren't well served by the fact that they arrived when synthesisers arrived, because they tend to sound very dated now. But they're clearly major composers along the lines of Schubert, Puccini and others. Even in the later years, with *Sugar Tax* and '*Talking Loud and Clear*', they have a great ear for a pop melody.

First time I saw them, at Hammersmith Apollo on the Architecture & Morality tour in 2007, I was in a great place. I was very busy at work, so I was thinking, 'Oh God, am I going to be able to get there?' But I did and it took me back to my childhood. I brought my wife, who really didn't know them, shamefully, and I just thought, 'This is so brilliant I think I'm going to burst into tears here.' And listening to 'Souvenir' did make me cry.

It really was fantastic to hear those songs again. They really gave it everything. You can just see Andy's love for music. That's what I love about it. Until I appeared on *Strictly Come Dancing*, there was a certain tragic quality to McCluskey's dancing. Now I completely understand. *Strictly* have got to get him on. It's the obvious booking!

ANCIENNE BELGIQUE

22 May 2007,
Brussels, Belgium

DAVID HAERINCK

My brother introduced me to OMD's music. 'Enola Gay' is a song I've heard at least a billion times. When they made their comeback and visited the AB in Belgium, I contacted them about my wedding and they allowed

↑ David Haerinck proposed to his girlfriend on stage at an OMD show in Brussels, Belgium

me to propose to my girlfriend on stage. That was the most beautiful day of my life.

PALLADIUM
26 May 2007,
Cologne, Germany

HAGEN SCHMITT

It was like getting an electric shock when I saw the band for the very first time, performing on a German quiz show in 1982. All four wore cool brown leather jackets and were standing behind strange looking boxes, with a big screen in the background running a movie of a young medieval lady on a horse. I'd never heard of Joan of Arc, or the 'Maid of Orleans.' I was electrified, fascinated and affected at the same time by this pure melody-magic and stoic-pumping, powerful waltz rhythm. Within four minutes and 12 seconds my whole life changed.

Aged 13, I placed an ad in a music magazine looking for other like-minded people who shared my passion for the music of OMD. I was surprised when the first handwritten letters rapidly rolled in from all over the country. The German media didn't publish very much about the band, so I was getting the bus to the nearest major city a few times a week to visit the only newspaper store where it was possible to read all the British music magazines without having to buy them. I only bought them when there was something about OMD inside.

With spare pocket money, I produced fan magazines for my newly-established German based fan club and we all were in active letter contact. Unfortunately, but inevitably, after two years I was no longer in a position to finance the fan club and had to close it. But, inspired by Mal Holmes and the song 'Southern', I began to play drums, starting my own bands and getting interested in other music directions, far away from synthesiser-oriented pop.

In 2002, I got access to the Internet for the first time. I remember sitting in front of the monitor and, not knowing exactly what to do, typed my first thought into the search engine, a word with three letters, 'OMD.' I landed on the website of US fan site pioneer Pat Fetty, who also offered links to other sites like Neil Taylor's 'Motion & Heart'.

I was so excited about finding all this information, a lot of which was new to me. Very little information was available in the German language about OMD, so I decided to change that and finally start the GermanManoeuvres site. A great community has grown up over 16 years, with strong cohesion and a lot of personal friendships.

I was pleased to be at the Motor Museum Studio in Liverpool in 2004, when Andy and Paul publicly spoke about a possible reunion. I also feel honoured to have been at their German chart show TV comeback a year later. Finally, last year I fulfilled a big wish - to see the band live in Liverpool. And the best thing - they're still making fantastic music.

MC VREDENBURG
27 May 2007, Utrecht, The Netherlands

MARISKA BARNIER MACGILLAVRY

It was around Christmas 1994 when I heard 'Maid of Orleans' on the radio. I asked my mother which band it was. She knew the song, but no more. I had to ask my stepbrother on New Year's Eve, so from 1 January 1995, aged 18, I became a fan, although having to wait until 2007 for my first OMD concert.

My second concert was on the History of Modern 2010 tour at the Paradiso in Amsterdam. I was seven and a half months pregnant with my youngest daughter, who was named after Andy. In 2013, I went to the English Electric tour at the Tivoli in Utrecht. My oldest daughter was seven, saw pictures from the concert and said, 'Mam, I want to go with you to an OMD concert sometime.'

In the meantime, I saw OMD

↑ Hagen Schmitt produced OMD fan magazines for the German-based fan club

in 2015 at Retropop. The day after Paul was still in the hotel while the others had left. Some fans said I should ask if I could have my picture taken with him. I was too shy, so my husband asked for me. In 2016 I went VIP to see Architecture & Morality and Dazzle Ships at the Royal Albert Hall in London - that concert was amazing!

A year later *The Punishment of Luxury* was released and I went to concerts at the Empire in Liverpool (with a VIP ticket), Glasgow's Royal Concert Hall and the Sage, Gateshead. In December I went with my oldest daughter to the Tilburg 013 concert. She was pretty nervous but enjoyed every moment. Andy gave her one of his Dunlop 1mm guitar-picks and from Ed she got the stage setlist. She was over the moon.

CITADEL SPANDAU

7 June 2007, Berlin, Germany

STEFFEN LÜSSING

Raised in East Germany, an hour south of Berlin, before 1989 there was no music to buy and no music magazines. The only music we heard was from West Berlin radio stations RIAS (Rundfunk im Amerikanischen Sektor) and SFB2 (Sender Freies Berlin). But in 1984 there was a music night on TV, on Channel ZDF, where I saw OMD for the first time live.

When the Wall fell, I drove to West Berlin and crawled through the record shops, buying LPs and maxi-singles, and discovering B-sides. Then I got my first CD player and bought *The Best of OMD* on CD. I only learned after that some of my favourite songs, like 'Genetic Engineering', 'Enola Gay', 'Souvenir' and 'Maid of Orleans', were by OMD.

Seeing OMD at Citadel Spandau was fabulous. These were the heroes of my youth, only a few metres away from me on stage. I could hardly believe it. And another curiosity was revealed. If you only know music from the radio, and you don't get any background information, you don't know that 'Souvenir' and '(Forever) Live and Die' are sung by Paul instead of Andy. I found that out at the show.

ROYAL CONCERT HALL

12 June 2007,
Nottingham, UK

ANDY HUTCHINSON

Eight of us, all massive electronic music fans, managed to get tickets dead central and near the front. As soon as the opening beats started we were on our feet. As most of us are six-footers, this meant everyone behind us had to stand, so from the off everyone was on their feet. I remember Andy saying, 'Blimey, you're all up for it - here we go…' And so it proved. A belter of a gig.

BRIGHTON DOME

22 June 2007,
Brighton, UK

JOHN MCSHANE

I was a fan in the 80s but never saw them back then, due to lack of funds. The first time was 2007 at Brighton Dome. The sound was crystal-clear, and I was immediately struck by Andy's relentless energy and quirky dancing and the superb musicianship of the band. They played a very non-self-indulgent set, hit after hit, and by the time of 'Maid of Orleans', with flashing strobes and Andy in full-flow dancing, the audience was going wild. Paul's smiling face showed they were enjoying the feedback from the cheering crowd. 'Talking Loud and Clear' is one of my all-time favourite songs, bringing back memories of driving around winding coastal roads in Scotland with my family in the summer of '84. I was nearly moved to tears when they played it. It was one of those rare concerts where I walked away with a big smile on my face, and a feeling of euphoria.

PARK BUEHNE
29 June 2007,
Leipzig, Germany

DIANA MÜLLER

My stepdad, 11 years older than me, has always been like a brother to me. Thanks to him I grew up with the best of electronic music: Kraftwerk, Jean-Michel Jarre, Depeche Mode, Simple Minds, and OMD. It was a dream come true to see OMD in 2007. And at 2017's meet-and-greet at Leipzig's Haus Auensee, Andy recognised the t-shirt I had bought 10 years before.

↑ Diana Müller with OMD in Leipzig, Germany

MONTE CARLO SPORTING CLUB
24 July 2007, Monaco

ANDY MCCLUSKEY

This was a very strange gig. All the crew had to wear long trousers, jackets and ties. We knew ticket sales had been awful. We just wanted to get this over with. The concert began with us behind a golden bead-curtain standing on a 70s-style disco-light floor, which slid forward as the music started. There were only a very few occupied tables, with people dressed in dinner suits and bow ties. It surely couldn't get any weirder. Yes, it could. There was Shirley Bassey in the front row!

AMBASSADOR THEATRE
28 September 2008,
Dublin, Ireland

ROGER LYONS
OMD road crew

We were touring with a very cool, new digital mixing desk, a Vi6. So new that we we're basically the guinea pigs. It sounded great, but 30 minutes into our Dublin gig that changed. The band were in full swing with 'Maid of Orleans' but the audience didn't look right. The main PA system had gone off. Normally in these situations we do that classic tech-support move - turn it off and on, but that didn't work! We dug deeper - turned it off and on again. Still no joy. The band were still on stage (always embarrassing, that) so Andy said, 'We'll get this fixed and be back in a mo.' Off they trooped.

To that point it had been a rocking gig, with a particularly rowdy crowd. I waited patiently for the sound-crew to sort the system, but it wasn't going well. The prototype desk wouldn't reboot. After 30 minutes without music the crowd were booing, a few things getting thrown at the stage. I suggested we forgot the main system, turned the side-fills around to face the audience and progressed that way. After 40 minutes it looked like it was going to turn into a full-on riot, all a bit scary. Then, all of a sudden, the desk decided its nap was over and it woke itself up. The band came back on to rapturous applause, starting 'Maid' again. Intermission forgotten. Absolute belter of a gig!

ANDY MCCLUSKEY

When a major piece of equipment fails, it ruins the whole vibe of a concert. There was a horrible moment at the Ambassador. I was windmilling around to 'Maid' and the audience didn't look right. I have side-monitors and an in-ear, so couldn't tell that the main PA had gone off.

Sat in the dressing room waiting for the desk to come back on was the most excruciating experience. You know there is no spare and you're trusting that the crew can fix it. But if digital desk software crashes and won't reboot, the gig is over!

↑
Andy and Mal on stage in Dublin 2008. Photo by Mark Crouch

MICK LYNCH

Me and my mate Pete went along to see the opening night of the tour. I'll always remember Andy's reaction and comments after the opening few songs. 'If we'd have known it was gonna be this good, we'd have done it sooner.'

What was memorable about the gig was that the mixing desk broke down. They went off stage for quite a long while, came back with it fixed, then proceeded to sing the same songs again, feeling we were robbed of them the first time. What other band would do that? I recall him saying something like, 'Irish sound system versus English mixing desk, and the English mixing desk fucked up.'

MESSAGES: GREATEST HITS WAS RELEASED

29 SEP 2008

SYMPHONY HALL

6 October 2008, Birmingham, UK

ROGER LYONS
OMD road crew

Andy arrived at the venue and he was grey. Not a good colour on a pop star. He'd basically done a me, staying up all night drinking. He was a real pro that day and I don't know how he got through it, as he had to have regular access to the 'Dazzle Bucket' as he puked and danced his way through the gig. Poor chap, great show nonetheless.

ANDY MCCLUSKEY

I have trouble sleeping on tour. It's hard when you come off stage, full of adrenalin, so I sometimes take sleeping pills. I didn't have any pills after the Birmingham show the night before and stupidly tried to anaesthetise myself with an entire bottle of Grey Goose vodka. I slept in the van outside the gig all afternoon. I had to do a sponsor meet-and-greet, feeling like death. Sat in the shower for two hours before the show, somehow I got through the gig despite feeling like I wanted to die. Never, ever, ever will I do that again!

ROUND HOUSE

7 October 2008, London, UK

LORI TARCHALA

I first heard OMD by pure fluke. My best friend got an LP from her brother for her birthday that had a collection of artists on it, most unfamiliar to us and almost all from outside the States. 'Joan of Arc' was the OMD song and I still remember my first listen. I actually got up to turn the volume knob. It has such a quiet beginning before building up. I loved it, grabbed the cover to see who the heck I was listening to and, once home, immediately asked for the album for Christmas!

A few months later my sister and I started watching a video show that came up on a smaller TV station called *MV3*, hosted by Richard Blade, an Englishman who moved to California, using his background to expose Americans to artists from 'across the pond'. He played the video

OMD - 1998-2010

OMD 2008: Andy, Mal, Martin and Paul

to 'Genetic Engineering' and I loved that even more than 'Joan of Arc.' Then my sister found a couple of cassettes of the first two albums. I was hooked.

I have vivid memories of hearing OMD on US radio for the first time for 'So in Love'. My sister surprised me shortly after with a copy of *Crush*. It skipped on 'So in Love' and '88 Seconds in Greensboro', but I didn't care. I listened so much that I still hear the skips when singing along to my non-skipping CD version.

Sadly, my parents wouldn't let me go to concerts until I was 18 so I missed the last American tour in 1988. Finally, in 2008, I was able to fly to the UK for two shows. My friends were all, 'You're flying to England for a concert?' But I told them, 'Not a concert - *the* concert I've waited 26 years to see. I'm not waiting any longer!' I had second balcony in Birmingham the first night and front-row on the floor at the Roundhouse in London.

There was talk of them coming to America and I told friends I'd do the entire tour if they did. Well, Spring 2011 they did, and I did. It was a life experience, not just to see so many awesome shows but to make many new friends, see places in America I'd not seen before and have the massive adventure of following a band for a month mostly on my own. OMD for me is a never-ending story of wonderful concerts, friends and experiences.

ANDY MCCLUSKEY

We were so humbled that Lori was doing the entire tour in 2011, (the first person to do so since the mid-80s) we gave her a AAA laminate.

CLARE BARBER

My partner and I drove from Plymouth. I said, 'If they play 'Statues' I will probably wee myself', that being one of my all-time favourites (along with 'The New Stone Age', which is being played at my funeral). Up until then I'd never experienced it live, so when they did play it, guess what happened? But only a little bit.

MARCO GOTTWALD

When I married my wife, her only wish was to hear 'Maid of Orleans' in the church. Her wish was my order. As we played the song I told my new wife we would spend our honeymoon in London in October. She looked at me and I saw the question marks in her eyes. I said, 'I've bought two tickets for an OMD concert!' She was a bit worried, as she was pregnant at the time.

In 2018 my wife, nine-year old daughter and six-year old son came to the concert in Bochum. When my daughter was born and was crying, my wife played a song from OMD and she stopped, having listened to it in the womb.

PHILHARMONIC HALL

20 June 2009,
Liverpool, UK

MARK WARRINER

It was a fantastic experience to be able to see Andy and Paul play live with a 75-piece orchestra. 'Maid of Orleans' was breath-taking.

LG ARENA

2 December 2009,
Birmingham, UK

LEE BURTON

In the summer of 1993, aged 14 and returning from visiting military airfields in Lincolnshire with best friend James, he asked his Dad, driving, to play a record copied onto cassette from his older brother. I soon heard 'Maid of Orleans,' with its stunningly atmospheric opening and tremendous drumbeat. I made my friend's father play it on repeat all the way home to Nottingham.

James couldn't identify the artist, as the track was one of many copied, and his brother had since moved out of the family home. But the next day I went to my local W.H. Smith and picked up a copy of the *Guinness Book of Hit Singles*. I knew from the lyrics the song had something to do with Joan of Arc. OMD had released a single called 'Joan of Arc', so I assumed that must be the artist. I immediately went and purchased *The Best Of* cassette and rushed home to play it. While I was enjoying the album, my heart sank a little when 'Joan of Arc' started. That wasn't the record my friend played. But my heart lifted again when the very next

ODYSSEY ARENA

10 December 2009, Belfast, UK

ALISON LYONS

Alison Lyons with Paul and Andy

song on the album started, 'Maid of Orleans'. Although slightly confused, I was absolutely delighted.

When the group disbanded in 1988 I didn't think I'd ever get the chance to see them live. But thankfully Andy and Paul made the wonderful decision to start performing and recording again, and I've been lucky enough to see them twice. The first time was with Simple Minds in 2009 and the second in my hometown of Nottingham in November 2017 with the wonderful Tiny Magnetic Pets.

I'm still blown away by their music. It helped get me through revision for my GCSEs, relationship ups and downs, and whiling away the hours in my bunk-bed out at sea after joining the Royal Navy at 18.

'Souvenir' was so hauntingly beautiful, unique and melodic. I couldn't get enough and bought the 10" version, which I played to death. Their visit to the Odyssey Arena was my first experience of hearing them live. I was blown away by Andy's energy and that they sounded like a recording of their songs.

In October 2017, they performed at Mandela Hall in Belfast, a challenging venue with low ceiling, bodies packed like sardines and no air circulating due to health and safety rules, demanding the doors remain closed. I was wilting doing very little, while Andy was windmilling during 'Joan of Arc' like a true pro, even though the sweat was literally dripping onto the stage from him. I was so impressed, I decided to do something I'd never done before and book and fly over to another gig on their European tour to the Isle of Man.

That gig was the icing on the cake for me and even better than the previous two for many reasons.

After being unable to secure a VIP pass before I left (and, believe me, I tried) I flew into the Isle of Man, got to my hotel room and rushed to meet two other fans, both with VIP passes. We had a drink, then it was time for the meet-and-greet. I went along in the hope I might be able to secure VIP there and then, which I did thanks to the wonderful tour manager. He was so lovely, going off to get me the necessary items.

Andy was very professional but friendly to us all. After that, we were ushered into a side-room, where my friend and I decided to go to the back of the queue in the hope of securing a bit more time with Andy and Paul. We were like giddy teenagers, and by the time we got there I'd forgotten what I wanted to ask. I managed to get a couple of pics with both, then asked Andy if I could have one with him alone. He duly obliged and gave me the most enormous hug. I was knocked sideways. We witnessed another fabulous gig to a very packed, happy audience.

The following morning, the weather was beautiful, and I had breakfast outside a cafe with my friend before catching a bus to the airport. We didn't realise we were on the same flight to Manchester. While in the airport lounge waiting for our flight, my friend said, 'I think Andy's here.' But we decided we wouldn't approach him as he had company, and he must be on a different flight.

We finally boarded, everyone taking their seats. Who should walk past, turn and say, 'Hello'? Mr McCluskey. He was sat seven seats in front (yes, I counted). We were totally in shock and enjoyed the fact that we shared the same airspace and extra meet-and-greet time. On landing, we decided to stay seated until he got off. As he walked by, I stuck my hand out, which he took with both of his, saying, 'Take care.' We finally got into the airport and to baggage-claim. Then who came sauntering down the hallway to collect his suitcase? Andy again.

CHRIS OATEN
photographer

My friend Andy Duffin introduced me to OMD. He played me 'Electricity' and 'Messages' and I immediately connected. I had never heard anything quite like this and 'Messages' remains one of my all time favourite singles.

I asked my friend to make me a copy on a tape which I played until I could afford to purchase the album and singles. There was no question that this was going to be the band that would shape my musical tastes and eventually inspire me to take up the bass guitar.

My mum, bless her, used to rearrange her bills so I always had money to be first in the queue at HMV to purchase releases which were out that week from OMD. I became such a familiar face at this music store that they used to save me all the window displays so I could plaster my bedroom walls with them.

THE MANOR

·Shipton-on-Cherwell·Oxford·(08675) 77551·

Reg. Office: Virgin Studios Ltd., 95-99 Ladbroke Grove, London W.11 Reg. No: 1214591 (England)

Dear Chris,

If I can find the infamous shirt — you can have it. But finding it may be difficult. Paul wore it in America and either left it in the USA at his wife's house or left it in our London office. I will get Ines from the fan club to try and find it.

By now I think it may have shrunk or got a bit faded. — I haven't seen it for 6 months.

PTO

If you still want it, how does £70 sound. (That £50 cheaper than I bought it for). No on second thoughts make it £50 — it probably smells since Paul's been wearing it.

For further reference contact Ines at the Fan club. 132 Liverpool Road. London N1 1LA.

Cheers

←

The letters to photographer Chris Oaten from Andy with the offer to buy *that* shirt

In 1984 I was at Sheffield City Hall to see the Junk Culture tour and I sneaked back stage. I was just about to be ejected by a security guard when Andy intervened Andy, shook my hand and we had a chat. From then on Andy allowed me backstage after gigs and we kept in touch ever since. I even named my first band Junk Culture where I met my future wife as when she auditioned. We have written music together ever since.

OMD played 'Locomotion' on the Multi-Coloured Swap Shop in 1984 with Andy wearing a geometric abstract-striped shirt in red, white and black. I was so blown away by this shirt that I wrote to Smash Hits and Linda Duff from the magazine contacted the OMD fan club to find out where I could buy one. I couldn't as the limited number was sold out. Not giving up on my quest, I wrote to Andy who replied on Manor Studios paper saying, 'Since Simon Le Bon has worn the same shirt on TOTP you can have mine for £70.' but also joked, 'Actually Paul has been wearing it so it probably smells.. you can have it for £50.' Sadly the shirt was stolen so Andy sent me a Crolla shirt and test pressings, which I treasured. I was still fixated on the original red shirt and had one made it up from my very crude drawings costing me £55. This doesn't sound a lot today, however at the time my mum missed bills and said it could be my early Christmas present. I even wore it for my 21st the following June.

Years later I found good photos of Le Bon wearing his version and I could work out that there was a system to the chaos print. My friend Paul Willerton and I spent 4 days designing another shirt, had it printed on best Egyptian cotton, and Sarah Bowes (award winning Hull fashion designer) made up the shirt. Total cost £350!

By 2009 I had my own photographic company (O-Ten Photography) and Andy Paul came for two shoots for their album History of Modern. I had an exhibition at Hull Truck Theatre and some of the large prints were auctioned for charity. I became great friends with Imogen Bebb, (she bought the big prints of Andy and Paul) so I decided that the old version needed a new home and a new journey, Imogen is the only person I would trust with this shirt as I know she will never part with it.

OMD did another shoot with me 2017. Never in a million years when I was sat in Andy Duffin's bedroom could I imagine making photos for two OMD albums. My mum, if she was still alive, would have probably taken out an ad in the local paper to tell everyone of my achievements, but more importantly how proud she was of her son.

BRADEN MERRICK
president, Bright Antenna

The band made a huge impression on me in '86 when I was 14. They were the gateway into my love of New Wave synth-pop. The girls I was into were those that looked kind of like Robert Smith (one, a Molly Ringwald doppelganger, worked at an ice cream parlour, and we'd talk about synth-pop), read the *NME*, watched *120 Minutes*, had black lights in their bedroom, and an insane music collection of almost everything British.

'If You Leave' was the gateway track from the *Pretty In Pink* soundtrack and from there I found more material from the band that suited me better and that led to me having debates about what I call the 'Big 3' of synth-pop. Kraftwerk were cool, but I love choruses with big vocal hooks, and the only bands doing that well from '79-'89 in my opinion were OMD, Depeche Mode, and The Pet Shop Boys.

Fast forward to 2002, when I discovered and started managing an unknown band from Las Vegas, The Killers. All I could think was here is my dream band. One-part Bowie, one-part OMD, and one-part U2. The success of that relationship with breakthrough LP *Hot Fuss* must have caught the attention of Andy McCluskey and Paul Humphreys, because there I was in Cannes, circa 2009, having drinks with their manager, Mirelle Davis, having become a partner in a record label called Bright Antenna, and she said without telling me who it was, 'I have something to play for you.' When I heard it, I knew who it was immediately, asking with a big smile, 'How do we get involved?' A couple of weeks later, Mirelle said I should call Andy.

Inside, I was nervous as hell but very excited to talk to one of my Big 3, and the best of the Big 3. I'll never forget that call. Andy mentioned The Killers' *Hot Fuss* to me and appreciated the work I'd done for that record, our conversation leading to Bright Antenna releasing *History of Modern*.

The all-original line-up tour was a fantastic success for the band worldwide and bringing Paul Humphreys to X96 in Salt Lake City for a radio interview was surreal. I was and still am very honoured and humbled to be part of the band's ongoing career story. And their music still stands the test of time.

OMD - 1998-2010

THE ONE SHOW PAUL'S OLD HOUSE

January 2010, Meols, UK

DAVE FROST

I am lucky enough to live in Paul's old house in Meols, where a lot of the early songs were written and demoed. I was delighted to host Andy and BBC TV's *The One Show* when they did a programme about the band. Andy and Paul also kindly came over and signed my framed 'Enola Gay', which I got for my 40th. I went to the re-opening of Eric's and saw the band with my good friend and next-door neighbour Mike Johnson. Waiting for the band to come on, he turned to me and said, 'Do you know I was stood in this exact spot for their first gig in October 1978?'

ANDY MCCLUSKEY

When the band reformed, Paul and I made ourselves a promise that we would undertake to try and actually do every crazy offer that came our way. And they didn't come crazier than doing a gig at Bletchley Park, home of the WWII Enigma code-breakers, for a vintage computer convention.

HISTORY OF MODERN (PART I)
WAS RELEASED

2 MAR 2010

Press advert for 'History of Modern (Part II)'

BLETCHLEY PARK
19 June 2010,
Milton Keynes, UK

SIMON FULLER
OMD tour manager
2013-2018

I first met OMD in 2009. I was a sound engineer and occasional backline tech, and initially filled in for someone looking after a few technical things for their performance with the Liverpool Philharmonic Orchestra. At the age of about 23 or 24, I confess I didn't really know who they were. I knew more about Atomic Kitten than OMD.

Sometime later, during 2010, I received a phone call. I was asked if I'd be interested in coming to help them out with a two-piece performance they were playing at a vintage computer fair in Bletchley Park.

The whole event was incredible. Someone programmed an Atari to play a kind of eight-bit version of 'Enola Gay', and there were all kinds of displays of computers and games from my childhood and way before.

When we came in to set up in a small ballroom, we encountered a few problems straight away. It's standard practice for bands to bring in their own sound engineer to mix the show, using in-house equipment. However, this show was far from standard. The PA and mixing desk was brought in by its owner, who was refusing to let anyone but themselves touch the desk. After a few calm discussions we were getting nowhere. The event organiser even came down to try and reason with the owner, to no avail.

There was a very loud, disconcerting low-end mains hum across the whole PA. There were wild accusations thrown around that it was our equipment causing it, but I knew this wasn't the case. After all, we only had a keyboard, a laptop and a bass guitar. I set about trying to isolate the problem until eventually I managed to figure out it was in fact the desk causing the hum. Our two problems had been rolled into one, yet neither was resolved.

Whilst deliberating what to do, someone helpfully piped up that they just happened to have another mixing desk sat in the back-seat of their car. They didn't really know how to use it, but perhaps it would help. It did. With the day saved, we brought the desk in and both of our issues were gone. The new owner was more than happy for me to use their desk, if anything honoured that it would be used for an OMD show.

I hadn't appreciated the significance at the time, but that show was the first performance of some of their first new material in years, so quite a few hardcore fans had travelled some distance to attend, and it nearly didn't happen. If I remember rightly, the band only had a few songs prepared in this new format, so when asked for an encore they just played the whole set again.

After this, the OMD two-piece show became more of a 'thing', and I continued to work on all those shows promoting the new album, *History of Modern*. During the following years, I stayed in touch with the band, nearly coming in as their monitor engineer a few times, but it never quite worked out.

Roll on to 2013, and by chance I was looking for work, and OMD were looking for a tour manager for four-piece shows, so everything aligned for me to come on board. This was a great opportunity and led to five great years working with the band. At that point I was 27 and 12 years younger than the next youngest person on the tour, but they made me feel welcome.

That show at Bletchley Park effectively served as my job interview for the two-piece shows, and to an extent, the tour manager job for the full band. Andy told me much later that he and Mirelle (the band's manager) were stood at the back while all the dramas with the desk unfolded. Andy had been unsure whether to even bring any crew, but after that vowed to always take someone. My handling of the situation had also hopefully been a good precursor to dealing with the inevitable stressful situations a tour manager often has to look after.

A RANDOM HEART BEAT

It was Mirelle's first official concert as our manager and I was worrying that it could be my last if I could do it all. I had recently been diagnosed with Atrial Fibrillation. A random heart beat, that when it triggered left me weak and breathless. I was waiting for an operation but had to get this gig done hoping that my heart wouldn't start misbehaving on stage! It didn't. Eventually, I required three operations. The first under local anaesthetic. It's rather a strange experience watching a live operation on your own heart via an X-ray monitor!

ANDY MCCLUSKEY

LIVE AT THE BEACH
21 August 2010, Büsum, Germany

MIRELLE DAVIS
OMD Manager

This one is important as it was my first gig as OMD's manager and I have the fridge magnet to prove it. I know it may seem odd that I ended up managing the band, but in many ways it was an obvious step for both sides. I'd worked in the music industry for years in UK and international marketing and as the UK office for a well-known American manager. I had the experience and who knew OMD and their career better? I also knew Anthony Addis, their manager, having worked with him at Mushroom Records on Muse.

The band originally reformed just to play live, but when they talked about putting records out Anthony got me involved. He looked after the live side and me the records. Eventually I took over the whole thing but at first it was always the live stuff I found most difficult, so used to just being a fan. As manager I had ultimate responsibility for everything, as I learned at SXSW when a camera crane collapsed. That day in Busum, things shifted for me. I was the band's manager now and I admit it took a while before it truly felt like that at a gig, but Busum is special as it was the first.

IF YOU WANT IT
WAS RELEASED

6 SEP 2010

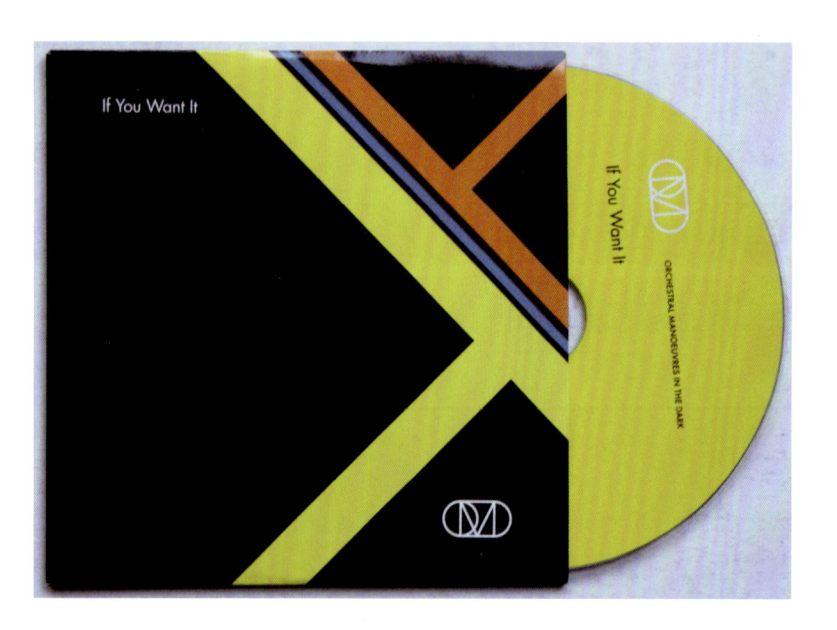

CLUB24

14 September 2010, London, UK

TRICIA ARNOLD

I was living in London, working in international music distribution, my friend and colleague Colleen and I having got to know OMD's manager Mirelle, working with her on other projects. When they played an album release show for *History of Modern* on Kingly Street in London, Colleen and I both got to go. That was my first opportunity to see them. It was such an amazing show at a relatively small venue and I got to meet Andy.

I then started working with Paul. He had a label being distributed by the company where I currently work and was heading up sales in Europe. I was star-struck but tried to play it cool.

They decided to put out the last album, distributed by my company. An incredible experience. By then I'd moved back to the States, heading up the North American retail marketing team. So we had *The Punishment of Luxury*, coming out. It was a big priority for us and me personally, OMD enjoying their highest-charting US album for a number of years.

I was so thrilled to have been able to work on that. So many times in the industry, people say not to work with bands you love, as it doesn't always go as you'd like. But OMD have been an immense pleasure to work with and are absolutely lovely guys, really positive. It's been an amazing experience for my fourth-grade self to end up with them and one of the best experiences of my professional career.

TOBY HARRIS

I signed OMD to 100% in 2010, ahead of their *History of Modern* release. The first time I saw them live was for the album release show on Kingly Street in central London, a two-man show to an intimate crowd. We had the bright orange artwork on screens around the bar and I was blown away by Andy's stage presence. The warm-up got me eagerly awaiting their tour and the Hammersmith Apollo show certainly didn't disappoint. It was an amazing performance by the full band, with a fantastic audience, and a special night, with clear evidence that the new songs blended seamlessly into the repertoire, fans knowing every word of every new song like they did the old.

ANDY MCCLUSKEY

Playing live again was such a delight, but after a few years we had to ask ourselves, 'Is this it now? Is this all we will ever do, playing the old songs live? Are we a tribute band to ourselves?' So we decided to do the crazy thing and see if we could create new music again.

History of Modern was really a mixture of various ideas that we had never quite finished previously being re-used, and some brand new tracks. It was a process of getting the engine running again. There were some really great ideas on the album, but stylistically it was not holistic for obvious reasons. Also, with Paul in London and me in Wirral we tried to use the Internet to send working ideas and song files. Understandably, It was not the same as being in the same room together.

HISTORY OF MODERN WAS RELEASED

20 SEP 2010

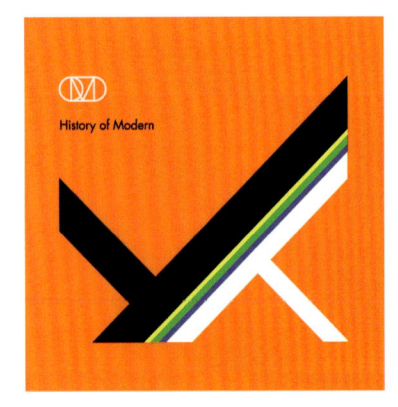

PHILHARMONIC HALL

2 October 2010,
Liverpool, UK

DEE WILLIAMS

The Wondrous Place celebration at the Philharmonic Hall with the Royal Liverpool Philharmonic Orchestra also featured OMD, The Scaffold and a Chinese Youth Orchestra. I was amused that just prior to OMD's performance, they took the precaution of removing a priceless Chinese musical instrument to one side, something they hadn't bothered to do with any of the other performers. Obviously, they knew about Andy's windmilling and feared for the instrument's well-being.

Afterwards, I was talking to a tres grande dame while waiting at the cloakroom. When I told her I was staying with family in Hoylake, she very kindly offered a lift as her chauffeur was picking her up. I accepted and in due course a rather smart Jaguar swept up, complete with driver. As we set off for the tunnel, I asked if she'd enjoyed the concert. It transpired that she was a member of the poshest RLPO friends' group, the real reason she decided to attend. She explained that she enjoyed the occasion far more than she expected, including 'all that pop-pop'.

I asked if she enjoyed OMD and she replied she had and, fortunately the 'head singer' looked 'clean.' Even though she was very kindly giving me a lift, I wasn't going to let her insult Andy like that. 'He's called Andy McCluskey', I said, 'and comes from The Wirral.' She seemed surprised, presumably thinking Andy had emerged from some hole. I added that he'd been educated at Calday Grange. Getting into the swing of things, I added for good measure that he had four A-levels. Hearing this, she was astonished but added, 'You'd think he would have been able to get a good job then, wouldn't you?'

Music

Orchestral manoeuvres in the Noughties

The stars of Eighties electro-pop are back, via a circuitous route that included the rise and fall of Kerry Katona. They confess all to **Neil McCormick**

"We feel like kamikaze pilots with a long-service medal," declares Andy McCluskey. "It wasn't supposed to be this way." Eighties synth pop stars Orchestral Manoeuvres in the Dark are back with their first album in 14 years. Which, according to the 51-year-old singer and bassist, would come as a grave disappointment to their younger selves.

"The 20-year-old Andy would be absolutely mortified. I used to tell my friends, 'If I'm still in this business when I'm 25 you can shoot me'."

"He's still wearing his bulletproof vest," interjects his partner in crime, Paul Humphreys, 50.

The duo originally formed "as a dare" for a gig at Liverpool punk club Eric's in 1978. "That's why we came up with such a preposterous name – it was just for one night, not world domination," insists McCluskey.

Schoolfriends from the Wirral, they played in "art-school rock bands". But they also shared a love of electronic music, inspired by seeing Kraftwerk in September 1975. "That was a life-changing gig," says McCluskey.

"We were looking for our own identity and found it in German electronic music. Our friends, who were into Genesis and the Eagles, just thought that we were mad. That's why there was only two of us and a tape recorder, cause nobody else wanted to play with us."

by Manchester music provocateur, Tony Wilson, who released their debut single, *Electricity*, on his Factory label. "He said, 'This is the future of pop music', and we were offended. 'We're experimental! How dare you call us pop!' We were completely unconscious of the fact that we had somehow distilled the Kraftwerk aesthetic into three-minute punky electro."

The song was a hit and OMD (as they quickly became abbreviated to) went on to become multi-million selling pop stars, with such distinctive hits as *Joan of Arc* and *Enola Gay*.

"We would find ourselves standing on stage at *Top of the Pops*, with Elton over there and Roxy Music over there, and we'd look at each other going, 'How the hell did this happen?'" says McCluskey. "I didn't enjoy it as much as I wish I had done. I was very nervous, very uptight, very intense. My younger self might be horrified to see me now, but my older self just wants to slap 20-year-old Andy round the head and go, 'Lighten up and enjoy it!'

"But OMD wouldn't have been what it was if I wasn't a complete pain in my own arse. Paul was there to balance it out. We are very different people. Two Pauls would get nothing done. Two Andys would have shot each other in the first six months."

McCluskey is a very live-wire character, loud, articulate, argumentative, witty with a sharp edge to his humour, and a gusty laugh. Humphreys, the synth wizard in the duo, is much softer and quieter, though they seem to genuinely enjoy the dynamic this creates. It is reflected in pop music that is full of complex, philosophical, downbeat lyrics and almost sickly-sweet singalong melodies. "The tension between technology and humanity is where we generate our romance," according to McCluskey.

Humphreys left OMD in 1989, when, he says, the band "were losing the plot", exhausted by constant touring and futile attempts to break the American market. McCluskey soldiered on alone until 1996. Both are fairly withering about the band's output after the first run of hits. "We were going back to an empty well too regularly. We'd run out of things to say," admits McCluskey.

McCluskey finally retired the OMD name in 1996, feeling adrift in a changing musical landscape. "Britpop had come along and, all of a sudden, our idea of modern wasn't modern anymore."

Which is when this rather polemical character had a second unlikely career as the Svengali behind manufactured girl band Atomic Kitten, featuring a young Kerry Katona. He claims it was Karl Bartos of Kraftwerk who first suggested he invent a band as a vehicle for his songs.

"It was very liberating, great, disposable junk-culture pop. I wrote five top 10 British singles, including *Whole Again*, of which I am very proud. But after 18 years in OMD, I thought I knew the music business. I had no idea just how nasty, dodgy, backstabbing and dirty the manufactured pop industry is."

After one album, McCluskey was deemed "surplus to requirements" by Atomic Kitten's record company, who didn't share his vision for the group. He recounts a meeting in which he was told, "We've got a winning formula now. I want *Whole Again, Whole Again* and more f—ing *Whole Again*."

When I ask if McCluskey feels responsible for inflicting Kerry Katona on the world, he snorts with laughter. "I feel more responsible for inflicting her upon herself than the rest of the world. I love Kerry to bits, but she is a Titanic looking for an iceberg. She was a beautiful girl, funny as hell, brilliant but totally insecure and screwed-up, who thought being rich and famous would change her life and make her happier. She is the classic case of 'Do not have your wishes and dreams come true'."

He had a second stab at manufactured pop with Genie Queen, featuring Abi Clancy, who became better known as England footballer Peter Crouch's girlfriend. When she left him in the lurch to pursue romance and modelling, McCluskey decided to stop expending time, effort and money on other artists.

"She's a great singer, one of the best voices I've ever heard. But she realised there was loads more money to be made taking your clothes off for FHM and dating footballers than there is out of working hard at music. And she's right. I don't think if we were 18 now we would be getting into the music industry. It really does feel like we're at the decline and fall of the pop empire."

And yet the duo are back in the fray. The pair remained friends, collaborating on songwriting projects, and began to detect a groundswell of interest in OMD, with young bands such as the xx, La Roux, the Killers and LCD Soundsystem namechecking them as an influence.

"It's cool to sound like OMD at the moment," says Humphrey's. "And if anyone has an excuse to sound like OMD, it's us." They initially reformed in 2007 to perform live, reviving only their early Eighties material, but soon found themselves back in their home studios. There was a sense, they admit, of unfinished business.

"We actually had some things to say," says McCluskey. "And we could talk in our own language: analogue synths, simple drum patterns, and songs about the end of the universe."

The result is the ironically titled *History of Modern*. And it's extraordinarily good, a belting synth-pop classic crammed with catchy tunes and complicated lyrics about matters of life and death, art and philosophy.

The pair are aware of all the contradictions in making a nostalgic comeback with music once considered boldly futurist, but seem to be really enjoying their foray into what might be deemed retro electro.

"We consider ourselves some of the last of the 20th-century modernists. It's like being 19 again. We're really talking to ourselves. If other people like to listen in to the conversation, that's great. That's the way we used to work. It took us 30 years to get back to that state of mind."

'History of Modern' is released on Sept 20

> **Britpop came along, and our idea of modern wasn't very modern any more**

Andy McCluskey and Paul Humphrys today. Above right, McCluskey in the Eighties

---

HAMMERSMITH APOLLO

7 October 2010, London, UK

JENNIFER PRUNTY

I was actually in London and realised they were playing. It was a great gig, but they didn't play 'If You Leave', which was confusing to me, having grown up in the States, where that song was huge. I accosted the sound guy, who explained that the song wasn't popular in the UK. Four months later though, they toured America and I finally got to hear it. It was everything I thought it would be.

↑ 2010 *Daily Telegraph* interview with Andy and Paul

1998-2010 | 355

Emma Toal and Steven with OMD in Glasgow 2010

he came up with the ingenious idea of sending the letter to each of the venues they hadn't yet played. Andy took the time to write back to Noah personally, sharing insights into making great music. That gesture alone fed Noah's enthusiasm for making music. We did as Andy suggested, got some equipment together and put Noah on the road to making his own music. Noah's now an accomplished pianist and guitarist, composing, recording and releasing his own music. The letter from Andy is a reminder of how it all started, and OMD still get played all the time in our house.

DOME
29 October 2010, Brighton, UK

MARK SIMMONDS

I'd already introduced my son Noah to OMD, as he'd shown considerable interest in playing and making his own music. I took him to see the *History of Modern* concert at Brighton Dome for his very first live concert, and he asked so many questions about how the band composed the songs. I didn't have a clue, so he decided to write to the band.

As the band were still on tour,

ROYAL CONCERT HALL
2 November 2010, Glasgow, UK

EMMA TOAL

My Mum, Lesley, discovered OMD in the early 80s, aged 10, listening to the charts every Sunday and buying *Smash Hits*. An avid fan, she had every album, single and 12". When the band reformed, she got tickets every time they were in Glasgow and checked the fan forum several times a day. Sadly and suddenly, in October 2010 Mum passed away. No longer would I come home to OMD blasting through the house and Mum dancing about.

We sent her off in her favourite OMD t-shirt, to one of her most-loved songs, 'Romance of the Telescope.' Mum had tickets for the Glasgow show and my Dad, Steven, and I decided to go in her memory. Dad posted on the forum about what had happened. Andy messaged us, inviting us to meet the band beforehand, even dedicating the last song of the night, 'Walking on the Milky Way' to me. It's my favourite song and a fitting tribute to Mum, who would have absolutely loved to have been there. Thank you, OMD, for creating a life-long memory.

ECHO ARENA
4 November 2010,
Liverpool, UK

SIMON GARLAND

I take my wife and son to the Echo Arena for the History of Modern tour. At one stage my lad cracked up laughing during 'Tesla Girls'. I asked what the joke was. He'd misheard the title as 'Testicles.' I will never hear that song by its original title again.

SISTER MARIE SAYS
WAS RELEASED

15 NOV 2010

←

One of the press advertisements that caught Andy's attention by Sister Marie Gabriel

THEATER HAUS
15 November 2010, Stuttgart, Germany

MAUREEN HOFMANN

Born in 1979, I grew up more with 90s than 80s music. Every day my colleagues and I listened to the radio station, Antenne Bayern. One day they played 'Walking on the Milky Way.' I have no idea why this song captivated me, because it wasn't the kind of music that usually caught my attention.

In September 1996 I went into a shop to buy a video cassette of my favourite TV series, *The X-Files*, saw a table with various albums on it, and recognised a sleeve design which reminded me of the CD cover of 'Walking on the Milky Way'. It was *Universal*, and I bought it.

In 1998 Andy gave an interview to German radio station MDR Life in which he said OMD were history. Slowly I realised I'd never ever have the chance to see them live. But everything changed with the reunion and *History of Modern*. I went with a friend to the Stuttgart show. We made it into the third row, closer than I ever expected, and I stopped breathing for a few seconds when Andy, Paul, Martin and Malcom walked on stage. I couldn't believe it.

↑ Maureen Hofmann with Paul in Luxembourg 2010

ANDY MCCLUSKEY

In 1994 I began reading some rather strange advertisements taken out in British newspapers by 'Sister Marie Gabriel' (a.k.a. Sofia Richmond, Sofia Paprocski, Zofia Sagatis and Sofia Marie Angel). She was born in Poland in 1941 and was predicting various cataclysmic Armageddon's if the world did not change its ways. I was fascinated. It seemed as though she was some new Joan of Arc. Determined to try to write a song, I dusted off an old synth melody that I had written in the early 80s and discarded for feeling a little too like 'Enola Gay'. For several years the song mutated into various styles but I could never get it right. After the band reformed I felt that a little nostalgia would not be too harmful and with the help of Guy Katsav the new arrangement finally made it to release.

DEN ATELIER

21 November 2010,
Luxembourg City,
Luxembourg

JEAN PIERRE AND REBECCA SOUDANT

When I was 14, living with my grandma, she bought me my first LP, *Dazzle Ships*. I had heard 'Telegraph' on the radio but then discovered 'International' and was hooked. OMD kept me on track through a real rough childhood. Their music kept me from going in the wrong direction.

We went for a walk before the concert in Luxembourg. I was wearing one of their t-shirts when someone called out, 'Hey OMD!' It was Andy, smoking a cigarette in front of his hotel. Now we go to as many concerts as we can and have met some great friends.

ROGER LYONS

In Luxembourg, at an odd venue with a tiny triangular stage, I was operating the Pro Tools computers and needed eye contact with Paul, but it was difficult to find space. I ended up hidden behind a curtain on stage. It was so hot that I stripped down to my underwear and fell asleep for a few seconds while the band played. I awoke to see a light flashing for me to start the next song. Terrified that someone would wonder why the track hadn't begun, I pulled open the curtain, revealing myself half-naked. Adrenaline kept me awake for the rest of the show.

↑
Lynn Vermoesen with OMD after the 2010 show in Brussels, Belgium

ANCIENNE BELGIQUE
22 November 2010, Brussels, Belgium

LYNN VERMOESEN

Part of the younger generation that likes OMD, one of my favourite songs as a child growing up in Belgium was 'Maid of Orleans', but I never knew who it was by until I started listening to the band. Then I realised I knew quite a lot of their songs. And 'Electricity' was the song that turned me into a fan.

I've been struggling with mental health issues for most of my life and have always wanted to go to gigs and see my favourite bands live, but there was always something holding me back. But OMD was the first band that made me want to overcome my fears, so I could see them live. I remember being very nervous. This was my first concert ever and I didn't know what to expect. But once I got inside the venue and the music started, everything was good. I had the time of my life.

That gig really changed my life. OMD really has had a positive impact on my life and I can't thank them enough for that.

PARADISO
23 November 2010, Amsterdam, The Netherlands

PAULA BLANK

I'm a Portuguese married to a Netherlander, living in Holland, and being an 80s teen, a lot of music from that decade is the soundtrack of my life, with OMD a very important part of that.

I remember perfectly the first time I knew OMD were special. I'm sure I'd heard them before, but it hadn't registered. It was 1981 and I was on the bus, on my way home from school in the metropolitan area of Porto. The radio was on and 'Souvenir' came on. All of a sudden, I had goosebumps all over, wondering who on earth it was. I got the name from the DJ, and that was that.

OMD never played in Portugal before 2016 and being a penniless teen unable to fly to concerts, the first time I saw OMD live was at the Paradiso in Amsterdam. But it was well worth the wait.

FRANK FABER

I was watching *TopPop*, a Dutch music programme, when I heard 'Maid of Orleans' for the first time. Next day I went to a music store, bought *Architecture & Morality* and played it over and over again. For some reason the first two albums escaped my attention, as did *Dazzle Ships*. A few years later, I was watching the *Music Box* on Sky and saw the 'Talking Loud and Clear' video. The next day I went to a record store to buy *Junk Culture* and the first, second and fourth albums.

In 2010 I had my first OMD gig opportunity, with my sister Sylvia. During 'Talking Loud and Clear' Andy asked Sylvia if she was taking photos and asked if we were married. 'No,' I replied, 'She is my sister.' The day after the Hamburg gig, in 2013, we were waiting for our train home to the Netherlands at a platform at Hamburg station when suddenly the band walked in a line in front of us. I was too astonished to say anything.

CASINO DE PARIS
25 November 2010, Paris, France

GENA PICKERING

My funniest memory is from the Casino de Paris gig. I met a few fans beforehand and when we got in to the venue we discovered no one was allowed to sit in the central section of the first two rows and we were all squashed in the side-sections. I decided to ask a security guard, in clumsy French, if we could move. 'Non,' I was told, they are reserved for 'the people.' I asked, 'Well if the people don't arrive, can we sit there?' I was met with a very Gallic shrug, which I took as a definite 'yes'. A lady called Rebecca, sat over in the other wings, was passing and overheard me. We decided as soon as OMD came out we were having those seats. At the very first drumbeat, Rebecca and I locked eyes across the room and led the sprint to the front-row.

Between Steph le Tissier and me, I don't know who first noticed Andy's zipper was down. But how should we tell him he's about to expose Little Andy to a roomful of people? We started miming, but it just wasn't working. I think he must've thought we wanted him to strip (it wouldn't be the first or last time the thought crossed my mind). Then we started pointing. Nope. Nothing.

We resorted to taking photos, trying to show him on our camera screens. But his eyesight was clearly as iffy as his zipper. In the end, someone had a word with one of the crew, who told him when he was at the side of the stage changing his shirt. As he came back to centre-stage he stopped for a second, stared at us both, raised an eyebrow and smirked. Finally, recognition that I was doing a good thing and not just being lecherous.

GRAEME COOPER

When I was at school I wanted to be a musician but wasn't any good on drums so in 1977, with the help of an old school friend, I got into theatre, working for a sound and light company based in London's Covent Garden. I worked on a couple of musicals, including Jesus Christ Superstar at the Palace Theatre before moving into lighting. During the early 80s, as a lighting tech, I was asked by a band if I could tour-manage them as well as do their lights, the start of my career as a tour manager.

Over time I worked with various bands and management companies, including Direct Management, who were managing OMD. I was on board in 2007 for the 25th anniversary of Architecture & Morality and long-awaited comeback, going on to do two further tours in 2010/11 in Europe and the US.

I clearly remember meeting the band in Liverpool at the rehearsal studio prior to the tour. It was a surreal experience, Andy, Paul, Mal and Martin and I in a small studio. I sat and listened to them bang out hit after hit, knowing the songs and amazed at having a private show for an audience of one.

For the 2007 Architecture & Morality tour, it was important to keep costs down. The production Andy wanted was great but wasn't cheap and there was much discussion about how to proceed. But Andy was very focused on what he wanted. The tour itself was a great success and proved to many people the band was still relevant, but it lost money largely due to the films and screen.

One of my tasks was to launder Andy's shirts. As you can imagine he perspires no end with the lights, the jumping around and the windmilling. I'd swap shirts with him during the show then wash them afterwards, soaked in sweat. That along with wiping sweat out of his shoes was a daily chore. Never let anyone tell you this job is glamorous.

2011

During 2011 OMD played two North America tours as well as summer dates in Europe

HISTORY OF MODERN (PART I)
WAS RELEASED

2 MAR 2011

9.30 CLUB
10 March 2011, Washington DC

WILLIAM CASHION
Future Islands

I first heard of OMD from a college friend around 2003/4. She let me borrow her copy of *The Best of OMD*, thinking Art Lord & the Self-Portraits, our band, sounded similar. I'd heard 'If You Leave' probably a hundred times on radio but never dug any deeper. I immediately recognised similarities in what we were doing or trying to do, and what they'd done 25 years earlier, especially on early singles, 'Electricity' and 'Enola Gay.'

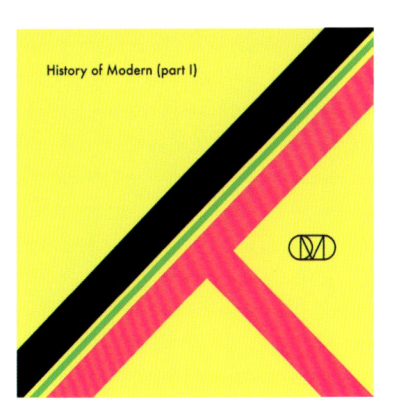

The simple yet sophisticated synthesisers, rhythmic, melodic bass on top of the classic four-on-the-floor beat. That was the first time I really dove into OMD's music. Flash forward to 2008, with Future Islands just

getting home from our second consecutive US tour, digging online to find if there was any positive press from the 60-plus shows and 100 or so people we played to each night. In an online review from *The Westword* reviewing a show we played at Denver's Rhinoceropolis, Dave Herrera wrote, 'The band's energetic and passionate performance made me think of what it would have been like to have seen Orchestral Manoeuvres in the Dark on its *Dazzle Ships* tour...' It was a really positive review for us at a time when we weren't getting much attention. Also, Sam and Gerrit hadn't really heard much OMD at that point, and I'd never heard that particular album. Sam was really intrigued by the comparison, and when we were in Chicago a month later, on another tour, he picked up a CD copy of *Dazzle Ships*. We listened in the van repeatedly and immediately fell in love.

Before that tour, we'd already begun writing new material for what would become our second album, *In Evening Air*, and when we returned home to continue, we kept coming back to *Dazzle Ships* as a reference. We loved all the little moments - the musical interludes and splotches of found sounds nestled between giant pop and burning ballads. We made a huge leap forward with our album because of *Dazzle Ships*' influence.

We finally saw OMD play live for the first time in 2011, and they absolutely blew us away with their energy. In 2014, Andy reviewed our album *Singles* for *Talkhouse*, and later that year we met him after a show at Liverpool's The Kazimier club. Since then, we've stayed in touch and become friends.

OMD's music has continued to be an influence for us, not only for their passionate and irresistible sound, but for the immense heart and soul of it all, keeping us coming back again and again.

CROFOOT BALLROOM
11 March 2011,
Pontiac, Michigan

JUSTIN ORMINSKI

My Dad and I, fans for years, finally saw them at the Crofoot. I'll never forget Andy announcing to a screaming crowd, 'If we'd known it would be like this, we would've come to Pontiac before.'

PARK WEST
12 March 2011,
Chicago, Illinois

MONICA ESPINOSA

Growing up in a small town in south-eastern New Mexico in the 80s, I was too young to go to concerts so lived vicariously through my older brother and his friends, who'd make mix-tapes for me featuring bands such as New Order, The Cure, Depeche Mode and Orchestral Manoeuvres in the Dark. Since I was 13, OMD's music and lyrics spoke to me and helped me through the ups and downs of life - those first crushes, first heartbreaks and rites of passage teenagers confront when starting the journey to adulthood. Never in my wildest dreams would I have imagined that 23 years later, I'd meet OMD in Chicago, opening the door to new friendships with them and fans around the US and the world.

That day in 2011 my friends, Dianne Davis and Jennine Goodman, and I, part of the Kansas City OMD crew (aka KC Souvenirs) bundled up in our best dresses, tights, warm coats and comfy dancing shoes, not knowing how much of an amazing night we'd soon be experiencing. It felt like our Moms going to see Elvis or that other band from Liverpool back in the 60s.

After an amazing soundcheck, we went to a sushi restaurant down the street. When we got there, I jokingly told my friends to save seats for Andy and Paul. Five minutes later, who should walk in but Andy and Paul. Coincidence? Serendipity? Of course. We instantly starting giggling like grade-school girls seeing their crushes stop by and say, 'Hi'.

After, we quickly returned to the venue and the front of the stage, Dianne, Jennine and I dancing like 80s teens at prom to every song, grateful for occasional slower songs to get our fans or towels out and dry our brows.

Then, after a phenomenal performance, Paul then Martin and Mal and soon Andy paid a visit outside the venue to their few but dedicated freezing fans on that cold Chicago night. Both Paul and Andy took the time to not only talk with us about the tour and album, but also chatted with us about our lives in Kansas City. It was refreshing to meet a famous band that were interested in talking with us as much as we were with them. Dianne and Jennine liked the show so much they drove to Dallas two days later with our friend Sunshine to see them again, giving Andy a 'McCluskey School of Dance: Established in 1978' t-shirt, a windmill on it resembling the A*rchitecture & Morality* cover.

ROGER LYONS
OMD road crew

In true *Spinal Tap* spirit, my fellow backline crewmate Baz and I always try to 'have a good time all the time.' Having accumulated a number of bottles of Jack Daniel's from the band's dressing room over previous nights, as the

After years of being a fan Vicki Hatfield gets to meet OMD in Philadelphia

bus sets off on a long overnight drive from Chicago to Atlanta we settled down in the front lounge. One by one the band and other crew started heading toward their bunks. Next thing I remember is getting quite confused because people started reappearing from the rear of the bus. We'd pulled up outside the hotel in Atlanta and Baz and I have been drinking round the clock. We hadn't moved, but the world had been put to rights in a marathon conversation.

Feeling very giggly, I stood up and immediately fell over, laughing my head off. Andy and our lovely soundman Chicky helped me up and I swayed gently off the bus with the legs of a new-born pony, staggered through the traffic and into the hotel. Next thing I remembered was Chicky waking me outside my hotel room, where I'd fallen asleep standing up with my key in the door. It was 24 hours before I woke up again, face down, fully clothed, with one of those hangovers that makes instant death feel like a viable option. Instead I had to load in at The Loft.

THE LOFT AT CENTER STAGE

14 March 2011, Atlanta, Georgia

JIM DONATO

OMD's infamous 'bank clerk fashion sense' had an impact on me as a youth. White dress shirts and thin ties had always been part of my fashion repertoire. Back in my younger days, I bought a lot of records via mail order and these included a listing for an official OMD promotional tie. Unworn until this evening and 100% polyester, my wife persuaded me to wear it at last.

VICKI HATFIELD

In the 80s, I was a big nerd, the kid in school that got hit in the face when a member of my team served the volleyball, picked last for all sports activities. I had an electric organ in my room and played Neil Diamond songs. I never learned to cartwheel like the cheerleaders but could conjugate a verb like no one's business. I wore clothes that were too big and out of style and pulled my hair back in barrettes. Even being in the band wasn't nerdy enough. I was a band-aide. I carried the instruments. The only time I ever skipped school, I asked my parents for permission. When the other kids were at parties, going to football games and dances, or trying out for cheerleading, I was in my room writing angst-filled poetry, listening to obscure British bands.

In 1983 we'd just moved from Atlanta, GA to Middle-of-Nowhere, Tennessee because my parents separated, moving in with my grandparents. I was 13, hard enough on its own, without the added misery of being ripped from your home, your school and your friends. My brother was 15 and made quick friends with another new kid, a boy that had just moved to Tennessee from London. He was the grand prize-winner in the 'my life sucks' contest but brought his music with him and made me mix-tapes of music I'd never heard. It filled a hole in my life and set my musical taste for the rest of my years.

OMD weren't exactly well known in the average southeastern US high school. Our teacher gave us a public speaking assignment in 1984 to speak about our favourite musical artist. While my classmates talked briefly about Van Halen and ZZ Top, I enthusiastically introduced bewildered classmates to the genius of Andy McCluskey and Paul Humphreys. I was so excited I didn't realise I'd strayed beyond an allotted three-minute limit. I can still see my classmates' faces as I launched into my seventh minute. I couldn't stop. The teacher finally pulled the plug at eight minutes. Oh, the shame.

My first OMD show was as an adult. I wasn't allowed to go when they toured the US in the 80s, so my first opportunity to see them live was when I was 41. I bought tickets for the closest show in Atlanta. We arrived in the afternoon, our hotel walking distance to the venue. Around 3pm we grabbed a late lunch at South City Kitchen, a short walk from the hotel. There was only one other diner, so we were immediately seated at a booth. I sat facing the man at the table behind, who was eating a salad and reading a book. My heart literally stopped beating. I picked up my phone, Googled 'Andy McCluskey'. When a photo came up, I pushed it across the table to my husband and said quietly, 'If you can do it without being obvious, glance at that man behind you.' Matt looked behind him at the gentleman, looked at my phone, and said, 'That's the same guy. Who is that?'

I've never considered myself the type of person to be star-struck. I imagined that if I ever ran into someone famous,

I genuinely wouldn't care. In reality, I was transformed into a stammering imbecile when I realised who was sat there, wearing a black turtle-neck and eating a salad. I regressed 28 years and forgot how to speak. 'You should go over and say something,' Matt said. I stammered, 'But what if he's an asshole?' It will ruin it. Or what if he's really annoyed by me? That would ruin it too.'

Matt simply sighed and said, 'I know, but you'll hate yourself if you don't.' I watched him eat another bite of salad. He didn't eat his salad like an asshole. I waited until he finished his food, paid his bill, closed his book and stood to leave. I had it all rehearsed in my head. I was going to be cool, calm, amazing. 'Hello,' I would say with breezy indifference, 'I'm a big fan and just wanted to tell you I'm really looking forward to your show tonight.' Instead, what came out was something like, 'Hi … Hi … Mr. McCluskey … you … I … you … I …. are great. No, you are great. I am excited. Your show … so excited … And your music is awesome, and I love you and can't wait for the show. That's all … um … okay … thanks. 'Bye.'

Instead of staring at me like I was an alien, Andy was incredibly kind and gracious. He welcomed me over, invited my husband over, shook his hand, let me take a terrible iPhone photo, and spoke to us for several minutes. He then waved at us during the show. What a class act.

Matt, who'd never listened to the music, loved the show and has patiently taken me to every North American tour since, including the Barenaked Ladies tour, where we didn't even wait for the headliner. I had no idea who they were. I'm 48 now, but still listen to OMD with the heart of that 13-year-old.

We saw them in Philly in 2013 and did the meet-and-greet. I figure the flight cost $500, the city centre hotel room $220, the taxi to Union Transfer $15 and the VIP tickets $300. And not realising my shirt was see-through until I got home and saw my meet-and-greet photo? Priceless!

PETER SWANK

My sister introduced me to '(Forever) Live and Die' during the summer of 1990. I was 13, that tune becoming a symbol of my friendship with my sister when she went to college.

Three years later, I'd just lost my first true love. My spirits fell and I searched for release and direction. In October 1993, I started smoking Djarum clove cigarettes and found a small group of misfits who welcomed me, especially a girl named Heather Chauvin. The buzz and sweet aftertaste of the cloves kept me away from mainstream drugs, for a while.

I picked up a used copy of *The Best of OMD* on cassette and played it incessantly while driving to meet my 'alternative' friends. 'Joan of Arc' and 'Maid of Orleans' enabled my imagination to travel back to Medieval France and launched a fascination with the girl messenger that persists today. Additionally, being captivated by vintage aviation and World War II, 'Enola Gay' cemented my understanding of the Hiroshima event and served as a foundation for further historic appreciations.

By chance, I heard OMD were visiting my then-home, Atlanta just before my birthday in 2011. I bought tickets for friends and me but honestly didn't comprehend what was about to happen. In a small, over-heated juke-joint downtown, OMD laid out an energetic, enthusiastic performance. During the show, hidden emotion volcanoed within. Bliss and awe took rein, and I was literally high on OMD by the time the encore began.

I phoned my sister during '(Forever) Live and Die' and also found 'Sister Mary Says' to be a new memory of my friendship with my sister.

Then in 2013, I died. I had an aortic aneurysm, aged 36. After emergency open-heart surgery, I was given a second chance by virtue of a partially-mechanical heart. Everything and every perspective in my life changed. Since then, I've lived in five countries and have committed myself to helping others while exploring life and culture. My soundtrack became ever more precious, and I try to attend performing art shows every month.

OMD sired many of my musical intrigues, and I treated OMD with a sort of ethereal reverence.

HOUSE OF BLUES
16 March 2011,
Dallas, Texas

KEVIN VALE

It was the mid-80s, my brother had a mix-tape with 12" versions of 'Tesla Girls' and 'Locomotion', with the rest B-sides that eventually became *Navigation*. What impressed me was the fullness of the music and that it wasn't traditional love songs, a quality to this day I enjoy about OMD. *Navigation* holds a special place in my heart, reminding me of when I was first introduced to the group. Andy called a girl out for talking on her cell-phone, incorporated into the next song, 'Green.'

MELLOW JOHNNY'S BIKE SHOP

17 March 2011,
Austin, Texas

CHICKY REEVES
OMD sound engineer

I knew Paul. We had friends in common. They saw me mix Grace Jones at the Roundhouse in London and liked the sound, hiring me on the spot.

I've been with OMD eight years now. One of my favourite shows was at Mellow Johnny's Bike Shop, part of South by SouthWest, just the two guys performing together in a shop owned by Lance Armstrong.

MOBY

Growing up poor white trash in Connecticut in the Seventies and 80s gave me an almost crippling obsession with anything even remotely European. My suburban world was one of food stamps, laundromats and second-hand clothes, so when I heard OMD on a college radio station in 1980 it was if I'd been handed a portal to a perfect European world wherein people played synthesisers, wore suits and stood around cathedrals having interesting, melancholy conversations.

Then a friend bought a British music magazine with a picture of OMD, and there they were; in Vienna, outside a cathedral, wearing suits, looking like they'd just finished having an interesting, melancholy conversation. I was hooked, going to all the local second-hand clothing stores in and around Darien, Connecticut to find suits and ties that looked like something I could wear on the streets of Vienna while casually bumping into my new synth heroes.

I couldn't afford to buy records, so I borrowed a friend's copy of the first American OMD compilation, taping it (early piracy). I listened to it on repeat in Mom's second-hand Chevy Vega as I went in search of places in suburban Connecticut that looked vaguely European.

Some 45 minutes away from our little house by the freeway was a town called Berlin. The town itself was typical suburban Connecticut banality, but the exit off the Merrit Parkway looked anonymous and green enough that, in my 16-year old mind, it could've been Germany.

So, when the malaise of suburban Connecticut life wore me down, I'd listen to my cassette of 'Enola Gay', 'Messages', 'Electricity' and 'Bunker Soldiers,' and drive up and down the Merrit Parkway, looking at the exit for Berlin and pretending I was a disaffected European in a trench-coat and an old suit, getting ready to meet up with my friends OMD, drink coffee and talk about Sartre and synthesisers.

Fast forward to Texas in 2011, OMD performing at South by Southwest in Austin, and via an e-mail chain they asked if I wanted to play bass with them on a few songs. I, without hesitating, responded, 'Yes.' We met 'backstage', a patch of grass by a parking lot. It was hot and sunny, and people were playing hacky sack and drinking beer. Paul and Andy and I were escorted to the side of the stage and, after being announced by a loud, local radio DJ, walked on stage. I'd grown up imagining meeting OMD in the late November crepuscular shadow of a Gothic cathedral somewhere in Europe, but here we were, smiling and shaking hands on stage at Stubb's Bar-B-Q under a cloudless blue sky in the middle of Texas.

But the opening drums for 'Enola Gay' started and I realised it didn't matter where we were. I was playing a beautiful song I'd loved for decades with two of the people who'd, through electronic music, shown me there was life outside suburban Connecticut. I'd substituted Berlin, Connecticut for Vienna, and with my eyes closed I could substitute the plywood stage at Stubb's Bar-B-Q for anywhere in the world.

STUBB'S BAR-B-Q

18 March 2011,
Austin, Texas

STEVE FERGUSON
APA, OMD's US live agent

One of my best friends from WSOU was a ginormous OMD fan. Unfortunately, Tom passed in 2011. Last time I visited him in hospital he was in a coma, but I gave him the *History of Modern* tour programme signed by all four members. It would have been one of his prized possessions had he lived to see it.

One of my most memorable experiences with OMD as their

↑
Andy and Paul at Mellow Johnny's Bike Shop, Austin, Texas (top)

↑
Moby and Andy onstage at Stubbs BBQ 2011 (bottom)

agent was in 2011. They were playing the annual SXSW festival. During an early promotional two-man mini-set in a bar called Maggie Mae's, OMD were forced to cut their set short. Acts prior to them took their time with equipment changeover and played longer than agreed to. Ironically, while OMD started to play 'Electricity' the bar cut their power. A resounding chorus of boos quickly began, but the venue staff could not give a shit. Needless to say, I was pissed (off). I found the venue's stage manager, told him I was their agent and they needed to play their last song. He said no. I demanded to see the owner, but the stage manager refused to get him, saying, 'Don't bother me.'

We argued some more, resulting in my telling him to go fuck himself. The booing continued. The stage manager then grabbed and pushed me out the back door, telling the band to follow and 'Get the fuck out.' We were all kicked out. Andy and Paul loved it all, laughing in the alley. They complimented me for standing up for them and called me a rock star. The whole incident always brings a smile to my face.

Next day, OMD were to play the 2,200 capacity Waller Creek Amphitheater at Stubb's Bar-B-Q. The show's corporate sponsor was filming the event, which included a large camera boom arm that could stretch over the crowd and climb as high as maybe 50 feet. Just before OMD were about to go on, the boom collapsed. Several fans suffered injuries, the show delayed while the injured were helped and the boom secured. Really scary.

OMD made sure that on their second US tour that year they came back to Austin to play a full show to the fans who didn't get to see the full set. That's the way the band's wired - fans come first.

PATRICK FABERBERG

I never had the chance to see OMD until they came to my adopted hometown of Austin, for the SXSW music festival. It was an evening that changed my life for ever. Just as the concert started, a 400lb camera boom fell into the crowd, hitting me directly on the head. I suffered a traumatic brain injury. I was a practicing lawyer at the time. One year into my recovery, a newfound artistic talent emerged. I suddenly had the ability to paint. I'd never painted before. Psychologists believe I am what is termed 'acquired savant.' I now make a living as a visual artist.

I've been in continuous contact with Andy since he reached out to me, concerned about my well-being. I visited him in Liverpool while filming a documentary set to be released in the fall of 2018. Andy spoke about creating a piece of music based on my art. He asked me while in Liverpool, 'Wouldn't you like to hear what your art sounds like?' It has been an amazing journey, ever since first hearing OMD and falling in love with their music. I don't think the final chapter of this improbable connection has been written.

SXSW

SXSW in 2011 was one of the most depressing few days I have endured in my time in the music industry. We were persuaded to go as part of our first tour in North America for 20 years. We had the power cut off at one gig, bad reviews for only being a two-piece and a weird audience at Stubb's one lunchtime that was only improved by Moby joining us for a couple of tracks. Then there was the ridiculous late-night gig at Stubb's with the full band where we were forced to go onstage after an audience member was almost killed by a camera boom. Who could have expected that the only enjoyable gig would be in a bicycle shop? Never again! What a total cluster-fuck SXSW was!

ANDY MCCLUSKEY

ROGER LYONS
OMD road crew

The camera boom sliced through the crowd. Lots of screaming and far too much claret on the floor around the heads of these poor folks. The band was in shock. Andy was visibly shaking, and all were white as sheets. Surely the gig would be cancelled, but the promoter was saying, 'It's going to be fine and we'll start a little later.' Paramedics had to fight their way through the crowd and we kept the band on standby. We should have pulled it, but the promoter was insistent the gig still happen.

While paramedics were taking care of the injured I had Andy and Paul next to me with a set-list, going, 'Right, that's another five minutes less, we'll have to pull another song'. We hacked the set to bits and did a greatest of the greatest hits gig for 25 minutes. Heavy night.

ANDY MCCLUSKEY

I saw the boom fall but didn't realise it had really hurt anyone, as I had a spotlight in my eyes as we walked onstage. I couldn't understand why Paul wasn't starting the gig. I've subsequently watched it all on YouTube. It took me ages to realise what was going on. Then I called for a doctor. I couldn't believe the concert wasn't cancelled. They insisted on us playing. We heard that the injuries were bad, but the promoter didn't seem interested. Horrible night!

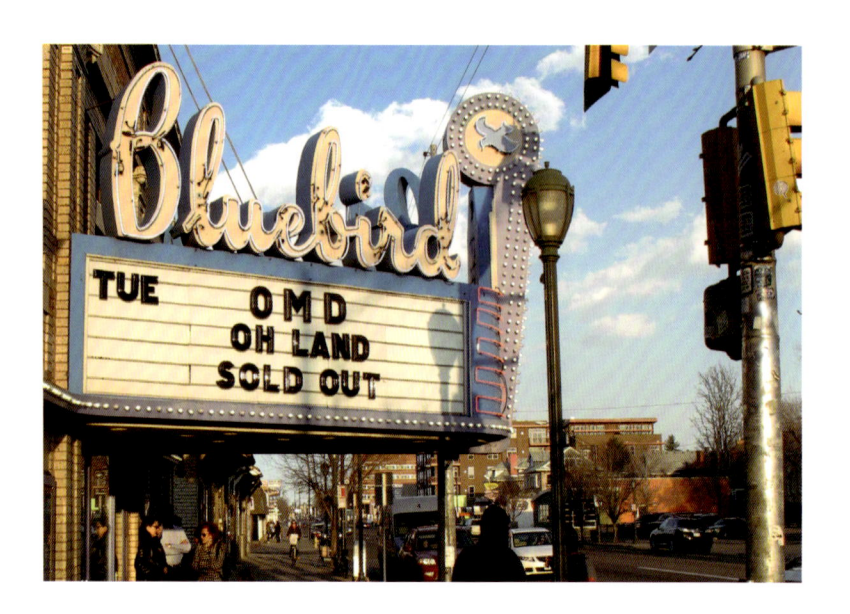

BLUEBIRD THEATER

22 March 2011,
Denver, Colorado

MARK SCHURER

Born and raised in the small town of Jupiter, Florida, I was a total redneck, mostly listening to country music. One day I heard 'If You Leave' on the radio and it resonated with me. A few days later, out with friends, I saw the album *The Pacific Age*. I bought it. We unwrapped it in the truck to listen on the way home. My country friends were unimpressed, but I was fascinated by this strange electronic music, transporting me to places I'd never been.

I went home with my 'weird' album' and fell in love with OMD. With my next pay I went to a music store to see if this band had other LPs, starting to buy them one by one. Each album has special meaning in my life. When I hear OMD I hear my own voice. And 25 years later at the tiny Bluebird Theater in Denver, Andy reached out from the stage and grabbed my hand, fulfilling a life-long dream. Thanks for making me a good part of who I am today.

DEPOT

23 March 2011,
Salt Lake City, Utah

↑
Sold out Bluebird Theater on 22 March 2011

ROGER ERICKSON

My brother and I overheard '(Forever) Live and Die' on the radio shortly after our father passed away in 1986, instantly falling in love with this unknown song. We had to call the station to learn it was by OMD and purchased *The Pacific Age*. We planned to catch them live in Salt Lake City in Summer 1991 but at the age of 14 I was hospitalised with type one insulin-dependent diabetes, fighting for my life. During my convalescence, my mother bought me *Sugar Tax* on cassette. The only album I had with me, I listened to it over and over.

I learned piano and synthesisers and in the late 90s started remixing my favourite bands, including OMD. These were released over the still-budding Internet and quickly earned me a small following. When OMD announced they would be reuniting and releasing new albums, I was contacted by the band and asked to submit an official remix. I was beyond elated. I ended up doing three remixes, 'History of Modern Part 1', 'If You Want It', and 'Metroland.' Even more amazingly, I finally got to see the band at the Depot.

FOX THEATER

26 March 2011, San Francisco, California

ELIZABETH EVANGELISTA

I first discovered Orchestral Manoeuvres in the Dark in 1984, hearing 'Tesla Girls' and 'Locomotion' on a radio station run by students at Robert Louis Stevenson School in Pebble Beach, California. I love their electronic music and lyrics about topics piquing my curiosity, but never got to any OMD shows.

Then came the possibility of shows in 2011, but tickets quickly sold out for the 1,000-capacity Mezzanine in San Francisco. I was crushed. Fortunately, the overwhelming demand resulted in a venue change to Oakland's Fox Theater. That show exceeded my expectations. A setlist of brilliant new songs and classics that had withstood the test of time, plus Andy's charisma and ability to connect with an audience made me want to attend more shows and buy new releases, for as long as OMD are still recording and touring.

Sold out sign at The Music Box, Los Angeles, California 29 March 2011. Photo by David Simmer II

4TH AND B
27 March 2011,
San Diego, California

JARET S YOUNG

A friend of mine told me to go to the backstage door after the show as I might be able to get an autograph. Soon as I got there, I saw Paul smoking a cigarette. I asked him to sign my copy of *Dazzle Ships* and he cheerfully obliged. Before signing, he inquisitively thumbed through the pages of the booklet, as though seeing it for the first time. Then it hit me. A band on this level may not necessarily be familiar with every thing out there with their name on it. I suppose he hadn't seen the new CD artwork reissued in the US. I guess that night was a first for us both.

SALA APOLO
15 June 2011,
Barcelona, Spain

MIGUEL ÁNGEL MEDINA VILLACRECES

In the 90s I bought my first OMD records, but wasn't a big fan until 2011, when my girlfriend bought me the *History of Modern* on double-vinyl and two tickets for a show in Barcelona for my birthday. When we married in 2013, we had 'Joan Of Arc (Maid Of Orleans)' play as we entered the Town Hall for the service. I'll never forget having OMD present for one of the best moments of my life.

SOUTH BANK THEATRE
16 June 2011, London, UK

MARTIN BAINBRIDGE

I'd play my Dad's *Live at Theatre Royal, Drury Lane* VHS incessantly, but never got to see OMD live until Paul Morley's *A Tribute to Tony Wilson* event at Ray Davies' Meltdown. It was the second of two Tony Wilson interviews Paul Morley conducted with Factory Records alumni. I'd been to the first, really enjoying seeing Durutti Column play and listening to Peter Saville's stories, so was keen to see Morley's second event, irrespective of who was playing or speaking.

As I was leaving work that night, confirmation came through that OMD were the musical guests, alongside Kevin Hewick. They played a great set, book-ended by 'Electricity', a rare outing for 'Almost' the highlight for me. Even Ray Davies snuck in for a bit.

ANDY MCCLUSKEY

This was the day Paul Morley finally publicly apologised for introducing us at Festival of the Tenth Summer as 'Two rich bastards from Los Angeles'.

ERIC'S
10 September 2011, Liverpool, UK

KAREN STROULGER

I was 18 when I heard 'Pandora's Box' on the radio, instantly loving it. Having then read about Andy and how his obsessions influenced his writing, I totally related to him and soon discovered and equally loved 'Enola Gay', 'Walking on the Milky Way', and 'All That Glitters.'

In 2011 I met the man who became my husband four years later. Another Andy, we discussed likes and dislikes. It appeared

↑ OMD played at the reopening of Eric's 30 years after it closed as a trip down memory lane and to celebrate a valuable live music venue opening rather than closing in Liverpool

we had nothing in common. We supported different football teams and our taste in music was worlds apart. Until OMD popped up in conversation. It turned out we both loved the group. Later that year we were lucky enough to win a pair of tickets for an intimate gig at Eric's in Liverpool. Our love for the group even played a part in our wedding, walking back down the aisle to 'Souvenir' in 2015.

GRAND CENTRAL

16 September 2011, Miami, Florida

RYAN WESTBROOK
OMD tour manager 2011/12 & 2018

This wasn't my first OMD show, but it was my first as tour manager. On the previous US tour, I looked after merchandise and handled soundcheck parties and VIP meet-and-greets. This time I was asked to step up, run the entire tour. I was honoured and excited by the opportunity. Every band is different so there's always a learning curve, but what happened that night in Miami was well outside the bounds of the usual curve. It could have been my last.

This wasn't a typical venue. It was more a dance club, its stage positioned awkwardly to one side, bulky patio furniture laid out everywhere, something wasn't right. I soon learned several owners had a hand in running the club, but none could agree on what type of club they wanted. It seemed the common thread was that they all enjoyed the nightlife too much to be in the business.

Every time I turned around, I met another owner and his entourage in the band's private space. There was an attitude that they'd come up with the money to get in a band they loved in high school, so we were there to honour their every wish. But that's not how it works.

The dressing rooms, if you can call them that, were upstairs. They'd not put much thought into that part of the venue. It was basically an abandoned attic space with a filthy bathroom, with dirty mops in mucky water in the tub where the band would be showering. I couldn't get anyone to understand that was unacceptable, but they eventually obliged and cleaned up.

As well as the usual first-night jitters, we all felt rushed. Then I realised I hadn't discussed the protocol for starting the show. Like most British crews I've worked with, OMD's didn't like wearing two-way radios. Maybe shouting across a room at someone all day was more their style. I walked downstairs and met each crew member individually. The general consensus was that the band was always on time, so as long as the show started at the advertised time, there'd be no issues. I prefer the more traditional radio call or flashlight signal, so was hesitant about this plan, but everyone seemed to think it was no big deal, so I went with it. We synchronised watches and I made the long trek back upstairs to find the band still behind schedule. I realised I didn't have enough time to go back and relay this to the crew. The clock struck 10pm, the house lights went off, the intro music from 'Dazzle Ships' began, and the light show began.

Unfortunately, the band was still in the dressing room getting ready, with Andy in the shower. The second he heard 'Dazzle Ships' rattle through the floor beneath him, he panicked, ran out of the bathroom with nothing but a towel around him. Somehow, they all got dressed and started moving down an incredibly long flight of stairs, expressing disbelief and dissatisfaction. We got to the side-stage just in time for the intro to end. The idea was to hold the band there and restart the intro, hoping no one would know the difference, but in the chaos and confusion half the band ran on stage awkwardly, while the other half stayed behind the curtain. This created an uncomfortable delay before the first song. I stood there in disbelief as the show finally started, processing what had happened. This wasn't how I envisioned my first show.

Despite the false start, the show was high energy and went off without a hitch. I was fully prepared to take the heat after but was confronted with such a whole new set of issues that I never got the opportunity. While the band was showering and changing, one of the club owners busted into the dressing room with a girl on each arm, wanting to hang with the band. He was intoxicated and under the impression he could breach the boundary between artist and promoter. I instinctively charged towards him to urge him out, defend the band's private space. Andy, stood behind in his underwear, asked me to calm down and be polite, as this was the promoter.

No sooner did I get rid of that guy, I had to deal with one of his partners to get OMD paid. I kept texting him, telling him to come and settle with me. Finally, he showed up with a sealed envelope

↑
OMD tour manager Ryan Westbrook with his boys

and piece of paper with scribble all over it. When I asked what it was, he said it was his settlement sheet., I've seen all kinds of show settlements, but this didn't appear to be anything close to the usual format. There was no ticket audit, no breakdown of expenses, and we'd sold enough tickets to receive an 'overage' but without a proper settlement, there was no way to determine the artist was receiving a fair share. This was all so amateur but at least there was a cheque in the envelope and I was ready to get on the road to Orlando for the next day's show.

As I returned to the stage the crew tell me the club was reopening as a disco and we wouldn't be allowed to move our equipment out until 5am - a five-hour wait. No way. I started raising hell. No one seemed to care. Confronted by a third, intoxicated club owner, following me around calling me names and cussing, finally a sympathetic security guard helps us get our gear out as the crowds piled back in. I called our driver, told him to pull the bus up to the door closest to the stage. I also asked if he had a gun. I was serious. I wasn't sure at this point we wouldn't need it. I had only known this driver about 48 hours and now I was asking him to watch my back in the streets of Miami.

I'll never forget the looks on everyone's faces when I got on the bus. There weren't words to describe the situation, but we all had the same thought. If tomorrow was anything like today, this was going to be a long tour.

It may have been the absolute worst start, but I'm happy to report the band was gracious enough not to fire me. We went on to have a splendid run across the US and all over the world. It's been six years since I've worked with OMD, but I got invited back for another North American outing and I'm quite relieved Miami is not on the itinerary.

CLUB NOKIA
7 October 2011,
Los Angeles, California

SURAJ MODY

I grew up in Bombay, India, listening to OMD on bootleg cassettes and *Top of the Pops* videos. My wife Christina grew up in East Germany listening to OMD on the radio, secretly exchanging OMD posters with a friend whose relatives smuggled them in from West Germany. Fast forward some 25 years later to sunny California. Both our dreams came true when we saw the band perform live in Los Angeles. It got even better on the Punishment of Luxury tour where I got to meet them, taking a priceless photograph which my wife and I will cherish forever.

HOUSE OF BLUES

8 October 2011,
Las Vegas, California

ROGER LYONS
OMD road crew

Climbing out of my bunk, bleary-eyed, pulling socks and trainers on before load-in at Irving Plaza, NY, one of our US-based guys looked at me and lost his shit. My socks were pink. He let loose a verbal tirade. 'What the fuck are you doing wearing pink socks! I know people in this venue and have friends there and refuse to go with you wearing pink socks! You're gonna make me look bad.' The whole bus waited for some kind of comedy punchline that never came. The guy was a raging homophobe.

There was only one thing to do. I ordered 15 pairs of pink socks online and we all wore them at load-in for the Vegas show. The look on his face was indescribable - like a purple berry ready to explode. Band and crew united against him. That was the last comment he passed on the subject for the rest of the tour.

OMD crew. L-R Stan, Andy, Ryan, Roger, Jason

NEIL HOLLIDAY

OMD crept up on me a bit like a girl you meet among friends – you meet, have a laugh, and gradually they fill up bits of your life you never knew were empty. I bought Organisation purely on the basis of 'Enola Gay' and for a long time that was the only track I was really listening to. But there was this dark track at the end of side one that just blew me away. I played it to my friends who were equally impressed and it became a sort of anthem with which we judged other songs. By the time I hit art college, it was anchored. I was beset by students who wittered on about The Doors or Led Zeppelin, but OMD had captured my heart and when things were tough, I could lie down in the dark and mutter, 'I can't imagine, how this ever came to be.' with the song playing in the background. 'Statues' was the song that really woke me up to what they could do.

CAROL SLIGER

My love for OMD started in college in 1978 when my friend Tom introduced me to their music. I thank him all the time for this as I loved their sound from the beginning. There is nothing like Andy's voice to make me emotional. My friend Leighsa and I would be at every show, always waiting until they came out. They always took the time to chat with fans which made us so happy. We went from seeing them at the smallest of venues on Long Island, where the theatre was more empty than full giving us so much room to dance, to larger venues where we were willing to wait in line to get up close. I moved from New York to California back in the 80s and got to see them in LA. Later in life I moved from New York to Ohio so I had to travel to Chicago to see them. I've seen them so many times now. I even bought a new car in the late 80s with the license plate OMINTHED.

2012

2012 and OMD played shows in Singapore, The Philippines, South Africa as well as UK dates

SMART ARANETA COLISEUM

12 March 2012, Manila, Philippines

MARK 'MERV' PEARSON
OMD drum-tech

We did a gig in Manila where these two guys said, 'We'll take you out after'. Manila is dodgy at the best of times, but we were with locals so thought we were covered. We said we wanted a casual bar with a couple of pool tables not too far from the hotel. They took us to a place with pool tables and I saw there was a downstairs. Being inquisitive, I went to suss it out. There were 15 to 20 girls there, 18 to 25 in age, wearing identical bikinis and dancing on the stage. I said, 'What's all this? Some sort of rehearsal?' I was calling the guys, saying, 'Come on lads, it's great down here. Have a look at this.' We all went down and sat at this big circular table when one girl swanned up to Ryan, the tour manager, and touched his leg. He freaked out and ran out, shouting, 'Guys, we've gotta get out of here!' We said, 'Why?' He said, 'I'm a fat guy from Nashville. She's talking to me like this. She doesn't want *me*.' I then noticed there were doors all the way round. It was a hookers' house downstairs and a bar upstairs. A scary place.

ANDY MCCLUSKEY

What a contrast to Singapore. When you land in Manila you can see the shanty town at the perimeter of the airport. As you drive into the city, you realise that if you know the right people you can have a nice life. But the 99 per cent who aren't in with the right

EMPEROR'S PALACE

4 & 5 August 2012, Johannesburg, South Africa

LORRAINE MEYER

OMD's music helped me through a divorce in the early 90s. I'd play their cassettes and my young boys would sit and play Lego blocks - soon they knew the words and bounced about the room. I wrote to Andy thanking him for the music, using the address inside the cassette. To my amazement, I got a hand-written letter back. I had to say thank you for that, so off went another letter from me. And, yes, another reply from Andy. And so it went on.

OMD came to South Africa with their Liberator tour. I missed it but taped it off the telly. It was a great show. Then the split, and I cried. But in August 2012 we got front-row seats, and at the meet-and-greet, Andy remembered me. That meant so much.

people, live in abject poverty.

The promoter introduced himself with his business card. Under his name in bold capitals, it said his primary job was arms and weapons trader. 'Okay,' I thought, 'We won't argue with him.'

We were playing the Coliseum, where Muhammad Ali and Joe Frazier fought the 'Thrilla in Manila' world heavy weight boxing match in 1975. It's an ancient, somewhat derelict indoor arena with no air conditioning. As we got into the second half of the set, I was exhausted and boiling hot, sweat pouring out. All that kept me going was the thought that, 'It could be worse. You're not doing 14 rounds with Joe Frazier punching you in the face.'

↑
Lorraine Meyer and grown up sons meet OMD on the Liberator tour in South Africa

100% RECORDS

I first saw OMD live in Clumber Park, Nottinghamshire, 18 August 2012. For them it was a routine festival appearance. For me it was the first day of the rest of my life. I work at 100% Records, the band's UK label since they reformed. My role with OMD is pretty broad. I've been responsible these last seven years for their social media platforms, much of the day-to-day admin at their label and (most excitingly) accompanying them on tour, running the VIP packages.

By my count I've seen them play live 54 times, in various contexts. Whilst every show is excellent and I'm truly thankful for the travel experiences I've had around Europe and the USA, there have been a few stand-out moments: The first show I ran the VIPs for was in Margate, 2013. I accidentally let everyone there on to the meet-and-greet. Really shouldn't have done that. Sorry, guys! I'm a bit better at running things now.

Having to explain to Andy and Paul that their dressing room at The Punishment of Luxury launch was, to all intents and purposes, a small cupboard. I remain in absolute awe of them for standing in an extremely claustrophobic space for an entire hour before taking to the stage. Taking my entire family to meet the band in Nottingham in 2017. A truly special moment in my home city, not least as my parents saw OMD in London very early in their relationship.

Finding myself and a number of VIPs locked in a goods lift in Hamburg, the only way to get through to a venue located in a market place, the gates of which are typically locked during the day. My German is adequate for basic conversations but not really up to explaining why we're stuck in a piece of industrial machinery. We did however make it in time for sound check.

Being so taken with the Museum of Liverpool during the 'Dazzle Weekend' in 2014, I completely forgot to do the Edmund Gardner Dazzle Ship tour.

Delivering the result of the set-list vote part of the 2017 European tour to the band. I was responsible for counting the digital votes and letting the band know what had been decided. I'm not so sure that Andy was thrilled to learn that he had to play a song he hadn't played live in a while ('The New Stone Age') while dealing with a truly catastrophic throat infection. Yet, as usual, he gave everything on stage. It was a truly memorable performance.

All that said, the moment I'll always remember is speaking to Andy backstage after the seminal Royal Albert Hall show in 2016. The words that came out of my mouth that night were, 'Shows like this are the reason I do the job I do'. I meant every word. OMD, you mean a great deal to me. Long may you continue.

**ED MACDONALD
100% RECORDS, SOCIAL MEDIA
AND VIP**

REWIND FESTIVAL

19 August 2012, Henley, UK

ANDY MCCLUSKEY

We were determined to re-cast ourselves as a stand-alone touring band and not join the heritage festivals. However, it was becoming obvious that we couldn't expand our touring attendances. Those who had seen us would always come again. Those who hadn't seen us just wouldn't consider attending gigs. Against our agent's advice, we chose to play Rewind. We headlined the Sunday night and loved it. What a huge crowd; and what a response! We've done more of these festivals in the last few years and it seems to be working. More and more people get to see us and come back to our own headline concerts.

↑
Tour poster for the
History Of Modern Photo
by Chris Oaten

2013-2018

In this year OMD released their twelfth studio album, *English Electric* as well as playing shows in the UK, USA and Europe.

KRAFT WERK'S RADIO ACTIVITY TATE MODERN

7 February 2013, London, UK

RUDI ESCH
author & bass player for Die Krupps

It may sound strange, but I knew Paul and Andy before I even truly discovered their music. Paul had a strong connection to my hometown of Düsseldorf through his then-partner, and we met several times playing the same summer festivals. As for Andy, he's a bass player so we connected easily and instantly. Bass Players United, they say. I loved their knowledge and passion about the music of others and the attitude towards their own; the incredibly humble appreciation they showed to the influential bands of my hometown. At the time I met them, I probably only knew one OMD song, 'Enola Gay', propelled by that growling bass tone. It's a song

↑
Rudi Esch, author & bassist for Die Krupps

I always loved and was part of my soundtrack to the summer of '81. Years later, we were invited to Kraftwerk's 'Radio-Activity' show at the Tate Modern in London. It was of course the perfect show to attend with Andy and Paul, as they always named *Radio-Activity* as their favourite, most influential Kraftwerk album. For me, the immense catalogue of OMD has always managed to retain, interpret and convey the atmosphere and themes of this incredible album. Intelligent songs about an unstoppable march of technology, driven by vibrant and creative soundscapes, continue to make OMD's music timeless. OMD don't sound like Kraftwerk, but they write songs that evoke the feel of *Radio-Activity*.

OMD are no electronic band, but they spearheaded and paved the way for many electronic bands in the UK. 'Electricity' is not 'Radioactivity', but it's the British answer. A song that started a new movement. And as influential as Düsseldorf may have been on their music, I know for a fact that in 1979 Düsseldorf was paying a lot of attention to the likes of OMD and Joy Division.

So, thank you OMD for all your amazing songs. 'Messages', my personal favourite, is surely the UK's answer to 'Antenna', right? Thank you for all the great laughs we shared and for lending out your song title for my own book (Electri-City: The Dusseldorf School of Electronic Music).

METROLAND

WAS RELEASED

25 MAR 2013

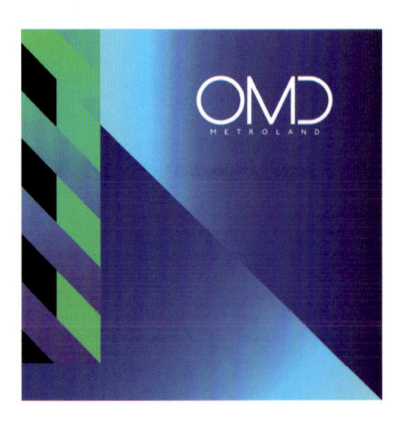

ENGLISH ELECTRIC
WAS RELEASED

5 APR 2013

HELOISA FLORES

OMD first appeared to me as a link. A link to a YouTube video, a still of the English Electric cover and the song 'Helen of Troy'. A friend of mine had sent it to me and I asked her who the band was. 'Oh, it's an 80s band. I listened to it again, loved it instantly.

Discovering the songs OMD made through the years, I couldn't help but be immensely fascinated about the themes - technology, history, outer space, art - all being portrayed as subjects of wonder and passion. As a person with Asperger's syndrome, the ambience and sounds comforted me, the lyrics interested me greatly, the songs kept me safe on rides to university, when alone late at night, in difficult times when life was overwhelming.

ANDY MCCLUSKEY

After *History of Modern* Paul and I felt we could push ourselves harder musically, but realised that we needed to spend more time actually in the same room (not sending files via the internet) for the chemistry to really work. There was also a conscious decision to revert back to more analogue synth sounds and be as minimal as possible. Working on a computer with the potential of over a hundred channels can lead to editorial decisions not being made. We both also liked the idea of exploring some of the more esoteric musical ideas that did not conform to traditional song arrangements.

↑ Signed *English Electric* boxset

THE FUTURE WILL BE SILENT (10" EP)
WAS RELEASED

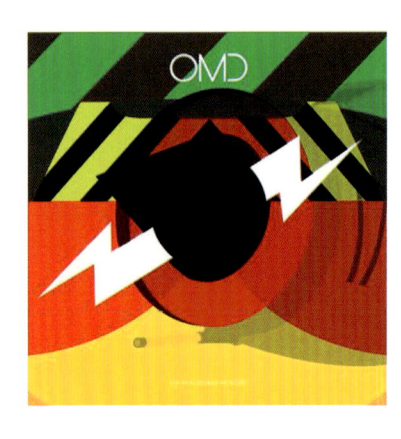

20 APR 2013

JON RUSSELL (JONTEKNIK)

I lived part-time and worked with Paul during his Onetwo project with Claudia Brücken. I learned so much about music production during that time. Paul is meticulous in his work and would be editing away hours after I'd gone to bed. I think myself so privileged to have had that time.

Years later, I was asked to remix the single 'Metroland'. I didn't have much time before it had to be submitted. I loved the track the very first time Paul played it to me. It is so vintage Kraftwerk-like, and that's like heaven to me. Luckily the remix fell into place quickly. I laid down some classic Roland drum machine samples and introduced the track with a 'Speak and Spell' machine saying 'OMD'. After the first submission, Paul said to take that bit out, then later I was asked to put it back in. I had the remix arrangement pretty close to the original track, but introduced the Orchestron choir, the same choir used by Kraftwerk on their *Trans Europe Express* album. I didn't have any drums in the second verse, as I recall, but Andy wanted the drums to be present and he was right. It flowed much better. It was a dream come true for me, and an absolute honour.

DELTIC DIESEL

The inspiration for the album title was circuitous as was the ultimate sleeve design. I fell in love with the English Electric Deltic diesel engine when I saw it at the Science Museum as a child in the Sixties. Paul and I liked the name English Electric as a metaphor for our music and wondered if a sleeve could be created using the distinctive front livery design of the Deltic. As the process continued, Tom Skipp the sleeve artist and Peter Saville as creative executive began talking the idea into the realms of various locomotive safety colours. It got too busy, I created the minimal version that was used in the 'Decimal' video and Peter finally suggested the brighter contemporary colour palette.

ANDY MCCLUSKEY

REGENT THEATRE

2 May 2013, Ipswich, UK

HILARY BATTYE

My husband Chris and I were listening to OMD before we even met; me on my mahogany-look record player with a brown-tinted plastic lid, and him on his sleek black music centre. When we married, we amalgamated record collections and found we had an extensive number of OMD albums. Even my Dad, who I lost a few months ago, recognised the wonderful sound when he heard it on the car radio. Although he could never quite bring the band name to mind, he always remembered I'd told him they came from Meols. His sister had lived in Meols Parade. Chris and I got to see them on the English Electric tour. As soon as the band took to the stage I had the most enormous smile. It felt as if the clock had been turned back as we sang, cheered and danced.

↑
Locomotive warning livery that inspired the English Electric album sleeve art

ROUND HOUSE
3 May 2013, London, UK

ANDREJ KOKOC

In Summer 2010, an 18-year old schoolboy from Lithuania was watching an episode of *Top Gear* in which the presenters visited Berlin with three second-hand cars. There was James May in a Mercedes, Richard Hammond in a BMW, accompanied by Phil Collins' 'In The Air Tonight', then Jeremy Clarkson in a Ford Sierra Cosworth, escorted by a melody I'd never heard before, yet one I loved from the off. But what was it? I went to the forums, asking what it was. Shortly after, someone explained it was the intro to 'Enola Gay', specifically the moment Malcolm Holmes goes heavy on the drums the first time, accompanied by the 'nasty little synths', as Andy McCluskey referred to them.

By early 2013, I'd moved to London to study for a university degree and bought a ticket to see OMD at the Roundhouse, excited beyond belief. I'd never seen a live concert. The lights went dark and the opening track of new album, *English Electric*, kicked in, followed by a loud roar as Paul, Malcolm and Martin emerged, followed by Andy in a white shirt.

I have to thank Jeremy Clarkson and *Top Gear* for helping me discover OMD.

ROYAL CONCERT HALL
12 May 2013, Glasgow, UK

RUTH CUNNINGHAM

On the Christmas 1981 edition of *Top of the Pops*, OMD were performing 'Souvenir' and I was three weeks short of my 13th birthday. You were known as 'the band with the funny name that sang that song about the bomb dropping,' but I hadn't taken any real notice until then. Off to the shops come New Year to spend some pressie money, I wanted to buy 'Souvenir', even though it wasn't in the charts. I went into the Edinburgh branch of Virgin Records and it was 99p, a fortune to a poor kid like me, but out came my purse, containing 99p all in one-penny pieces. The look on the sales assistant's face was priceless.

I spent 1982 catching up, buying OMD records when money allowed me to do so, and distinctly remember Dad buying me *Architecture & Morality* that Christmas.

When in 1983 my bible, *Smash Hits*, informed me they were about to bring out a new album, for the first time I could afford to buy it on release, so I started saving. It cost £4.99. I waited patiently, squirreling away money. Then my mother put a spanner in the works. I needed new shoes for school and she wasn't going to buy me them unless I was prepared to contribute the £5 I'd saved. A bit scared of my mother, I complied, handing over my *Dazzle Ships* money. I hated those bloody shoes. They were beautiful, soft black leather with a four-inch heel. They cost £25 and Mum paid the other £20. They were totally unsuitable for a gawky schoolgirl with NHS specs and hand-me-down clothes. They fell apart the very first day I wore them. Sabotage wasn't involved. I didn't twist the metal bit on the heel so it fell out. Neither did I pull it out with pliers, as was suggested. We went back to the shop and I chose a pair for £20. And yes, you guessed it, I ran all the way to the record shop and there it was. *Dazzle Ships*, in all its green and grey glory. I was back on track.

I loved it. No one else did. It was my defining album, the LP that convinced me I was an OMD fan. I wasn't allowed to go to see them that year, but I bunked off school because Andy was doing an interview on local radio.

When my school years were over, oh boy was I in trouble. Handing over the little brown envelope containing my exams results, I can still hear my father say, 'Too busy listening tae yer OMD to pass yer exams!' Little did he know I probably learned more from listening to them than I did from being in school.

In 2013 I had the best ever OMD experience at Glasgow's Royal Concert Hall. Row A Seat 29. I met them all for the very first time - Andy, Paul, Martin and Mal, in the flesh. God, I was nervous; dry-mouthed and unable to speak. And I was given the best souvenir of all, a towel thrown to me by Andy, which now lives in my drawer. I still take it out now and again for a cuddle.

EMPIRE
14 May 2013, Liverpool, UK

SIMON IRVING

Despite being a fan since 'Messages' was on *Top of the Pops*, I never saw OMD live until relatively recently. I was a very poorly bear, full of man flu, my hearing affected by a head cold. But I still loved it. Andy, Paul and Martin were utterly brilliant, while my abiding memory is of Mal's drumming, particularly on 'Maid of Orleans' and 'Talking Loud and Clear.'

TIVOLI

17 May 2013, Utrecht, The Netherlands

PASSENGER S (SVEN)
Metroland, mixed 'Night Cafe' & 'Metroland'

We arrived at the venue mid-way through a soundcheck. We said hello to the person behind the mixing desk and stayed to listen. When OMD started rehearsing 'Metroland', we decided to play a practical joke, asking the mixing desk guy to give clear instructions to Andy to no longer use the word 'Metroland', saying our group had a patent on the name. Each time Andy sang 'Metroland', he'd have to pay us a serious amount of money. Andy liked the joke so much, he continued the rehearsal but replaced 'Metroland' with 'Legoland'. The look on Paul's face was priceless.

DRESDEN
WAS RELEASED

20 MAY 2013

DOCKS
21 May 2013,
Hamburg, Germany

MARTIN
Vile Electrodes

OMD were 'my' band', the band I loved as a teenager, my bedroom covered in their Peter Saville album artwork. They were the first band I saw live, and that gig is still the most amazing gig I've ever seen. The closing moments of 'Romance of the Telescope', with synchronised lights and drums, is seared onto my retinas. They write songs with ostentatious titles about difficult subjects, but even when they're exploring the outer reaches, thematically and sonically, the songs - the stories - are still accessibly human, no matter how inhumane the subject matter.

   Meeting them when Vile Electrodes toured Germany was a lovely experience. Common wisdom says never meet your idols, but they were exactly how I imagined them. Intelligent, caring, witty, modest and very human.

JANE
Vile Electrodes

Considering OMD's enduring musical influence, and the creative impact they've had on Martin, to receive an out-of-the-blue invitation to tour Germany with them was mind-boggling. They were so supportive and encouraging throughout the tour - though they did enjoy ribbing us about all the hardware we brought on the road with us.

DANFORTH MUSIC HALL
19 July 2013,
Toronto, Canada

MALCOLM HOLMES

After 33 years and a ton of hits, gigs, hotels, flights, TV shows, managers, record labels, accountants, crew, producers, laughs, beers and tears, this was meant to be a day off. However, an extra gig had been added because of the success of the show we did there previously.

   We travelled from New York overnight and arrived late afternoon in Toronto on 18 July. I've no idea why they call it a sleeper bus. More like an 'awake all the time' bus. I was tired when we arrived in Toronto. It had been a hard tour for me this time. After checking in at the hotel I went for a bite to eat around the corner and a drink in the bar opposite the hotel. It was about 6pm. I was tired, so it was an early night for me.

I arrived at the Danforth gig the next day after meeting with my cousin and some of his friends. It was hot, the hottest day in Toronto that year, with an ambient street temperature of 48 degrees. The gig was an old venue with a small dressing room above and to the right of the stage, the stage door underneath the dressing room. I went into the gig before the soundcheck to find the dressing room and have a mooch. It was oppressively hot in the gig and on stage, with no room in the dressing room to chill out. People were coming and going, which was getting under my skin.

I went back to the bus, parked opposite the venue to get some space, escape the heat and people in the dressing room. The bus also had air conditioning while the gig didn't. The bus was empty, cool and peaceful. As I sat in the back lounge looking out of the window something didn't feel right. I had an anxious feeling.

I've always been really aware of how heat can knock the stuffing out of you on stage, and it was this that was going through my mind. This was no normal day and no normal temperature. There was a foreboding hanging over it. I was worried but talked myself through it, saying 'I need to really pace myself, get a feel for it, take it easy tonight on stage.'

Back over the road I joined everyone for the soundcheck. A couple of small cooling fans had been placed at the front of the stage. A nice idea, but totally incapable of cooling anything down. They were just blowing hot air around. We did the soundcheck and 'meet and greet' and I headed back to the bus, returning to the back lounge and watching the crowd arrive.

From the comfort of the back of the bus I watched a huge rainstorm blow in. A massive amount of rain, I thought it might clear the air. It didn't. As I got off the bus, I walked down a little alley, into the venue for showtime, and noticed a fire department truck parked just around the corner. I didn't think too much of that, but the people in the truck would play a big part in the events that followed.

In the venue I had a shower before the show. The dressing room was still crowded and incredibly hot. We walked on stage. Nothing could prepare me for walking on that night. If I thought the dressing room was hot, the heat on stage hit me like a train. It had got hotter. With me at the back, a full house and each of the lights above kicking about a kilowatt I sat on my kit.

The foreboding and anxiety hit me again. My mind went from my performance to just getting through. I wasn't 30 seconds into the first song before the heat and thin air took its toll. I realised how difficult it would be to get through an hour and 40 minutes with such heat and little air.

I stopped thinking about playing

and left it to muscle memory. Everything I played that night, my muscles and limbs did on auto-pilot. Things started to become surreal early on, as if I was in a dream. I had my ear monitors in, detaching me from what I was seeing. My eyes didn't match what my ears were hearing. I hit 'Maid of Orleans', muscle memory on overdrive. The reaction we got was incredible, I looked over at Mart as if to say, 'Did that really happen?' They were an amazing audience. Either that or I was starting to hallucinate. A bit of both maybe.

I slowly counted down the tracks, all the time not feeling right. I was exhausted, with very little left. 'Sailing on the Seven Seas' was next. The song is played across the tom-toms, so I need more oxygenated blood to the muscles in my upper body. It was this that was going to tip the balance. Not only was my heart trying to provide enough oxygenated blood to my muscles, it also had to pump more blood around to cool me down. At the end of 'Seven Seas' I realised it was game over. I literally had a voice shouting at me (my inner voice, I've been told). It was all I could hear. 'Mal, leave the stage now, go, don't think, just go now, leave now' I can still hear that voice shouting.

I had to think of the best way off the drum-riser and to the stage door. I needed air. I managed to get off stage and into the alley, but there was no respite there. The air was thin and incredibly humid as I tried to get my shirt off. I had no strength to unbutton it. I was soaked through. I couldn't breathe. Merv tried to cool me and Mart was comforting me, trying to help get my shirt off. However, my heart had reached about 200 beats per minute, the cylinders of my heart (like a car) starting to misfire. Once that had started, they would never get back in sync. My ticker had nowhere to go, and it stopped.

That was it. Lights out. Black. For the next three to four minutes I was dead. No pulse. I don't know what happened during this time, only what I've been told. There were a couple of strange things I saw - a flash of light and in the blackness far away I saw another light.

Next thing I remember, I was staring up at a paramedic. I could feel my body but could hardly open my eyes. I had an oxygen mask on and the paramedic said if I could hear him to say so. I could but didn't know how to say 'yes'. I knew what 'yes' was but couldn't speak. I gave out a huge grunt, my way of saying, 'Yeah, I can hear you'. He told me to hang in there. I was in and out of consciousness in the back of the ambulance. It was quiet, it was cool, and I could breathe. I'd finally got out of the madness of the heat of the gig.

I woke again in A&E and recognised Mart at the foot of the bed. The next bit will always make me laugh. I was now conscious, although I didn't know what had happened. I remember looking at Mart and thought, 'Mart doesn't look very well. I wonder what's wrong with him, he looks really pale and worried.' I think I said, 'Flippin' heck, mate. I must have fainted.' He explained to me what had actually happened and said they'd had to restart my heart with a defibrillator and I'd been dead. This went completely over my head, but I knew it was serious, because Mart was really shaken and looked probably as bad as me.

A doctor came over and asked a few questions. I'd had no oxygen to my brain for a while, so he was checking to see if it was damaged. I was wheeled up to a ward, with Mart there throughout. They plugged me into all sorts and the nurse asked if there was anything she could get me. I asked if they had a fan. She brought a fan over, put it on the table next to me. The fan's motor gave a slow reassuring drone as it rotated and blew a gentle cool breeze over me as I lay there. For the first time in 24 hours, I felt safe. The foreboding had gone. I was so lucky. So many things could have gone wrong, but when I needed them I managed to roll a few double-sixes at the right time. As I lay there late in the night, I knew things had changed forever. Playing the drums might have just ended, along with the laughs I had with my friends.

MARK 'MERV' PEARSON

It was me, Martin and Mal in the alley for a good 10 minutes before anyone came out. I was the one who called the ambulance. I knew it was serious. I knew his history. There was no way Mal would stop a show if it wasn't serious. Every minute that went by, he was looking worse. He just wasn't responsive. He was awake but wasn't talking, and it was melting hot.

At most places there'll be a medic on site. But there were none. I was screaming at the promoter, 'Are there no medics?' He said, 'No, but I know of a friend of mine whose wife is an ex-nurse. I'll go and get her.' I said, 'Let's get an ambulance.' Stupid things go through your head, like, 'It's going to cost the band if there's nothing wrong with him.' While we were waiting, it got progressively worse. Then this ex-nurse came out, took one look at him, dragged me aside so Mal couldn't hear and said, 'I hope you called an ambulance.' It was then that I knew how serious it was.

I started tearing up. Then Paul came out and started tearing up. It was fortunate we were in Toronto, because they've got good public services. I must have counted about four to five minutes, and I could hear the sirens. As I heard the first siren, Mal completely passed out. I think that's when his heart stopped. I honestly thought the worst had happened.

What saved Mal was that the guys already had the defibs in their hands when they came down the alley. They had his shirt off, went straight in and zapped him a few times. Then they got him on the stretcher and he was off.

PAUL HUMPHREYS

I'll never forget what happened in Toronto. It will be etched in my memory for as long as I live. We went back there in 2018r with Stuart as drummer and I started to write about it from the perspective of returning and the feelings that invoked. But Mirelle said, 'You should just let Mal tell that story.' It was very strange. The chair was still there that Mal was sitting on in the side alley where he crashed. It was a very emotional return. It was one of the most traumatic moments of my life to see Mal, who I'd known since I was 13, effectively dead on the floor.

We were playing 'Sailing on the Seven Seas' and Mal was putting cymbals in the wrong places. I remember thinking, 'Why is he putting that there? That's completely the wrong spot. What's happening? What's he doing?' Then we got to the end of the song and I was about to start the drum machine for 'Enola Gay' and heard this voice from behind. It was Mal saying, 'Don't start the drum machine, don't start the drum machine. I need to get off stage.'

Merv was already there and taking care of him, helping him off the stage. Andy and I stayed on stage, talking to the audience. It was the perfect storm, really. Everything conspired against Mal that night. He was really hungry. He had some food before the gig, which he wasn't supposed to as part of his regime. That didn't help. The worst thing was that it was the hottest day of the year in Toronto and we were in this old venue, and the air conditioning wasn't working properly.

It was over 40 degrees on stage. We were dying in the heat. Andy was reining in his dancing as best he could. But Mal couldn't rein it in, because he was always full on. If you don't hit the snare at the volume Mal hits it, the noise gates don't open, which means the drums don't come out of the PA. He has to hit it. He couldn't dial it down. He still had to be full on in that temperature.

It was towards the end of the show and we were exhausted. People were passing out in the crowd. We thought Mal was suffering from heat exhaustion. Andy and I said to the crowd. 'It's almost the end of the show. We're not going to come back. Mal's obviously exhausted from the heat and we're sorry but there's things more important than music.'

We left the stage. Andy thought Mal was tired, so went to have a shower. I went out to the alleyway where they'd taken Mal to get some air. When I got out there, I heard Merv saying, 'Dial 911. I'm gonna dial 911 right now.' I thought he must not be feeling very good. I went outside to find him and he looked like hell. All of sudden he dropped to the floor off the chair and we couldn't find a pulse. He's so lucky, Mal, because the Fire Department paramedics arrived in about three minutes and basically saved his life. He was fortunate that it happened in Toronto. The next night we were going to be in Detroit. Detroit had at that point declared bankruptcy, with the emergency services taking 45 minutes-plus to respond to calls. Mal would be dead now if that had happened in Detroit.

We went to the hospital to see him and it just sums up Mal really. The doctor said, 'We don't know how long he didn't have a pulse for. It could have been more than four minutes without any oxygen to the brain. You need to put him through his paces, see how lucid he is. There could be some brain damage.' In the background we heard Mal say, 'But I'm a drummer. How can you tell if I've got brain damage?' At that point we thought, 'He's fine', and we all had a sigh of relief, because that's the Mal we knew and loved, able to come up with a quip like that after all he'd been through.

ANDY McCLUSKEY

We shouldn't have done the gig, but there were 2,000 people there, and we didn't want to disappoint them. We'd played there the week before and sold it out and they asked us if we'd come back on a day off between other gigs, so we were squeezing it in.

It was unbelievably hot. We'd been on the road for a while, so it wasn't like I was unfit, but I couldn't move. I was having to stand in the two corners of the stage by the fan. I normally dance around like an idiot, but I was just walking from side to side. I just couldn't do it.

Of course, Malcolm had to keep playing. He'd done an hour and 25 minutes and he was exhausted. And the guy had a heart attack and triple bypass several years earlier. It was a miracle he was drumming in the first place. We got to the end of 'Seven Seas', the most aerobic of the drum tracks, and I strapped my bass on and thought, 'Praise be, it's 'Enola Gay'. We get to finish after this, and I can stop for a few minutes.'

I'm standing there waiting for the drum machine to start, and it wasn't. So I turn round and Paul's making cut-throat gestures, going, 'Stop, stop, stop!' Malcolm is walking away. I said to the audience, 'Okay, we've got a problem here, folks. That's the end of the gig. We're really sorry. We've got a problem.'

Malcolm is saying, 'I feel ill. I need air.' We opened the door and Mal went out and sat in the alleyway, but it wasn't much cooler outside. A piece of tree had come down in the alleyway by the stage door, because there had been a tropical downpour.

We looked at Malcolm, and Paul and I went back on stage, saying, 'We're really sorry. Malcolm's not well. Health is more important than songs. I hope you've enjoyed the show. I'm really sorry we can't finish, but that's it. Good night. Thank you.'

Martin was out there. I spoke to Merv, Malcolm's backline guy who does drums and bass, and Merv said, 'We've called an ambulance just in case.' At that stage, it was 'just in case'. He's okay, he's outside, Martin's with him. I went, 'I need a shower.' I really thought everything was going to be okay.

I got in the shower. I'm very nesh. I don't like cold water. But I was having a cold shower because I was so exhausted. When I got out, there's a window going up the corridor to the main road and all I could see were flashing lights. I could hear lots of commotion outside. I shouted to the tour manager, 'What's happening?' He said, 'Malcolm's dead.' I went, 'What?' 'No, the paramedics are here. He's alive again.'

I missed the whole thing. It all happened while I was in the shower. Malcolm had basically started to slump off the chair and Martin was holding him. He was collapsing into Martin's arms. The paramedics arrived in four minutes. They zapped him and brought him back to life. By the time I came back out, he was breathing again but unconscious.

Martin was ashen-faced. His mate had died in his arms. Paul was ashen-faced. Everybody was in shock. I stood there with a towel round me and no clothes on. We were all in shock.

We went to the hotel. The rest of the gigs had to be cancelled, and I felt really guilty - I'd been in the shower and hadn't been looking after my mate. But I thought he was all right. So I felt really weird, quite down on myself: 'Oh yeah, Malcolm's dying and you're having a shower.' I still feel pretty shit about that.

MARTIN COOPER

I met Mal when we were around 19. We quickly became good friends and firm allies. My memories of OMD's early years are firmly entwined with him and our experiences are so interlinked he feels more like a brother than a friend.

Consequently, trying to write about this memorable day has proved very difficult. Words can't describe the emotions I went through that night.

Mal has written movingly about the sequence of events that led us into the alley. Once there, Merv and I sat him on a chair and while Merv was off getting ice to cool him down. Mal's eyes started to roll back into his head. It was time to call an ambulance!

Merv then disappeared to call for help and I stayed with Mal. I held him in my arms and tried to comfort him, but the overriding emotion was one of panic and terror. Mal was dying in front of me.

All of a sudden there seemed to be chaos all around us. People were arriving and shouting instructions from all directions. I held onto Mal tightly while we moved him onto the ground, and there the recently arrived paramedics started working on him. After what seemed like an

Mal and Andy share a joke on stage at Latitude Festival 17 July 2011

age, actually only a few minutes, they managed to restart Mal's heart.

Later Mal was moved into the ambulance and I accompanied him. He was still being worked on frantically. Suddenly the mayhem stopped. Everything was calm. I knew Mal was out of the woods when the ambulance driver turned to me with a smile and said my friend's stars had been aligned that night. He was stable and was going to be OK. That was a special moment and the sense of relief was overwhelming.

I'll never be able to look back on the night of 19 July 2013 without experiencing a chill down my spine. It was my last ever performance with Mal. Take care Mal. I miss you.

KEVIN D. TERRY

I've been a fan since I was a teenager in the 80s, but never had the chance to see them live until 2013. OMD didn't fail to impress, but unfortunately it turned out to be the last show on that tour. Oddly enough, after the show my friend and I ran into Paul outside the hotel where we were staying. Paul was obviously a bit sombre but very friendly.

MALCOLM LEAVES & STUART JOINS

ANDY MCCLUSKEY

We promised Malcolm we wouldn't do anything without him. He went back to Germany. The band stopped. We didn't do anything for a year, because we didn't want to put any pressure on him.

A year later, on his birthday we spoke on the phone. I asked, 'How are you doing? Where's your head?' He just said, 'I can't do it anymore. I want to, I really want to, but can't take the chance.' I said, 'Okay. How would you feel if we carry on without you?' He said, 'I'll hate it, but you have to.'

That was really hard, because Mal's been a drummer since he was 13 or 14. In many ways, it's how he defined himself. Mal *is* a drummer. People used to hold up signs saying 'Mal is God'. Before shows, Paul and I would be doing vocal warm-ups and Malcolm, who'd never sung in his life, would always do scales too, 'La-la-la-la-LA—la!' Mal's always funny. Mal is the joker. He could be a grumpy bastard, but he was always great.

We eased ourselves in. In 2014, Paul, Martin and I did a gig at the Museum of Liverpool, where we did a bit of *Dazzle Ships* and a small thing for real hardcore fans where we said we'd play things we'd never played before, just testing the water to see how we felt without Mal behind us.

Once we'd all decided we wanted to carry on, we logically turned to Stuart Kershaw, because he was still part of the family. He'd written with me, he'd toured with me, we'd done TV shows with him. Stuart was retired, doing a degree to become a history teacher. He was a stay-at-home dad. So that was strange, to drag him out of retirement. Funny thing is, we just did the *Ultimate Chart Show* again in Germany, with Stuart wearing his third hat. In 2005 Stuart stood in for Martin when Martin couldn't do that show. Stuart also stood in for Paul when he couldn't do it, and in 2018 Stuart was there drumming on that show. Next time we do it, Stuart will be singing!

However, in 2015 Stuart hadn't played drums for 12 years. He was going to have to learn again, pretty quick.

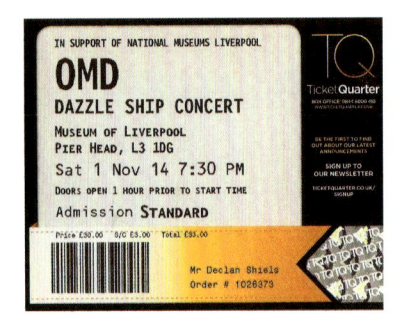

MUSEUM OF LIVERPOOL

2 November 2014, Liverpool, UK

LEONOR GOMES

When I was six, 'Souvenir' was No.1 in Portugal. This led my Mum, a Beethoven and Beatles fan, to buy *Architecture & Morality*. I listened to the album in full. It sounded so arty and unique. I felt I'd finally found my band.

Soon after, I found *The Pacific Age* in a record store, the first record I ever bought with money I'd earned myself. I painted my own OMD t-shirt, inspired by the cover.

I first saw OMD live at the Museum of Liverpool, when I was just shy of 40. It was a dream: hearing the missing parts of the *Dazzle Ships* piece in a dazzle ship installation, seeing Winston brought back to life, and the band playing at being a living museum exhibit.

ANDY MCCLUSKEY

Being a trustee at the Museums of Liverpool certainly helped in planning these concerts. I knew exactly who to call, but had no idea just how complicated it would be to arrange to play in a museum. Vibration tests needed undertaking to ensure that we didn't rattle any priceless artefacts loose from their display cabinets. No smoke machines, and stage and lights all had to be on rolling wheels to get them in and out to allow normal visiting in the daytime.

I had thought that persuading Paul and Martin to wave flags again would be the difficult part, but that turned out to be easier than convincing Martin to play bass onstage for the first time in 30 years. Needless to say he played 'Julia's Song' better than I ever could have! And what a delight to play 'International' and '4-Neu'. The emotions etched on the audience's faces were worth overcoming all the complications.

ALI FILDER

We gathered in the atrium of the museum with bated breath, waiting for our three boys to enter, holding the much-loved semaphore flags from earlier videos and album cover. The silent energy was so tense. A recording of Malcolm's playing accompanied the boys, the fourth member of the original line-up present by sound recording on an updated Winston. For us die-hards this acknowledgement of Malcolm was a must.

PRIMAVERA SOUND FESTIVAL

27 May 2015,
Parc Del Fòrum,
Barcelona, Spain

AIDA ARCAS

In 1994 my parents bought a new hi-fi. The guy from the department store asked if I could check during the afternoon that everything worked fine. He would be in the neighbourhood if required. I arrived home from high school and got to work. With no vinyl of my own, I went to my parents' collection (four metres of tightly-packed albums on the upper part of a built-in wardrobe) and picked one record randomly. I looked at the cover and thought, 'This must be something like electronic classical music. This will do.'

I put side A on the turntable, pressed play and, unexpectedly, heard a song I knew perfectly - 'Enola Gay.' 'Wow, I didn't know my parents had this.' When it finished I asked Mum if we had more albums by the band. She didn't know, so I checked where I had taken *Organisation* from, but didn't find anything, waiting impatiently for my father to return from work.

As soon as he opened the door I asked, pointing frantically to the album, 'Dad, do you have anything else by these guys?' He thought they had another album but didn't remember the cover. I climbed onto the chair again and started pulling and pushing back every LP in the wardrobe. After having checked more than 350 albums, I finally found what I was looking for. I ran back to the turntable, played the album and again had that magic feeling when after so many years you hear, smell or taste something familiar from your early childhood: 'I know this song!' 'Souvenir', 'And this one too!' 'Joan of Arc', 'Oh my God, this song also!' 'Maid of Orleans.'

I told my parents that I remembered several of the songs. They looked at each other, saying, 'How strange. We barely played those records. We bought them because a friend owned a music shop and recommended them.' Mum added, 'When you were a little child I used to have the radio on. Maybe that's why these songs rang a bell.'

I guess it was just fate that I rediscovered OMD. I couldn't believe it had taken me so long to find out that all these beautiful and fantastic songs were by a band called Orchestral Manoeuvres in the Dark.

I remember reading the text about 'Genetic Engineering' in the *Dazzle Ships* leaflet, thinking, 'This is really interesting, this is the future - I have to study this!' Now, I'm a scientist who works in biomedical research, I've been fascinated by technology (new and old) for as

Paul and Andy greet Marina Palamos in Barcelona, Spain

MARINA PALAMOS

It was in 1982 when, having listened to 'Joan of Arc', I decided to buy my first OMD cassette, *Architecture & Morality*. I fell in love with the songs, the sensitivity imparted and feeling transmitted, and although I could only understand some words in English, I knew it was beautiful because of the emotion in Andy's voice.

I was interested in the lyrics of each song, so I bought a dictionary to translate to Spanish. When I had them all translated, I liked them even more. It confirmed it was an extraordinary piece of work. The little English I know is thanks to these translated songs.

When I saw they were scheduled to perform in Barcelona, I thought, 'This is the moment'. I designed banners; 'Tonight the universe conspires to make my dream come true', '34 years waiting for this moment' and 'Can I sing 'Secret' with you, Andy?'

My first OMD concert was spectacular, in the first row with those banners. Andy blew me a kiss from the stage during 'Talking Load and Clear'. I have lots of memories from seeing them in 2018 too, the most magical when Andy, before 'One More Time', talked to the audience and said when he comes to Barcelona, a lady welcomes him at concerts with banners, dedicating the song to her. Listening to the first verse with him looking at me, I nearly died.

I want *Architecture & Morality* to play at my funeral. It will be my earthly farewell and my best entrance to the universe. Whatever is waiting for me there, it will be with an OMD melody.

STUART KERSHAW

My first gig back was at Primavera. It had been hot with a clear blue sky. The warm evening had turned to dusk. As I paced around back and forth behind the stage in the open air, from the gloom I saw a tall, dark figure walking towards me with arms stretched out like an aeroplane. He came in for a big hug and said, 'Here we go again - glad to have you back'. It was of course Andy. It had been 22 years since I last played live with OMD, with 25,000 punters out front to play to. In addition to this, it was being

---

long as I remember, and have always been interested in history, literature, art and architecture.

I was delighted to read they had reunited. Taking advantage of having to go to Barcelona to collect my PhD diploma, I travelled there to see them play at Primavera. I arrived too early to check into my hotel room and waited in the lobby. I sat on a sofa and started sending mails. Suddenly, I heard a voice I knew. I turned back and there were Andy and Paul being interviewed. I couldn't wait to see them on stage.

transmitted live on Spanish TV. I remembered, all of a sudden, the pressure of playing in a top pop band like this. That's never easy, but it always becomes a dream come true.

REWIND NORTH

9 August 2015, Capesthorne Hall, Cheshire, UK

GLENDA MITCHELL

I first heard 'Enola Gay' on the radio when I was 14, at the very bottom of the South Island, New Zealand. I saved all my pocket money, walked uptown in my lunch hour from school and bought *Organisation*. I remember how I felt as I put the tape into my pink Walkman and heard the magic in my ears all those years ago. I bought *Pacific Age* while on a youth exchange in Tasmania, Australia in December 1986 and away from home for my birthday and Christmas. Every song on that album filled me with joy and I stopped feeling homesick and alone. I had my safe place, Mr McCluskey's voice in my ears making my heart soar.

Living in New Zealand doesn't offer many opportunities to see OMD live. In 2015, I interrupted a tour of Italy and Germany for Rewind North. I flew from Cologne to Manchester, then took a train to Stockport and a bus to the venue. I lay on the grass and snoozed through the other acts until OMD were on.

I stood alone at the back, singing my heart out to every song. It was the most surreal and incredible moment in my life. One person walked past a couple of times and told me to get up the front since I knew every word, but I was too shy for that. On the bus on the way back to the hotel, someone else tapped me on the shoulder, asking if I'd really come all the way from New Zealand just to see OMD. I was so proud to say I had.

Hans Lampe, Andy and Michael Rother

Andy on the phone at Kling Klang

DUSSELDORF ELECTRIC CITY CONVENTION

30 October 2015

ANDY MCCLUSKEY

Rudi Esch kindly invited me to do a Q&A at the inaugural Electri-City Convention. Then he went one better, inviting me to dinner with Michael Rother (Neu) and Hans Lampe (Neu, La Düsseldorf) before the gig. When I mentioned how much I loved the Flammede Herzen album, Michael apologised that they weren't playing anything from it that night. However, they played 'Karosel', and I found myself being a fan boy again, grabbing the nearest person by the lapels (Martin Swan from Vile Electrodes) shouting, 'This is for me!' Then Rudi delivered a killer punch. 'I have the keys to Kling Klang. Wanna go?' 'Do I wanna go?'... Hell, yes!' This was Mecca. Kraftwerk's studio, where the magic was born, the music that changed my life. Just after midnight we walked in. For once in my life I was dumbstruck, kissing the walls.

PLAYING LIVE

We're loving playing live! And I think as a band we've really gone from strength to strength live over the last 10 years or so. We put on such a good show. We've got such energy. Stuart Kershaw has done brilliantly well. It was a difficult job to come in after Mal and he's a different kind of drummer, but he's really made being OMD's drummer his own thing, and I love playing with him, as I do Martin and of course Andy. We're a really powerful unit and I love every moment of playing with the guys.

I never get stage-fright. I used to be terrified. I used to have the worst stage-fright. As a kid, I never wanted to publicly speak. I'd hate it if I got picked on in the English lesson to read aloud in front of the class. I'd rather have climbed a tree, fallen and broke my leg than have to stand in front of assembly or something, just to get out of it. In the early days of OMD it was difficult. I'd role-play to pretend I was someone else to get through it. I'd be acting on stage and pretend to be this other person. It's like a mind-game I had to play until I reached the point where I was actually me. It took years and years of doing it all the time, but now I can walk on stage in front of 30,000 people and it's all good. I look forward to walking out there and just playing and singing.

The only time I get nervous is if we haven't had a sound check and we've got technical issues. It's all digital desks, so everything should be normal.

PAUL HUMPHREYS

ROYAL ALBERT HALL

9 May 2016, London UK

MIRELLE DAVIS
OMD manager

Having been in the music industry over half my life - more than 25 years - and a fan of OMD even longer, it seems only right to talk about their Royal Albert Hall show, a major highlight, the band playing there for the first time, performing Architecture & Morality and Dazzle Ships, two records that definitely influenced the next 30 years of my life.

I first wrote about this so my family and friends had more of an idea of what goes into putting a show together, but I'm hoping this may be of interest to other OMD fans too.

I'd temporarily stopped managing the band, but when we met to discuss the future, I jokingly said I'd return as manager if I got the show of my choice. So the idea was born. Our agent had serious concerns about whether we could sell this show, as did the promoter, but tickets prices were agreed, and on-sale dates planned. We could only book a Monday at the venue though, so the band were concerned, thinking that an awkward day for people travelling to London. The Royal Festival Hall was touted as an alternative, but I held firm. I wanted the Royal Albert Hall. I just hoped the budget improved. The fee gave us no money for production, so I was going to have to perform miracles to make it financially viable. It was a very expensive venue, and I stupidly told the band we didn't need to make money. Any profit could go into making the show amazing. That's what happens when you have a 'fanager' - common sense goes out the window.

We picked 4 December for the on-sale date – Fridays are good days to sell tickets, and it was pre-Christmas. I was volunteering in Cambodia on the lead-up, but still nervous. Yet we sold out in less than three hours. Bloody incredible! And was I the only one not surprised that others felt like me, knowing this would be an evening not to be missed?

With the show six months away, Paul needed to program a considerable amount of material that hadn't been played live in years, some for the first time ever. The band then needed to rehearse, not least considering that 90% of the set-list would be new ground for Mal's replacement, Stuart.

Simon Fuller, our tour manager, needed to find a crew. Most would be our regulars, but there would be additions, the band going off for a seven-week US tour shortly after. Andrew Liddle needed to build a light-show for a one-off gig, a near-impossible task with a restricted budget, while I had to talk the band into lights rather than screens. Not just because of the money. I honestly believed this was the better option and would add to the atmosphere. With the venue visited, the band were convinced and trusted Andrew as one of the best lighting designers around.

We then looked at each other, already slightly stunned by the knowledge that in a few months OMD would be playing this iconic venue.

I also needed to ensure the books balanced. That meant VIP ticket sales, a live recording sold on the night (released on triple-vinyl six weeks later), and a full range of merchandise. I added considerably to my task, being nostalgic, trying to create a tour programme mimicking those OMD made in the early Eighties. That meant digging out old copies, wading through Virgin's photo archives, painstakingly tracking down photographers 30 years on to negotiate purchase of their work. The same went for clearing quotes. It took weeks, so it meant a lot when our agent, Ian texted to say the programme was a nice touch.

That work goes into every tour, but usually a full tour with many shows. This was for one night, so margins on merchandise and VIP slots were lower. But it was such a special show. We wanted everything to be perfect. The good news was that we were way above our guarantee, the marketing spend drastically cut as we sold out so fast, and had the money for the kind of light-show we wanted. I could breathe easier. And the band were happy with their rehearsals, starting to feel more confident, while the 36th version of the poster was approved and sent to the printer.

There was one final nightmare before the show - the guest-list, the bane of every manager and tour manager's life, taking care of friends, family, various dignitaries, press, music industry, accountants, lawyers, designers, labels, even the odd MP.

I met my friend Pauline at 12.30pm for sushi, arriving at the venue at 1.30, a conscious move, wanting the band to settle in and feel comfortable with their surroundings. I watched the band as they walked out on to that historic stage, a mixture of excitement and fear. Martin said later he was so terrified he nearly fainted. The sound-checked lasts an hour and a half, much longer than normal, and the only people in that huge venue were the band, the crew, Pauline and I. I'd stopped being a manager by then, spellbound by songs I hadn't heard in decades, thrilled by the venue. Pauline burst into tears during 'Almost', and hairs on the back of my neck stood up for 'Julia's Song' and 'International.' The band thought 'Julia's Song' was my favourite. In fact, 'International' and 'Romance' pip it to the post. That night I got all three.

After 4pm we let 160 paying VIPs troop in for a further half-hour soundcheck. A quarter of those stayed for a meet-and-greet. All 160 had seats in the front eight rows. The meet-and-greet idea wasn't ideal on such a big day, but the band did it with good grace

Andy finally replied to my 8am text asking how he was. I saw that as a good sign. He was finally relaxing.

I had my own dressing room space, knowing this would come in useful later when I needed to hide. It's also pleasant not to have to float around corridors like a spare part. Show-day is a weird one for a manager, with 90% of the work done in the months leading up to the gig. You inevitably feel a little lost. It also meant Pauline and I could get dolled up, so after a trip to catering in the bowels of the building, we changed for the performance.

It was time to wish the band luck, and I nipped into the dressing room to see them before they went on stage, then headed to our first-floor box, where my friends and I would see the show. Pauline and I had two of the front four seats, but part of me wished we were alone and could lose ourselves in the show. It's embarrassing to be so excited around friends, but they're my friends, so they understand.

There was a problem with the guest-list. The queue was horrendous, and the list wasn't yet at the door, everyone texting me in a panic. I contacted Simon, who hurried along to sort it. Stage time went back a few minutes to allow everyone time to find seats before the lights dimmed and the show began.

Dazzle Ships has a unique beginning. Last time I heard it live I was 17, watching a show at Nottingham University. As my friend Jan reminded me, our Economics teacher took the piss, implying we were too incompetent to take a bus on our own. Also, there was the embarrassment of

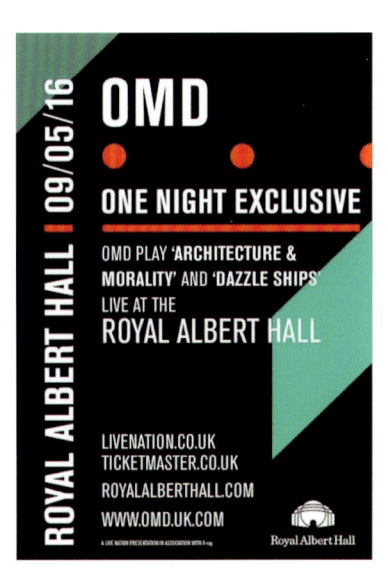

↑ 'The beginning and the End' at the Albert Hall with Stuart on guitar. Photo by Steve Morley

Dad striding backstage to haul me into the car while I queued for autographs. On this occasion, I wasn't counting my change for the bus, but managing a band playing the Royal Albert Hall, yet I briefly shut my eyes, imagining I was that girl again, Dad in the car outside, waiting to drive me home.

Later, the after-party, but as ever these things were awful. I didn't get to enjoy any of it, running around sorting out people who thought they needed to be there for various reasons, never thanking us. Then I slipped out unnoticed, went home. No party for me. I was totally overwhelmed and just wanted my kitchen, Pauline, and a nice cup of tea. There would be more gigs, more of the same work, yet I couldn't imagine anything would feel like this show. But when Andy texted to say pretty much the same, I was happy, and proud.

The show was everything I hoped it would be. I loved it, beginning to end, and hoped and believed the band did too. They were amazing, and I'll never forget hearing 'International', 'Julia's Song' and 'Romance of the Telescope' in that building. In fact, every single song sounded fresh and exciting. That show will remain in my heart forever, one of the most incredible nights of my life and a constant reminder of who I am and what I've done with my life.

BARBARA CHARONE
publicist

I'd had the pleasure of working with OMD since 2013's gem, *English Electric*. My fondest memory is when they played the Royal Albert Hall. It was nothing short of magical. Andy and Paul were almost as happy as a delirious audience. It was one of those 'you had to be there' nights. Unforgettable!

ANDY McCLUSKEY

I was certainly nervous about whether we could sell out the Albert Hall. I have to thank Mirelle for her absolute confidence. So much work went into what was only supposed to be one concert; it was frankly a crazy idea. But we said we would do crazy! And I loved learning songs we hadn't played for decades, some of which we'd never played before. We were offered to take the show to Germany, so I was able to make an excuse to leave the after-show party early and go to the bus for the overnight drive. I asked to be let out of the south exit to avoid a large number of people at the stage door. There were only a couple of clever people waiting for autographs and hugs. I climbed into my little coffin-sized bunk on an empty bus after just playing to a sold-out Albert Hall. I felt elated and empty, all at the same time. I remembered Mirelle had said she felt emotional, so texted to say I felt the same and thanked her.

FRIEDRICH STADT PALAST
11 May 2016, Berlin, Germany

GEIR JONNY VIK

In 1984 I moved with my mother and stepfather from Ålesund in Norway, where there was only one TV channel, to Oslo, where there were seven or eight. A new world opened up to me, with lots of music videos every day. I'd spend at least two hours a day watching. Nik Kershaw was my first idol but in 1985 when OMD released 'So in Love' and 'Secret', they became favourites.

I got to see them live in 2016. The sun was shining, the weather was warm, and I had a Toto t-shirt on. I was early and wanted to find the stage entrance. I went around the corner of the building and saw a lady a few metres ahead. She started talking to me in German. I did not understand much of what she was saying. She then told me in English that she had the same t-shirt and was hoping Andy and Paul would come out of the stage entrance to smoke. She was right. Andy came out first, then Paul. We chatted a few minutes. I got an autograph and a photo. It was a great moment. And the concert was awesome.

ALTE OPER
15 May 2016,
Frankfurt, Germany

MAUREEN HOFMANN

My friend Kornelia and I went to our fourth OMD concert. They played the whole of *Dazzle Ships*.

After, we waited patiently at the rear exit. Andy came out. I couldn't believe my eyes. I walked up to him and instead of introducing ourselves, asked for some photos and autographs. I also thanked him for a wonderful evening.

THE CABOOZE
3 June 2016,
Minneapolis, Minnesota

KEVIN HEARN
Barenaked Ladies

In Toronto in 1985 I was in a basement with my high school band, recording our version of 'Secret' by OMD live to cassette. My voice was still cracking, because I was in grade ten. I never would have dreamed that 30 years later I'd be playing that tape for Paul Humphreys and Andy McCluskey in a dressing room over a post-show glass of wine, having a good laugh.

Falling in love with the song 'Secret' led me to loving the album, *Crush*. The title track, with its wonderfully strange sequence of samples, particularly appealed to my expanding musical tastes. I put the song on

↑
Kevin Hearn from Barenaked Ladies invited OMD on their 2016 tour

a mix-tape. Side B, track 1. That song was playing the first time I made love.

About five years later, living with my cousin, comedian Harland Williams, in a dingy Toronto apartment, a mentor to me in many ways, he was playing some amazing music. I had to know what it was. It was the *Architecture & Morality* album. He added, 'You know what I love about these guys? They're not afraid to do whatever they want. They make the music they feel like making.' I really liked that idea, adopting it as a personal creative credo.

In 2016, sat with my Barenaked Ladies bandmates planning our summer tour, we made a wish-list of bands we'd love to tour with. Out of the blue, I suggested OMD, a suggestion met with surprise and one, 'Yeah … right'. I knew it was a long shot. I had a feeling they hadn't toured North America in some time. I wasn't sure if they were even touring anymore, so I was shocked and over the moon when we were told OMD would love to do a tour with us.

Our first show was in Minneapolis, a very unglamorous venue, The Cabooze. I was seeing them live for the first time and it was incredible. I had no idea what a great front-man Andy was. And hearing Paul sing 'Secret', so many memories came rushing back.

I watched their set every night, until they invited me to join them on accordion for 'Maid of Orleans.' I'd be okay as long as I stayed out of the way of Andy's dancing. Stuart whispered, 'You know Kevin, OMD never have guests sit in!' It was indeed an honour.

I loved getting to know Andy, Paul, Martin and Stuart, and here are some of my favourite OMD facts:

- Stuart is very serious about proper tea etiquette
- Martin is an amazing painter
- Paul irons everyone's shirts before the show
- Andy's serious air is often betrayed by a wonderful, mischievous laugh
- OMD remain an inspiration to me, both as a band and as people

ANDY MCCLUSKEY

We were amazed to be asked on to the BNL tour, but what a wonderful experience, and must thank them and their amazing crew for their warmth and generosity. And we got to catch up with Howard Jones after 32 years. The tour really gave us an opportunity to play to people who hadn't seen us in a long time or even ever. And I learned something. BNL's stage banter is great and our audiences have noticed we now talk more and crack jokes on stage. Thanks Ed, Kev, Jim and Ty.

↑ Kansas City Massacre. Martin, Stuart and Paul passed out after a tequila afternoon in Kansas City on the Barenaked Ladies tour

STARLIGHT THEATER

4 June 2016,
Kansas City, Kansas

KURT IVERSON

I moved to Kansas City with my wife in 2002 after my girls were born. We both lost our jobs after 9/11 and there was really nothing for us in California. But, 15 years later, I got to see OMD with Howard Jones and Barenaked Ladies. It was the best concert in a long time, like reliving all the greatest moments of the most formidable years of my life. Like key frames in an animated version of my history, I can pinpoint every emotion and event that impacted me through an OMD song.

VERIZON AMPHI THEATER

28 & 30 June 2016, Alpharetta, Georgia

DERIC SHAW

I first heard OMD on Sirius XM. When I found out they had a new album, *History of Modern*, I had to buy it. I appreciate that they haven't messed around with their style. Too many bands well known in the 80s sound nothing like they did. When I saw OMD in Alpharetta, Howard Jones was also there. My wife came along. She didn't know of OMD, but she's now a fan as well. Andy mentioned how they don't 'get around to these parts too much'.

TERESA CHILDERS

I first got to see OMD at Encore Park, touring with Barenaked Ladies and Howard Jones. Sorry to admit, but I really didn't know too much about the band until I researched them and realised I knew most of their songs. But I was so thrilled to see them.

LET'S ROCK THE MOOR

20 May 2017, Cookham, UK

AARON BUCK
OMD's Monitor Engineer

On my 30th birthday, OMD headlined Let's Rock the Moor. Most times, when a band headlines a festival, they're offered a morning set-up and soundcheck before the site opens. I met the band, we played a few songs, and all was well. We headed back to our hotel for the afternoon and got some rest. Then, 30 minutes before stage time, I came down with a horrific case of food poisoning. I'm sure you've heard the phrase 'out of both ends', and this certainly applied in the backstage loo, not knowing whether to sit on it or stand over it.

But the show must go on, and it wasn't going to stop for me. The tour manager got me a bucket and we started. The bucket got used, and because my condition was obvious to all on stage, I think they gave me an easy ride. I left straight after with the band in their luxury van, which I threw up all over the side of out of the window as we were drove back to the hotel.

I'm happy to report we've done around 60 shows around the world since, without further incident. And, all credit to the guys, they were incredibly sympathetic and saw the funny side.

BBC RADIO 6 MUSIC DAY
15 June 2017, Salford, UK

ANDY MCCLUSKEY

I got a call from my sister Helen to say Mum has been admitted to hospital. Our mother, Margaret had not long celebrated her 86th birthday, but her health was slowly failing. She'd been confined to her bed and living for seven years with Helen.

Between the sound check and returning to the Cunard Building for our live radio broadcast, I was at Mum's bedside. Before leaving, my two sisters and I were summoned into a side-room, an anxious young doctor informing us we should be prepared for the worst. He feared that Mum was in her last few days. We were shocked, but frankly not convinced. She'd been extremely sick on several previous occasions and rallied again to be quite healthy. However, negative thoughts and fears for Mum's health were in my mind.

Standing on the stage inside the Cunard Building at Liverpool's Pier Head, converted for the British Music Experience exhibition, started to feel rather surreal for me. I was in that very room where I was employed in my one and only nine to five job, for three months in 1979. As we played live on the radio I couldn't help but reflect on the last time I was in there, the day I left the Civil Service. My head wasn't in the moment at all. At the end of the performance I decided to say something live on the radio. I spoke about how my mother encouraged me to follow my dream and leave that building. I recalled her very words. 'If you don't try, you could spend the rest of your life wondering, 'What if?' So I tried, and for the next 40 years I never, ever needed to wonder, 'What if?'

I returned to the hospital that evening. Mum was well enough to understand that I had mentioned on the radio how her words had inspired me all those years ago. I kissed her and thanked her. Margaret Agnes McCluskey passed away seven weeks later on July 4.

CHILFEST

8 July 2017, Tring, UK

ELIZABETH MARSHALL

I wasn't a huge fan in the 80s, but a year or so back, going through some of my stuff, I listened to 'Enola Gay' again and was sufficiently hooked to travel more than 22,000km from my home in New Zealand to Chilfest in England. Would I do it again? In a heartbeat!

REGENCY BALLROOM

28 July 2017, San Francisco, California

KRISTA HAMBY

I was third in line, determined to be at the barricade at the front of the stage. Standing in line, chatting with new friends I made there, I saw Andy drive by towards the alley entrance. We ran around the corner and met him. Later, I saw Paul in the alley on my way back. I had to approach. An incredible day. Both Andy and

↑
OMD at the Regency Ballroom, San Francisco, 28 July 2017

Paul had pictures taken with us and were so nice. It's refreshing to meet celebrities that are kind and thoughtful and really care about and appreciate their fans.

PEPSI CENTER

2 August 2017, Mexico City, Mexico

DIEGO JUDEZ

While 2011's Corona Capital Music Festival was sold out and my girlfriend and I had to listen from outside, when OMD came back in 2013 I was in the first five rows. And in 2017 I met them and they all signed my question printed in the 2013 tour book. Andy wrote, 'To Diego, all the best!'

MARIANA DOM

I was 12 when I heard 'Secret'. Then my uncle bought me *Crush*. My English teacher translated the lyrics, because I had no idea what was being sung. I've now seen OMD twice, at the Metropolitan then at the Pepsi Center, when my daughter was at my side, listening to my favourite song. My tears would not stop, but I was immensely happy.

HARD ROCK CAFÉ

5 August 2017, Punta Cana, Dominican Republic

ANDY MCCLUSKEY

We played Mexico in 2017 and got offered a concert in the Dominican Republic, which we did as a two-piece as we couldn't afford to take everyone. The city's history was interesting, and the promoters were great guys, but this was possibly one of the worst concerts we've ever done.

They'd extended the stage. It looked like it was built out of metal tables. The bass sub-speakers in the PA were 10ft behind us, the entire stage vibrating. There was a terrible noise in my ears, but if I took my microphone off the stand it stopped. The stage was making the mic stand shudder so much that there was a constant rumble. Our cables weren't long enough to get the Pro Tools computer off the stage, so the backing tracks kept stopping, the shaking making the computer buffer or disconnect. It was excruciating. We had to go off stage several times.

It was a very wealthy audience at the front, sat at tables in long rows drinking champagne, paying top dollar for tickets, because it was the first time we'd ever performed in the country. When we played a song the audience knew, they all got up and partied. When we played one they didn't, they sat down and ignored us, like we were the lounge piano act in a hotel lobby.

We were supposed to do more concerts in South America but, as is often the case, we discovered the promoter hadn't deposited the money promised. You never go to South America unless you've got money in advance, because very often promoters are a bit suspect.

THE PUNISHMENT OF LUXURY

WAS RELEASED

1 SEP 2017

OMD - 2013-2018

Imogen Bebb in that Dazzle Shirt

BARRY SMITH

In September 2017, I suffered a mental breakdown. A very scary time. I was listening to *The Punishment of Luxury* on repeat, and while I was massively struggling to cope, that album kept me going. It means a lot to me, but 'The View from Here' meant the most, particularly the lines, 'Sliding backwards down the slope, clinging desperately to hope, watching you untie the rope, cast away, couldn't cope. Climb the mountain of your fear, you should see the view from here.' An incredible lyric to a beautiful song.

IMOGEN BEBB

The Dazzle Shirt, as it became known, is a copy of one Andy McCluskey wore on *Top of the Pops* in 1984. It was sent to me by OMD photographer Chris Oaten in 2017, as he knew I was an avid fan. It was such a great design that I've worn it to most of the OMD gigs and events I've attended since, and often get asked where it came from. It does get heavy and warm when worn indoors (and dancing) though.

TAPE LONDON

1 September 2017,
London, UK

WILLIAM DIXON

I entered the world of OMD after watching the film, *Alan Partridge: Alpha Papa* in 2014. 'Enola Gay' was used in a montage scene, and I was instantly drawn to the synth sounds and craved more. OMD quickly became my favourite band, my addiction so prevalent that I was known around college as 'The guy who only listens to OMD'. I even inherited Andy's infamous windmill dance, my go-to dance move.

I saw a competition on 100% Record's Facebook page for a chance to win free tickets to the launch party for *The Punishment of Luxury*. I entered on a whim and ended up winning. It was my first OMD live show and the best day of my life. Being ridiculously close to Andy and Paul, hearing so many of the new songs played live, was a real treat.

BRADLEY ROGERS

My Dad and I got word that there would be a fans' launch party in London, so I said, 'Try and get tickets - we can't miss it'. And by

↑
William Dixon discovered OMD through Alan Partridge

some miracle we did. I woke up that morning, went straight to my Apple app and downloaded the new album. A band my parents had seen in their younger years had rubbed off on me and they had released the *Architecture & Morality* of today.

We entered the nightclub that evening with such anticipation. I remember seeing the set-list, thinking, 'Wow, no hit singles,' which was joked about later when Andy told the audience they weren't playing any, and there was dead silence.

PAULA GILMER
Tiny Magnetic Pets, 2017 UK & Ireland tour support

In 2017 out of the blue, OMD approached Tiny Magnetic Pets, inviting us to be the opening act for the UK and Irish leg of the Punishment of Luxury tour. From one end of the UK to another, Eugene, Sean and myself watched all 20 shows, never failing to be mesmerised. Their showmanship and total commitment to their audience, crew and everyone involved made us proud to part of the OMD family.

VICAR STREET
23 October 2017, Dublin, Ireland

SEÁN QUINN
Tiny Magnetic Pets

I became aware of OMD when my brother's schoolmate, Eamonn, asked if we'd heard this new electronic band. He said, 'They have this record called 'Electricity.' I thought it was a very long name for a band, remember thinking it was English guys playing German music. I was intrigued at how they'd combined Teutonic synths with new wave - and I liked it - it was the future.

I'd never seen them live before the first night in Dublin and once our set was over I went with Una, our manager, to find a good spot. I wasn't sure what to expect but wasn't expecting the energy that came off the stage that night - especially from Andy, windmilling all over like the Duracell Bunny gene-spliced with Ian Curtis.

Another fond memory was in Liverpool. We took the opportunity to visit (accidentally via Penny Lane) the phone box (632 3003), which was in the process of being restored. It was interesting to see the streets where they grew up and the environment, which triggered the emotions in the music. I grew up in a very different place, but we both looked to Düsseldorf (and Liverpool for me) when it came to music and bought our first instruments from a catalogue. We then headed back for the soundcheck, only to find ourselves on Menlove Avenue. We thought being on Penny Lane, Birkenhead Road and Menlove Avenue on the same day was a good omen for the tour - and we were right.

ANDY MCCLUSKEY

I first heard of Tiny Magnetic Pets when they gave me their CD whilst I was watching Michael Rother in Dusseldorf. I'd just missed them play. It took me months to get around to listening, but I truly adored their music. It was an obvious choice to ask them to support us.

GREENWOOD ROAD

29 October 2017, Meols, UK

STEPH MCCAHILL
Friends of 632 3003

'Red Frame/White Light' will always be the most special track for me. Being a Hoylake girl, I'd hang around the Meols phone box this track was written about when I was 10, hoping to catch a glimpse of Andy or Paul as they used it as their unofficial office in the early days.

The phone box was removed by BT in August 2017 and, following a successful campaign by locals and fans around the world, put back in its rightful place two months later in Greenwood Road, in time for OMD's 40th anniversary. Fans visited the box before the Liverpool Empire show to celebrate its return. To hear OMD perform 'Red Frame/White Light' again was fantastic. It brilliantly pays homage to an important, cultural, iconic landmark.

OMD - 2013-2018

↑
Inside the refurbished phone box

→
Steph McCahill outside the Meols phone box

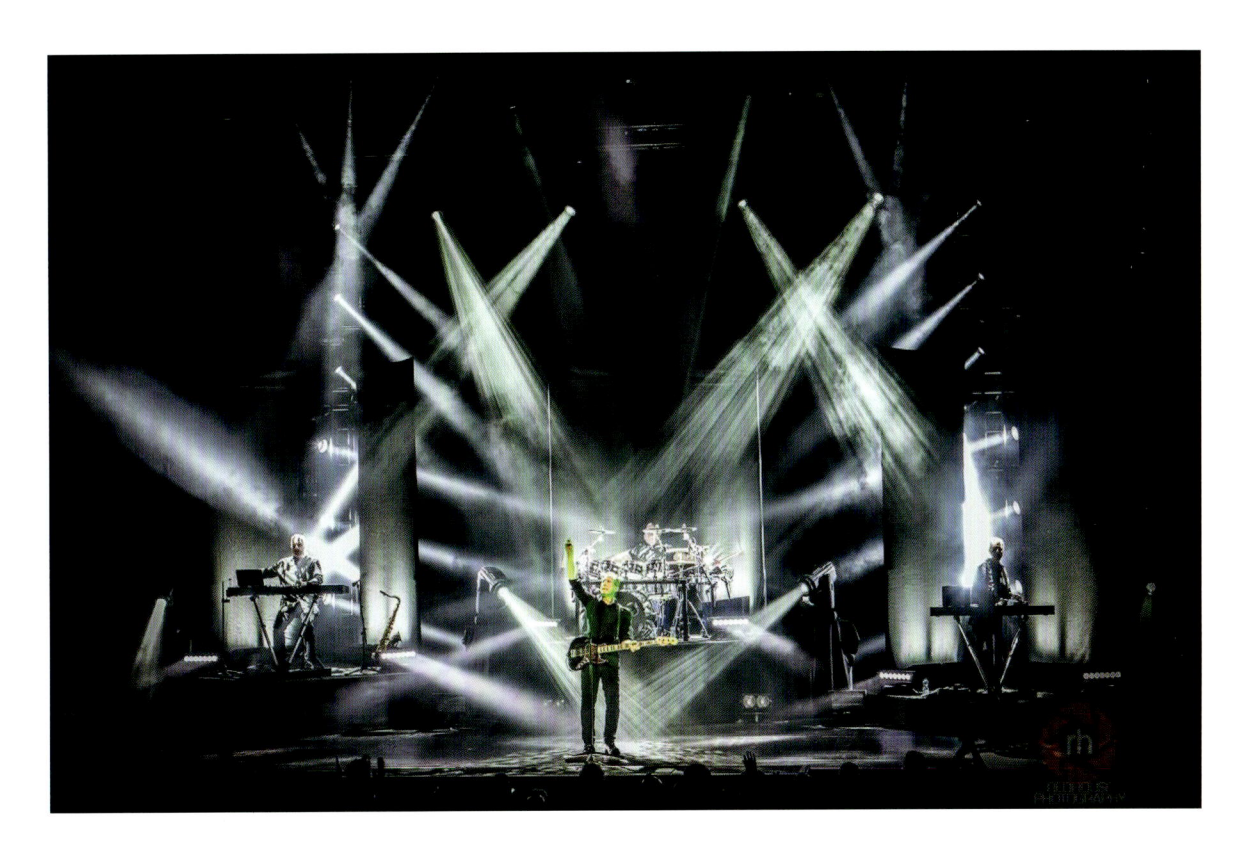

EMPIRE

29 October 2017,
Liverpool, UK

LYNNETTE HOWLETT

I discovered OMD while studying my A-levels. I bought a vinyl 12" of 'Maid of Orleans' at a second-hand stall on the market. I flipped it over to discover the B-side, 'Of All The Things We've Done'. The layering and build-up of instruments, the powerful energy, the haunting voice, the lyrics and breakdown of instruments as it fades away make it an absolute masterpiece. At the time, I was suffering with exam stress, revising and feeling overwhelmed. That song was my salvation - the stress would just melt away as I got lost in the music, the rhythmic drumbeat taking me to a calm, peaceful place.

Now, 29 years on, I still regard that song as my salvation. In 2017 I was very lucky to be able to attend gigs in Liverpool and Manchester. And on the set-list was 'Of All The Things We've Done'. I'd never heard it live before.

← Friends of 632 3003

↑ OMD live at the Liverpool Empire 2017

OMD – 2013-2018

check we met the band. What a great day. About 15 minutes later, we met Andy outside and I asked him to dedicate a song to me, Ian and his brother Colin. He dedicated 'Electricity'. While talking to Andy, Ian said, 'You know my wife.' Andy said, 'Do I?' Ian said, 'Yes, she was one of your dancers in the 'Telegraph' video. Her name is Lorraine, the one with the red hair.' Andy replied, 'Susie's sister.' Ian said, 'Yes.' Andy said Susie told him we were coming but didn't know it was us until then.

Guido Mussehl brought a VCL 11 valve to Liverpool as a gift for Paul

ANDY PINNINGTON

In the early 80s, my friend lived in Birkenhead and invited me over. He said, 'Bring a copy of *Smash Hits* with OMD on the front.' We called at Andy's mum's house on the Wirral, knocked on the door and she invited us in. Andy was away on tour, but she showed us his discs on the stairs. She also said, 'Leave your stuff here and I'll get Andy to sign it.' She kept her promise and I have the cover to this day with my collection.

When OMD played the Empire in 2017, I met Andy and Martin outside before the gig, telling them me and my best mate Ian were going to fly out to Boston for the gig and asked if they could sort out free passes. Luckily, Mirelle, their manager, was there. She told me to e-mail her. True to her word, when we got to Boston we had backstage passes. After the sound

RACHEL EACOTT

As kids growing up in the 80s, my husband and I both loved OMD, so when our son Kristian took an interest in playing synthesisers we pointed him to them. Gradually we started to hear him picking out bits of songs, like 'Souvenir', and when we had the chance of two tickets for Liverpool Empire we knew one of us had to take him to his first concert. Luckily it was me.

The gig was fantastic from beginning to end and he was buzzing. As we were staying just up the street from the stage-door, we decided to wait around. After a long, cold wait we were rewarded as Paul appeared. What a lovely man, taking the time to speak to Kristian, sign his ticket and pose for a pic. I thought my son was going to burst. It spurred him on with his music and was a night neither of us will forget.

THE SHOW MUST GO ON

The UK section of the tour had started brilliantly in terms of audience feedback, but very badly for my health. I was already carrying a sinus infection before we started. Then I damaged my 'good' knee in Liverpool. In Leicester the doctor took one look in my mouth and exclaimed, 'SHIT!' Not the words that a singer wants to hear a doctor say when looking down his throat. 'You've got septic tonsillitis. The bad news is that it will hurt. The good news is that as long as the pustules don't burst and run into your vocal chords you can still sing.' I went onstage so full of medication that I didn't know what planet I was on. And then the crowd went ballistic. What a great gig!

ANDY MCCLUSKEY

SABINE CONRADI

My best mate is from Liverpool and when I visited her, I fell in love with the city and the Wirral. One day my flatmate urged me to watch a documentary, *Souvenir*, and I realised I knew more songs than I thought.

My love for the band took off when, after an emotional couple of weeks, I watched *Architecture & Morality & More* on DVD and 'The Romance of the Telescope' came on. The way Mr McCluskey sang and portrayed the emotions of the song seemed to express what I felt. My first live experience was when someone sold me his ticket because he couldn't go, meaning I would see the band on their home turf. I cried when 'Ghost Star' started - I'd never heard an audience sing along to a synth-line in a song. Brilliant.

EDWARD VAUGHAN

Aged 13 I caught the back end of a song I'd never heard before. It was so catchy and full of life. It was 'Electricity'. And the DJ? None other than the late John Peel.

Sometime later I came across 'Red Frame/White Light' and loved that too. With the release of 'Messages', my journey had begun. I got no end of ridicule from my peers, especially in school. I was always a fringe-dweller, never one of the 'follow me' brigade. I remember painting the lid on my haversack in white gloss paint, using black permanent marker to clearly define in large letters, as artistically as I could, 'Orchestral Manoeuvres in the Dark', reversing the e's for effect.

I even got my little cousin into them. Being quite industrious, my cousin and I acquired Andy McCluskey's home telephone number and had the gall to phone him. He was at first annoyed, but quickly realised we meant no harm and spoke to us for well over an hour.

Some years later, my cousin Dave and I met Andy in Victoria Park, Tranmere. He was doing the Atomic Kitten thing and we spoke at length. My lady had never done a concert, so I bought two VIP tickets for Liverpool. I was lucky, Pledge going into meltdown with demand.

DE MONTFORT HALL

5 November 2017,
Leicester, UK

ANNA-MARIE UNDERWOOD

Discovering OMD when I was 18, absolutely loving 'Sailing on the Seven Seas', I bought *Sugar Tax* and discovered they weren't a new band. My son now has custody of my vinyl collection, and we were lucky enough to see the band play in Leicester. They were brilliant, despite Andy's tonsilitis and my vertigo.

MASON UNDERWOOD

My earliest memory of OMD involved a TV ad for a *Ministry of Sound* 80s compilation, using the melody from 'Enola Gay'. I instantly liked it. My mum seemed to get excited too, and we nipped to HMV to pick up some CDs. OMD's music quickly became the soundtrack to my brother and I playing in the back garden, as Mum blaring them from our windows. A decade or so later, studying at Guildford's Academy of Contemporary Music, at the end of each trimester, Mum picked me up and we'd drive back to Leicester for the holiday. On one such drive our selection of music included a greatest hits compilation. That's when I rediscovered OMD. 'Walking on the Milky Way' stood out. Lyrics about getting older seemed rather pertinent to me in my early 20s.

I treated Mum to see you live, which was brilliant. Andy looked directly at me during the chorus of 'So In Love', giving me a look of utter bewilderment. I'm not totally sure why, but I suspect it's because I'm not 40, as a woman next to me made a point of mentioning before.

↑
Anna-Marie Underwood and her son Mason

ROYAL CONCERT HALL

6 November 2017, Nottingham, UK

DAVID HANSON

Almost 40 years ago, I was listening to *Architecture & Morality* in my bedroom.

Fast forward to 2017. After a quick chat with the wife, two tickets were booked. We arrived way too early and made our way to Row D, Seats 37/8, in an almost empty hall. After the support and obligatory dash for the men's room, I was back and my 38-year dream was fulfilled. From the intro and 'Ghost Star' through to 'Messages' and our request, 'The New Stone Age', could this get any better? Then 'Joan of Arc' and 'Maid of Orleans', a 50-something man almost losing it. I could feel the bottom lip start to go and a tear in my eye.

EDWARD HAMMOND

I first heard OMD aged about four, my parents playing their songs in the car when we were going on holiday. I distinctly remember the feeling of adventure and excitement 'Sailing on the Seven Seas' gave me. It became my 'holiday music'.

What I find especially insightful is exploring the meaning behind each song and the message it's attempting to convey. *The Punishment of Luxury* is proving the most relatable so far.

CHRIS INNS

I took my 26-year-old William for his first OMD experience. He was introduced to OMD as a baby, bouncing in his static walker, hanging from my lounge doorframe. En route to the gig, he said, 'Do they do 'Tesla Girls'?' Leaving the de Montfort Hall he said, 'Dad, they are good, aren't they? And they can sing.' I gave him a big smile, and said, 'Yes, son.'

DAVE BIGGS

I was desperate for VIP tickets in Nottingham on the Punishment of Luxury tour. I was online at work while my daughter, Stacey, was online at home. I had trouble connecting but she managed to get tickets. It's daft at 56 getting so excited. My grandchildren would laugh, seeing their grandfather almost shaking with anticipation.

Stacey called me at work with the good news but was miffed when I responded, 'Okay, thanks, goodbye.' I could almost hear her say she wished she hadn't bothered. As it happened, unbeknown to me, I was having a stroke. Work colleagues, seeing I was ill, called an ambulance and I was rushed to hospital. Fortunately, although ill for a good while and still feeling the effects, I was well enough to attend with my wife, having an amazing day and night. I'll still try to be first in line for future gigs, but OMD should come with a health warning. Even after all these years, they can still have a serious effect on their fans.

CITY HALL
7 November 2017, Sheffield, UK

DANIEL LEE

Playing pool in a bar, I heard 'Enola Gay' and was inspired to look them up online, when it all came flooding back to me. Playing those songs again I knew I had to see OMD live. A year later I found out they were playing not far from where I live, and when tickets went on sale I got mine. They were awesome, interacted with the audience, humoured us, and played fantastically.

HEXAGON THEATRE
9 November 2017, Reading, UK

ADAM KING

In 1980 in Blackpool, I was a Rocker and my best mate was a Mod. In the record shop, he bought a new LP by OMD and I bought Status Quo's *12 Gold Bars*. Within two days I returned to buy *Orchestral Manoeuvres in the Dark*. I've never looked back. The last time I saw them live was in Reading in 2017.

MARTIN STRIKE

I first heard 'Enola Gay' on a cassette player at school, while in room B10 before Piggy Stockton returned to take us for double physics. Much of my adolescence was spent with OMD's aural company in my bedroom, performing solitary, Middle Ages-type dance to 'Maid of Orleans', inspired by the TV show *Blackadder*. God knows what my folks thought, their ceiling reverberating to 'Joan of Arc', my size 11's performing quadrilles. My old pal, Clive, who also survived those daily bundles at grammar school, suggested we go to watch you at Reading Hexagon.

Okay, they may look like Rob Brydon and Barry from *Eggheads* these days but proved themselves as electro-gods that night. As they came on, we stood centrally, maybe 15 people deep, when two drunk women pushed in front. We are both six feet tall, so it was no problem. One seemed to latch on to me, turning to smile (and stagger), using me as support for her wavering. Through a mist of prosecco, she told me she last saw you guys at 15, was now 50 and 'far too old' for me. Being 54, I didn't attempt to contradict her. During 'Messages' this harmless, almost amusing behaviour turned into bump and grinding on her part. As a happily married man, I passed her gyrating self on to some apparently single chap next to me. Why did this never happen to me during my single days? I should have been to an earlier OMD gig.

GUILDHALL
10 November 2017,
Southampton, UK

PAULINE TARR

I have only had two dedications in all these years. One was in sound-check at Ipswich Gaumont in 1984. The band started playing 'Almost' - my favourite - and Andy said, 'This is for you Pauline.' I'd been nagging all tour for them to play it.

The second was more recent, on the Punishment of Luxury tour in Southampton. It's no secret that I loathe 'If You Leave'. Knowing the fan vote that day had been a dead-heat, I knew that meant it would be in the encore. The time came and over the intro came words from Paul. 'This is for Pauline. We love you.' The joke had been turned in on me. Now I have to like it, as it's my song.

G LIVE
11 November 2017,
Guildford, UK

EUGENE SOMERS
Tiny Magnetic Pets

We invited our good friend Chris Payne to see the Punishment of Luxury show in Guildford. One of my favourite moments was Chris

ROUND HOUSE

13 November 2017, London, UK

L-R. Martin, Stuart, Chris Payne (keyboard player on '79 Numan tour), Eugene TMP, Paul TMP, Paul, Sean TMP and Andy

coming backstage to see OMD, as the last time they were together was on tour with Gary Numan playing the very same venues as we did in 1979. It was amazing to see the guys catch up after all that time. One story I'll always have was hearing Chris tell the story of when Gary Numan's mother ironed Andy and Paul's shirts before the show. Fantastic.

JOHN SAMUEL

I've been a fan since the early 80s and my most treasured record is a 12" single of 'Enola Gay'. One of my best father and son moments was taking my 18-year old son, James, to G Live. We really need another fix soon.

LUCY BOUGHTON
PR

One of the first albums I bought was *Architecture and Morality*. It was one of only a handful of records I owned, and I played it over and over again on my parents' record player.

In a strange twist of fate, it transpired that Aunty Connie, my Grandma's friend, was Paul's Aunt. She arranged for autographs to be sent, with a signed photo. I still have it on my office wall. Dad fixed the autograph to my A&M album with sticky-back plastic.

Fast forward 36 years, and I was working with the band. I never had a chance to see OMD live back in the day, as I was so young, so it was fantastic to go to the Roundhouse show in 2017.

DANCING

When the band reformed I intended to have some dignity and not dance. No chance! Faced with live music and an audience, I reverted to type. I now claim it's a shamanic trance I descend into. For 90 minutes I'm purged of anxiety and spiritually connected to so many others. Or maybe I'm just a sad old man dancing badly.

The left knee has suffered for my art on stage. Now I have a cortisone injection in my knee before I start a tour, greatly reducing the pain. But all it's doing is masking the damage. Scans show my left knee is a complete mess. There's no cartilage, the bones are out of alignment, and I've got lots of arthritic growth.

Before I go on, I take quite heavy-duty cocodamol and wear a knee-brace, adrenalin and a shot of neat vodka seeming to anaesthetise me while I'm on stage. I walk around like a 90-year-old man on tour, apart from when I'm on stage, when I don't seem to feel it.

I've tried to modify my dancing. I do less jumping up and down than I used to. But when you want an audience to jump up and down, as I do for 'History of Modern (Part 1)', you have to lead by example. When you're in the middle of the moment on stage, it's very hard to remind yourself you have to lift up onto your toes but don't leave the ground, so there's no impact coming back down.

I should probably sit in an ice bath for half an hour when I come off to reduce the inflammation, but there are few concert halls with ice baths backstage.

ANDY MCCLUSKEY

DE LA WARR PAVILION

15 November 2017, Bexhill-on-Sea, UK

LAURENCE COLMAN

I got the bug to meet them again in 2017, this time in God's Waiting Room, Bexhill. I loved the soundcheck again and meeting the guys for the second time, and Stuart Kershaw for the first time. After the final encore, I was lucky enough to catch Stuart's drumstick. It takes pride of place on my mantelpiece.

JON RUSSELL

Two buses and one train journey to get their sounds was simple enough, but when you're bipolar, life can be a right unpredictable friend. The amount of gigs I've bought tickets for and not attended, because the very thought has overwhelmed me too much.

Fast forward to a day of meeting the band. I already knew Paul, which made the whole situation that bit easier. I was quite in awe of Andy. I wanted to ask him so much, but no words would come. Stu's drumming at the soundcheck left me gob smacked. Martin was so friendly, asking me to sign the CD of my music I gave him. I sat at the front of the balcony for the gig. Having that space in front helps me settle. It was wonderful to see the enthusiasm below. I'd never witnessed such euphoria, the music seeming to encapsulate every soul and carry each person, creating over a thousand memories. Depression, anxiety, and unpredictable moods can rule your life, and it's hard, but thanks to OMD that night music was again my friend, and nothing else mattered.

BARBICAN THEATRE

18 November 2017, York, UK

MIKE GARRETT

I got into OMD through accidentally ripping them off. I'd just written a new song with the catchiest hook ever. It was a blend of synth, heavy metal guitar and frantic jungle drum-beats. I could see it roaring to No.1 and my act giving an impressive performance on *Top of the Pops*. I burnt a CDR and took it to my dad, who would always get the first listen to any demos I did. He looked at me with a different set of eyes than usual and if I recall correctly, a smirk. He knew it was familiar but couldn't put his finger on why. After some frantic CD searching, he dug out *The Best Of OMD* and played 'Enola Gay'. My heart simultaneously sank and fell in love. The former, because my No.1 hit's best bit was 'Enola Gay's' hook, and the latter due to the sheer awesomeness of what I was hearing. Fast forward to 2017 and I bought my Dad and I tickets to see OMD in Bexhill, one of the best gigs I've been to.

ISABEL HEADON

After we heard 'Going Down to Liverpool' by The Bangles in Tesco, my Mum and I were helped by Dad to make a playlist of bands from and songs about Liverpool. One was 'Enola Gay'. My mum told me she discovered them in Houston supporting The Thompson Twins, not knowing who they were.

I had to go. My Dad tried to book tickets for Glasgow's Royal Concert Hall, but it was sold out. For the Manchester show, we said Orchestral Manoeuvres in the Dark, but the people on the phone were confused. They only knew the band as OMD. That sold out too. York was the last straw and a month before the show Dad got the last ticket. With a wheelchair-user, the carer usually goes free. I went with Mum. In February 2018, as a memento, I ordered some custom Lego mini-figures. They were Paul and Andy of OMD from the night I saw them in concert.

ROYAL CONCERT HALL

19 November 2017, Glasgow, UK

ANGELA COUSTURES

At 10-years-old I was addicted. They had me at Malcolm's drum intro to 'If You Leave.' But soon that became a distant introduction to a powerful passion I couldn't get enough of. Working odd jobs for neighbours and friends I'd take my earnings to a small record shop, where the owner would keep OMD albums behind the counter just for me. I was too young to go to the concerts, so instead I created my own concert playlist. I played my records and with my headphones on I'd pretend I was there in the front row, just off centre.

The lyrics made me curious about the world I was in. I learned about history, about profound love and the pain that comes from it. I was transported far away. As I listened I melted with Martin's every breath into the saxophone, Malcolm's hypnotic beat of the drums, and swayed to Paul's sweet rhythmic sounds. But Andrew became my weakness. His voice enslaved me, his energy ignited me.

OMD would be my first love. To me they were further away than the moon, but I was utterly and completely infatuated with their art and what it stood for. It wasn't until 30 years later that I finally found myself there in my spot - front row, just off centre. It was more exhilarating than I ever imagined.

Andy and Julia sound check at The Barbican 18 November 2017

SYMPHONY HALL

21 November 2017,
Birmingham, UK

STUART RICHARDS

The energy and joy from the band radiated across the crowd and gave me an unforgettable experience. I feel slightly disappointed sometimes that I missed certain bands from the 80s and 90s back in their prime, but OMD certainly proved to me that despite being around for 40 years, fans shouldn't worry about their heroes not sounding their best. And younger fans should go see them whenever they can.

SAGE

22 November 2017,
Gateshead, UK

TOMMY DRAPER

In 1985 a girl borrowed my tape of 'Enola Gay' so she could play it in her car. She played it at maximum volume, so you heard her coming. In 2018 that same girl and I celebrated our 30th wedding anniversary, and the year before we had one of our best days ever, meeting the band at the Sage in Gateshead.

MITSUBISHI ELECTRIC HALL

3 December 2017,
Düsseldorf, Germany

ROGER KAMP

For a fan of electronic music, it's always something special playing in Düsseldorf. The connection to Kraftwerk can't be overlooked. I heard that OMD didn't like the former Philips Halle but it was a good decision to play there again. A lot of people from the electric music scene have been there, so it felt like a family meeting.

013

5 December 2017,
Tilburg, The Netherlands

YAËL POL

My father, Ronald, grew up loving OMD's music and, when I was about eight, regularly took me out for a drive, playing the *Universal* CD in the car. I called it the 'bubble CD' because of the album cover. When I was 11, my father and I were listening to *Universal* at home when 'Too Late' came on. I started crying. It was the first time a song really got to me in such an emotional way.

As I grew older, I got to understand what 'Too Late' was about, which made me love it even more. It's helped me through some hard times these last few years. Tilburg, Andy explained the song was about a personal relationship that he knew would end someday. It was a very emotional moment, so when Andy gave me a big hug, it felt like someone finally understood how I feel about this beautiful song.

LES DOCKS

8 December 2017,
Lausanne, Switzerland

MIRELLE DAVIS
OMD Manager

It was my idea the band did this book. The minute I saw The Wedding Present's book I knew I wanted OMD to do one. As somebody whose life literally

↑
Roger Kamp makes everyone give the thumbs-up after the Düsseldorf show

```
ART EATS ART / LA MITRAILLEUSE
                    GHOST STAR
                       ISOTYPE
                      MESSAGES
                   TESLA GIRLS
        HISTORY OF MODERN PART I
                  ONE MORE TIME
                      FAN VOTE
              FOREVER LIVE & DIE
                      SOUVENIR
                   JOAN OF ARC
                MAID OR ORLEANS
                    TIME ZONES
       OF ALL THE THINGS WE'VE MADE
              WHAT HAVE WE DONE
                     SO IN LOVE
                    LOCOMOTION
         THE PUNISHMENT OF LUXURY
         SAILING ON THE SEVEN SEAS
                     ENOLA GAY
          WALKING ON THE MILKY WAY
                        SECRET
                    ELECTRICITY
```

OMD setlist from December 2017

changed because of OMD's shows, it seemed the best way to celebrate their 40-year career. A concert isn't just about those on the stage but, as OMD know only too well, it's about the audience and both the shared and personal experience. Every show means something different for every person in the room. And every show has meant something different to me, first as a fan and then as a manager. Some have been joyous, some sad, some pleasure and some work. If I am honest, these days it can be hard to be just a fan.

London, New York and LA shows will always see me running around, looking after label and media guests and generally being driven crazy by the guest-list. So I've chosen Lausanne in Switzerland, the final show on the European run in 2017, as the last show I'm going to write about, because I felt like a fan again. I managed to lose myself in the music, in the concert, in the memories and in the now, and I had fun. I let my hair down literally and figuratively and became that 18-year old girl again. OMD will always be able to do that for me, and that will always make our relationship special.

HANNAH BADERTSCHER

Growing up in Chester in the 80s and 9os, I'm ashamed to say OMD meant nothing to me. Kylie, Jason and Take That were what young girls listened to. Fast forward to 2001, my German degree taking me to Switzerland and my Swiss boyfriend and now-husband, Urs. His CD collection is so big it needs its own room and I discovered a host of new bands, including OMD.

Ironically, it took a move to Switzerland to discover links with the band's history. My Dad's from the Wirral, I'd driven past infamous Stanlow more times than I could count, and from chatting with Andy at a concert I discovered that his local bank was the same Heswall branch where Dad once worked.

PAUL HUMPHREYS

We don't want to play for more than two hours, because I think that's the maximum time you have the attention of an audience. I hate bands that play for three and a half hours. I lose the will to live after two. Having said that, there are a lot of songs that people expect to hear every time we play, which means that in some ways, we're the victims of our own success. So we have to try and do a balancing act - playing the hits but also new stuff. We dared play six tracks from the new album on the Punishment of Luxury tour. Not a whole section - we spread them through the show. And they went down surprisingly well. We also try to bring in more obscure tracks for the more hardcore fans. On the last tour we did 'Of All the Things We've

Made' from *Dazzle Ships*, where we all went down the front in very Kraftwerkian style. Stuart played one drum, Martin and I played mini-keyboards, and Andy played guitar and sang. It's as close as you can get to OMD unplugged.

Luxury tour dates were released I asked my dad to come with me to Oslo. I'd heard about Andy's 'energetic' dance, but to see it for myself – wow! I also found it funny that I was most likely the youngest person in the audience, at 20. I returned home inspired.

ROCKER FELLER
7 February 2018, Oslo, Norway

HANNE SYNNØVE W PEDERSEN

I struggled throughout my teens with mental problems. Nothing severe, but enough to make it difficult for me to function normally in everyday life, especially at school. I was 17 when Dad brought me a book about Kraftwerk and encouraged me to read it.

The book resulted in me searching for 'old' electronic music, my renewed interest for OMD following a car trip when Dad was playing 'Tesla Girls'. OMD became one of the bands I listened the most to, and the music was one of the things that helped me make it through the day in a good mood.

When The Punishment of

DR KONCERT HUSET STUDIE 2
9 February 2018, Copenhagen, Denmark

LEIF PLITH LAURITSEN

In the summer of 1982, aged 15 and visiting my Danish uncle in Norway watching a music programme on TV, a catchy sound came out of the speakers and a very captivating video started. A female knight was riding through a beautiful snowy landscape with a frozen crossbow soldier and a wonderful castle ruin. The video, and most of all the music and the words, made me want to know more about Joan of Arc and the medieval period in general. So even though I'm a bit dyslexic, I threw my energy and myself into books and started reading. Today I'm a medieval archaeologist and castle researcher and now work in a leading role at a local museum. I'm also still a big OMD fan, and 2018 in Copenhagen was fantastic.

PROGRESJA
11 February 2018, Warsaw, Poland

DARIUSZ FIGIEL

In 1983, as a teenager behind the Iron Curtain, it wasn't easy to find foreign bands' records. We mostly had to tape things off the radio. Sat in a schoolfriend's flat, his older brother played a tape. We started with 'Radio Prague' and finished with 'Enola Gay'. It was the start of my OMD adventure.

I saw them most recently in Warsaw in 2018. A gold disc of *Dazzle Ships*, signed by Andy and Paul in Warsaw, hangs on my wall.

ANDRZEJ 'ANDY' KUCZKOWSKI

Seeing OMD live in 2018 was one of the most important events in my life. To be well prepared for the concert, I spent the whole night before learning the lyrics. That gig was a really moving experience for me - no taking photos, no recording videos, just dancing and singing along to almost every song.

BATACLAN
12 February 2018, Paris, France

DOUG DAVIE

Serving in the Royal Navy in 1981, a friend who had the first album played it to me and I was immediately taken. I first saw the band later that year at the Southampton Gaumont and on every tour from then on. In 1982 when I was in the Falklands War, 'Bunker Soldiers' and 'Enola Gay' seemed strangely apt. There seemed to be a tie to my military life throughout the Cold War era, played out in songs like 'Georgia', 'Radio Waves' and 'Silent Running'. Being in the Royal Navy, 'Sailing on the Seven Seas' was a given, while as an aviator, 'Gravity Never Fails' was always a cause for concern.

After seeing both nights at Hammersmith Apollo in 2007, I decided to try getting to know the band better. That led to blagging my way into more intimate gigs at Bletchley Park, Absolute Radio and even the launch party for *History of Modern* in London.

Life changed massively for my wife, Mandy, and I when in 2015 a genetic illness resulted in her suffering kidney failure, meaning dialysis and waiting for a transplant. An amazing friend was an exact match and donated a kidney in 2017. However, the operation didn't go well, with things touch and go for a while. Mandy pulled through slowly and, as she was unable to travel abroad for many years due to her condition, one year post-transplant we decided to combine her first trip abroad with an OMD gig at the Bataclan in Paris. We were lucky enough to have VIP tickets and attend the afternoon soundcheck. Andy and Paul were their usual relaxed chatty selves, and it felt great to be back in the OMD family. The evening gig was amazing, and despite the Bataclan's sombre setting, it lent itself perfectly to the way OMD perform.

AULA MAGNA
16 February 2018,
Lisbon, Portugal

NICK WALSH

I've seen OMD about 40 times but the best was in Lisbon in 2018, with front-row seats and a VIP upgrade to watch the sound check and meet Andy and Paul. During the sound check, while the engineers worked on something, Andy chatted with us. I asked what song he likes performing best. He said it's like playing blackjack. He has songs that are like having a king and an ace in his hand. When he lays them on the table he kills it and he's won.

↑
Andy on stage in Lisbon.
Photo by Nick Walsh

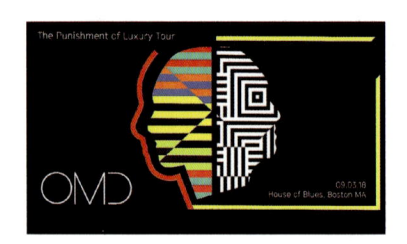

VILLA MARINA HALL

20 February 2018,
Douglas, Isle of Man

RICHARD HULME

My first memory of OMD was as an 11-year-old watching one of my favourite sports, rallying. The 1982 Monte Carlo Rally was on TV and the intro was the start of 'Joan of Arc'. It was music like I'd never heard before. I've been a fan ever since.

9.30 CLUB

6 March 2018,
Washington DC

COEN MARCH

My uncle recognised my obsessive love for 80s music and gave me an entire library featuring new wave and synth artists. 'Tesla Girls' was the first song I listened to. I was immediately hooked. I was overjoyed to find OMD were playing the 9.30 Club. My father purchased tickets and I enjoyed every minute.

My adrenalin pumping, I convinced my father to let me wait outside in the cold. It was snowing, but I didn't care. I waited and waited. Eventually, someone had the idea to wait in the front of the building, so that's where everyone went.

My father, waiting in the car, told me I had 10 minutes before I had to get in. I darted back and forth between the side of the building and front door. Going down the alley again, my father ran after me and shouted at the top of his lungs. I thought he was angry with me, but he wasn't. Paul Humphreys had walked through the front door. The small crowd of fans swarmed him, signing all sorts of merchandise. I, with extreme nervousness, approached. He kindly and warmly greeted me, and I got a picture with him.

EDGAR ORTIZ

I first listened to OMD when I was 10 in my native Puerto Rico, a beautiful island recently ravaged by a nasty hurricane but with the pride and resilience to roar back into its beauty. We didn't have *MTV* but we did have Channel 13, an American station. I religiously sat in front of the TV after school, and caught Richard Blade's *Video One* show, which exposed me to so many bands, one being this cool one with catchy synth sounds, infectious rhythms and melancholic lyrics.

I moved to the States almost 20 years ago, and one of my hopes was to catch OMD live. I was finally able to see them in 2018, in Washington, DC. It was amazing. I can't wait to experience it again, hopefully next time with some of my friends from the island. They deserve that joy too.

TERMINAL 5
10 March 2018,
New York, New York

KIP KOURI
OMD's US publicist

Working with Paul and Andy has been a dream come true. I grew up in Washington, DC in the early 80s, listening to early OMD in my bedroom and dancing. Cut to 40 years later as their publicist. I'm beyond words. We were at a sound check recently and there was an incident where a fan cycled from Harlem to catch an autograph and photo with Paul and Andy, almost getting into an accident in traffic - twice. We laughed our heads off. I remember being that little boy.

14 MARCH 2018

VAL DEACON

'The View from Here' is not the usual song you expect at the funeral of a 75-year old. My Mum, Jean, devoted her whole life to looking after others. A strong robust woman with a crippling anxiety about the big C who in May 2017 had ovarian and breast cancer diagnosed. Two days before Mum passed away that August, my husband sent me a YouTube link to 'The View From Here' and I listened to it with Mum and my sister, unable to contain my tears. The lyrics were the most poignant I'd heard. The family agreed this was the song to be played at her funeral.

2017 was dire and the nightmare continued into 2018. My retirement present from my husband Tosh was tickets for three dates on the Punishment of Luxury tour.

Tony 'Tosh' Deacon became ill shortly after Christmas, my

husband of 36 years. Our first concert together was OMD at Victoria Hall, Hanley, Stoke-on-Trent, in 1980. Tosh's taste for music was diverse but OMD were always top of the list. He played OMD at full blast on his home surround-system. Periodically, neighbours would complain and ask for it to be turned down. 'Funny that,' Tosh would reply, 'as we live in a detached house.'

In February 2018 Tosh was admitted to our critical care unit with multiple organ failure. At times barely conscious, he responded to the sound of his favourite band. 'It's your last chance for a dance' was a remark on one of his last lucid moments. 'Metroland' was the last song he heard before he slipped into a coma.

Tosh's wish was to see OMD with the Liverpool Philharmonic Orchestra and he bought two tickets a week before he was taken into hospital. He passed away on 14 March 2018, at the tender age of 56, a devoted husband, father and grandad.

We had a celebration of his life and young kids who had never heard of OMD were up and dancing to Tosh's two favourites, 'Electricity' and 'Enola Gay.' 'If You Leave' was played at his funeral.

ROCKWELL @ THE COMPLEX

21 March 2018, Salt Lake City, Utah

JOHNATHON TEODOSIO

Age 12, I discovered big hits like 'Messages', 'So in Love', 'If You Leave' and 'Electricity' on Depeche Mode radio on Pandora.

I was right up front for the show in Salt Lake City and able to catch Andy and Stuart's attention a couple times. At one point I was the only one grooving to 'Of All the Things We've Made'. Stuart saw me and started to chuckle. He also saw me doing the dance my high school friends and I do during 'Secret'. We both began to laugh.

RYAN MICHAEL PAINTER

If you weren't at The Complex, you missed what will be remembered as one of the greatest OMD gigs. No amount of words, regardless of language, can describe the kinetic and symbiotic energy exchanged between band and audience.

Andy and Paul took the stage, flanked by Martin and Stuart to the sounds of 'Art Eats Art/La Mitrailleuse'. McCluskey stood with back to audience as the ambient atmosphere of 'Ghost Star' filled the room. It's something of a red herring. The majority of the night was filled with a collage of electronic pop songs that have rattled the status quo and filled dance floors for 40 years.

Full-bodied cheers and chants brought the band back for 1988's 'Dreaming,' *Crush*'s 'Secret', and 'Electricity.' If you were there, you know the joy that passed between audience and band. If you weren't, you missed out on something special.

REGENCY BALLROOM
27 March 2018, San Francisco, California

STORMY PHOENIX
(aka Jisselle Fernandez)

OMD stepped on stage as the stars they are and opened with 'Ghost Star'. McCluskey excited the audience, saying, 'You know when I play bass, it's an old song'. Even while singing, McCluskey did his new wave club dance. The man is 59 and still knows how to move across the stage. He even offered life advice to everyone: 'Dance like nobody's watching.'

THE WILTERN
29 March 2018, Los Angeles, California

CAROL COMPTON

As a teenager I watched OMD on *Top of the Pops* every Thursday night in England. I moved to America and never forgot about them, but only recently did I get to see them, with my boys Toshiro and Saburo. We were able to see their sound check, then meet them and watch an amazing show. We don't have normal lives like most other families, as my husband's a quadriplegic after a near-fatal motorcycle crash 19 years ago. The moments we spent with OMD at the Wiltern were so magical, very precious and special.

THE VAN BUREN

2 April 2018,
Phoenix, Arizona

KENNETH MILLER

OMD's unique mix of technology with humanity struck a chord that resonates to this very hour. Andy and Paul sounded as if in a time machine. Every song I wanted to hear was played, and the new songs meshed with classic hits flawlessly. But that wasn't why this concert was phenomenal, it was the unexpected element of love - the absolute adoration of us crowded masses, and the reciprocal appreciation extended from the band. I felt moved in a way I'd never experienced at a concert venue, bonding with an audience of varying ages, the likes of which I'd never seen. Best concert ever.

CIVIC THEATRE

9 April 2018,
New Orleans, Louisiana

HUONG NGUYEN

I only saw OMD recently, but it reminded me how in 2007 I dated a wonderful guy who drove a red convertible Porsche 911. I have happy memories of listening to *The Best of OMD* in his car, the top down while cruising around New Orleans. Our relationship didn't work out and he and I broke up a year later. I forgot my OMD CD and never asked for it back. Let's just say that was his souvenir.

CENTER STAGE

10 April 2018,
Atlanta, Georgia

KEVIN MURRAY

I woke to the summer sounds of Syracuse, New York. A small city, the Big Apple was at least four hours away but might as well have been a million miles. The windows were open and the weather perfect. I was looking forward to my birthday. I was going to be 11 and music was furthest from my mind.

I heard a skateboard gliding up our blacktop driveway. I couldn't see the rider but knew who it was. A crash from an unsuccessful kick-flip gave it away, my brother's friend Dave had come to hang out. Dave was cool. As far as I knew, he was the only punk in Syracuse. Dave gave a series of high fives and took off upstairs, returning a few minutes later with my brother's boom-box.

He pulled two cassettes out of his backpack, put the first one in and explained, 'This music is totally awesome. It's punk. It's loud and offensive.' It was the Sex Pistols. We listened a while and I couldn't get my head around it. I felt like I was involved in something bad, something deviant.

Dave popped the tape out and plunked another one in. He said, 'Now this. This music is made with synthesisers and computers.' That got my attention. I had no idea, prior to that very moment, that I even cared about computers or synthesisers. Dave pushed the play button. Suddenly I hear, 'No. No. No,' followed by an arpeggiated synth-line. This was perfect. Amazing. Incredible. This was OMD. This I could listen to for days on end, and I did.

It eventually led to my interest in making my own music and my first sampler, the Casio SK-1. It was a toy, but I wrote songs with it when I was 12. Over the years I wrote hundreds of songs and nearly got signed to a dance label in the 90s. My musical career never got grip, but I was honoured to have my cover of 'Julia's Song' included on the *We Love You* fan tribute to OMD CD.

And I got the band to sign my micro-preset at the Atlanta show.

↑
The end of tour meal in Florida, USA. From left to right Martin, Dusty (tour bus driver), Andy, Danny Davies (backline technician - keyboards), Merv Pearson (backline technician - drums & guitars), Paul Bird (lights), Aaron Buck (monitors), Simon Fuller (tour manager), Paul, Chicky (front of house sound), Stuart and Jeff De Bryun (merchandise)

SECRET GIG

After 40 years we're still learning. We played a little alleyway in Liverpool. All the art galleries and museums were open until 10 as part of the Lightnight Festival. Lucy Byrne, agent for John Petch, who designed the *Punishment of Luxury* sleeve, asked if we would play to support John's exhibition, hoping fans would buy his work.

Health and safety said the alley could only hold 250 people. We thought, 'We've just sold over 3,000 tickets for the Philharmonic.' Mirelle, our manager, said, 'It'll leak out. People will know. Let's not advertise it and cause chaos.' All we announced was, 'There will be a secret concert by a band who cannot be named.' We thought, 'Surely they'll get the message.'

Come 6.30, half an hour before we were due to go on, there was nobody there. We called Ed, who runs our social media, saying 'I think you'd better make it explicit that *we* are playing, as there's nobody standing in front of the stage.' A few got the message and rushed down. In the end there were probably about 70 people. There should have been a lot more. Fortunately, John sold more than 30 pieces of art, so the gallery and John were happy. Bless our hardcore fans who worked out we were there and who supported a great artist. Moral of the story: be careful just how secret you make a secret gig.

ANDY McCLUSKEY

LET'S ROCK FESTIVAL

26 May 2018, Earlham Park, Norwich, UK

GAIL PATRICIA STANLEY

'Joan of Arc' was one of the first two records I owned. I got it for Christmas, 1981, and played the B-side over and over. I knew how special and unique OMD were right then.

In 2004 I wanted a large screen TV for Christmas, but my husband got me a new-fangled iPod mini. I was unimpressed. However, he said, 'It's great. Just listen'. I put the headphones on and heard 'Enola Gay'. I burst into tears. The fact that he put OMD on it saved his Christmas.

I saw OMD at Norwich's Let's Rock Festival and they were the best performers that day by miles. The following day my knees were slowly recovering. 'Electricity' is a thrilling song that demands jumping around to.

SOMMER NACHTS TRAUM FESTIVAL

7 July 2018, Munich, Germany

KIRSTIN WITT

When Anja (from Düsseldorf) and I (from Berlin) heard OMD were playing in Munich, we

← The band invite fans who have been to multiple gigs onto the stage at the last gig of the North American tour 2018. From L-R: Diane, Mark, Monica, Andy, Lori, Stuart, Kim, Martin, Paul, Elizabeth, Madison, Pam, Bill. Kim Tang came to every concert

↑ Kirstin and friends in their hand-made OMD style traditional Bavarian dress

OMD – 2013-2018

Stuart Kershaw at Suikerrock (top)

Enola at Suikerrock Festival 29 July 2018. Photo by Anja Minnemann (bottom)

had the idea to meet there in a traditional Bavarian dress called Dirndl. I took the *Dazzle Ships* cover and the cover of *The Punishment of Luxury*, printed them on textiles, then sewed the three matching aprons to our dresses. It was an unforgettable day in beautiful weather, with 30,000 people, and OMD in high spirits, a great mood, and full of energy.

SUIKERROCK FESTIVAL

29 July 2018,
Tienen, Belgium

JURGEN DEBEDTS

When our daughter was born in 1999, we named her Enola after the mischievous little girl in the Kevin Costner movie, *Waterworld*. As young as she was, she decided 'Enola Gay' was her song. At Suikerrock, she was holding up a sign saying, 'Enola is here'. Halfway through the show, Andy surprised everybody, pausing to ask if it was really her name, telling everyone his own daughter is also called Enola. He then autographed the sign. Enola was delighted.

KELVIN GROVE PARK

3 August 2018,
Glasgow, UK

ANDY McCLUSKEY

Paul played a clanger at Kelvingrove in 2018. We were playing 'She's Leaving' and he played this sequence part that's got a long delay in it. Paul hit a bum note and it went down the echo for three or four seconds. I had to take the mickey out of him about that afterwards. But then I forget the words rather too often.

When the band reformed, I

hadn't sung the songs for a very long time. The memory had started to fade. 'Talking Loud and Clear', 'Sister Marie Says' and 'Joan of Arc' were a problem. I managed to get 'Talking Loud and Clear' sorted out. I worked out how to remember that. The first phrase is, 'Talking loud and clear', in the second the phrase begins with 'o', the third is 'Talking loud and clear', and the next one is 'Promises'. So it's T-O-T-P - *Top of the Pops*. As long as I remember that, I can start each verse with the right word.

We played outdoors in Hamburg and there were people in the front row holding up the lyrics as a joke. I'd get flustered and angry if I forgot the lyrics. Now I just start singing, 'I've forgotten the lyrics, what the hell comes next, oh its, 'Should have known better …' I work it into the song and make a joke of it.

REWIND NORTH FESTIVAL

5 August 2018, Capesthorne Hall, Cheshire, UK

LINDSAY READE

When I listened to 'Electricity' that day in the car with Tony (Wilson) I never imagined that the group would be playing a huge stadium with such energy nearly 40 years later.

But what a gig it was. Andy and Paul are terrific musicians and singers, and the crowd loved them. I was very touched by some of the songs and their tribute to me, which meant a great deal. Great performers and great guys. Long may they thrive.

↑
Lindsay Reade with Andy and Paul at Rewind North Festival

The band says goodnight at Rewind. Photo taken by crew member Merv Pearson from side stage

REWIND SOUTH FESTIVAL

19 August 2018,
Henley-on-Thames, UK

RICKY WILDE

The year was 1980. I was an 18-year old sat in my bedroom with a Wasp synthesiser and Teac four-track tape machine, harbouring huge dreams of becoming a successful songwriter and producer.

One day I came home from meeting legendary record producer Mickie Most, securing a promise of studio time at RAK Studios. This could be my big break. Only problem was, I was a 'reluctant' artist with no interest in being a 'star' after releasing 'I Am an Astronaut' at the age of 12.

Thankfully, Mickie had seen and heard my sister Kim recording backing vocals on my demos and was interested in her as an artist. Maybe if I could write or produce a smash hit for Kim, that would tick all the boxes. I called on my Dad, Marty, to co-write a song with me. I played him a few ideas, and within an hour 'Kids In America' was born.

The sublime 'Messages' had only recently been released, and after hearing only the first two bars I was transfixed. The hypnotic synth-line unerringly rising and falling in fifths so brilliantly. Simple, yet so gorgeous. I had to get my fix and buy it immediately, playing it over and over.

'Kids' was progressing - sounding better and better, but to me the second verse seemed like it needed a slight lift. I got out my Wasp and before I knew it that killer hypnotic 'Messages' synth-line was bellowing out. To this day it remains a key part, not only in the song but possibly to the success of it.

Roll forward 38 years, sat backstage at the Rewind Music Festival in Henley and Andy appeared from nowhere and sat next to me, and I finally thanked him for all the inspiration. Who knows where Kim and I would be now had 'Messages' not been heard?

DAVEY HAVOK
AFI, Blaqk Audio, XTRMST & Dreamcar

When OMD unveiled the groundbreaking (Electricity) to England I was squirming in a crib in New York. *Architecture & Morality* arrived years before I became perpetually stuck to my single speaker cassette player, fingers poised to hit record when 'that so in love with you' song came on the radio. It's warm croon masked cold sentiment that that my impressionable young self couldn't have recognized, if not subconsciously. I didn't know who OMD were then. Being a very young American, John Hughes soon changed that. I learned. As I grew into a backwards life dedicated to music, my OMD education furthered as did the thrall of Orchestral Manoeuvres in the Dark. Even the name itself is enthralling. Seeing Andy sing 'If You Leave' only months ago still sent me and thousands of Californians twirling, teary eyed. OMD are purveyors of astoundingly intricate intellectual perfection for the pop scene yet revolutionary in the creation of dark electronic art that speaks to the hearts of the disaffected dancer in the shadows. These boys taught me that I may be both. They are one of the few groups to carry me my whole life. OMD have and will continue to musically and emotionally inspire me. Yes, I'm so in love.

ERIK STEIN
singer songwriter
Cult With No Name

Although they were born of that era, I've never seen OMD as a synth pop band. I still don't. For me, they had very little in common with the all the artists they are constantly being compared to. Saying OMD were synth pop just because they used synthesisers was as lazy as somehow labeling both Slipknot and Belle and Sebastian as guitar bands. From day one, OMD were much, much more than this and a quick listen to an early B-side and personal favourite in 'I Betray My Friends' tells you all you need to know. The sounds seemed to directly reflect and amplify the increasingly industrialised environment around us. No wonder they'd record an album called *Architecture & Morality*. It's true, though, that they are phenomenal songwriters. The sounds are not enough. Their seemingly endless talent for finding that elusive earworm seems so effortless that it often serves to distract us from the serious, intellectual heart beating behind it all. Whilst others are raging against the machine, OMD are generally trying to seduce it. Time after time they've succeeded. So, OMD may not be synth pop, but as brilliantly subversive as they are, they'll have you believe anything anyway.

OMD - 2013-2018

↑
Paul and Andy end the concert at Leipzig, Germany, 23 August 2018 the last show before the 40th Anniversary celebrations

›
Paul and Martin live on stage in Belgium

ROBOT MAN

'Robot Man' is a classic piece of OMD recycling. I originally wrote the song for The Genie Queen, a girl band that I created after Atomic Kitten. My producer friend Mike Crossey reminded me of it when I visited him in LA in 2015. He said that it was so good that I should redo it for OMD. Fortunately, I could not find the computer files from 2004 so had to start from scratch with a backing track that was absolutely intended to be a homage to 'Warm Leatherette' by The Normal. And I had to completely re-write the verse lyric so that I could sing it. When Stuart Kershaw heard the track he asked, 'Isn't that the same chorus melody to your early 90s unreleased song 'Yellow Press'?' It was! I had not even realised what I had done. Finally 25 years after the first chorus tune was created, a song was finally completed and released. One of our longer creative journeys.

ANDY MCCLUSKEY

← The Robotmen! Andy meets his match on holiday in Figueres, Spain

THEA DAHLMAN

I started to listen to Orchestral Manoeuvres in the Dark in 2018 and it all happened by coincidence. I was searching for a song I had heard a long time ago, and all I could remember was the music video and the main tune of the song. I described it to my father and said that the song sounded 'synth-ish' and 'pop-ish'. He answered, 'Could it be OMD?' I had no idea who he was talking about, but my father played me 'Souvenir' and I forgot all about the song I had been looking for (Fiction Factory's '(Feels Like) Heaven').

My first feeling was that I had heard this song before. It transported me back to my childhood days, when I was little and my father constantly played OMD when we were living in the south of Sweden. After the discovery of 'Souvenir', I listened to *Architecture & Morality* and learned all the lyrics. My favourites are 'Joan of Arc', 'She's Leaving' and, of course, 'Souvenir'. When I listen to 'Sealand' I can see before me a monster from the sea, who turns into something vulnerable and good-hearted.

OMD were in Stockholm recently, but the concert had an age limit of 18 years and I was still only 17.

BUTCHER & THE SURGEON

Paul is a more fastidious and patient music programmer than I ever could be. He knows his studio technology and has a much more reliable pair of ears for mixing than I do. My technique is to want everything as loud as everything else. However, Paul is not great at making executive decisions regarding arrangements and the number of parts in a song.

I recall him arriving at my house for a songwriting session with a track he had begun programming on the train to Liverpool. (Yes, he also has a tendency to do things at the very last possible minute). There were 10 sequencer tracks all playing variations on the same theme. I went through them.... 'No, no, delete, no, yes, no, no, delete, delete, alternative for change section. Ok and what is this 11th track here?' 'Just a sonic doodle that I was trying out,' comes the reply. 'That's a bloody main melody Paul. We're keeping that!' I deleted all his drums too, and in five minutes we had the three tracks that were the basis of 'Metroland'.

I have no patience! I want to hear the big picture ASAP! Thus, my programming is appalling. Unfinished parts, terrible edits, and one take vocals done on my battered old studio microphone. I refuse to let Paul re-record or reprogram (it would add years to any project) so he has to carefully re-stitch my brutal edits, polish my rough vocals and heal the wounds that I leave. He claims that this adds years to his work! It probably does. We call each other the 'Butcher' and the 'Surgeon'. We are a good team.

ANDY MCCLUSKEY

DARYN BUCKLEY
2018 – The View From Here

Orchestral Manoeuvres in the Dark are still a major part of my life. I've seen them live about thirty times (probably not as many times as many who have contributed to this book) but plenty nonetheless. I've been lucky enough to meet them, I've interviewed them on radio and I still seem to be symbiotically linked to their music; it continually pulls on my heart and draws me towards it. In these days of Spotify, their music is never far away. They are an intrinsic part of my life.

In March 2018, I was lucky enough to visit Anaheim in California with my family. I chose it as a destination not only for the proximity to Los Angeles or to Disneyland (I didn't even know Disneyland was there to be honest) but for the fact that one of the OMD Facebook followers, who had turned into something of a personal Facebook friend, lived there.

'You must come over,' said Laura Hesser when I told her I would be visiting Anaheim. So I did.

Laura, this wonderful OMD fan who regularly corresponded with me on Facebook and listened to my radio show each week, threw opened her doors and welcomed me into her house without hesitation. We sat and chatted whilst our children played together and talked music, mainly OMD and how they had pervaded our lives. We spent a lovely evening there and, as I was driving back to our hotel, it struck me that none of this would ever have happened had my uncle decided to listen to Visage or Joy Division that afternoon instead of the debut album by that weird band from Liverpool with the cool record sleeves who did that 'Dancing' song that was quite funny.

ANDY MCCLUSKEY

We were initially unsure about accepting the offer to tour with a-ha, but decided that we would use the opportunity to continue expanding our live audience. The response from their fans was incredible, with many suggesting that we stole the show. They loved the energy and humour that we display on stage. But then, we don't arrive in separate limousines, hide in separate depressing rooms and depart again separately at the end of the show! Very strange and sad really.

↑ Andy on stage in Doncaster, England, 16 June 2018

PHILHARMONIC HALL

6 & 7 October 2018, Liverpool, UK

ANDY MCCLUSKEY

The concert in 2009 with the Royal Liverpool Philharmonic Orchestra had been very special and we were delighted when they approached us again as it coincided with our fortieth anniversary. This time we determined to go even further outside our comfort zone. Conveniently for me, the arrangers Gary Carpenter and Ian Stephens both live in West Kirby only a few miles from me. I could easily go to listen to their ideas as they were formulated. I loved the slower songs for this performance but was worried that we would be too ambient for too long. Hambi Haralambous created the Motor Museum Studio that I now own. Since 2007 he has been working with us creating the films that we use live, and also the Energy Suite, and live performance films of the 2009 concert at the Liverpool Philharmonic and Museum of Liverpool. When he showed me the drone camera footage for 'Stanlow' and 'The View From Here' to use at the Philharmonic in October 2018 I was so moved. From that moment I knew that the decision to play the more subtle tone poem tracks in the first half of the concert was the correct decision.

DEBBIE PARKINSON

We arrived at the Phil for the Sunday night performance and slipped into our seats just as Paul and Andy, both suited and booted, walked on stage. Backed by the Royal Liverpool Philharmonic Orchestra, they started with 'Stanlow' and proceeded to play a 45 minute first half that Andy explained was going to be 'esoteric', with a collection of songs for the die hard fans. And the die hard fans loved it. Andy couldn't stand still and it didn't take much for the crowd to be on their feet and clapping along. I don't think the orchestra, led by conductor Richard Balcombe, had witnessed anything quite like it.

Except, of course, that the orchestra had played with Andy and Paul just the night before. Tongue firmly in cheek, Andy said, 'Last night's dress rehearsal went well.' The concerts were, he told us, just a week before what would mark the 40th anniversary of that first ever OMD show at Eric's back in 1978 and this really was a celebration of their whole career, from 'Electricity' through to tracks from *The Punishment of Luxury*.

THE TIMES | Monday October 8 2018

Pop
OMD
Philharmonic Hall, Liverpool
★★★★☆

When rock and pop bands do concerts with an orchestra it can often seem as if the classical players are there only to make simple songs sound sophisticated and the band look posh. Perhaps the clue to why this 40th anniversary concert by Orchestral Manoeuvres in the Dark (OMD) worked is in the name. Despite being a synth-pop act associated with the early 1980s new-romantic movement, they always had a semi-classical sense of grandeur.

Combined with OMD's Andy McCluskey and Paul Humphreys dressing like bank managers while their contemporaries were in blusher and frilly shirts, you can see why they never really fitted in. Forty years on from their first gig at Eric's Club in Liverpool, McCluskey's buttoned-up appearance and awkward dance moves still brought unwelcome visions of a businessman at the disco, but the nuances of the music worked perfectly with the orchestra and demonstrated how uncompromising OMD have been.

The first half of the concert featured *Stanlow* and *Statues*; icy, atmospheric tracks from the second album *Organisation*, while *The New Dark Age* took the band's image as doom-mongers to its logical conclusion by putting footage of war-torn Syria to a melancholic Scott Walker-like song about the apocalypse.

"If you've got a 75-piece orchestra," said McCluskey, referring to the Royal Liverpool Philharmonic Orchestra, "you may as well throw in an obscure B-side from the mid-1990s."

The big hits came in the second half, and what hits they were: a lament on the atomic bomb (*Enola Gay*), two songs about the same French 15th-century saint (*Joan of Arc*, *Maid of Orleans*), a tribute to the German electronic pioneers Kraftwerk (*Electricity*). The orchestra brought out the strength of the melodies and the richness of the arrangements.

There were shades of Burt Bacharach to *Walking on the Milky Way* and Ennio Morricone to *Native Daughters of the Golden West*, and a sense throughout that this was a band rejecting every rock'n'roll cliché going. It made Philharmonic Hall seem like their spiritual home.
Will Hodgkinson

After the interval came the hits and an hour and a quarter long set in which they did 'Souvenir', 'Enola Gay', 'Maid of Orleans', 'Joan of Arc', 'Messages', 'Sailing on the Seven Seas' and 'Walking on the Milky Way'. Andy was tie-less for the second half, had a prompt sheet for 'Talking Loud and Clear' and was exhorting the audience to clap along throughout. They needed no second bidding and were on their feet throughout the rest of the performance. This wasn't a 'sit quietly and listen carefully to the orchestration' kind of evening. It was a revivalist meeting, with a room full of true believers come to worship at the altar of Andy and Paul. At one point I definitely saw one of the violinists getting into the groove and swaying from side to side instead of staying still and studying her sheet music. It was that kind of night. A fantastic celebration of 40 years of fabulous music, with a venue packed with fans delighted to be sharing this landmark event with their heroes and two of the nicest guys making music today.

WILMA MISSENDEN

'Ghost Star' was phenomenal and 'Sealand' is a perfect reflection of Shetland. Well worth the 1,140 mile return trip in 24 hours!

ROZ BOWDEN

What a magical evening! Thank you so much for an unforgettable experience. My 90 year old mum (your oldest fan?) would have loved to have been there too and sends her regards. She remembers going to the Phil in the 1930s for concerts of a rather different ilk!

↑
Review from OMD at The Philharmonic Hall, Liverpool in *The Times* 8 October 2018

Andy and Paul live at The Philharmonic Hall, October 2018. Photo by Mark McNulty

The first half may have been atmospheric but even the casual fan could have appreciated how wonderful the musicianship was from the orchestra and how well OMD's catalogue translated to such a stage. It showed the depth of music OMD has and how after 40 years they can adapt and keep pushing into new territory.

New favourites such as 'Ghost Star' really added to the occasion for me as I was not alive for the first round of OMD fun in the '80s so the new releases have been pivotal for me as a fan. We even got a brand new song at Liverpool.

PAUL HUMPHREYS

Every year we sit down and think, do we still want to do this?

Do we still have the energy? We only want to do OMD if we still have lots of ideas for records, if we've still got the energy to tour – because we're not getting any younger. But the thing is, we still have oodles and oodles of energy. If you see our full band show, we're pumping. I think I enjoy being in OMD now more than I ever have before. It's more relaxed now. We all get on great. It's almost like we're kids again in my mum's back room, and we're back together doing it for the fun of it. And I think that shows in our records, in our performances. So … long may it continue.

AARON LAW

Liverpool was the obvious choice for such an event and I love visiting (I am from Coventry but have seen OMD in a number of cities across the UK). It was a wonderful occasion. I was in the same hotel as some other fans that have been to countless shows and they were very emotional about the set list choices and how well it worked with the orchestra. 'Sealand', we all agreed, was majestic.

ANDY MCCLUSKEY

One thing we were really keen to do with Liverpool Philharmonic was to not just turn up with all our instruments, play the song as we normally do, and find some half-hearted way to gratuitously weld on a few strings. Once we were told we could use the entire orchestra, we just thought 'let's completely de-construct our songs and have the orchestra play everything, then somehow we'll find
 a way to fit ourselves precariously on top of these amazing musicians.' It really felt like you were hanging on to the coat tails of this vast wave of music that you didn't feel you had a right to be surfing quite frankly. But we've got back on the board with slightly more confidence this time..

WAYNE BILLING

I live very close to Stanlow and it was fascinating watching the video with the Wirral and Liverpool in the backdown. I was at work the other day and was talking to the Architect about the concert and he told me his dad used to work with Andy's dad at Shell at Stanlow.

ANDREW STEVENS

I worked on Stanlow during a student placement on my engineering degree (1987). Seeing it again on this video really brought it back...... And the song itself....wow!

↑
View from the audience, OMD live at The Philharmonic Hall, October 2018

OMD - 2013-2018

A still from Henning Lederer's remarkable animation for 'La Mitrailleuse'

STEPHANIE LE TISSIER

I couldn't believe what I was seeing and hearing. The visuals which fitted in so well with the songs, the depth of music played by the orchestra and the tone and strength of Andy's voice. Such a moving experience. You both took this gig to such a higher level.

ANDY MCCLUSKEY

I was first alerted to the work of Henning Lederer by a lady named Iris who bought me a poster of the painting Watch by Gerald Murphy, then told me of an amazing German artist who had animated the painting. I loved the work so much that I found his website and emailed asking if he would do something with us in future. The wonderful results have been the films for 'Decimal', 'Atomic Ranch', 'Please Remain Seated', 'Isotype' and 'La Mitrailleuse'.

THE FUTURE

I don't want to still be doing it when I'm in my seventies, but there's life left in OMD yet. We've got lots of ideas still. There's definitely another album in us. I never say more than one.

What works best with Andy and I is if we sit in a room together and one of us has a small kernel of an idea, just something to start us off. It can be a lyric, a chord sequence, a sound, a rhythm. Something basic that sounds interesting. And then we'll throw ideas at it together. I'll come up with something and Andy says, 'Okay, I like your first phrase but your second phrase is shit'. Okay, so I'll play the first phrase and, 'No, not that one. Oh yeah, that one. That's good.'

I remember when we were doing 'Isotype' at Andy's house and we went through so many tunes. And I said, 'Andy, just go and make a cup of tea. Just leave me with it for a minute.' And I tried a few things. And then I hit on the main theme, the main tune, and Andy came running upstairs, tea spilling, going, 'That's the one, that's the one! I'm going to drop you into record!' If he hadn't have been there I probably would have moved on to something else. That's the way we work, and that's the way we've always worked best.

PAUL HUMPHREYS

← Martin (Vile Electrodes) Swan's very impressive OMD collection including rare vinyl picture discs, 7" and 12" imports, 'She's Leaving' 7", and one lonely 'Vile' cushion

OMD - 2013-2018

OMD on stage in North America in 2018 performing 'Of All the Things We Made'. Photo by Ruta Degutyte-Humphreys

WHY WASN'T SUSIE THERE?

MIKE HUMPHREYS

I wrote this poem/prose piece after the Liverpool concert in 2017. When I saw her cousin and her friend dancing that night, I thought of Susie, our sister, who died when Paul was six and I was sixteen, and how she'd loved to have been there.

OMD Concert!

*Always a heady experience
This time Jane and Julie were with us.
I watched them dancing in the aisles
And suddenly
My heart was in my throat;
Why wasn't Susie there,
Dancing with her cousin and her friend?
A choke of deep sadness,
Pained wistfulness.
A cloudburst of nostalgia
Sets an old video playing in my head:
Family, holiday, laughter.*

*Why wasn't Susie there?
She'd have seen Paul,
Her little brother,
Now keyboard ace,
Confident vocalist,
Famous, up there on stage!
She'd have seen Andy,
Gleefully working the audience,
Belting out their songs –
Those great and lasting melodies;
The pulsating, hypnotic beat,
The scatter-gun lights,
Spot, laser, strobe;
And all the time
A smooth, seamless performance,
So professional –
The cool presence of the whole band.*

*They've come so far
Since the late Seventies
And that modest hobby of sound-making
In Mum's back room…
Oh, why wasn't Susie there?
We are buoyed up among crowds of fans,
Unified with excitement and awe;
Nobody wants to leave.
She'd have seen fun and joy in all our eyes,
A defining inspiration,
A red-hot warmth in the senses.
How do we preserve such moments?
Susie – I desperately wish you'd been there;
Maybe you were there, after all,
Watching over us,
Feeling all the love.*

Mike Humphreys, 2017

Pink noise

low rate
Low transpose
75 attack
½ decay
½ sustain
0 release
5 VCF bpf

Vibrato
growl
aDSR
Hold
32.8
Noise

Start with fade in glide synth
or preferably organ (phased swelling)
1) Chords D   D-C   C-E   E-D
   slow time 4/4   3/4   3/4   3/4
   repeat etc.

2) Bass - high pitch echo (fast double repeat)
   Bass plays two riffs to every keyboard one
   continue for 4 keyboard times

3) Synth joins in
   with 3 wind D C low E mech

E = echo
wind swell

British Rail Young Persons' Railca
Valid until 15 OCT 85
Issued to
Address
Issued at
I agree to the conditions set out and referred to on the back hereof.
Signature
YP 2044587
Not valid without issuing office stamp
To be carried on all rail journeys

ACKNOWLEDGEMENTS

We received many other stories that we just couldn't find room for but thanks for sending them in and posting them on Facebook as we enjoyed reading them all. Particular thanks to:

Aaron James, Adam Stevenson, Alan Varley, Andee and Emma, Andreas Stahlberg, Andrew Speakman, Andy Clarke, Anne Schofield, Anthony Ricciardi, Arthur Croonenberg, Barry Rogers, Barry Walton, Berry Groot, Cecilia & Cesar, Cheryl Wright, Chris Mack, Christina Nysten Justesen, Christophe Duron, Christophe Vindevogel, Clare Edwards, Claudia Salvermoser, Dalida, Dan Williams, Daniel O'Neil, Darren Wortley, David Booker, Deb Alderson, Debra Hayden, Deenie Gumina, Dirk Wellborn, Duane Mayhew, Elizabeth O'Leary, Emma Smith, Frederica Zhu, Gabriela Orth, Gary Churchward, Gina McHale, Gita Andani. Graham Snape, Gustavo Campos, Helga Sandmeier, Ian Plested, Jacek Stryjek, Jackie Murray, Jeanette Severn, James Parker, James Plaj, James Rae, Jane Weaver, Jo Burrows, Joanna Ciechowska, Joe Flammensbeck, John Barba, John de Heer, John Redmond, Jools Cartwell, Juan Fo, Juan Jesús López, Karen Blake, Karen Greenwood, Kevin Annetts, Lauren Moore, Len Lumbers, Magnus Ramström, Mags Dearden, Maika Hoffmann, Manuela Heilmann, Margaret Broughton, Marjolein Wilson, Mark Rogers, Martin Hughes, Mason Porter, Matthew Suffidy, Michael Cuthbert, Mike Whelan, Nao H, Neil Taylor, Nic Blinston, Nico van der Breul, Pammy Paulson, Patrick Burke, Paul Hermansen, Paul Whitehouse, Philip Ruffley, Rachel Quilter, Rebecca Deriemacker, Richard Burbage, Rigel Keffer, Rob Forsdyke, Rob Garrett, Rob van Roijen, Robert Cunningham, Robert Glebocki, Rodney Meiklejohn, Rubén Dīaz Alvarez, Ryan Quinn, Sean Damer, Sharon Simpson, Shayla Day, Simon Davies, Steve Morley, Stuart Morris, Sue Cartwright, Toni Argilo , Vanessa O'Neil, Wendy Hunt, Wilma Missenden, Yogi / Mario, Yvette Darrington, Erik Stein, Lyndon Brock, Chris Van Der Linde, Sally Langley,

Kimberly Buffington, Pablo Safe, Lee Harnett, Judy Vargas, Richard Prentice, Dale Allen, Andy Jennings, Maciej Zrobek, Lucienne Vossen, Iain Docherty, Karen Rendell, Justyna Potopa, Henrik Erichsen, Judith Crosier, Michael Connelly, Craig Martin, Guido Mussehl, Robert Farrah, Vic Fernandez, Edwin Cole, Graca Ribeiro, David Richards, David Rush.

Special thanks to Daniel Summersgill at Robot Mascot for the interior pages design and layout, patience, late nights and understanding.

Pretending To See The Future is also available as a digital eBook with extra fan's stories

For everything OMD
www.OMD.uk.com

THIS DAY IN MUSIC BOOKS
www.thisdayinmusic.com